Mia's
MATH
SERIES

GEOMETRY

HERMONHOUSE

Mia's Geometry

발 행　2025년 5월 9일　초판 1쇄

저 자　소미혜
발행인　최영민
발행처　헤르몬하우스
주 소　경기도 파주시 신촌로 16
전 화　031-8071-0088
팩 스　031-942-8688
전자우편　hermonh@naver.com
출판등록　2015년 3월 27일
등록번호　제406-2015-31호

ⓒ 소미혜 2025, Printed in Korea.

ISBN　979-11-94085-50-8 (53410)

- 책 값은 뒤 표지에 있습니다.
- 헤르몬하우스는 피앤피북의 임프린트 출판사입니다.
- 이 책의 어느 부분도 저작권자나 발행인의 승인 없이 무단 복제하여 이용할 수 없습니다.

❖ 저자직강 인터넷 강의는 SAT, AP No.1 인터넷 강의 사이트인 마스터프랩 (www.masterprep.net) 에서 보실 수 있습니다.

Why? Mia's Geometry

'이해하기 쉬운 개념 + 다양한 example 문제 + 심화응용문제'

삼중 그물망구조로 Geometry에 필요한 모든 토픽 및 개념과 실전 능력을 한 번에 잡는다!

지난 10년간 결과로 증명된 학교 GPA관리용 최적의 교재!

이해하기 쉽고 친근한 이미지를 활용하여 어려운 수식을 빠르게 이해!

1. '이해하기 쉬운 개념 + 다양한 example문제 + 심화응용문제'

   그 동안의 Geometry 교재에서는 볼 수 없었던 삼중 그물망구조로 Geometry에 필요한 모든 토픽 및 개념과 실전 능력을 한 번에 잡는다!

2. 스스로 빈칸을 채워가며 개념을 꼼꼼히 공부할 수 있도록 설계한 교재

3. 그저 그런 교재가 아니다!

   지난 10년간 현장에서 수많은 학생들에게 결과로 증명된 학교 GPA 최적의 교재!

Preface

미국의 Geometry는 도형, 각도, 입체, 증명 등을 통해 공간 감각과 논리적 사고를 기르는 미국 중고등학교 수학 과목입니다. 한국의 중학교 수학과는 달리, 미국 Geometry는 도형에 대한 다양한 이론(정의, 공리, 정리 등)을 바탕으로 증명 문제를 중점적으로 다루며, 도형의 성질을 논리적으로 설명하는 훈련이 핵심입니다.

하지만 많은 학생들이 이론을 단순히 암기하는 데 그치고, 이를 실제 증명 문제에 적용하는 데 어려움을 겪는 모습을 보며, 학생들이 충분히 연습하고 사고력을 기를 수 있도록 증명 문제를 집중적으로 훈련하고 깊이 있는 도형심화 문제를 경험할 수 있는 교재를 제작하게 되었습니다.

교재 제작을 위해 수많은 Geometry 교과서의 내용과 문제들을 분석하고 연구하였습니다. 또한 학원 수업과 개인 지도를 통해 접한 국내외 다양한 국제학교 및 외국인학교 학생들의 Geometry 학습을 지도하면서, 각 학교 선생님들의 수업 방식과 커리큘럼을 벤치마킹하였습니다.

이 과정에서 학생들이 어려워하는 개념과 문제 유형을 면밀히 분석하고, 실제 학생들의 피드백을 바탕으로 교재를 지속적으로 개선하며 완성도를 높였습니다. 그 결과, 이 교재를 통해 많은 학생들이 매년 Geometry 학교 시험에서 좋은 성과를 거두고 있습니다.

이 책을 통해 학생들이 Geometry가 충분히 doable이라는 자신감을 얻고, 문제를 해결했을 때의 즐거움을 느끼며, 더 깊이 있는 문제들을 통해 사고력과 응용력을 한층 더 키우기를 바랍니다.

마지막으로 이 책을 함께 만들기 위해 애써준 사랑하는 남편TY와 잘생긴 아들 주원이, 그 동안 함께해 준 고마운 학생들, 그리고 헤르몬하우스 관계자 여러분과 마스터프렙의 권주근 대표님께 감사의 마음을 드립니다. 그리고 무엇보다도 소중한 기회를 주신 하나님께 감사와 찬양을 올려드립니다.

Mia Mihye So

이 책의 특징

1. 교재의 모든 개념 설명과 문제 해설은 유학 인터넷 강의 전문 사이트인 마스터프렙(www.masterprep.net)에 Mia쌤의 쉽고 명쾌한 해설 강의와 함께 제공됩니다.

2. '이해하기 쉬운 개념 + 다양한 example 문제 + 심화응용문제(*표시 문제)'의 삼중 구조로, 개념 학습과 실전 연습을 한 번에 잡을 수 있도록 구성되어 있습니다. 어려운 개념도 쉽게 배우고, 다양한 예제로 연습한 뒤, 심화 응용 문제를 통해 완벽하게 개념을 정리할 수 있습니다.

3. 개념을 빈칸 채우기 형식으로 꼼꼼하게 학습할 수 있도록 설계되어 있습니다. 각 빈칸의 정답은 페이지 하단에 수록하여, 필요 시 바로 참고할 수 있도록 하였습니다.

4. 이해하기 쉽고 친근한 이미지와 함께, Geometry에서 꼭 알아야 할 정의(Definition), 공리(Postulate), 정리(Theorem)뿐만 아니라, 어려운 수식도 빠르게 이해할 수 있도록 시각적으로 정리하였습니다. 반드시 암기해야 할 핵심 개념과 공식은 쉐이드 박스(shaded box) 안에 따로 정리하여 한눈에 파악할 수 있도록 구성했습니다.

5. 이 책의 모든 그림은 실제 비율(크기)에 맞게 그려진 것이 아닙니다. (The figures are not drawn to scale.) 그림을 보고 직관적으로 판단하지 말고, 문제의 수치, 조건, 이론을 기준으로 논리적으로 풀어야 합니다.

◆ 기호 정리

* (star): 심화 응용 문제

$\mathbb{R}$: Real numbers
$\mathbb{Z}$: Integers
$\mathbb{N}$: Natural numbers
∪ : or
∩ : and

∅ : empty set (no solution)
∞ : infinity
∴ : Therefore
∵ : Since

저자 소개

Mia(소미혜) 선생님은 지난 10년 이상을 유학 수학 현장에서 다양한 학생들과 호흡하면서 최적화된 미국 수학 및 국제학교 수학에 대한 솔루션을 제공해온 수학 전문가이다.

압구정 미국수학 전문강사라는 타이틀이 위의 노력들을 통해서 자연스럽게 얻게 된 선생님의 별칭이다.

미국에서 인증된 수학전문강사(Texas 8-12 미국수학교사자격증 content exam + PPR exam 통과)로 관련된 전문자격증을 소지하고 있으며, 특히, 해외 엄마들 사이에 입 소문난 실력파 강사이다.

Geometry, Algebra 2, AP Precalculus, AP calculus AB BC, AP Statistics, SAT math, IB Math 등에서 12년이상의 경력을 가지고 있다. 또한 한국 수능수학 강의 경력도 4년 이상을 가지고 있어서 한국 수학과 미국/국제 학교 수학에 대해서 모두 정통한 수학 전문가이다.

- 8-12 Texas Mathematics Teacher Certificate (content exam + PPR exam 통과)
- (현) No.1 유학 인터넷 강의 사이트 마스터프렙(www.masterprep.net) 수학강사
- (전) IBAdvance IB, sat 수학대표강사
- (전) 해커스유학 미국수학강사
- (전) PSU Edu AP, SAT 수학강사
- 미국텍사스고등학교, 국내국제고등학교 수학교사 경력 6년.
- 수능수학강의 경력 4년
- 용인외대부고, 경기외고, KIS, 제주KIS, SIS, 청라달튼, 브랭섬홀, 미국, 중국, 일본, 싱가포르, 베트남 국제학교 등의 학생들의 온라인/오프라인 개인지도
- College Board certification for AP Calculus AB, BC
- College Board certification for AP Statistics

- 저 서 -
Mia's ALGEBRA2 / Mia's PRECALCULUS
Mia's AP PRECALCULUS / Mia's AP CALCULUS AB BC

Contents

1. Basic words for Geometry 11
   - 1.1 Basic Words_ Points, Lines, and Planes 12
   - 1.2 Basic Words_ Angles 15
   - 1.3 Basic Words_ Special Pairs of Angles 18
   - 1.4 Basic Words_ Polygons 21

2. Geometric Reasoning 25
   - 2.1 Conditional Statements 26
   - 2.2 Inverses and Contrapositives 30
   - 2.3 Postulates and Theorems 35
   - 2.4 Writing Proofs 41
   - 2.5 Segments and Angle Relationships 49
   - 2.6 Special Pairs of Angles 58
   - 2.7 Perpendicular Lines 67
   - 2.8 Theorems about Special Pairs of Angles 72
   - Postulates or Theorems from Chapter 2 78

3. Parallel Lines 81
   - 3.1 Parallel Lines and Transversals 82
   - 3.2 Angles and Parallel Lines 88
   - 3.3 Proving Lines Parallel 95
   - 3.4 Angles of Triangles 104
   - Postulates or Theorems from Chapter 3 110

4. Congruent triangles 115
   - 4.1 Congruent Polygons 116
   - 4.2 Proving Congruence_ SSS, SAS, ASA 119
   - 4.3 Proving Congruence_ AAS, HL 126
   - 4.4 CPCTC 132
   - 4.5 Isosceles Triangles 139
   - 4.6 Using Congruent Triangles 147
   - Postulates or Theorems from Chapter 4 150

5. Relationships in Triangles 153
    5.1 Median, Altitude, and Bisectors 154
    5.2 Centers of Triangles 161
    5.3 Midsegment Theorem 174
    5.4 Properties of Inequalities 179
    5.5 Inequalities in One Triangle 186
    5.6 Inequalities in Two Triangles 192
    Postulates or Theorems from Chapter 5 198

6. Quadrilaterals 201
    6.1 Angles of Polygons 202
    6.2 Parallelograms 210
    6.3 Tests for Parallelograms 218
    6.4 Rectangles, Rhombi and Squares 225
    6.5 Trapezoids 238
    Postulates or Theorems from Chapter 6 247

7. Similarity 251
    7.1 Proportions 252
    7.2 Identify Similar Figures 257
    7.3 Proving Similar Triangles 261
    7.4 More Theorems about Similar Triangles 275
    Postulates or Theorems from Chapter 7 283

8. Right Triangles and Trigonometry 285
    8.1 Right Triangle Similarity 286
    8.2 The Pythagorean Theorem 291
    8.3 Special Right Triangles 299
    8.4 Trigonometry of Right Triangles 305
    8.5 Angle of elevation or depression 311

9. Circles 317
    9.1 Basic words _Circles and Arcs 318
    9.2 Tangent Lines 322
    9.3 Common Tangents and Tangent Circles 333
    9.4 Chords and Arcs 341
    9.5 Inscribed Angles 355
    9.6 Secants, Tangents, and Angle Measures 373
    9.7 Secants, Tangents, and Segments 382
    Postulates or Theorems from Chapter 9 390

10. Areas of Plane Figures 393
    10.1 Area of polygons 394
    10.2 Area of regular polygons 402
    10.3 Area of Circles and Sectors 408
    10.4 Areas and Ratios 419

11. Areas and Volumes of Solids 429
    11.1 Basic words _3D Solid 430
    11.2 Surface Area 435
    11.3 Volume 443
    11.4 Sphere 456
    11.5 Area and Volume of similar Solids 464

12. Coordinate Geometry 473
    12.1 Transformation 474
    12.2 Distance and Midpoints 482
    12.3 Equation of Circle 486
    12.4 Slope of a Line 493
    12.5 Coordinate Geometry Proofs 498

Abbreviations 507
Answers 509

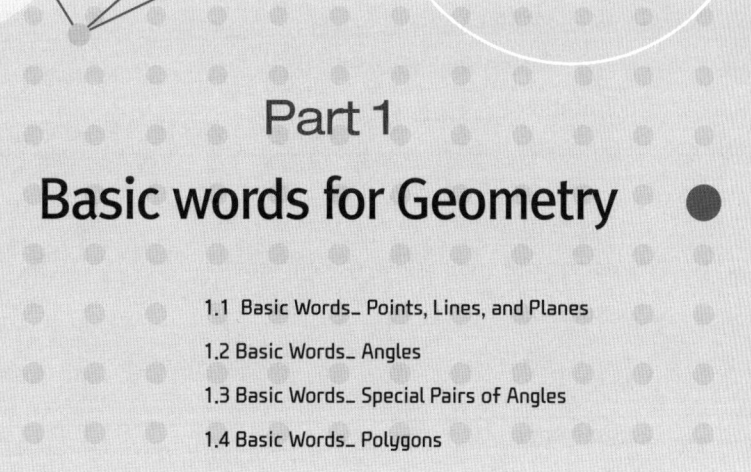

Part 1
Basic words for Geometry

1.1 Basic Words_ Points, Lines, and Planes

1.2 Basic Words_ Angles

1.3 Basic Words_ Special Pairs of Angles

1.4 Basic Words_ Polygons

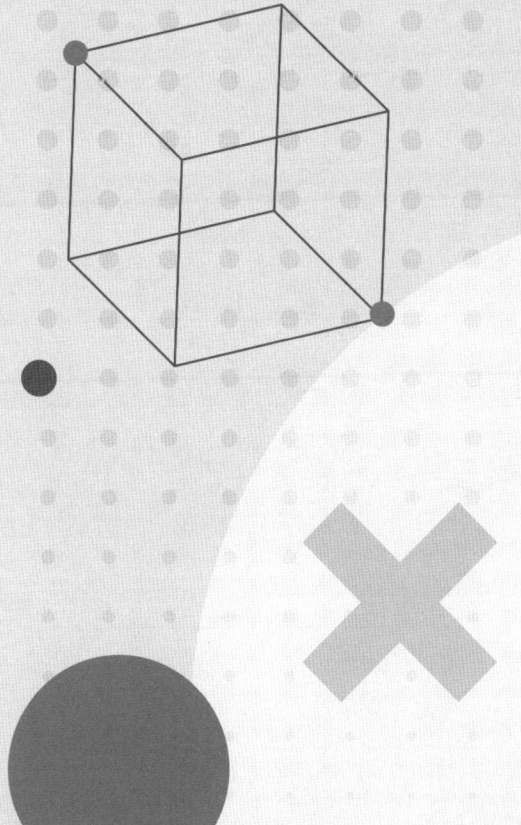
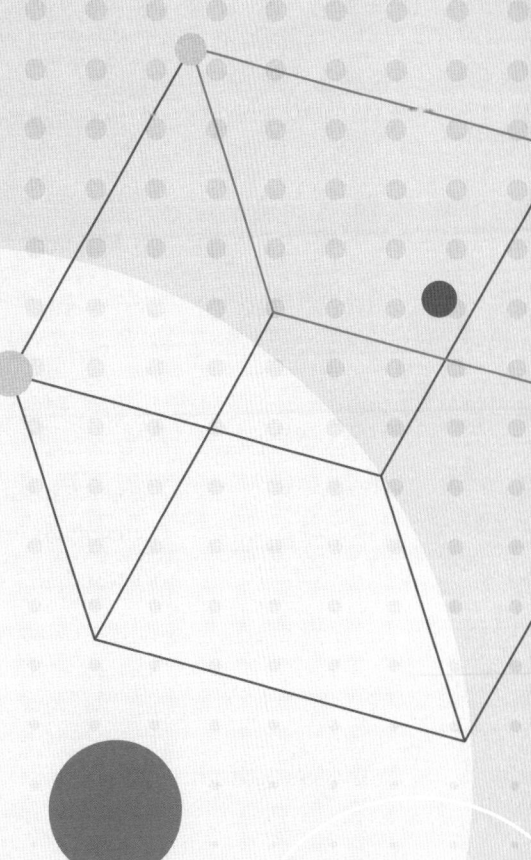

Mia's Geometry

1.1 Basic Words_ Points, Lines, and Planes

1. Points, Lines, Planes

Vocabulary	Meaning	Notation and Figure
Point	: is a location. : has no size, only position. • Notation : ①_____	Point A
Line	: contains infinite set of points. : is straight (no curves), has no ends. • Notation : ②_____	line l , $\overleftrightarrow{AB}$
Segment	: has ends. • Notation : ③_____ • Length of $\overline{AB}$ = ④_____ (⊗ We write AB = 5 not $\overline{AB}$ = 5)	$\overline{AB}$
Ray	: has one end. • Notation : ⑤_____ • The endpoint of a ray is always named first. • $\overrightarrow{AB} \neq \overrightarrow{BA}$	$\overrightarrow{BA}$ $\overrightarrow{AB}$
Plane	: is a flat surface. : contains infinite set of points and lines. • Notation : ⑥_____	N

Blank : ① Point A   ② $\overleftrightarrow{AB}$ or $\overleftrightarrow{BA}$ or line l ③ $\overline{AB}$ or $\overline{BA}$ ④ AB ⑤ $\overrightarrow{AB}$ ⑥ Plane N

collinear	: points are on the same line ex) Points A, B, and C are ①_____.	
noncollinear	: points are NOT on the same line ex) Points A, B, and C are ②_____.	
coplanar	: points are on the same plane ex) Points A, B, and C are ③_____.	
Intersection	: Where two figures meet or cross each other ex) Lines l and m has an ④_____ at point A. Lines l and m intersects at point A.	
Congruent segments	: Segments that are equal in length. ($\cong$ means 'congruent') ex) If $\overline{AB}$ ⑤____ $\overline{CD}$, then AB ⑥____ CD. (⊗ Do not write $\overline{AB} = \overline{CD}$ or $AB \cong CD$)	congruent to $\overline{AB} \cong \overline{CD}$ equal to $AB = CD$
Segment bisector	: a line, segment, ray that cuts a segment exactly in half ex) If $\overline{CD}$ is a segment ⑦_____, then $AM = MB$.	Segment Bisector

Blank : ① collinear ② noncollinear ③ coplanar ④ intersection ⑤ $\cong$ ⑥ = ⑦ bisector

Vocabulary Check True or false?

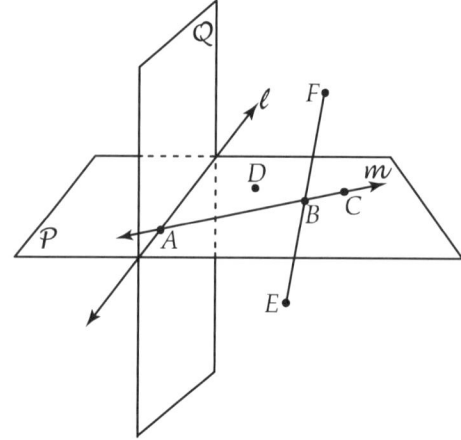

① $\overrightarrow{AB}$ is same as $\overrightarrow{BC}$

② Point C is on line m.

③ $\overrightarrow{AC}$ contains point D.

④ $\overrightarrow{AC}$ and $\overline{EF}$ intersect at point D.

⑤ Lines l and m intersect at point B.

⑥ Plane P and Plane Q intersect at line l.

⑦ Points A, B, and C are collinear.

⑧ Points A, C, and F are collinear.

⑨ Points A, B, and D are coplanar.

⑩ If $EB = BF$, then $\overleftrightarrow{AC}$ is the segment bisector of $\overline{EF}$.

Mia's Geometry

1.2 Basic Words_ Angles

1. Angles

Vocabulary	Meaning	Notation and Figure
Angle	: A figure formed by two rays with same endpoint. The rays are called the ①_____ of the angle. The common endpoint is called the ②_____. • Notation: ③_____	side A vertex 30° side B C ∠ABC or ∠B or ∠1
Measure of an angle	: The number of degrees (or radians) that an angle sweeps out. (=size of an angle) ex) The measure of ∠B is 30° : ④_____ (✗ Do not write ∠B = 30°)	measure of ∠ABC m∠ABC = 30°
Acute angle	: angle < 90°	acute ∠
Right angle	: angle = 90°	right ∠

Blank : ① sides   ② vertex   ③ ∠ABC or ∠B or ∠1   ④ m∠B = 30°

Obtuse angle	: 90° < angle < 180°	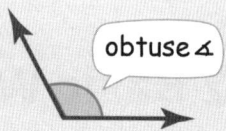
Straight angle	: angle = 180°	
Reflex angle	: 180° < angle < 360°	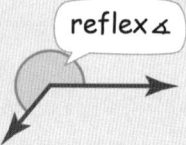
Complete angle	: angle = 360°	
Congruent angles	: Angles that have the same measure. ($\cong$ means 'congruent') ex) If $\angle 1 \underset{①}{\rule{1cm}{0.4pt}} \angle 2$, then $m\angle 1 \underset{②}{\rule{1cm}{0.4pt}} m\angle 2$. (⊗ Do not write $\angle 1 = \angle 2$ or $m\angle 1 \cong m\angle 2$)	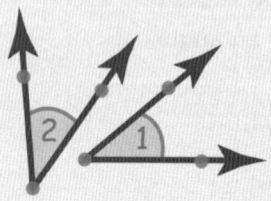
Angle bisector	: A ray that divides an angle into two congruent angles. ex) If $\vec{BS}$ is an ③ _____, then $m\angle ABS = m\angle SBC$.	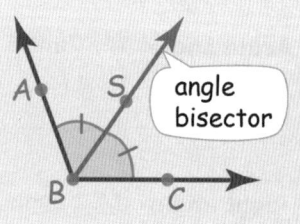

Blank : ① $\cong$ ② =   ③ angle bisector

Vocabulary Check Fill in the blanks.

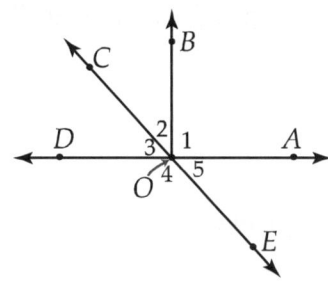

① If ∠1 is a right angle, then $m\angle 1$ = _____.

② ∠3 is formed by two rays _____ and _____.

③ ∠5 can be also written as ∠_____.

④ If ∠2 ≅ ∠3 then $\overrightarrow{OC}$ is an _____ _____.

⑤ Obtuse angle is ∠_____.

Mia's Geometry

1.3 Basic Words_ Special Pairs of Angles

1. Pairs of Angles

Vocabulary	Meaning	Notation and Figure
Complementary angles	: Two angles that add up to ①_____ ex) $m\angle A + m\angle B = 90°$. $\angle A$ and $\angle B$ are ②_____. $\angle A$ is complement of $\angle B$.	Complementary 63° 27°
Supplementary angles	: Two angles that add up to ③_____ ex) $m\angle A + m\angle B = 180°$. $\angle A$ and $\angle B$ are ④_____. $\angle A$ is supplement of $\angle B$.	Supplementary 145° 35°
Adjacent angles	: Two angles that have a common vertex and a common side. ex) $\angle 1$ is ⑤_____ to $\angle 2$.	Adjacent ∠s 1 2

Blank : ① 90°   ② complementary   ③ 180°   ④ supplementary   ⑤ adjacent

Linear Pair	: Two angles that are ①_____ and ②_____ ex) ∠1 and ∠2 are ③_____ _____.	

Vertical angles	: Two angles that are opposite each other when two lines intersect. ex) ∠1 and ∠2 are ④_____ angles.	

※ Supplementary Angle VS Linear Pair

Two angles are 　　　　　　　　　Two angles are

(⑤Supplementary angles/Linear pair).　(⑥Supplementary angles/Linear pair).

All linear pair angles are supplementary. (⑦True/False)

All supplementary angles are linear pair. (⑧True/False)

Blank : ① adjacent　② supplementary　③ linear pair　④ vertical

⑤ supplementary angles, linear pair (both)　⑥ supplementary angles　⑦ True　⑧ False

Vocabulary Check Identify and choose each pair of angles as complementary, Supplementary, vertical, adjacent angles, and/or linear pair. There can be more than one answer.

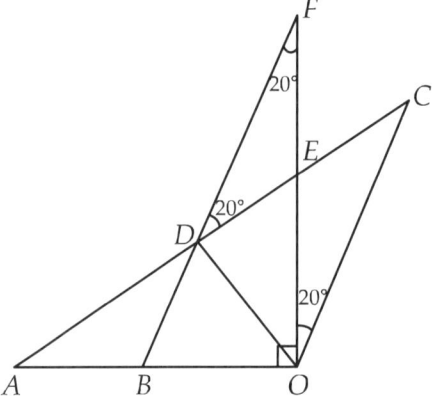

① ∠AOD, ∠EOD are (complementary ∠s / supplementary ∠s)

② ∠BDO, ∠ODF are (supplementary ∠s / linear pair)

③ ∠BDC, ∠EOC are (supplementary ∠s / linear pair)

④ ∠ADB, ∠FDE are (vertical ∠s / linear pair)

⑤ ∠ADO, ∠FDO are (vertical ∠s / adjacent ∠s)

⑥ ∠EOD, ∠EOC are (complementary ∠s / adjacent ∠s)

Mia's Geometry

1.4 Basic Words_ Polygons

1. Polygons

Poly- means "many" and *-gon* means "angle or corner".

Polygons are 2-dimensional shapes with many angles or sides.
They are made of (①straight lines/curved lines/ mixed)
, and the shape is (②closed/ opened).

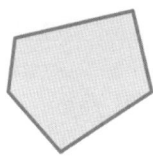
Polygon

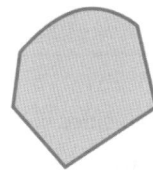
Not a polygon
(has a curve)

Not a polygon
(open, not closed)

2. Names of Polygons

Vocabulary	Meaning	Notation and Figure
Triangle	Polygon with 3 sides (*tri-* means 3)	triangle
Quadrilateral	Polygon with 4 sides (*quad-* means 4)	quadrilateral
Pentagon	Polygon with 5 sides (*pent-* means 5)	pentagon
Hexagon	Polygon with 6 sides (*hex-* means 6)	hexagon

Part 1_Basic words for Geometry

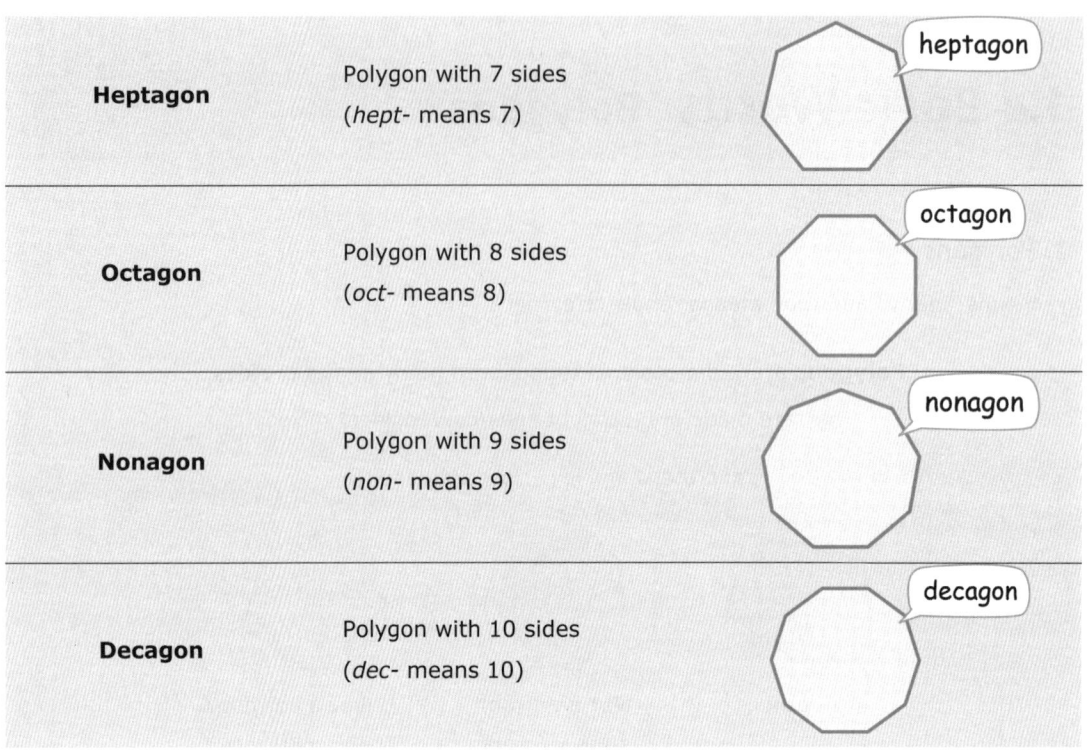

A ③_____ polygon has all angles equal and all sides equal, otherwise it is **irregular.**

A ④_____ polygon has all interior angles less than 180° (all vertices pointing outwards from the center). If any interior angle is greater than 180° then the polygon is ⑤_____.

Blank : ① straight lines   ② closed   ③ regular   ④ convex   ⑤ concave

Vocabulary Check Name each polygon by its number of sides. Then classify it as *concave* or *convex* and *regular* or *irregular*.

①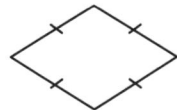

②

③

④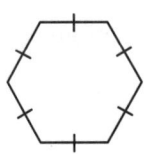

⑤

3. Names of Triangles

Vocabulary	Meaning	Notation and Figure
Scalene Triangle	Has no congruent sides	Scalene △
Isosceles Triangle	Has at least two congruent sides	Isosceles △
Equilateral Triangle ('*Equal+lines*')	All sides are congruent	Equilateral △

We will learn more details in the 'Triangle' chapter!

4. Names of Quadrilaterals

Vocabulary	Meaning	Notation and Figure
Parallelogram	Has two pairs of parallel sides.	Parallelogram
Rectangle	Has four right angles.	Rectangle
Rhombus	Has four congruent sides.	Rhombus
Square	Has four right angles and four congruent sides.	Square
Trapezoid	Has one pair of parallel side.	Trapezoid
Kite	Two pairs of adjacent sides of the same length.	kite

We will learn more details in the ' Quadrilateral' chapter!

Part 2
Geometric Reasoning

2.1 Conditional Statements

2.2 Inverses and Contrapositives

2.3 Postulates and Theorems

2.4 Writing Proofs

2.5 Segments and Angle Relationships

2.6 Special Pairs of Angles

2.7 Perpendicular Lines

2.8 Theorems about Special Pairs of Angles

Postulates or Theorems from Chapter 2

Mia's Geometry
2.1 Conditional Statements

1. If-then Statements

In geometry, many statements are written in 'If *something*, then *something*.' form. We call this form a ①_____ statement.

※ Conditional Statement

Conditional Statement (If-then form)
If p, then q. 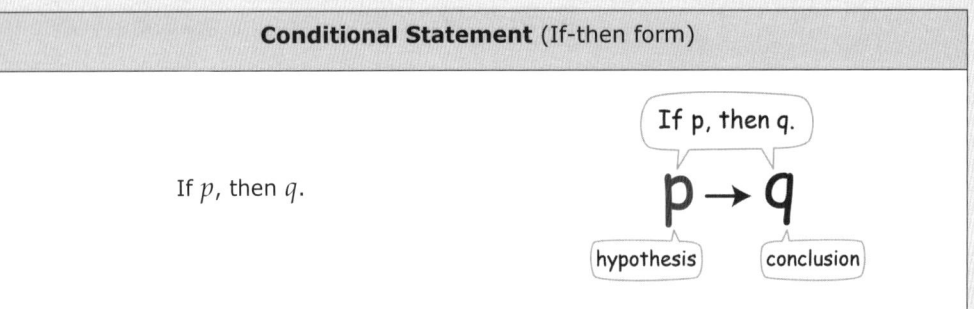

The 'if' part is ②_____, and the 'then' part is ③_____.

ex) <u>If you are living in Seoul</u>, <u>then you are living in Korea</u>.
        (hypothesis)   (conclusion)

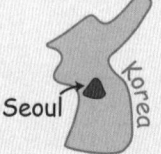

※ Other form:

$p \to q$	: Living in Seoul → Living in Korea.
p implies q	: Living in Seoul implies living in Korea.
p only if q	: You are living in Seoul only if you are living in Korea.
q if p.	: You are living in Korea if you are living in Seoul.

Blank : ① conditional　　② hypothesis　　③ conclusion

EXAMPLE 1. Write each statement in if-then form. Then underline the hypothesis and conclusion.

① A polygon with three sides is a triangle.

② All birds have feathers.

③ Two angles are supplementary if they add up to 180°.

④ A right angle has a measure of 90°

⑤ I'll go to the movie only if today is Saturday.

⑥ Jeff is a dog only if it is a mammal.

⑦ $x > 5$ implies $x > 1$.

⑧ $x = 2$ if $x^2 = 4$.

2. Is a Statement True or False?

※ How to determine if a statement is True or False

1) Conditional statement is TRUE, if the conclusion is ALWAYS TRUE when the hypothesis is true.
Conditional statement is FALSE, if the conclusion CAN BE FALSE when the hypothesis is true.

ex) If a number is divisible by 2, then it is even. (①True/False)

If a number is divisible by 3, then it is odd. (②True/False)

Sometimes it's easier to think of it in terms of sets.

※ How to determine if a statement is True or False

2) Conditional statement is TRUE, when *hypothesis* is the subset(=belongs to) of *conclusion*.

ex) If you are living in Seoul, then you are living in Korea. (③True/False)

If you are living in Korea, then you are living in Seoul. (④True/False)

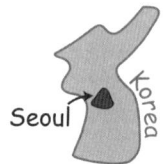

3. Counterexample

A **counterexample** is an example that shows you the statement is false.
The counterexample must have ⑤_____ hypothesis and ⑥_____ conclusion.

ex) If a fruit is yellow, then it is pineapple. (⑦True/False)

Counterexample: ⑧_____

Blank : ① True   ② False   ③ True   ④ False   ⑤ True   ⑥ False   ⑦ False   ⑧ banana

EXAMPLE 2. Determine whether the given statement is true or false. If it is false, find the counterexample.

① If $|x|=2$, then $x=-2$.

② $x=-2$ only if $x^2=4$.

③ $x<0$ if $x<-2$.

④ $x>2$ implies $x>5$.

⑤ $x^2>9$ implies $x>3$.

⑥ $\overline{AB} \cong \overline{BC}$ if $AB = BC$.

⑦ $A=0$ if $AB=0$.

⑧ If a shape has 3 sides, then it is isosceles triangle.

⑨ All figures with four sides of equal length are squares.

Mia's Geometry
2.2 Inverses and Contrapositives

1. Negation

※ Negation (=Not)

① Negation (~) means "not."

Not p
~p

② Negating "all" becomes "①_____",

Negating "positive" becomes "②_____",

Negating "greater than" becomes "③_____"

2. Converse, Inverse, and Contrapositive

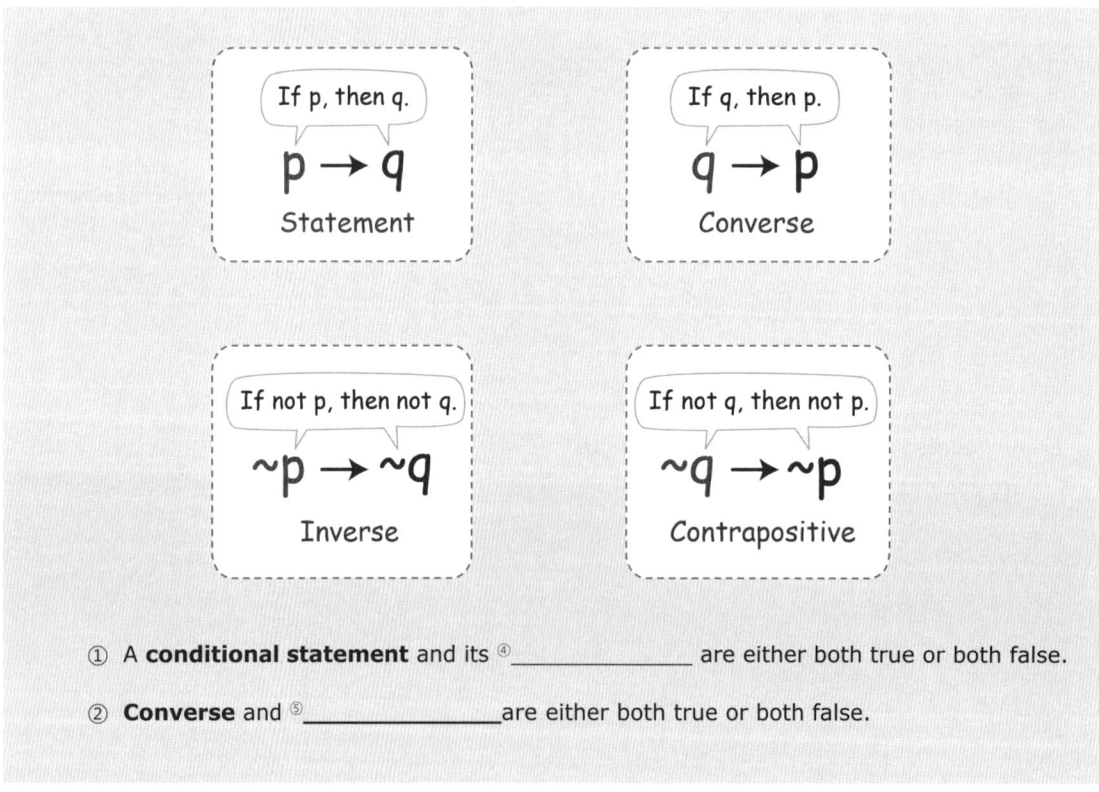

① A **conditional statement** and its ④_____ are either both true or both false.

② **Converse** and ⑤_____ are either both true or both false.

Blank : ① some　② negative or 0　③ less than or equal to　④ contrapositive　⑤ inverse ex) Statement: If you are living in Seoul, then you are living in Korea.

　　　　　　　(①True/False)

Converse: If you are living in ②_____, then you are living in ③_____.

　　　　　　　(④True/False)

Inverse: If you are not living in ⑤_____, then you are not living in ⑥_____.

　　　　　　　(⑦True/False)

Contrapositive: If you are not living in ⑧_____, then you are not living in ⑨_____.

　　　　　　　(⑩True/False)

EXAMPLE 1.   Write the converse, inverse, and contrapositive of each conditional statement. Tell which statements are true and which statements are false.

① If $x \neq 2$, then $x^2 \neq 4$.

Converse:

Inverse:

Contrapositive:

② If $x^2 = 9$, then $x = -3$.

Converse:

Inverse:

Contrapositive:

Blank : ① True ② Korea ③ Seoul ④ False ⑤ Seoul ⑥ Korea ⑦ False ⑧ Korea ⑨ Seoul ⑩ True

③ If x is positive, then x is at least 2.

   Converse:

   Inverse:

   Contrapositive:

④ If $x > 2$, then $x > 5$.

   Converse:

   Inverse:

   Contrapositive:

⑤ If a polygon is not a rectangle, then it is not a square.

   Converse:

   Inverse:

   Contrapositive:

⑥ If two angles are supplementary, then the sum of their measures is 180°.

   Converse:

   Inverse:

   Contrapositive:

3. Biconditional Statement

When a conditional statement (p only if q) and its converse (p if q) are both ①_____, you can write them as a single ②_____ statement.

※ Biconditional Statement

Biconditional Statement

When $p \to q$ is true, and $q \to p$ is true,
we can combine the statements and write :

p if and only if q.

(abbreviation: p iff q.)

p if and only if q

$$p \leftrightarrow q$$

★ Any definition can be written as a biconditional statement.

ex) Statement : If an angle is a right, then it has a measure of 90°. (③True/False)

Converse : If an angle has a measure of 90°, then it is a right angle. (④True/False)

Biconditional: An angle is right if and only if it measures 90°.

This statement is the ⑤_____ of right angle.

EXAMPLE 2. Write the converse of each statement. If the converse is true, write the biconditional statement.

① If an angle measures less than 90°, then it is an acute angle.

Converse:

Biconditional:

Blank : ① true ② biconditional ③ True ④ True ⑤ definition

② If the sum of the measures of two angles is 90°, then they are complementary.

Converse:

Biconditional:

③ If an animal is an owl, then it lives in the forest.

Converse:

Biconditional:

④ If an animal is a penguin, then it is black and white.

Converse:

Biconditional:

⑤ If $AB = CD$, then $\overline{AB} \cong \overline{CD}$.

Converse:

Biconditional:

⑥ If a circle has a radius of r, then it has an area of πr^2.

Converse:

Biconditional:

⑦ If two lines are perpendicular, then they intersect to form right angles.

Converse:

Biconditional:

Mia's Geometry
2.3 Postulates and Theorems

1. Inductive Reasoning

In geometry, we do a lot of reasoning to understand geometric concepts, solve problems, and prove theorems.

Reasoning is an act of drawing conclusions from patterns, facts, evidence etc.
We have two different types of reasoning;
      Inductive reasoning and *Deductive* reasoning.

Vocabulary	Definition	Notation and Figure
Conjecture	A guess based on the pattern.	
Inductive Reasoning	Uses ①_____ to arrive at a conclusion (=Making a conjecture after looking at several situations)	□ ▦ ▦ ?

EXAMPLE 1. Make a conjecture about the next item in each sequence.

① A, C, E, _____

② January, March, May,_____

③ −6, 12, −18, _____

④ $\frac{1}{2}, -\frac{1}{4}, \frac{1}{8}$, _____

⑤

⑥

Blank : ① pattern

2. Deductive Reasoning

Vocabulary	Definition	Notation and Figure
Definition	A statement that explains the meaning of a word or phrase. All definitions are ① _____ in geometry.	ex) Vertical angles are two nonadjacent angles formed by two intersecting lines. (Just explaining.)
Postulate (=axiom)	A statement that is accepted as true without proof.	ex) If two lines intersect, then their intersection is exactly one point. (So obvious.)
Theorem	A statement that has been proven true.	ex) Vertical angles are congruent. Proof: $m\angle 1 + m\angle 3 = 180°$ $m\angle 2 + m\angle 3 = 180°$ $m\angle 1 + m\angle 3 = m\angle 2 + m\angle 3$ $m\angle 1 = m\angle 2$ (Can prove.)
Deductive Reasoning	Uses DPPT(definitions, properties, postulates, or theorems) to arrive at a conclusion	ex) Two column proofs, flow chart proofs, paragraph proofs ...

Blank : ① biconditional

※ Inductive Reasoning VS Deductive Reasoning

Inductive Reasoning : Uses ①_____ to arrive at a conclusion

Deductive Reasoning : Uses ②_____ (definitions, properties, postulates, or theorems)
to arrive at a conclusion

ex) In the previous geometry class, Jay's teacher assigned him homework. Today, his teacher gave him homework again. Jay concludes that he will have homework in the next geometry class.

    Jay uses ③_____ reasoning to make a conclusion.

    It was based on past observation.

ex) In Julia's geometry class, the teacher introduced a new theorem: 'Vertical angles are congruent.' Julia notices that ∠1 and ∠2 are vertical angles, so she concludes that ∠1 ≅ ∠2.

    Julia uses ④_____ reasoning to make a conclusion.

    It was based on theorem.

EXAMPLE 2. Determine whether each conclusion is based on inductive or deductive reasoning.

① Hanna knows that the sum of two complementary angles is 90°. She has two angles, A=35° and B=55°. She concludes that A and B are complementary angles.

Blank : ① pattern   ② DPPT   ③ inductive   ④ deductive

② Joshua calculated the sums of the interior angles of several triangles. He noticed that they were all 180°. He concluded that the sum of the interior angles of a triangle is 180°.

③ Maria calculated that 1+2 is an odd number, 3+4 is an odd number, and 11+12 is an odd number. She concluded that the sum of two consecutive numbers is an odd number.

④ A car that parks illegally gets a ticket. Jack parked illegally. Therefore, Jack will get a ticket.

⑤ Students at Kelly's high school must have a B average in order to participate in sports. Kelly has a B average. She concludes that she can participate in sports at school.

⑥ Claire notices that every Saturday, her neighbor mows his lawn. Today is Saturday. Claire concludes her neighbor will mow his lawn.

3. Postulate

A **postulate** is a statement that is accepted as *true* (①with/without) proof.

※ Basic Postulates

Postulate
If two lines intersect, then their intersection is exactly one point.
If two planes intersect, then their intersection is a line.
Through any two points, there is exactly one line.
A line contains at least two points.
Through any three noncollinear points, there is exactly one plane.
A plane contains at least three noncollinear points.
If two points lie in a plane, then the line containing those points lies in the plane.

Blank : ① without

EXAMPLE 3. Use the postulates to determine whether each statement is *always, sometimes*, or *never* true.

① A line contains exactly two points.

② If two points are collinear, then they are coplanar.

③ Any two lines intersect.

④ Any two planes intersect.

⑤ Two points determine a line.

⑥ Three planes intersect in exactly one point.

⑦ A line and plane intersect in exactly one point.

⑧ Two points determine a plane.

⑨ Three points lie in exactly one plane.

⑩ Two intersecting planes intersect in exactly one point.

⑪ Three points are coplanar.

⑫ Three points are collinear.

Mia's Geometry

2.4 Writing Proofs

1. Writing Proofs

Proofs are a key part of geometry because they show us why a statements or properties about shapes, angles, sizes or other geometric concepts are true.

Most geometric proofs start with a **Given** and a **Prove** (or To Prove) section.

ex)

'Given'

Given: ∠1 and ∠2 are vertical angles.

Prove: $m\angle 1 = m\angle 2$

'Prove'

2. Types of Proof

1) Two Column Proof

These proofs are most often seen in high school textbooks including this book.

In a two-column proof,

we list the steps of the proof on the left column (① _____ part),

and the reasons for each steps in the right column(② _____ part).

ex)

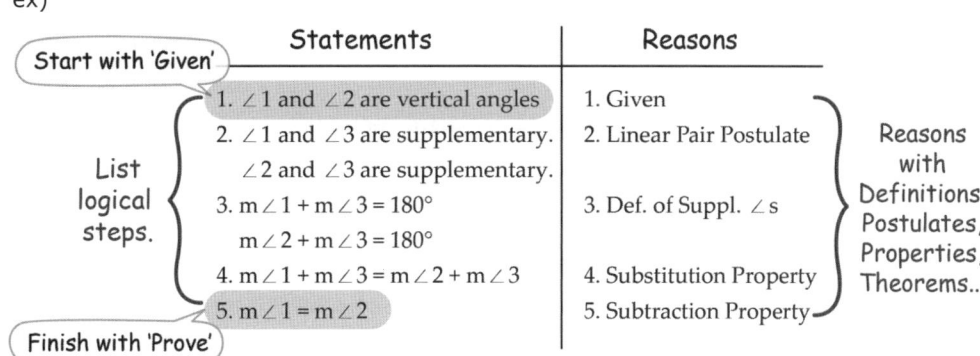

Start with 'Given'

Statements	Reasons
1. ∠1 and ∠2 are vertical angles.	1. Given
2. ∠1 and ∠3 are supplementary. ∠2 and ∠3 are supplementary.	2. Linear Pair Postulate
3. $m\angle 1 + m\angle 3 = 180°$ $m\angle 2 + m\angle 3 = 180°$	3. Def. of Suppl. ∠s
4. $m\angle 1 + m\angle 3 = m\angle 2 + m\angle 3$	4. Substitution Property
5. $m\angle 1 = m\angle 2$	5. Subtraction Property

List logical steps.

Finish with 'Prove'

Reasons with Definitions, Postulates, Properties, Theorems…

Blank : ① statements   ② reasons

When we write reasons, we use DPPT (Definitions, postulates, properties, and theorems.)

2) Flow chart Proof

These proofs use flowchart to visualize the process and the sequences of the statements. We write the reasons below each box.

ex)

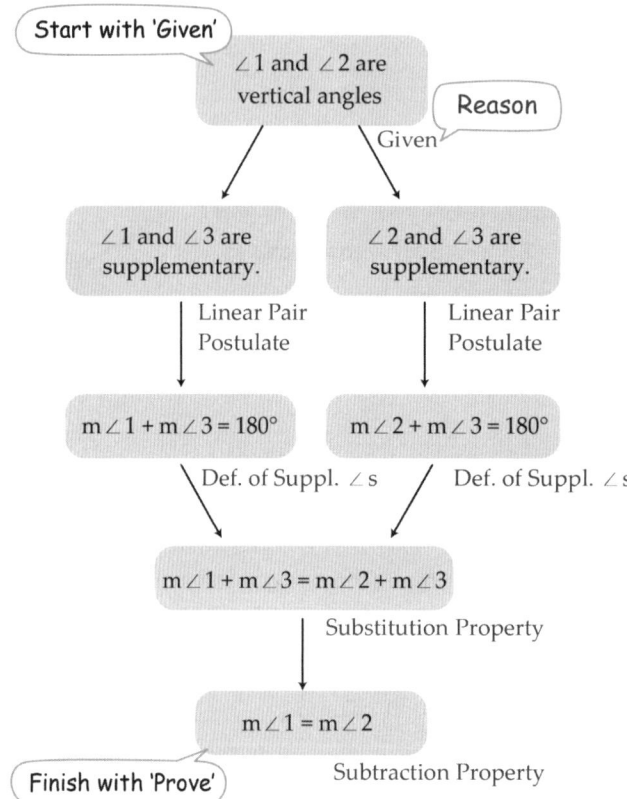

3) Paragraph Proof

These proofs are written in paragraph form using complete sentences.

ex) "∠1 and ∠2 are vertical angles. By linear pair postulate, ∠1 and ∠3 are supplementary, ∠2 and ∠3 are supplementary. By definition of supplementary angles m∠1 + m∠3 = 180° and m∠2 + m∠3 = 180°. By substitution property, m∠1 + m∠3 = m∠2 + m∠3. So, m∠1 = m∠2 by subtraction property."

3. Steps for Writing Geometric Proof

1. **Identify** what is given and what you need to prove.
2. **Draw or label** the points, angles, and segments according to the information from 'Given' part.
3. Ask yourself : "What do I need to show in order to conclude this?" The postulates, definitions, or theorems you are learning in each chapter can be a BIG HINT.
4. Write down the path of your thought in the **'Statements' column** with appropriate statements, clear notations, and accurate words.
5. Write the reasons in the **'Reasons'** column using DPPT(Definitions, postulates, properties, and theorems.)

☺ Tips

- The proof is **always true**.
- There can be **more than one correct way** to do a proof.
- If a certain word is used in the 'Given' part, we usually use the **definition** of that word.
- All definitions are **biconditional** so you can use in either direction.
- In the 'Reason' column of your two-column proof, you should write the *name* of the DPPT(Definitions, postulates, properties, and theorems.) you're using. **Memorize the *name*** of the DPPT!
- You **may use abbreviated words** for the DPPT.
- If you are stuck, sometimes **working backwards** could help you.
- The more you **practice proofs**, the more familiar you'll become with the logical patterns.

4. Basic Properties

Here are some common properties you might use in a two-column proof.

※ Basic Properties

For all numbers a, b, c and d,

	Property
Reflxive Property	$a = a$. (A segment or angle is congruent to itself)
Symmetric Property	If $a = b$ then $b = a$. (If one segment or angle is congruent to another, the reverse is also true.)
Transitive Property	If $a = b$ and $b = c$ then $a = c$. (If first is equal to second and second is equal to third, then first and third are equal.)

Addition Property	If $a = b$ then $a + c = b + c$.
	If $a = b$ and $c = d$ then $a + c =$ ①_____.
Subtraction Property	If $a = b$ then $a - c = b - c$.
	If $a = b$ and $c = d$ then $a - c =$ ②_____.
Multiplication Property	If $a = b$ then $a \cdot c = b \cdot c$.
	If $a = b$ and $c = d$ then $a \cdot c =$ ③_____.
Division Property	If $a = b$ then $a / c = b / c$. ($c \neq 0$)
Distribution Property	$a(b + c) =$ ④_____.
Substitution Property	If $a = b$ and $a = c$, then $b = c$. (a may be replaced by c)

☺ The Transitive Property is about connecting relationships.

$$\text{If } a = b \text{ and } b = c \text{ then } a = c.$$

The Substitution Property is about replacing.

$$\text{If } a = b \text{ and } a = c, \text{ then } b = c.$$

Blank : ① $b + d$ ② $b - d$ ③ bd ④ $ab + ac$

EXAMPLE 1. State the property that justifies each statement.

① If $m\angle 1 = m\angle 2$, then $m\angle 2 = m\angle 1$.

② $AB = AB$

③ If $AB = 5$ and $AB = BC$, then $BC = 5$.

④ If $2AB = 40°$, then $AB = 20°$.

⑤ If $m\angle 1 = m\angle 2$ and $m\angle 2 = 60°$, then $m\angle 1 = 60°$.

⑥ If $AB = CD$ and $CD = EF$, then $AB = EF$.

⑦ $\angle A \cong \angle A$

⑧ If $AB = 2$, then $2 = AB$.

⑨ If $AB = CD$, then $2AB = 2CD$.

⑩ If $m\angle 1 + m\angle 2 = 70°$ and $m\angle 1 = m\angle 3$, then $m\angle 3 + m\angle 2 = 70°$.

⑪ If $AB + CD = 7$ and $CD = EF$, then $AB + EF = 7$.

⑫ If $AB = CD$ and $EF = GH$, then $AB + EF = CD + GH$.

⑬ If $m\angle 1 = m\angle 2$, $m\angle 2 = m\angle 3$, and $m\angle 3 = 30°$ then $m\angle 1 = 30°$.

⑭ If $AB = CD$, then $AB - EF = CD - EF$.

⑮ If $m\angle 1 + m\angle 2 = m\angle 1 + m\angle 3$, then $m\angle 2 = m\angle 3$.

EXAMPLE 2. Complete each proof.

① Given: $2x+6=7x-14$
Prove: $x=4$

Statements	Reasons
1. $2x+6=7x-14$	1.
2. $6=5x-14$	2.
3. $20=5x$	3.
4. $4=x$	4.
5. $x=4$	5.

② Given: $\dfrac{9x-6}{3}=4$
Prove: $x=2$

Statements	Reasons
1. $\dfrac{9x-6}{3}=4$	1.
2. $9x-6=12$	2.
3. $9x=18$	3.
4. $x=2$	4.

③ Given: $3(x+4)=15$
$x+y=10$
Prove: $y=9$

Statements	Reasons
1. $3(x+4)=15$ $x+y=10$	1. Given
2. $x+4=5$	2.
3. $x=1$	3.
4. $1+y=10$	4.
5. $y=9$	5.

④ Given: $2(-y-1)=14$
$y=2x+1$
Prove: $x=-\dfrac{9}{2}$

Statements	Reasons
1. $2(-y-1)=14$ $y=2x+1$	1. Given
2. $-2y-2=14$	2.
3. $-2y=16$	3.
4. $y=-8$	4.
5. $-8=2x+1$	5.
6. $-9=2x$	6.
7. $x=-9/2$	

Part 2_Geometric Reasoning 47

⑤ Given: $\overline{AB} \cong \overline{AC}$
Prove: $x = 11$

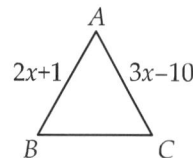

Statements	Reasons
1. $\overline{AB} \cong \overline{AC}$	1. Given
2. $AB = AC$	2.
3. $2x + 1 = 3x - 10$	3.
4. $2x + 11 = 3x$	4.
5. $11 = x$	5.
6. $x = 11$	6.

⑥ Given: $\angle A \cong \angle B$
Prove: $x = 5$

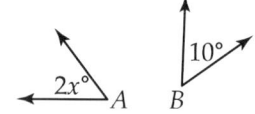

Statements	Reasons
1. $\angle A \cong \angle B$	1. Given
2. $m\angle A = m\angle B$	2.
3. $2x = 10$	3.
4. $x = 5$	4.

☺ Definition of $\cong$ segment : $\overline{AB} \cong \overline{AC} \rightleftarrows AB = AC$

Definition of $\cong$ angle : $\angle A \cong \angle B \rightleftarrows m\angle A = m\angle B$

Mia's Geometry
2.5 Segments and Angle Relationships

1. Basic Postulates or Theorems about Segment

These postulates and theorems are the foundations for solving problems involving line segments in geometry. Must memorize!

※ Segment Addition Postulate

Segment Addition Postulate
B is between A and C if and only if $AB + BC = AC$.     ☹ Do not write $\overline{AB} + \overline{BC} = \overline{AC}$

※ Midpoint

Definition of Midpoint
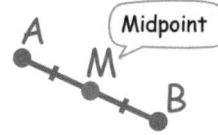 M is the midpoint of $\overline{AB}$ if and only if $AM = MB$. 

Midpoint Theorem
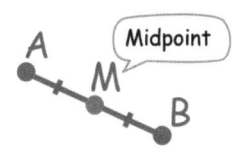 If M is the midpoint of $\overline{AB}$, then $AM = \dfrac{1}{2} AB$ and $MB = \dfrac{1}{2} AB$. 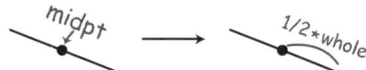

☺ Memorizing Tip: Definition of Midpoint VS Midpoint Theorem
　　Definition: Parts are ≅
　　Theorem : Part = 1/2 * whole

※ Segment Bisector

Definition of Segment Bisector

$\overline{CD}$ bisects $\overline{AB}$ if and only if $AM = MB$.

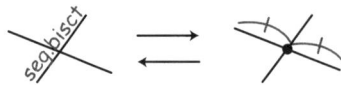 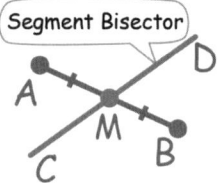

EXAMPLE 1. M is the midpoint of $\overline{AC}$ and $\overline{BD}$. $\overline{LN}$ bisects $\overline{AD}$ and $\overline{BC}$. Name the definition, theorem, or postulate that justifies the given statements.

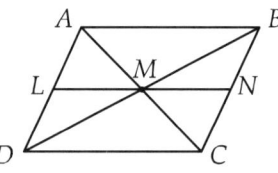

① $AM = MC$

② $MC = \dfrac{1}{2} AC$

③ $DM = \dfrac{1}{2} DB$

④ $AM + MC = AC$

⑤ $DM + MB = DB$

⑥ $DM = MB$

⑦ $AL = LD$

⑧ $BN = NC$

⑨ $AD = AL + LD$

⑩ $LN = LM + MN$

EXAMPLE 2. Complete each proof.

① Given: $BC = DE$
Prove: $AB + DE = AC$

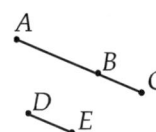

Statements	Reasons

② Given: $AB = CD$
Prove: $AC = BD$

Statements	Reasons

③ Given: B is midpoint of $\overline{AC}$
C is midpoint of $\overline{BD}$
Prove: $AC = BD$

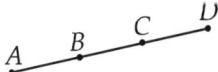

Statements	Reasons

④ Given: $AB = CD$, $AO = CO$
Prove: $DO = BO$

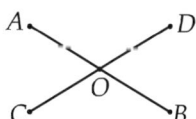

Statements	Reasons

⑤ Given: $AB = CD$

M is midpoint of $\overline{AB}$

M is midpoint of $\overline{CD}$

Prove: $AM = CM$

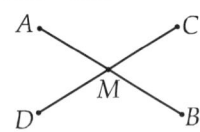

Statements	Reasons

⑥ Given: $AC = DF$

B is midpoint of $\overline{AC}$

E is midpoint of $\overline{DF}$

Prove: $BC = EF$

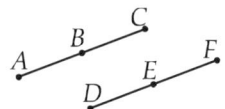

Statements	Reasons

⑦ Given: $\overline{AD}$ bisects $\overline{CE}$
    $BC = EF$
Prove: $BD = DF$

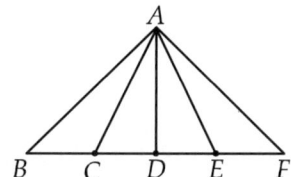

Statements	Reasons

⑧ Given: $\overline{BE}$ bisects $\overline{AC}$ and $\overline{DF}$
    $BC = EF$
Prove: $AB = DE$

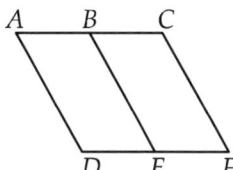

Statements	Reasons

⑨ Given: $\overline{AC} \cong \overline{BD}$
Prove: $AB = CD$

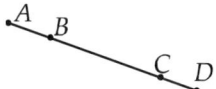

Statements	Reasons

⑩ Given: $AC = DF$, $AB = EF$
Prove: $BC = DE$

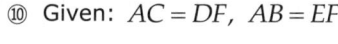
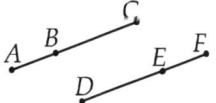

Statements	Reasons

2. Basic Postulates or Theorems about Angles

These postulates and theorems are the foundations for solving problems involving angles in geometry. Must memorize!

※ Angle Addition Postulate

Angle Addition Postulate

Point R is in the interior of $\angle ABC$ if and only if

$m\angle 1 + m\angle 2 = m\angle ABC.$

 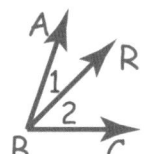

☹ Do not write $\angle 1 + \angle 2 = \angle ABC$

※ Angle Bisector

Definition of Angle Bisector

$\overrightarrow{BX}$ bisect $\angle ABC$ if and only if

$m\angle 1 = m\angle 2.$

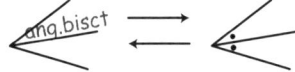 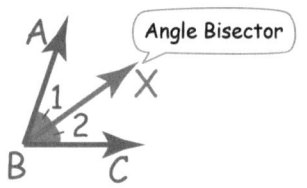

Angle Bisector Theorem

If $\overrightarrow{BX}$ bisect $\angle ABC$

, then $m\angle 1 = \dfrac{1}{2} m\angle ABC$ and $m\angle 2 = \dfrac{1}{2} m\angle ABC$.

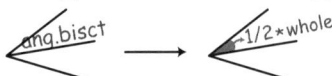 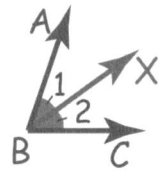

☺ Memorizing Tip: Definition of Angle Bisector VS Angle Bisector Theorem
  Definition: Parts are ≅
  Theorem : Part = 1/2 * whole

EXAMPLE 3. Name the definition, theorem, or postulate that justifies the given statements.

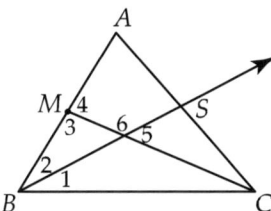

① If M is the midpoint of $\overline{AB}$, then $AM = \dfrac{1}{2} AB$.

② $m\angle 1 + m\angle 2 = m\angle ABC$

③ If $\angle 1 \cong \angle 2$, then $\overrightarrow{BS}$ bisects $\angle ABC$.

④ If $\overline{AM} \cong \overline{MB}$, then M is the midpoint of $\overline{AB}$.

⑤ $m\angle 5 + m\angle 6 = 180°$

⑥ If $\overrightarrow{BS}$ bisects $\angle ABC$, then $\angle 1 \cong \angle 2$.

⑦ If $\overrightarrow{BS}$ bisects $\angle ABC$, then $m\angle 1 = \dfrac{1}{2} m\angle ABC$

⑧ $AS + SC = AC$

EXAMPLE 4. Complete each proof.

① Given: $\angle 1 \cong \angle 3$
Prove: $m\angle DAB = m\angle CAE$

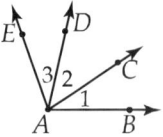

Statements	Reasons

② Given: $\angle ABC \cong \angle ABD, m\angle 2 = m\angle 4$
Prove: $m\angle 1 = m\angle 3$

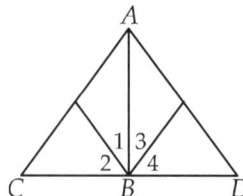

Statements	Reasons

③ Given: $m\angle DAB = m\angle CAE$
Prove: $m\angle 1 = m\angle 3$

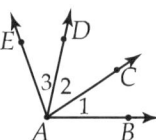

Statements	Reasons

④ Given: $m\angle 1 = m\angle 3, m\angle 2 = m\angle 4$
Prove: $\angle ABC \cong \angle ABD$

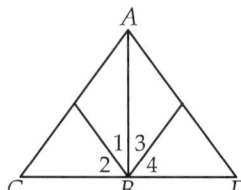

Statements	Reasons

⑤ Given: $m\angle 2 = m\angle 3$
Prove: $m\angle 1 = m\angle 4$

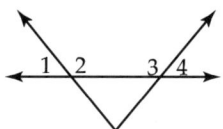

Statements	Reasons

⑥ Given: $\overrightarrow{BD}$ bisects $\angle ABC$
$\overrightarrow{FH}$ bisects $\angle EFG$
$m\angle ABC = m\angle EFG$
Prove: $m\angle 1 = m\angle 3$

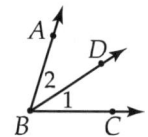 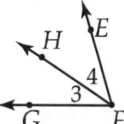

Statements	Reasons

⑦ Given: $\overrightarrow{BE}$ bisects $\angle ABC$
$\overrightarrow{CD}$ bisects $\angle ACB$
$m\angle ABC = m\angle ACB$
Prove: $m\angle 1 = m\angle 2$

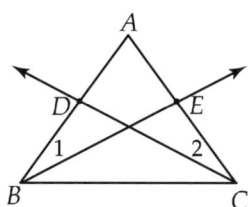

Statements	Reasons

Mia's Geometry

2.6 Special Pairs of Angles

1. Postulates and Theorems about Pairs of Angles

※ Complementary angles

Definition of Complementary angles
Two angles are complementary if and only if they add up to 90°. 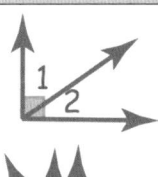   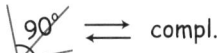 compl.   ex) $m\angle 1 + m\angle 2 = 90°$ ⇌ angles are complementary.

Complement Theorem
If the noncommon sides of two adjacent angles form a right angle, then the angles are complementary. 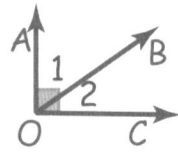    → compl.   ex) $\overrightarrow{OA} \perp \overrightarrow{OC}$ → angles ($\angle 1$ and $\angle 2$) are complementary.

☺ Memorizing Tip: Definition of Compl. ∠s VS Complement Theorem

Definition: <u>add up to 90°</u> ⇌ complementary

Use it to show that two angles are complementary based on their measures.

Theorem : <u>form right ∠</u> → complementary

Use it when you know two angles form a right angle, and you want to conclude that they are complementary.

※ Supplementary angles

Definition of Supplementary angles

Two angles are supplementary
if and only if they add up to 180°.

180° ⇌ suppl.

ex) $m\angle 1 + m\angle 2 = 180°$ ⇌ angles are supplementary.

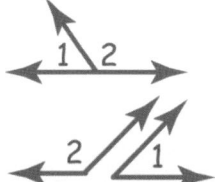

Supplement Theorem (Linear Pair Postulate)

If two angles form a linear pair, then they are supplementary.

lin. pair ⟶ suppl.

ex) $\angle 1$ and $\angle 2$ form linear pair(straight line) → angles($\angle 1$ and $\angle 2$) are supplementary.

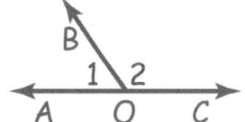

☺ Memorizing Tip: Definition of Suppl. ∠s VS Supplement Theorem

Definition: <u>add up to 180°</u> ⇌ Supplementary

Use it to show that two angles are supplementary based on their measures.

Theorem : <u>form straight line</u> → Supplementary

Use it when you know two angles form a straight, and you want to conclude that they are supplementary.

Vertical Angles Theorem

Vertical angles are congruent.

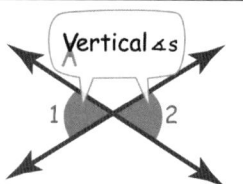

☺ Proof of Vertical Angles Theorem:

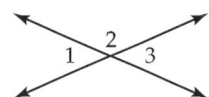

Given: ∠1 and ∠3 are vertical angles
Prove: $m\angle 1 = m\angle 3$

Statements	Reasons
1. ∠1 and ∠3 are vertical angles	1. Given
2. ∠1 and ∠2 are supplementary. ∠2 and ∠3 are supplementary.	2. ① _____
3. $m\angle 1 + m\angle 2 = 180°$ $m\angle 2 + m\angle 3 = 180°$	3. ② _____
4. ③ _____	4. Substitution Property
5. ④ _____	5. Subtraction Property

Blank : ① linear pair post.   ② Def of suppl. ∠s   ③ m∠1 + m∠2 = m∠2 + m∠3   ④ m∠1 = m∠3

EXAMPLE 1. The line $\overleftrightarrow{AE}$, $\overleftrightarrow{BF}$ and the ray $\overrightarrow{OB}$, $\overrightarrow{OD}$ is shown. Name the definition, theorem, or postulate that justifies the given statements.

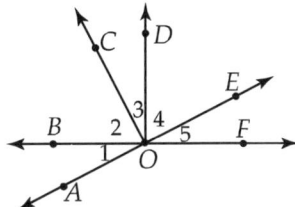

① If $m\angle 1 + m\angle 2 = 90°$, then $\angle 1$ and $\angle 2$ are complementary angles.

② If $\angle DOF$ and $\angle BOD$ are linear pairs, then $\angle DOF$ and $\angle BOD$ are supplementary angles.

③ $m\angle 1 + m\angle 2 = m\angle AOC$

④ If $m\angle DOF + m\angle BOD = 180°$, then $\angle DOF$ and $\angle BOD$ are supplementary angles.

⑤ $\angle AOB$ and $\angle BOE$ form a straight line, so $\angle AOB$ and $\angle BOE$ are supplementary angles.

⑥ If $\angle 3$ and $\angle 4$ are complementary angles, then $m\angle 3 + m\angle 4 = 90°$.

⑦ If $\angle AOB$ and $\angle BOE$ are supplementary angles, then $m\angle AOB + m\angle BOE = 180°$.

⑧ If $\overrightarrow{OA} \perp \overrightarrow{OC}$, then $\angle 1$ and $\angle 2$ are complementary angles.

⑨ If $\overrightarrow{OB} \perp \overrightarrow{OD}$, then $\angle 2$ and $\angle 3$ are complementary angles.

⑩ $m\angle BOE = m\angle AOF$

⑪ $m\angle 1 = m\angle 5$.

Part 2_Geometric Reasoning 61

EXAMPLE 2. For the given diagram, Find the value of x, y, or z.

①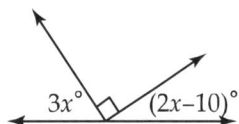

②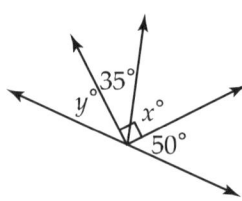

③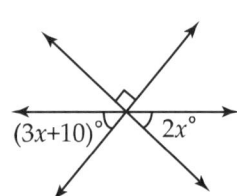

④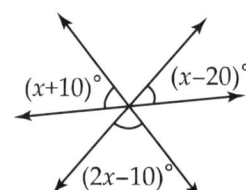

⑤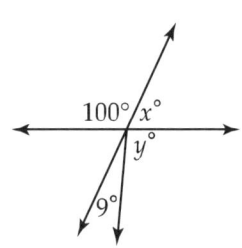

⑥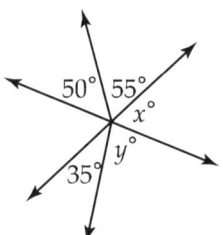

EXAMPLE 3. What is $x-y$?

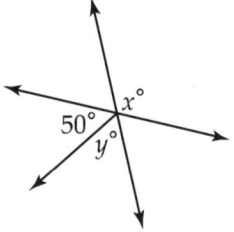

EXAMPLE 4. What is $x+y+z$?

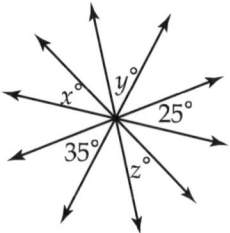

EXAMPLE 5. Complete each proof.

① Given: ∠1 ≅ ∠4
   Prove: ∠2 ≅ ∠3

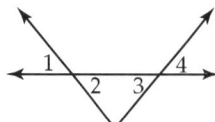

Statements	Reasons

② Given: $m\angle 1 = m\angle 3$
   Prove: $m\angle 2 = m\angle 4$

Statements	Reasons

③ Given: $\overrightarrow{OB}$ bisects ∠AOC
   Prove: ∠2 ≅ ∠3

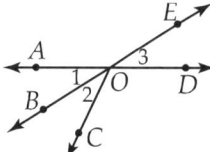

Statements	Reasons

④ Given: $m\angle 1 + m\angle 2 = 90°$
   Prove: ∠2, ∠3 are complementary

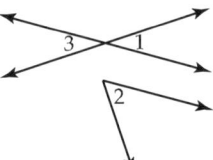

Statements	Reasons

⑤ Given: $\overrightarrow{OA} \perp \overrightarrow{OC}$
Prove: ∠1, ∠3 are complementary

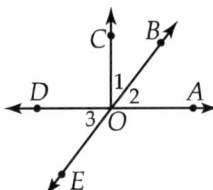

Statements	Reasons

⑥ Given: ∠1, ∠2 form a linear pair
∠3 ≅ ∠4
Prove: ∠2, ∠4 are supplementary

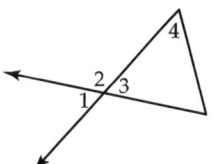

Statements	Reasons

⑦ Given: ∠1, ∠2 form a linear pair
∠3 ≅ ∠5, ∠2 ≅ ∠4
Prove: ∠4, ∠5 are supplementary

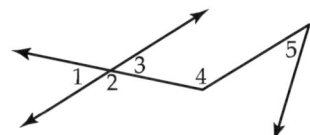

Statements	Reasons

EXAMPLE 6. Fill in the blanks with *always, sometimes*, or *never* to make each statement true.

① If two angles form a linear pair, they are _____ complementary.

② Supplementary angles are _____ congruent.

③ Two vertical angles are _____ supplementary.

④ Complementary angles are _____ adjacent angles.

⑤ Complementary angles are _____ congruent.

⑥ Adjacent angles are _____ supplementary.

⑦ Supplementary angles are _____ adjacent angles.

⑧ Vertical angles are _____ congruent.

⑨ If two angles form a linear pair, they are _____ adjacent angles.

⑩ Vertical angles are _____ adjacent angles.

⑪ Two adjacent angles _____ form a linear pair.

Mia's Geometry
2.7 Perpendicular Lines

1. Perpendicular Lines

※ Perpendicular lines

Definition of Perpendicular lines

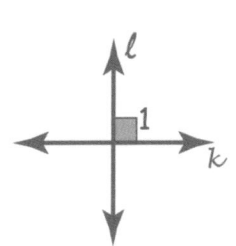

Two lines are perpendicular
if and only if they form right angles.

ex) If $k \perp l$, then $\angle 1$ is a right angle (or $m\angle 1 = 90°$).

If $\angle 1$ is a right angle (or $m\angle 1 = 90°$), then $k \perp l$.

Perpendicular lines Theorem ($\perp \rightarrow$ form $\cong \angle$s.)

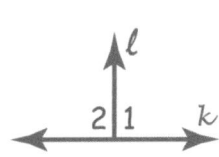

If two lines are perpendicular,
then they form congruent adjacent angles.

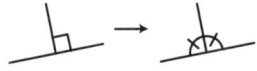

ex) If $k \perp l$, then $\angle 1 \cong \angle 2$.

Converse of Perpendicular lines Theorem ($\cong \angle$s. $\rightarrow \perp$)

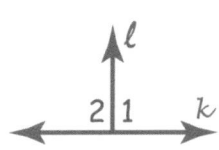

If two lines form congruent adjacent angles,
the lines are perpendicular.

ex) If $\angle 1 \cong \angle 2$, then $k \perp l$.

☺ Memorizing Tip: Definition of ⊥ lines VS ⊥ lines Theorem

Definition: $k \perp l \rightleftharpoons$ form right angle (90°)

Theorem : $k \perp l \rightarrow$ form congruent angle

☺ Proof of Perpendicular lines Theorem:

Given: $k \perp l$
Prove: $m\angle 1 = m\angle 2$

Statements	Reasons
1. $k \perp l$	1. Given
2. $m\angle 1$ = 90° $m\angle 2$ = 90°	2. ①_____
3. $m\angle 1 = m\angle 2$	3. Substitution Property

Blank : ① Def of ⊥ lines

EXAMPLE 1. Name the definition, theorem, or postulate that justifies the given statements.

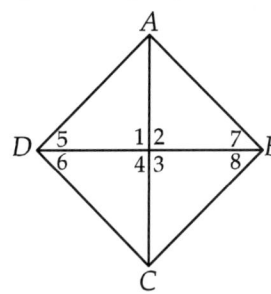

① If ∠1 is a right angle, then $\overline{AC} \perp \overline{DB}$.

② If $\overline{AC}$ is perpendicular to $\overline{DB}$, then ∠1 ≅ ∠4.

③ If $\overline{AC} \perp \overline{DB}$, then ∠3 ≅ ∠4.

④ If $\overline{AC} \perp \overline{DB}$, then ∠1, ∠2, ∠3, and ∠4 are right angles.

⑤ If $\overline{AB} \perp \overline{BC}$, then ∠ABC = 90°.

⑥ If ∠3 and ∠4 are complementary angles, then $m\angle 3 + m\angle 4 = 90°$.

⑦ If $m\angle 2 = m\angle 3$, then $\overline{AC}$ is perpendicular to $\overline{DB}$

⑧ If ∠4 ≅ ∠3, then $\overline{AC} \perp \overline{DB}$.

⑨ If $m\angle 5 + m\angle 6 = 90°$, then ∠5 and ∠6 are complementary angles.

EXAMPLE 2. Write a two column proof.

① Given: $\overline{AB} \perp \overline{BC}, \overline{BC} \perp \overline{CD}$
Prove: $\angle B \cong \angle C$

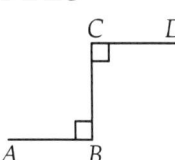

Statements	Reasons

② Given: $\overline{AC} \perp \overline{AB}, \overline{BD} \perp \overline{CD}$
$\angle A \cong \angle C, \angle D \cong \angle B$
Prove: $\angle B \cong \angle C$

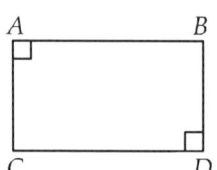

Statements	Reasons

③ Given: $m\angle 1 = m\angle 2$
$m\angle 3 = m\angle 4$
Prove: $\overleftrightarrow{BC} \perp \overrightarrow{OA}$

Statements	Reasons

④ Given: $\overline{AB} \perp \overline{CD}$
$\angle 1 \cong \angle 3, \angle 2 \cong \angle 4$
Prove: $\angle 3 \cong \angle 4$

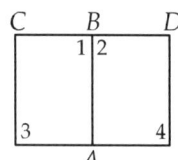

Statements	Reasons

70 Mia's Geometry

⑤ Given: $\overline{AB} \perp \overline{CD}$
$\angle 1 \cong \angle 3$
Prove: $\angle 2 \cong \angle 3$

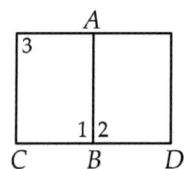

Statements	Reasons

☺ All right ∠s are ≅: If $m\angle A = 90°$, $m\angle B = 90°$ then $\angle A \cong \angle B$.

Mia's Geometry
2.8 Theorems about Special Pairs of Angles

1. Congruent Complement and Supplement Theorem

※ Congruent Complement and Congruent Supplement Theorem

Congruent Complement Theorem

Angles complementary to the same angle
or to congruent angles are congruent.
 ex) If ∠4 is compl. to ∠5
 and ∠6 is compl. to ∠5,
 then ∠4 ≅ ∠6.

Congruent Supplement Theorem

Angles supplementary to the same angle
or to congruent angles are congruent.
 ex) If ∠1 is suppl. to ∠2
 and ∠3 is suppl. to ∠2,
 then ∠1 ≅ ∠3.

☺ Memorizing Tip:

Definition of Supplementary angles : Two ∠s add up to 180° ⇌ Suppl.

Supp. Theorem (Linear Pair Postulate): Two ∠s form straight line → Suppl.

Congruent Supplementary Theorem: ∠1 Suppl. to ∠2, ∠3 Suppl. to ∠2 → ∠1 ≅ ∠3

We usually use Congruent Suppl./compl. Theorem to show that two angles are ①_____ based on their supplementary/complementary relationships.

☺ Proof of Congruent Supplement Theorem:

Given: ∠1 is suppl. to ∠3
∠2 is suppl. to ∠3
Prove: ∠1 ≅ ∠2

Statements	Reasons
1. ∠1 is suppl. to ∠3 ∠2 is suppl. to ∠3	1. Given
2. $m\angle 1 + m\angle 3 = 180°$ $m\angle 2 + m\angle 3 = 180°$	2. ②_____
3. $m\angle 1 + m\angle 3 = m\angle 2 + m\angle 3$	3. Substitution Property
4. ③_____	4. Subtraction Property
5. ∠1 ≅ ∠2	5. ④_____

Blank : ① congruent   ② Def of suppl ∠s   ③ m∠1 = m∠2   ④ Def of ≅ ∠s

EXAMPLE 1. A) Make a conclusion that two angles are congruent using the information given.
B) Name the definition, theorem, or postulate that justifies conclusion.

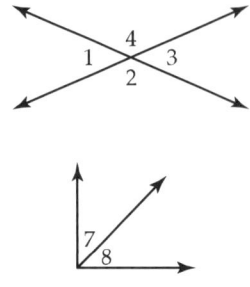
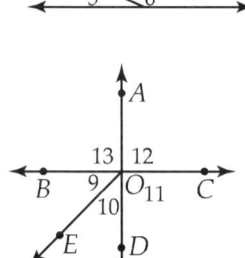

① ∠1 is supplementary to ∠6
∠5 is supplementary to ∠6

② ∠9 is complementary to ∠10
∠8 is complementary to ∠10

③ ∠7 is complementary to ∠8
∠9 is complementary to ∠10
∠8 ≅ ∠10

④ $\overline{AD} \perp \overline{OC}$

⑤ $\overline{AO} \perp \overline{BC}$

⑥ ∠5 is supplementary to ∠6
∠2 is supplementary to ∠3
∠2 ≅ ∠6

⑦ $\overrightarrow{OE}$ bisects ∠BOD

74 Mia's Geometry

EXAMPLE 2. Complete each proof.

① Given: $\overrightarrow{OA} \perp \overrightarrow{OC}$
∠2 is complementary to ∠3
Prove: ∠1 ≅ ∠3

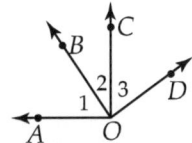

Statements	Reasons

② Given: $\overline{AB} \perp \overline{BC}, \overline{ED} \perp \overline{EF}$
∠2 ≅ ∠4
Prove: ∠1 ≅ ∠3

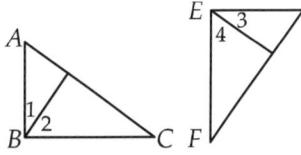

Statements	Reasons

③ Given: $m\angle 1 + m\angle 3 = 180°$
∠2 is suppl. to ∠4
Prove: ∠3 ≅ ∠4

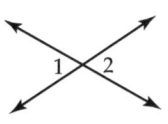

Statements	Reasons

④ Given: ∠1 is compl. to ∠2
∠3 is compl. to ∠4
Prove: ∠1 ≅ ∠4

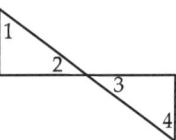

Statements	Reasons

⑤ Given: ∠2 is suppl. to ∠3
   Prove: ∠1 ≅ ∠3

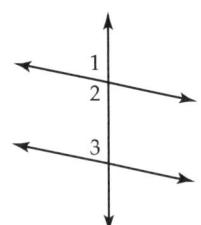

Statements	Reasons

⑥ Given: $m\angle 1 + m\angle 3 = 180°$
   Prove: ∠2 ≅ ∠3

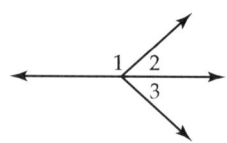

Statements	Reasons

⑦ Given: ∠1 ≅ ∠4
   Prove: ∠2 ≅ ∠3

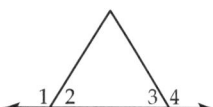

Statements	Reasons

⑧ Given: ∠2 ≅ ∠3
   Prove: ∠1 ≅ ∠4

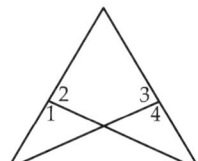

Statements	Reasons

⑨ Given: $\overrightarrow{OC}$ bisects $\angle AOB$
   Prove: $\angle 3 \cong \angle 4$

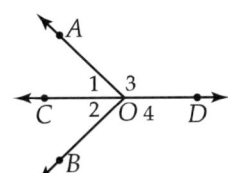

Statements	Reasons

⑩ Given: $\overline{AD} \perp \overline{BC}$, $\angle 3 \cong \angle 4$
   Prove: $\angle 1 \cong \angle 2$

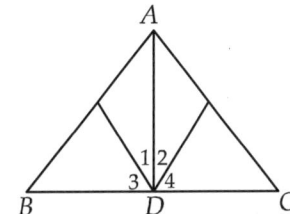

Statements	Reasons

⑪ Given: $\overline{AD} \perp \overline{DC}$, $\overline{BC} \perp \overline{DC}$,
   $\angle 1 \cong \angle 3$
   Prove: $\angle 2 \cong \angle 4$

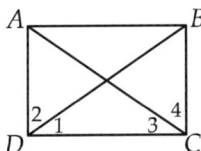

Statements	Reasons

⑫ Given: Two lines intersect at one point
   Prove: $\angle 1 \cong \angle 3$
   [Vertical angles theorem]

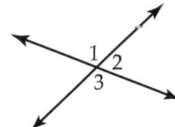

Statements	Reasons

Mia's Geometry
Postulates, Theorems from CH2

***All in One** (sorted by Miamath)

	...Property
Reflxive	$a = a.$
Symmetric	If $a = b$ then $b = a.$
Transitive	If $a = b$ and $b = c$ then $a = c.$
Addition	If $a = b$ then $a + c = b + c.$
	If $a = b$ and $c = d$ then $a + c = b + d.$
Subtraction	If $a = b$ then $a - c = b - c.$
	If $a = b$ and $c = d$ then $a - c = b - d.$
Multiplication	If $a = b$ then $a \cdot c = b \cdot c.$
	If $a = b$ and $c = d$ then $a \cdot c = b \cdot d.$
Division	If $a = b$ then $a / c = b / c.$ ($c \neq 0$)
Distribution	$a(b + c) = ab + ac.$
Substitution	If $a = b$ and $a = c$, then $b = c.$ (a may be replaced by c)

About Segments	About Angles
Segment Addition Postulate $AB + BC = AC.$	**Angle Addition Postulate** $m\angle 1 + m\angle 2 = m\angle ABC.$
Definition of Midpoint M is the midpoint of $\overline{AB}$ if and only if $AM = MB.$	**Definition of Angle Bisector** $\overrightarrow{BX}$ bisect $\angle ABC$ if and only if then $m\angle ABX = m\angle XBC.$
Midpoint Theorem If M is the midpoint of $\overline{AB}$, then $AM = \frac{1}{2}AB$.	**Angle Bisector Theorem** If $\overrightarrow{BX}$ bisect $\angle ABC$, then $m\angle ABX = \frac{1}{2}m\angle ABC$.
Definition of Segment Bisector $\overline{CD}$ bisects $\overline{AB}$ if and only if $AM = MB.$	
Definition of ≅ segment $\overline{AB} \cong \overline{AC} \rightleftarrows AB = AC$	**Definition of ≅ angle** $\angle A \cong \angle B \rightleftarrows m\angle A = m\angle B$

About Complementary angles	About Supplementary angles
Definition of Complementary angles Two angles are complementary if and only if they add up to 90°. ∠90° ⇌ compl.	**Definition of Supplementary angles** Two angles are supplementary if and only if they add up to 180°. 180° ⇌ suppl.
Complement Theorem If two adjacent angles *form a right angle*, then the angles are complementary. → compl.	**Supplement Theorem** **(Linear Pair Postulate)** If two angles *form a linear pair*, then they are supplementary. lin. pair → suppl.
Congruent Complement Theorem If ∠4 is compl. to ∠5 and ∠6 is compl. to ∠5, then ∠4 ≅ ∠6.	**Congruent Supplement Theorem** If ∠1 is suppl. to ∠2 and ∠3 is suppl. to ∠2, then ∠1 ≅ ∠3.

About Perpendicular Lines and others	
Definition of Perpendicular lines Two lines are perpendicular if and only if they form right angles. 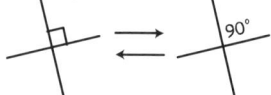	**Perpendicular lines Theorem** If two lines are perpendicular, then they form congruent adjacent angles. 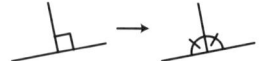
Vertical Angles Theorem Vertical angles are congruent. 	**Converse of Perpendicular lines Theorem** If two lines form congruent adjacent angles, the lines are perpendicular. 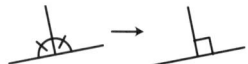

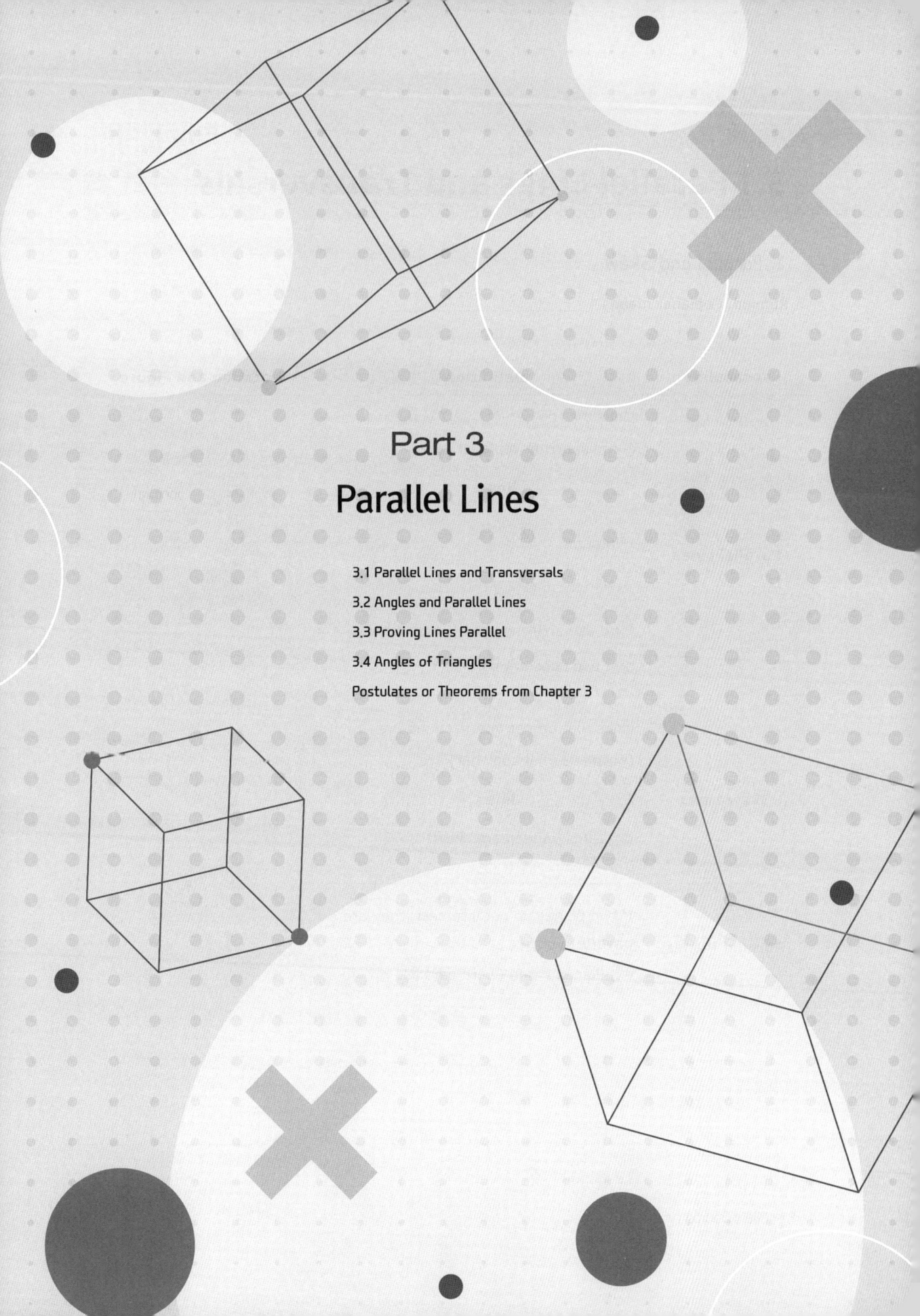

Part 3
Parallel Lines

3.1 Parallel Lines and Transversals

3.2 Angles and Parallel Lines

3.3 Proving Lines Parallel

3.4 Angles of Triangles

Postulates or Theorems from Chapter 3

Mia's Geometry

3.1 Parallel Lines and Transversals

1. Parallel and Skew

☺ Remind: Coplanar means ①_____

Vocabulary	Definition	Notation and Figure
Parallel Lines	Lines that do not intersect and are (②coplanar/not coplanar) are ③_____ **lines**. • Notation: $\overleftrightarrow{AB}$ ④___ $\overleftrightarrow{CD}$ or l ⑤___ m • We use arrowheads to show that two lines are parallel.	(figure showing parallel lines with points A, B on line l and C, D on line m)
Skew Lines	Lines that do not intersect and are (⑥coplanar/not coplanar) are ⑦_____ **lines**. ex) Lines l and m are skew.	(figure showing line l in plane P and line m in plane Q)
Parallel Planes	If two planes do not intersect, they are **parallel planes**. ex) Planes P and Q are parallel.	

Blank : ① on the same plane ② coplanar ③ parallel ④ ∥ ⑤ ∥ ⑥ not coplanar ⑦ skew

EXAMPLE 1. Using the figure, solve the problem.

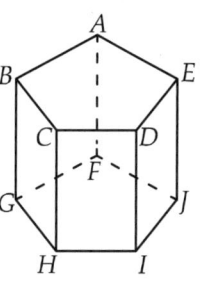

① Name one plane that is parallel to the plane $ABCDE$.

② Name one plane that intersects the plane $DEJI$.

③ Name one segment that intersects $\overline{AB}$.

④ Name one segment that is parallel to $\overline{EJ}$.

⑤ Name one segment that is skew to $\overline{BG}$.

⑥ Name one segment that is skew to $\overline{EJ}$.

⑦ Name one coplanar segment that do not intersect and not parallel to $\overline{DE}$.

EXAMPLE 2. Fill in the blanks with *always, sometimes*, or *never* to make each statement true.

① Two coplanar lines are _____ parallel.

② Two parallel lines are _____ coplanar.

③ Two coplanar lines are _____ skew.

④ Two skew lines are _____ coplanar.

⑤ Two noncoplanar lines _____ intersect.

⑥ Two lines that lie in parallel planes are _____ parallel.

⑦ Skew lines _____ intersect.

⑧ Two lines are _____ coplanar.

⑨ If two planes do not intersect, then they are _____ parallel.

⑩ Two lines in intersecting planes are _____ skew.

⑪ Two planes parallel to a same line are _____ parallel to each other.

⑫ Two lines parallel to a third line are _____ parallel to each other.

2. Transversal

A ①_____ is a line (or segment) that crosses at least two other lines (or segments).

(*trans*-means across)

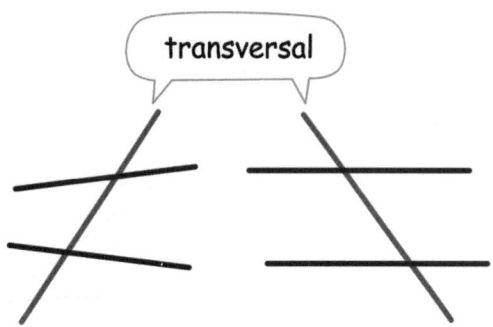

EXAMPLE 3. Name the followings that form each pair of angles.
a) the two lines   b) the transversal

① i) ∠1 and ∠2
   a) Lines :_____
   b) Transversal:_____

② i) ∠1 and ∠2
   a) Lines :_____
   b) Transversal:_____

ii) ∠1 and ∠3
   a) Lines :_____
   b) Transversal:_____

ii) ∠1 and ∠3
   a) Lines :_____
   b) Transversal:_____

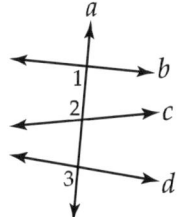

Blank : ① transversal

③ i) ∠1 and ∠2
   a) Lines :_____
   b) Transversal:_____

   ii) ∠3 and ∠4
   a) Lines :_____
   b) Transversal:_____

④ i) ∠1 and ∠2
   a) Lines :_____
   b) Transversal:_____

   ii) ∠2 and ∠3
   a) Lines :_____
   b) Transversal:_____

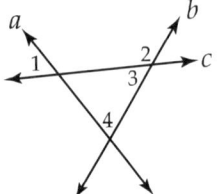

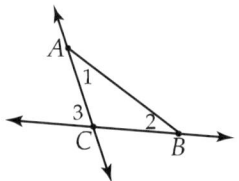

⑤ i) ∠1 and ∠2
   a) Lines :_____
   b) Transv :_____

   ii) ∠3 and ∠4
   a) Lines :_____
   b) Transversal:_____

⑥ i) ∠1 and ∠2
   a) Lines :_____
   b) Transversal:_____

   ii) ∠3 and ∠4
   a) Lines :_____
   b) Transversal:_____

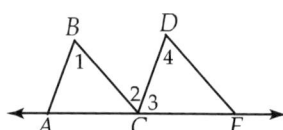

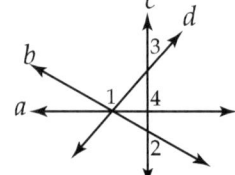

86 Mia's Geometry

We can name the angles that are formed when a transversal crosses two lines.

Vocabulary	Definition	Notation and Figure
interior angles	Angles on the ①_____ part of two lines	
exterior angles	Angles on the ②_____ part of two lines	
alternate **interior** angles	Angle pairs are on ③_____ sides of the transversal, and on the **interior** of the two lines.	
alternate **exterior** angles	Angle pairs are on ④_____ sides of the transversal, and on the **exterior** of the two lines.	
consecutive **interior** angles	Angle pairs are ⑤_____ (they follow each other), and on the **interior** of the two lines.	
corresponding angles	Angles in matching corners	

Blank : ① inside ② outside ③ opposite ④ opposite ⑤ consecutive

EXAMPLE 4. Identify the special name for the angle pair.

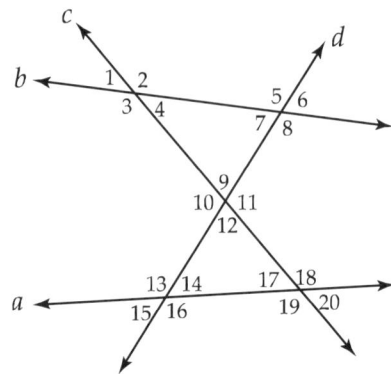

① ∠1 and ∠10

② ∠9 and ∠18

③ ∠4 and ∠18

④ ∠12 and ∠14

⑤ ∠7 and ∠11

⑥ ∠4 and ∠17

⑦ ∠10 and ∠20

⑧ ∠9 and ∠16

EXAMPLE 5. Find the sum of all the corresponding angles for ∠1.

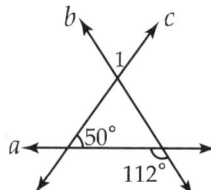

88 Mia's Geometry

Mia's Geometry

3.2 Angles and Parallel Lines

1. Parallel Lines and Angle Pairs

When *two parallel lines* are cut by a transversal, the following pairs of angles are ① _____.

- corresponding angles
- alternate interior angles
- alternate exterior angles

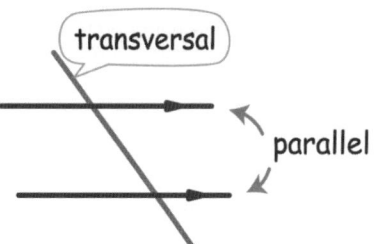

Consecutive interior angles are ② _____.

※ Theorems and Postulates about Parallel Lines and Angle Pairs

Corresponding Angle Postulate
(∥→ Corresp. ∠s are ≅)

If two parallel lines are cut by a transversal then *corresponding angles* are congruent.

ex) If $l \parallel m$, then ∠1 ≅ ∠5, ∠2 ≅ ∠6
∠3 ≅ ∠7, ∠4 ≅ ∠8.

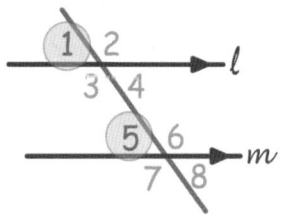

Alternate Interior Angle Theorem
(∥→ Alt. int. ∠s are ≅)

If two parallel lines are cut by a transversal then *alternate interior angles* are congruent.

ex) If $l \parallel m$, then ∠3 ≅ ∠6, ∠4 ≅ ∠5

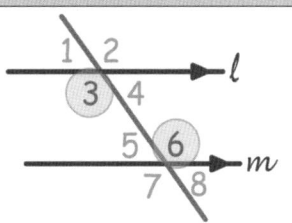

Alternate Exterior Angle Theorem
(|| → Alt. ext. ∠s are ≅)

If two parallel lines are cut by a transversal then *alternate exterior angles* are congruent.

ex) If $l \parallel m$, then ∠1 ≅ ∠8, ∠2 ≅ ∠7

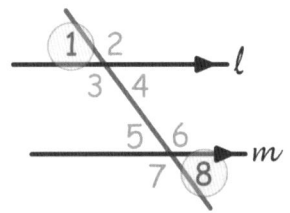

Consecutive Interior Angle Theorem
(|| → Consec. int. ∠s are suppl.)

If two parallel lines are cut by a transversal then *consecutive interior angles* are supplementary.

ex) If $l \parallel m$, then ∠3, ∠5 are ③_____

∠4, ∠6 are supplementary.

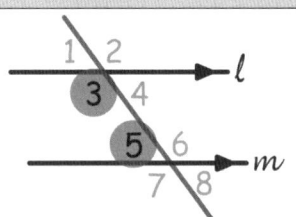

☺ Memorizing Tip:

※ Theorems about Parallel and Perpendicular Lines

Perpendicular Transversal Theorem (⊥ to one ||, ⊥ to other)

If a transversal is perpendicular to one of two parallel lines, then it is perpendicular to the other one.

ex) If $l \parallel m$ and $t \perp l$, then $t \perp m$.

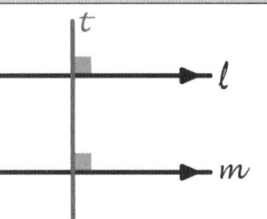

Blank : ① congruent ② supplementary ③ supplementary

EXAMPLE 1. Name the definition, theorem, or postulate that justifies conclusion.

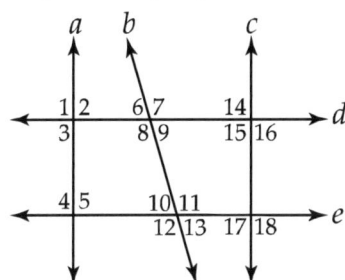

① If $d \parallel e$, then ∠8 and ∠10 are supplementary.

② If $d \parallel e$, then ∠3 ≅ ∠5.

③ If $a \parallel c$, then ∠3 ≅ ∠15.

④ If $a \parallel c$, then ∠2 + ∠14 = 180°.

⑤ If $d \parallel e$, then ∠7 ≅ ∠12.

⑥ If $d \parallel e$, then ∠6 ≅ ∠10.

⑦ If $a \parallel c$, then ∠5 ≅ ∠17.

⑧ If $d \parallel e$ and $c \perp d$, then $e \perp c$.

⑨ If $a \parallel c$ and $a \perp d$, then $c \perp d$.

⑩ ∠11 ≅ ∠12.

EXAMPLE 2. Find the value of the variable(s) in each figure. The figures are not drawn to scale.

①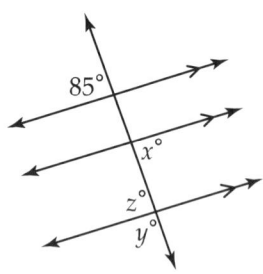

②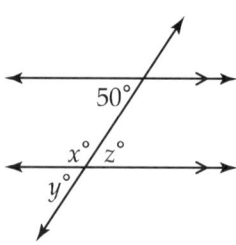

③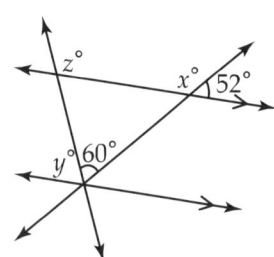

④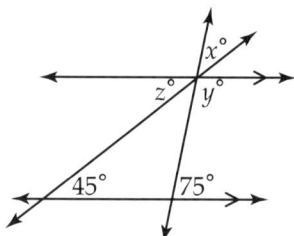

⑤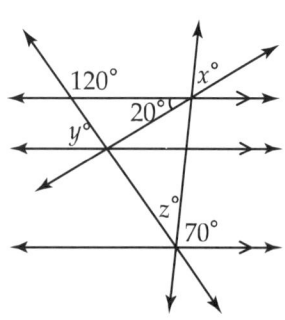

⑥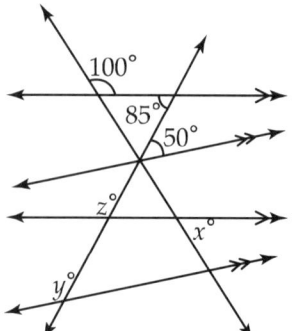

⑦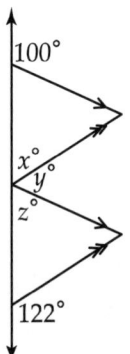

⑧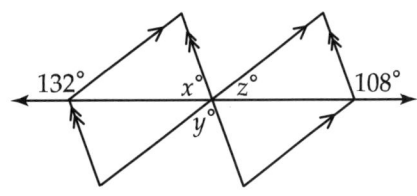

⑨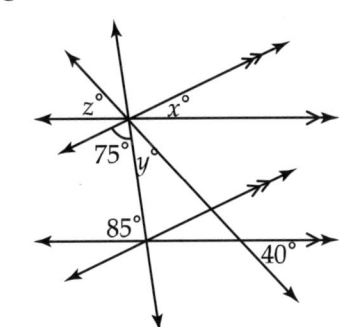

EXAMPLE 3. Find the value of x in each figure. The figures are not drawn to scale.

☺ Tip: Draw an auxiliary line (= helping line).

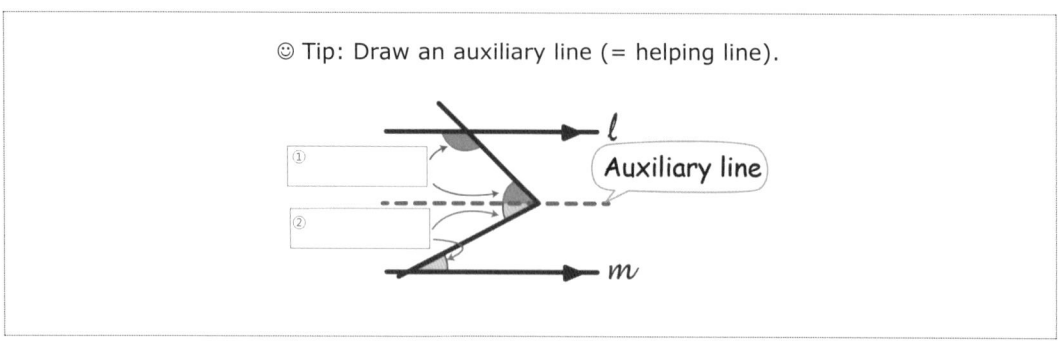

①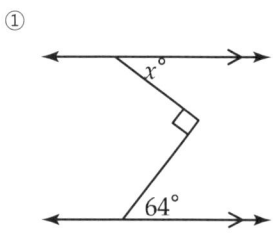

②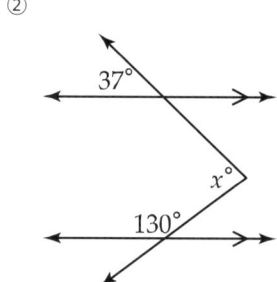

③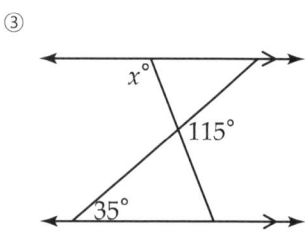

④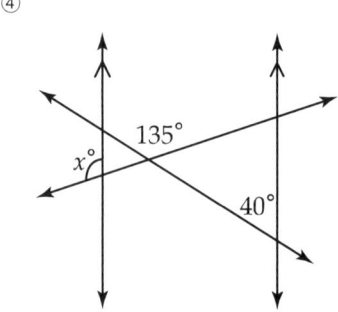

Blank : ① Consec. int. ∠s ② Alternate int. ∠s

94 Mia's Geometry

⑤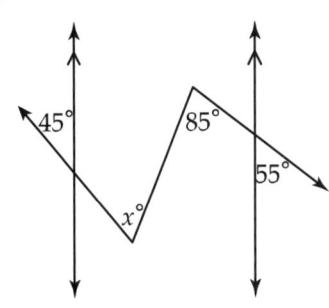

⑥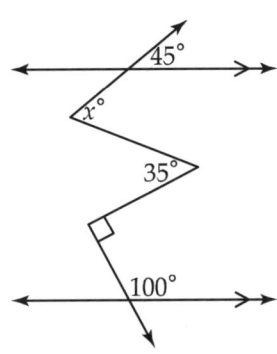

⑦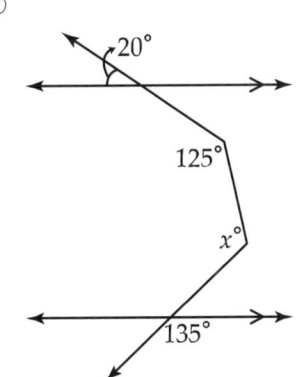

⑧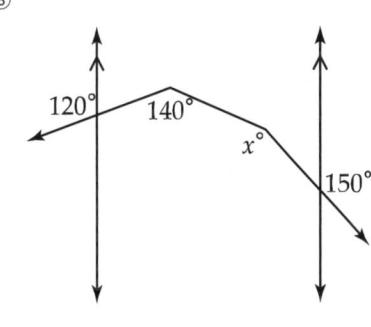

⑨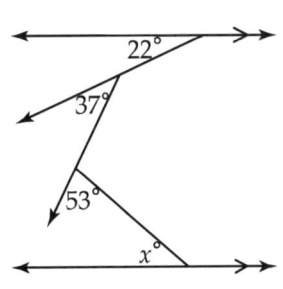

⑩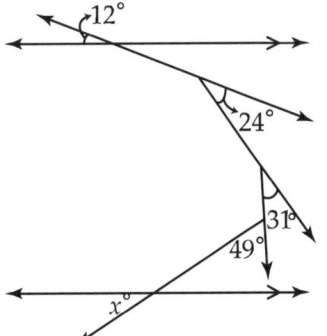

Part 3_Parallel Lines 95

EXAMPLE 4. * Ray l and m are parallel. What is $a+b+c+d$?

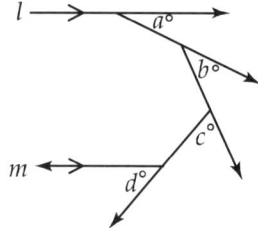

Mia's Geometry
3.3 Proving Lines Parallel

1. Identify Parallel Lines

※ Theorems about Parallel Lines and Angle Pairs

Converse of Corresponding Angle Postulate
(Corresp. ∠s are ≅ → ∥)

If corresponding angles are ①_____

, the lines are *parallel*.

ex) If ∠1 ≅ ∠5, then $l \parallel m$.

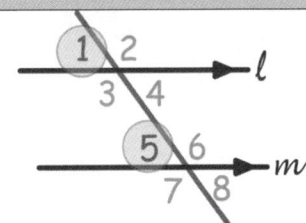

Converse of Alternate Interior Angle Theorem
(Alt. int. ∠s are ≅ → ∥)

If alternate interior angles are congruent,

, the lines are *parallel*.

ex) If ∠3 ≅ ∠6, then $l \parallel m$.

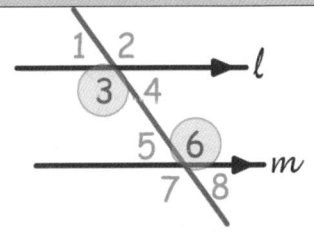

Converse of Alternate Exterior Angle Theorem
(Alt. ext. ∠s are ≅ → ∥)

If alternate exterior angles are congruent,

, the lines are *parallel*.

ex) If ∠1 ≅ ∠8, then $l \parallel m$.

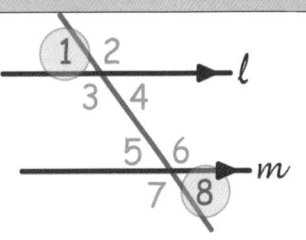

Converse of Consecutive Interior Angle Theorem
(Consec. int. ∠s are suppl. → ∥)

If consecutive interior angles are ② _____,
, the lines are *parallel*.
ex) If ∠3 and ∠5 are supplementary, then $l \parallel m$.

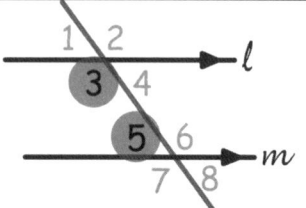

☺ Memorizing Tip:

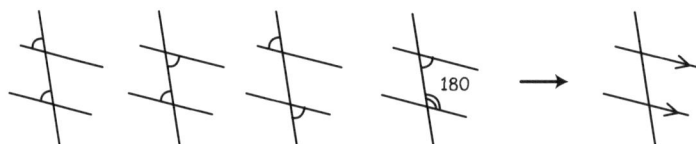

EXAMPLE 1. Determine which lines, if any, must be parallel. State the postulate or theorem that justifies your answer.

①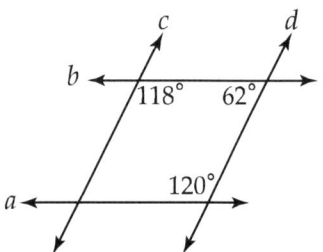

②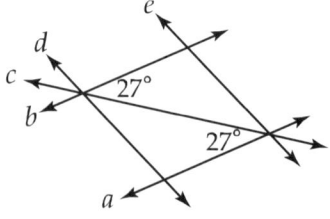

Blank : ① Congruent   ② supplementary

③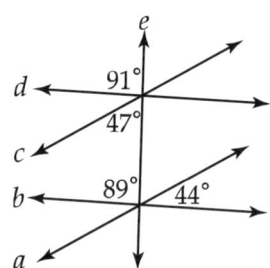

④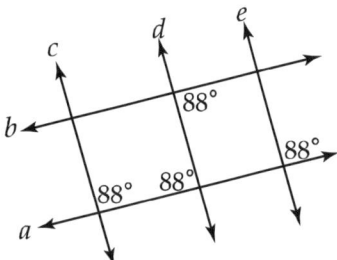

⑤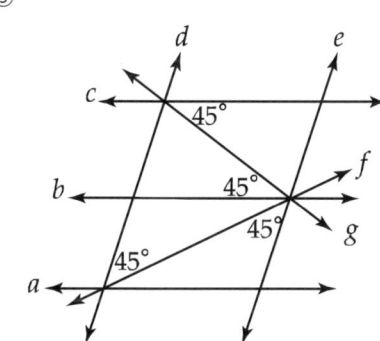

※ **Theorems about Parallel and Perpendicular Lines**

Two Perpendiculars Theorem
(Two ⊥ make ∥)
If two lines are perpendicular to the same line, the lines are *parallel*. 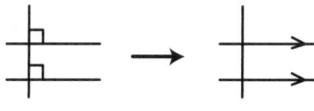 ex) If $t \perp l$ and $t \perp m$, then $l \parallel m$. 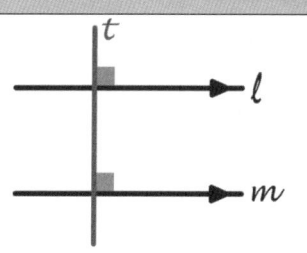

This is also called the 'Converse of Perpendicular Transversal Theorem'.

☺ Perpendicular Transversal Theorem : ⊥ to one ∥, ⊥ to other.
  Two Perpendiculars Theorem: Two ⊥ make ∥.

EXAMPLE 2. Determine which lines, if any, must be parallel. State the postulate or theorem that justifies your answer.

①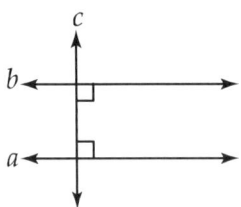

②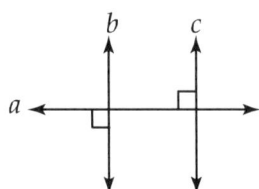

③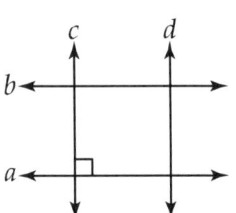

④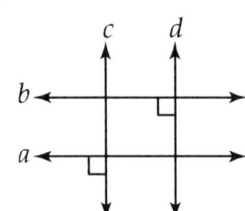

⑤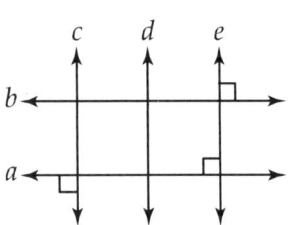

⑥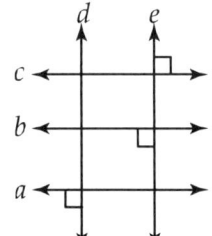

EXAMPLE 3. Write a two column proof.

① Given: $\angle 1 \cong \angle 2$, $\angle 3 \cong \angle 4$
   Prove: $\overline{AB} \parallel \overline{DE}$

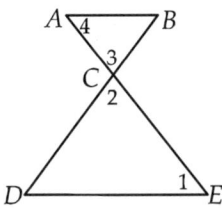

Statements	Reasons

② Given: $m\angle 3 + m\angle 8 = 180°$
   Prove: $a \parallel b$

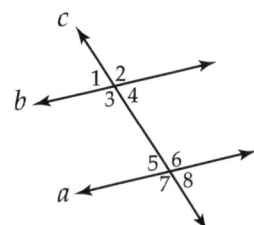

Statements	Reasons

③ Given: $\angle 1 \cong \angle 5$, $\angle 4 \cong \angle 5$
   Prove: $\angle 3 \cong \angle 5$

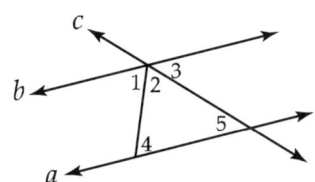

Statements	Reasons

④ Given: $m\angle 4 + m\angle 7 = 180°$
   Prove: $\angle 4 \cong \angle 5$

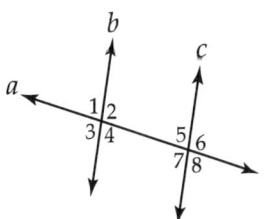

Statements	Reasons

⑤ Given: $\angle 1 \cong \angle 5$, $\angle 9 \cong \angle 18$

Prove: $\angle 20$ is suppl. to $\angle 26$

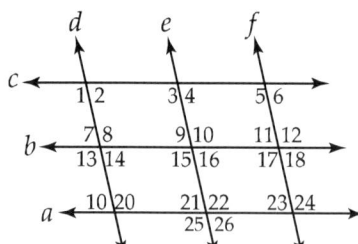

Statements | Reasons

⑥ Given: $\angle 2 \cong \angle 4$, $\angle 7 \cong \angle 10$

Prove: $a \parallel b$

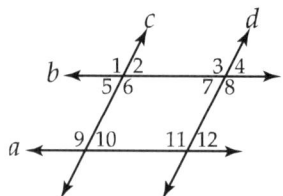

Statements | Reasons

⑦ Given: $a \parallel b$, $\angle 3 \cong \angle 8$

Prove: $m\angle 2 + m\angle 5 = 180°$

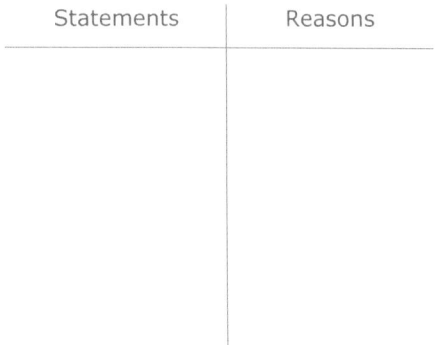

Statements | Reasons

⑧ Given: $\overline{BC}$ bisects $\angle ABE$

$\angle 1 \cong \angle 3$

Prove: $\overline{BC} \parallel \overline{DE}$

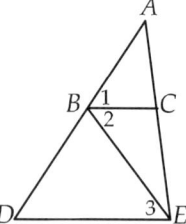

Statements | Reasons

⑨ Given: $a \perp d, b \perp d$
Prove: $\angle 1 \cong \angle 2$

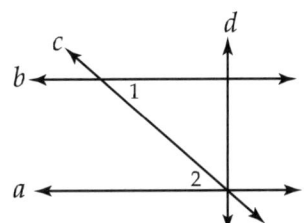

Statements	Reasons

⑩ Given: $a \perp c, b \perp c$
Prove: $m\angle 1 + m\angle 2 = 180°$

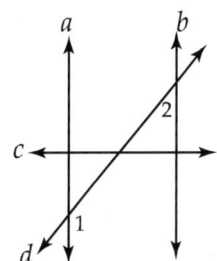

Statements	Reasons

☺ Transitive property of ∥ lines : If $a \parallel b$ and $b \parallel c$, then $a \parallel c$.

Mia's Geometry

3.4 Angles of Triangles

1. Triangles

A **triangle** is a three sided polygon that has three angles, vertices, and sides.

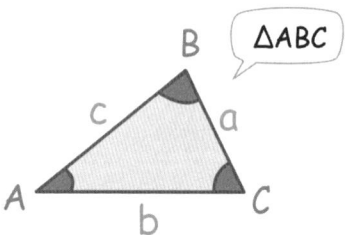
△ABC

△ ABC has three angles: ∠A, ∠B, ∠C

three vertices: A, B, C

three sides: $\overline{AB}, \overline{BC}, \overline{CA}$ or a, b, c

(The side opposite from an angle gets the same letter in lower case)

2. Classify Triangles by Angles

Triangles can be classified by the angles.

Vocabulary	Definition	Notation and Figure
Acute Triangle	All angles are acute ∠s	acute ∠
Right Triangle	Has one right ∠	right ∠
Obtuse Triangle	Has one obtuse ∠	obtuse ∠
Equiangular Triangle ('Equal+angle')	All angles are congruent	

3. Classify Triangles by sides

Triangles can be classified by the number of congruent sides.

Vocabulary	Definition	Notation and Figure
Scalene Triangle	Has no congruent sides	Scalene △
Isosceles Triangle	Has at least two congruent sides	Isosceles △
Equilateral Triangle ('*Equal+lines*')	All sides are congruent	Equilateral △

EXAMPLE 1. Match the triangle that satisfies the given statement.

① Acute scalene triangle

② Acute isosceles triangle

③ Right isosceles triangle

④ Right scalene triangle

⑤ Equilateral triangle

⑥ Obtuse scalene triangle

⑦ Obtuse isosceles triangle

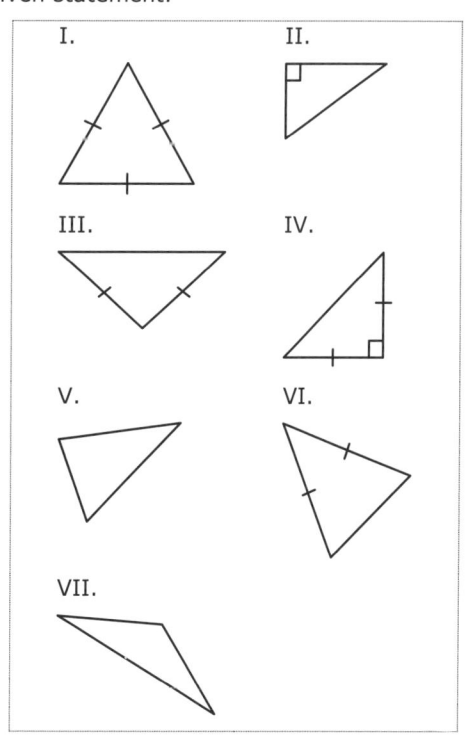

EXAMPLE 2. Fill in the blanks with *always, sometimes,* or *never* to make each statement true.

① An obtuse triangle is _____ isosceles.

② A right triangle is _____ scalene.

③ An equilateral triangle is _____ isosceles.

④ An equilateral triangle is _____ a right triangle.

⑤ A scalene triangle is _____ isosceles.

⑥ A scalene triangle is _____ obtuse.

⑦ An acute triangle is _____ isosceles.

⑧ An isosceles triangle is _____ an equilateral triangle.

4. Triangle Sum Theorem

※ Triangle Sum Theorem

Triangle Sum Theorem
The sum of the measures of the angles of a triangle is 180°.   ex) $m\angle A + m\angle B + m\angle C = 180°$. 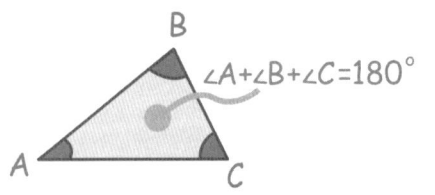

☺ Proof :

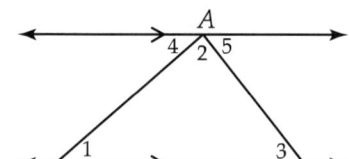

Given: △ABC
Prove: $m\angle 1 + m\angle 2 + m\angle 3 = 180°$

Statements	Reasons
1. Draw a line through A parallel to $\overleftrightarrow{BC}$	1. Auxiliary line
2. $m\angle 4 + m\angle 2 + m\angle 5 = 180°$	2. Definition of straight line
3. $m\angle 4 = m\angle 1$	3. ① _____
4. $m\angle 5 = m\angle 3$	4. ② _____
5. $m\angle 1 + m\angle 2 + m\angle 3 = 180°$	5. Substitution property

EXAMPLE 3. Find the value of the variable(s) in each figure. The figures are not drawn to scale.

①

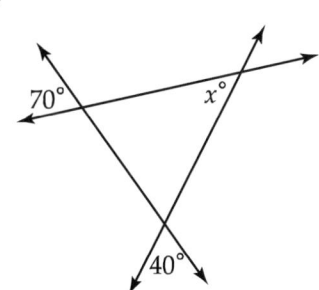

②

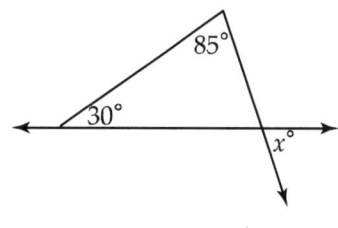

Blank : ① ∥ → Alternate int. ∠s are ≅   ② ∥ → Alternate int. ∠s are ≅

③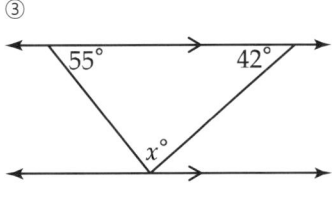

④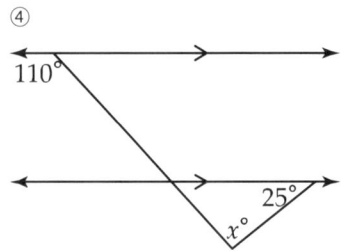

⑤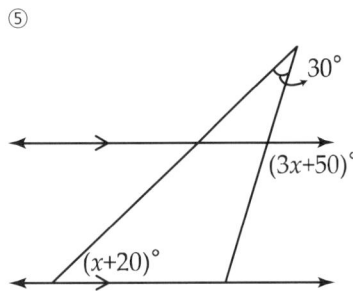

⑥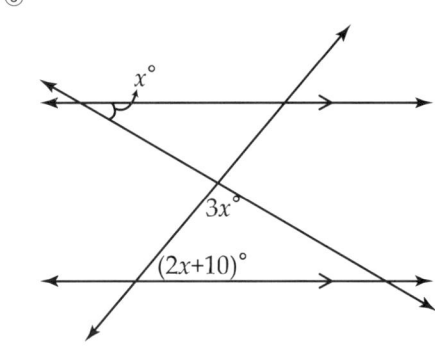

⑦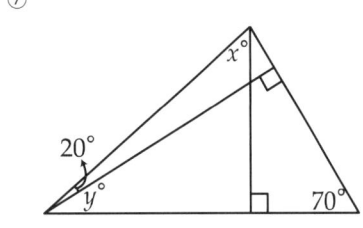

⑧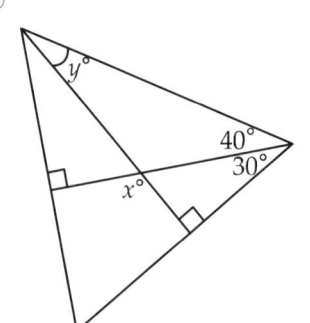

5. Exterior Angle Theorem

remote interior angles

exterior∠

If we extend on side of the triangle, then we can make an **exterior angle**. The interior angles on the other side of the triangle are called the ①_____ _____ **angles**.

(Remote means 'far away')

※ Exterior Angle Theorem

Exterior Angle Theorem
The measure of an exterior angle of a triangle is equal to the sum of the measures of the two remote interior angles. ex) $m\angle A + m\angle B = m\angle BCD$

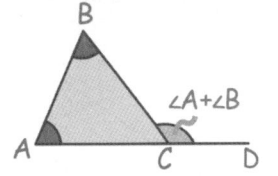

☺ Proof :

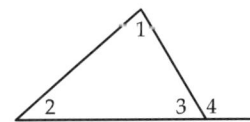

Given: $\angle 4$ is an exterior angle of $\triangle ABC$
Prove: $m\angle 1 + m\angle 2 = m\angle 4$

Statements	Reasons
1. $\angle 4$ is an exterior angle of $\triangle ABC$	1. Given
2. $m\angle 3 + m\angle 4 = 180°$	2. Definition of straight line
3. $m\angle 1 + m\angle 2 + m\angle 3 = 180°$	3. ②_____
4. $m\angle 1 + m\angle 2 + m\angle 3 = m\angle 3 + m\angle 4$	4. Substitution property
5. $m\angle 1 + m\angle 2 = m\angle 4$	5. Subtraction property

Blank : ① remote interior ② Triangle sum thm.

EXAMPLE 4. Find the value of the variable(s) in each figure. The figures are not drawn to scale.

①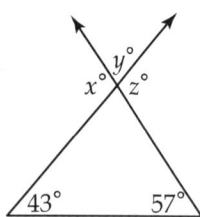

②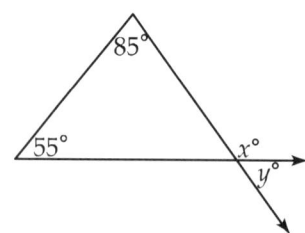

③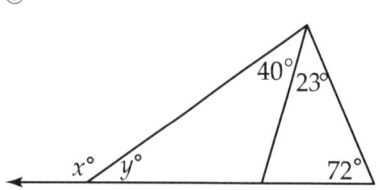

④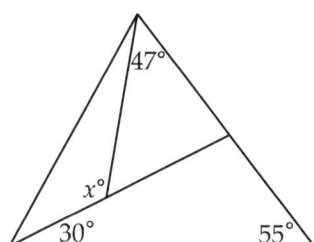

⑤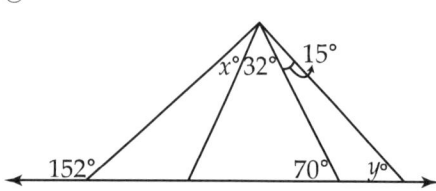

⑥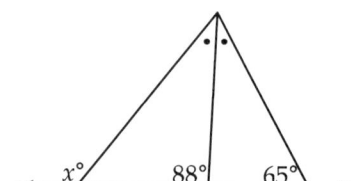

⑦

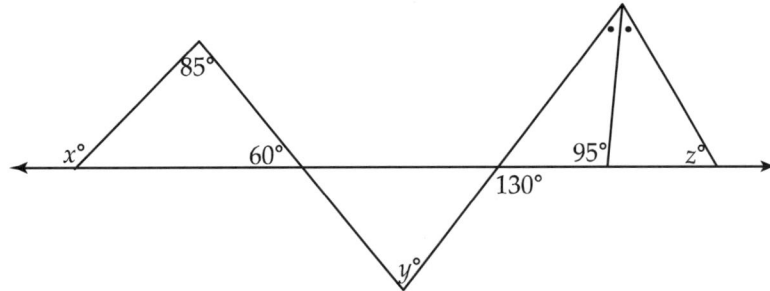

⑧

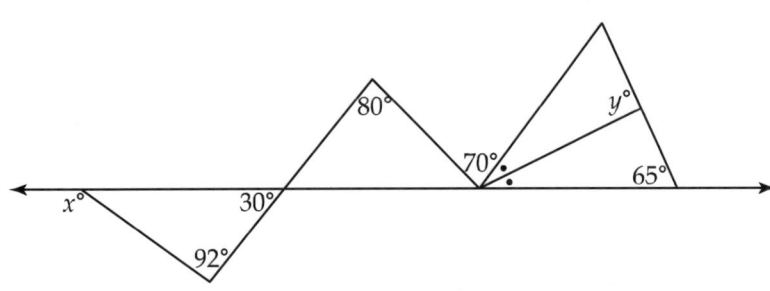

⑨

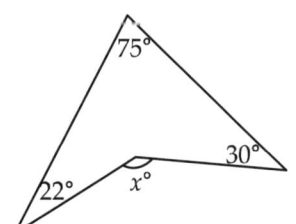

⑩

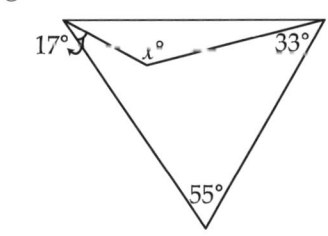

Part 3_Parallel Lines 111

⑪ *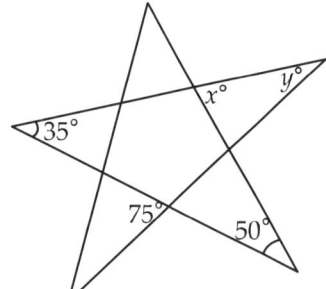

⑫ *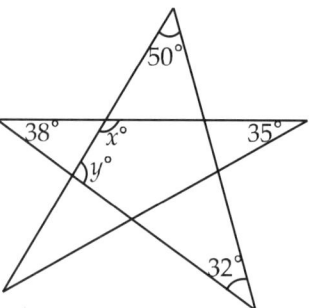

EXAMPLE 5. * What is $a+b+c+d+e$?

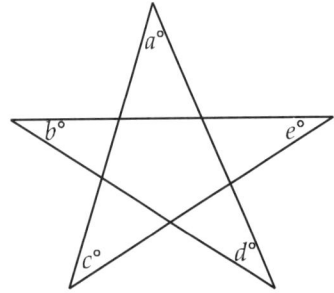

Mia's Geometry

Postulates, Theorems from CH3

*All in One (sorted by Miamath)

When we have two parallel lines..	
Corresponding Angle Postulate (∥ → Corresp. ∠s are ≅) If two parallel lines are cut by a transversal then *corresponding angles* are congruent.	
Alternate Interior Angle Theorem (∥ → Alt. int. ∠s are ≅) If two parallel lines are cut by a transversal then *alternate interior angles* are congruent.	
Alternate Exterior Angle Theorem (∥ → Alt. ext. ∠s are ≅) If two parallel lines are cut by a transversal then *alternate exterior angles* are congruent.	
Consecutive Interior Angle Theorem (∥ → Consec. int. ∠s are suppl.) If two parallel lines are cut by a transversal then *consecutive interior angles* are supplementary.	180
Perpendicular Transversal Theorem (⊥ to one ∥, ⊥ to other) If a transversal is perpendicular to one of two parallel lines, then it is perpendicular to the other one.	

To prove that two lines are parallel..	
Converse of Corresponding Angle Postulate (Corresp. ∠s are ≅ → ∥) If corresponding angles are congruent, the lines are *parallel*.	
Converse of Alternate Interior Angle Theorem (Alt. int. ∠s are ≅ → ∥) If alternate interior angles are congruent, , the lines are *parallel*.	
Converse of Alternate Exterior Angle Theorem (Alt. ext. ∠s are ≅ → ∥) If alternate exterior angles are congruent, , the lines are *parallel*.	
Converse of Consecutive Interior Angle Theorem (Consec. int. ∠s are suppl. → ∥) If consecutive interior angles are supplementary, , the lines are *parallel*.	180
Two Perpendiculars Theorem (Two ⊥ make ∥) If two lines are perpendicular to the same line, , the lines are *parallel*.	

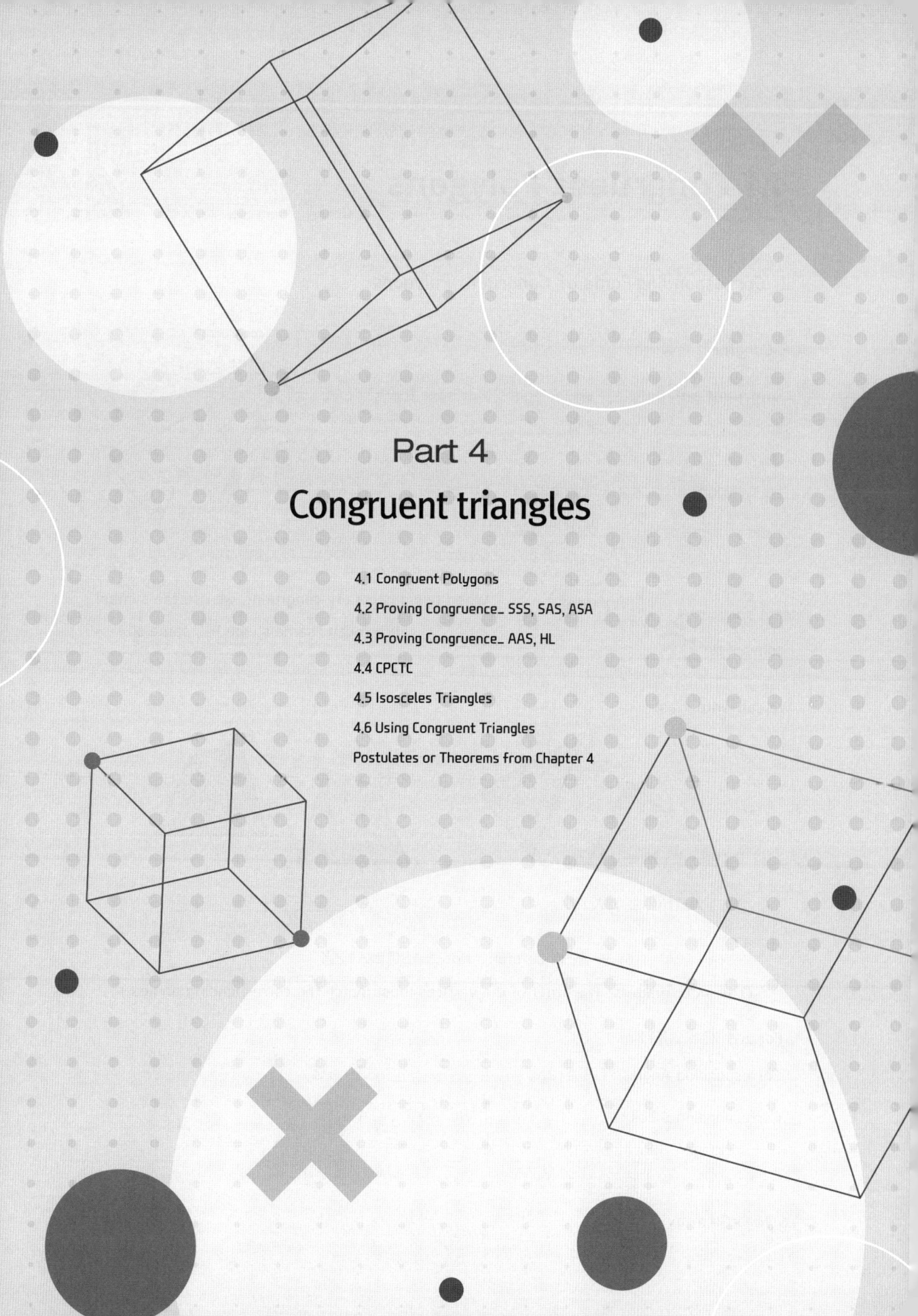

Part 4
Congruent triangles

4.1 Congruent Polygons

4.2 Proving Congruence_ SSS, SAS, ASA

4.3 Proving Congruence_ AAS, HL

4.4 CPCTC

4.5 Isosceles Triangles

4.6 Using Congruent Triangles

Postulates or Theorems from Chapter 4

Mia's Geometry
4.1 Congruent Polygons

1. Corresponding Parts of Congruent Polygons

※ **Congruent Polygons**

Congruent polygons are the polygons that have the same ①_____ and same ②_____.

Two polygons are congruent if and only if their ③_____ parts are congruent.

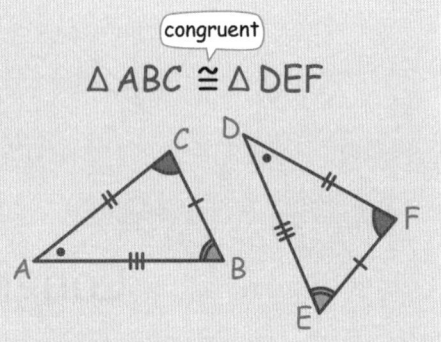

△ABC ≅ △DEF

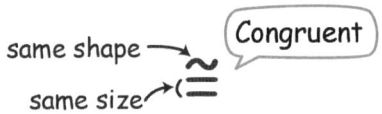

same shape → ~
same size → =
Congruent

When two objects are congruent, we use the symbol ④_____ which means same shape '~', same size '='.

We can write it as;

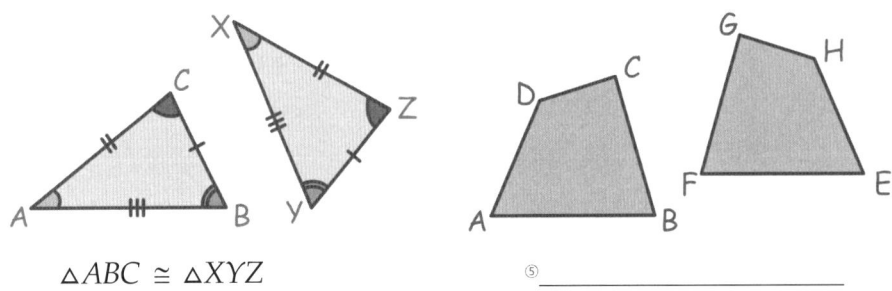

△ABC ≅ △XYZ

⑤_____

☺ Careful: Not △ABC ≅ △YZX .

(The order matters! The order of the vertices must match the corresponding angles.)

For △ABC ≅ △XYZ;

Corresponding Angles : ∠A ≅ ∠X, ⑥_____, ∠C ≅ ∠Z

Corresponding Sides : ⑦_____, $\overline{BC} \cong \overline{YZ}$, $\overline{CA} \cong \overline{ZX}$

Blank : ① size   ② shape   ③ corresponding   ④ ≅   ⑤ □ABCD ≅ □EFGH   ⑥ ∠B ≅ ∠Y   ⑦ $\overline{AB} \cong \overline{XY}$

EXAMPLE 1. Suppose $\square ABCD \cong \square AFED$. Fill in the blanks.

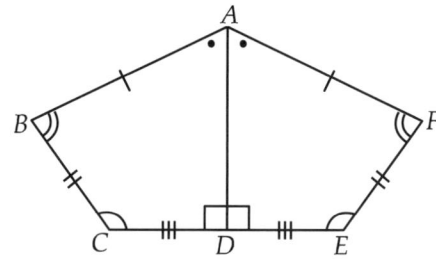

① $\angle B \cong$ _____

② $\overline{CD} \cong$ _____

③ $\overline{AF} \cong$ _____

④ $\angle E \cong$ _____

⑤ $\angle FAD \cong$ _____

⑥ $\angle ADC \cong$ _____

⑦ $\square CDAB \cong$ _____

EXAMPLE 2. Identify the congruent triangles in each figure.

①
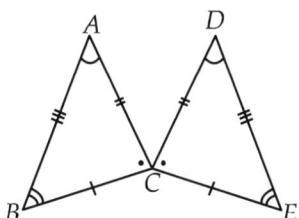

②
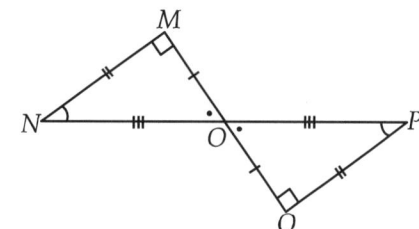

③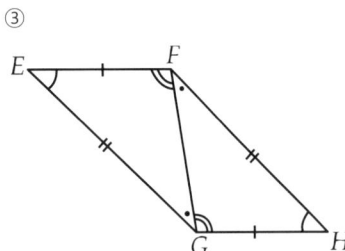

④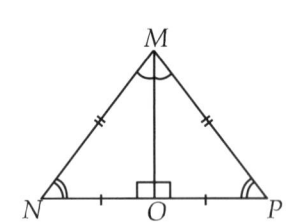

⑤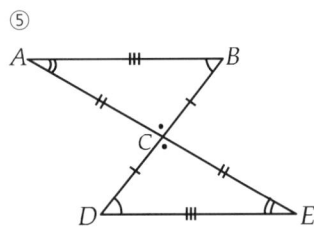

⑥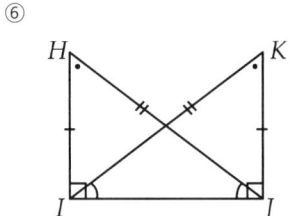

⑦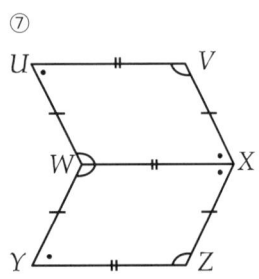

⑧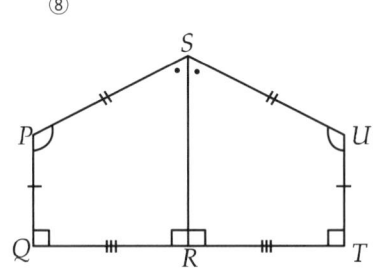

Mia's Geometry

4.2 Proving Congruence_ SSS, SAS, ASA

1. SSS, SAS, ASA Postulate

It is helpful to use these words to describe the parts of a triangle;

∠C is an ①_____ to $\overline{AB}$

$\overline{AB}$ is an ②_____ to ∠C

∠B is an ③_____ between $\overline{AB}$ and $\overline{BC}$.

$\overline{AC}$ is an ④_____ between ∠A and ∠C.

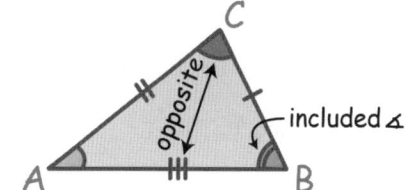

To prove that two triangles are congruent, we need to show that they satisfy one of these postulates or theorems. These are the postulates you can use;

※ Proving Triangle Congruence

SSS Postulate (side-side-side postulate)

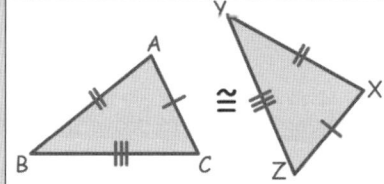

If $\overline{AB} \cong \overline{XY}$, $\overline{BC} \cong \overline{YZ}$, and $\overline{CA} \cong \overline{ZX}$,

then △ABC ≅ △XYZ.

SAS Postulate (side-angle-side postulate)

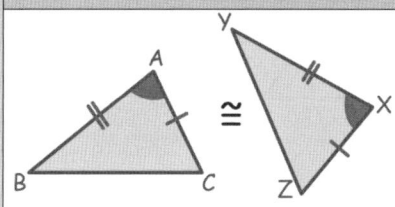

If $\overline{AB} \cong \overline{XY}$, $\overline{AC} \cong \overline{XZ}$,

and ∠A ≅ ∠X (⑤_____ angle),

then △ABC ≅ △XYZ.

Blank : ① opposite ∠   ② opposite side   ③ included ∠   ④ included side   ⑤ included   ⑥ included

Part 4_Congruent triangles   119

ASA Postulate (angle-side-angle postulate)

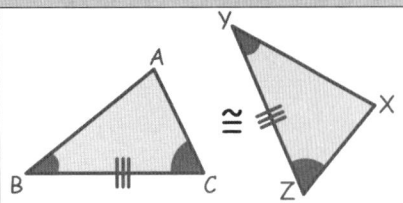

If $\angle B \cong \angle Y$, $\angle C \cong \angle Z$,

and $\overline{BC} \cong \overline{YZ}$ (⑥_____ sides),

then $\triangle ABC \cong \triangle XYZ$.

☺ Memorizing Tip:

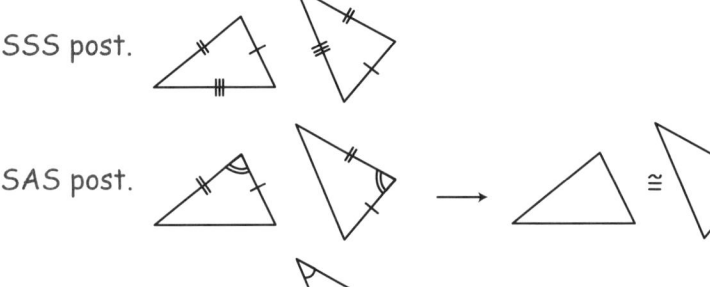

SSS post.

SAS post.

ASA post.

EXAMPLE 1. Determine which postulate (SSS or SAS or ASA) can be used to prove that the triangles are congruent. If it is not possible to prove that they are congruent, write not possible.

①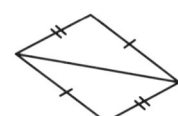

②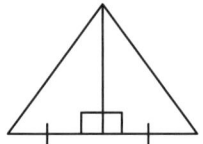

③ 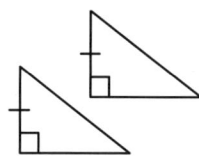 ④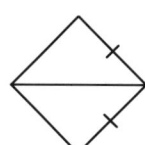

⑤ 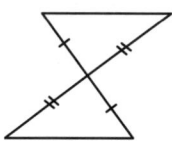 ⑥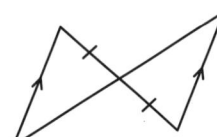

⑦ 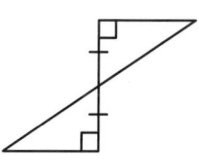 ⑧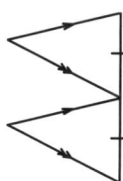

⑨ 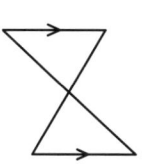 ⑩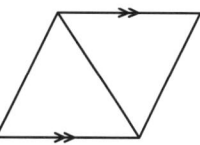

⑪ 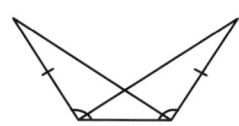 ⑫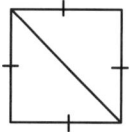

EXAMPLE 2. Write a two column proof.

☺ Steps for Congruence Proof
- Step1. Mark the 'Given'.
- Step2. Mark the reflexive sides or angles, vertical angles, or the implied infomation from 'Given' part.
- Step3. Choose the congruence postulate or theorem.
- Step4. Fill in the statements in the order of the method.
- Step5. Fill in the reasons with definitions, postulates or theorems.

① Given: $\overline{AB} \perp \overline{AC}$, $\overline{CE} \perp \overline{DE}$
  C is midpoint of $\overline{AE}$
  Prove: $\triangle ABC \cong \triangle EDC$

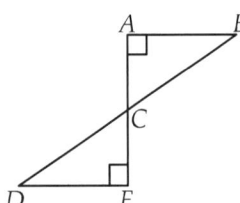

Statements	Reasons

② Given: $\overline{AC} \perp \overline{BD}$
  $\overline{BC} \cong \overline{CD}$
  Prove: $\triangle ABC \cong \triangle ADC$

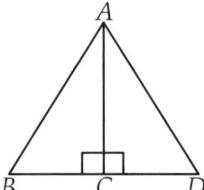

Statements	Reasons

③ Given: $\overline{AB}$ and $\overline{DF}$ bisect each other

Prove: $\triangle AEF \cong \triangle BED$

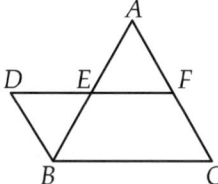

Statements	Reasons

④ Given: $\overline{AB} \cong \overline{AD}$

$\overline{AC}$ bisects $\overline{BD}$

Prove: $\triangle ABC \cong \triangle ADC$

Statements	Reasons

⑤ Given: $\overline{AB} \parallel \overline{DC}$, $\overline{AB} \cong \overline{DC}$

$\overline{AN} \cong \overline{MC}$

Prove: $\triangle ABM \cong \triangle CDN$

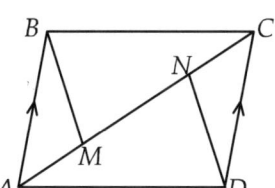

Statements	Reasons

⑥ Given: $\overline{BD}$ bisects $\angle ABC$

$\overline{AB} \cong \overline{CB}$

Prove: $\triangle ABD \cong \triangle CBD$

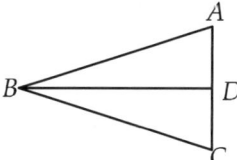

Statements	Reasons

⑦ Given: $\overline{AB} \cong \overline{AE}$, $\overline{AC} \cong \overline{AD}$
$\overline{BC} \cong \overline{DE}$

Prove: $\triangle ABD \cong \triangle AEC$

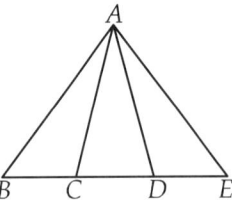

Statements	Reasons

⑧ Given: $\overline{AF} \parallel \overline{BE}$, $\overline{CF} \parallel \overline{DE}$
$AB = CD$

Prove: $\triangle AFC \cong \triangle BED$

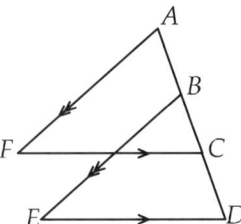

Statements	Reasons

⑨ Given: H is midpoint of $\overline{AB}$
$\angle A \cong \angle B$, $\angle 1 \cong \angle 2$

Prove: $\triangle AHE \cong \triangle BHD$

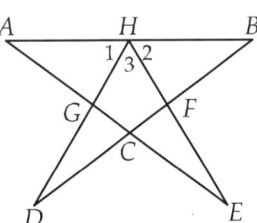

Statements	Reasons

⑩ Given: $AB = AE$, $BC = ED$

Prove: $\triangle ACE \cong \triangle ADB$

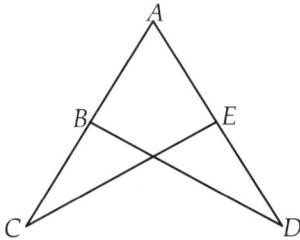

Statements	Reasons

⑪ *Given: ∠1 ≅ ∠2, $\overline{AB} \cong \overline{CD}$

Prove: △ABD ≅ △DCA

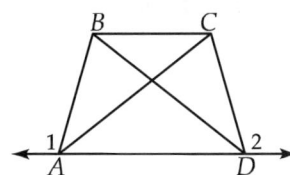

Statements	Reasons

⑫ *Given: ∠1 ≅ ∠4, $\overline{AB} \cong \overline{AE}$
∠5 ≅ ∠7

Prove: △BAD ≅ △EAC

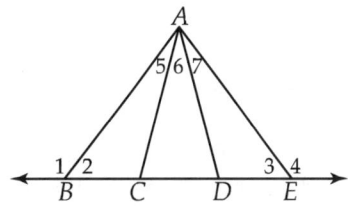

Statements	Reasons

☺ Tips: Implied information from 'Given'

midpoint : ① _____

parallel : _____

segment bisector : _____

angle bisector : _____

perpendicular : _____

Blank : ① This is explained in Mia's Geometry video from www.masterprep.net.

Mia's Geometry

4.3 Proving Congruence_ AAS, HL

1. AAS Theorem

To prove that two triangles are congruent, we need to show that they satisfy one of these postulates or theorems. These are the theorems you can use;

※ Proving Triangle Congruence

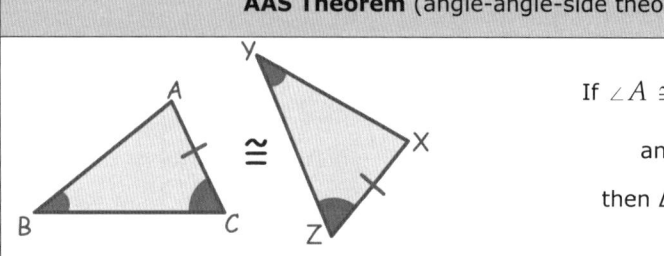

AAS Theorem (angle-angle-side theorem)

If $\angle A \cong \angle X$, $\angle B \cong \angle Y$,
and $\overline{BC} \cong \overline{YZ}$,
then $\triangle ABC \cong \triangle XYZ$.

2. HL Theorem

The next theorem ONLY belongs to right triangles.

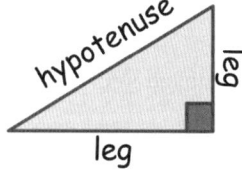

When we have a right triangle;

The perpendicular sides are called ① _____

The longest side, opposite the right angle, is called
② _____.

Blank : ① legs ② hypotenuse

※ Proving Triangle Congruence

> **HL Theorem** (Hypotenuse-Leg theorem, Right Δs ONLY)
>
> If the **H**ypotenuse and a **L**eg of one right triangle are congruent to the corresponding parts of another right triangle, then the triangles are congruent.
>
> When you are doing proof:
> HL Theorem is for only right Δs, so you must state the two Δs are right Δs.

☺ Memorizing Tip:

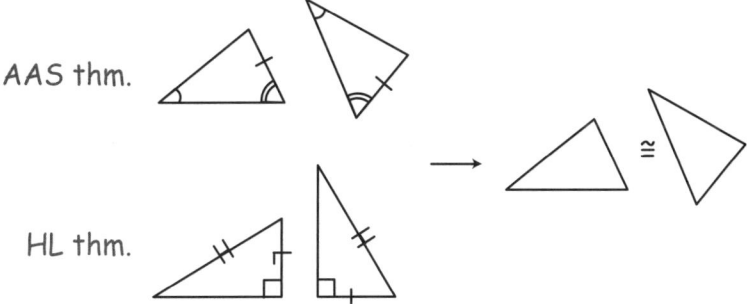

AAS thm.

HL thm.

EXAMPLE 1. Determine which theorem (AAS or HL) can be used to prove that the triangles are congruent. If it is not possible to prove that they are congruent, write not possible.

①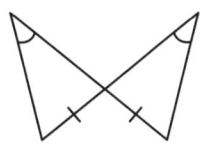

②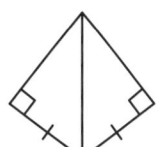

③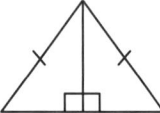

④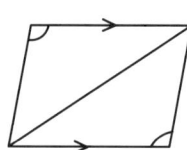

⑤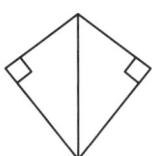

⑥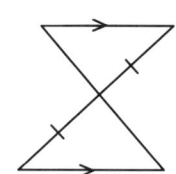

⑦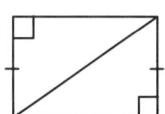

⑧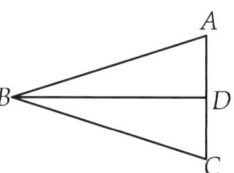

EXAMPLE 2. Write a two column proof.

① Given: $\overline{AD} \cong \overline{BE}$, $\angle A \cong \angle E$
Prove: $\triangle ACD \cong \triangle ECB$

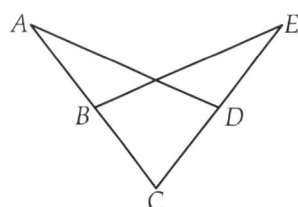

② Given: $\angle A \cong \angle C$
$\overline{BD}$ bisects $\angle ABC$
Prove: $\triangle ABD \cong \triangle CBD$

Statements	Reasons

Statements	Reasons

③ Given: $\overline{AB} \perp \overline{CD}$, $\overline{AC} \perp \overline{BE}$
   $\angle EBC \cong \angle DCB$

Prove: $\triangle DCB \cong \triangle EBC$

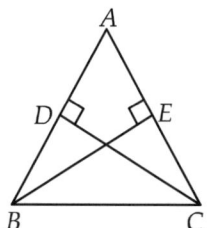

Statements	Reasons

④ Given: $\overline{AB} \cong \overline{AE}$, $\angle C \cong \angle D$

Prove: $\triangle ACE \cong \triangle ADB$

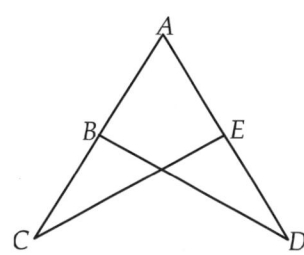

Statements	Reasons

⑤ Given: $\overrightarrow{AB} \parallel \overrightarrow{DE}$
   $\overline{BD}$ bisects $\overline{AE}$

Prove: $\triangle ABC \cong \triangle EDC$

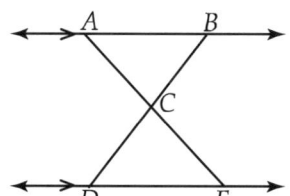

Statements	Reasons

⑥ Given: $\angle A, \angle D$ are right $\angle$s,
   $\overline{AC} \cong \overline{DB}$

Prove: $\triangle ABC \cong \triangle DCB$

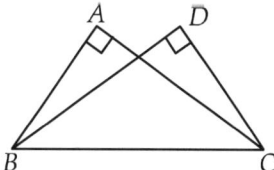

Statements	Reasons

⑦ Given: $\overline{AB} \perp \overline{AC}$, $\overline{DE} \perp \overline{DF}$
$\overline{AB} \cong \overline{DF}$, $\overline{BE} \cong \overline{FC}$

Prove: $\triangle ABC \cong \triangle DFE$

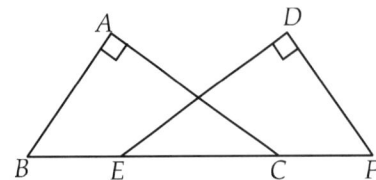

Statements	Reasons

⑧ Given: $\angle 1, \angle 2$ are right $\angle$s,
$\overline{FC} \cong \overline{EA}$, $\overline{BC} \cong \overline{DA}$

Prove: $\triangle BCE \cong \triangle DAF$

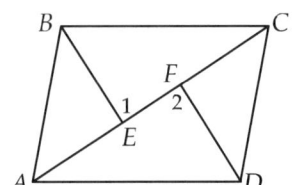

Statements	Reasons

⑨ Given: $\overline{AE} \perp \overline{BD}$, $\overline{AB} \cong \overline{ED}$

C is midpoint of $\overline{BD}$

Prove: $\triangle ABC \cong \triangle EDC$

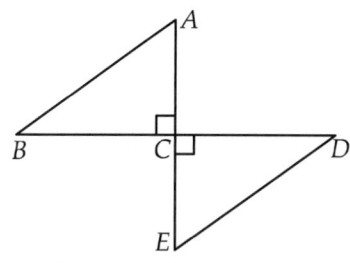

Statements	Reasons

You now have five ways to show that two triangles are congruent.

SSS, SAS, ASA postulate

AAS, HL theorem

Careful! There is no SSA or AAA!

 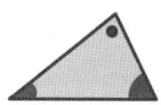 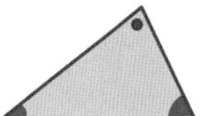

 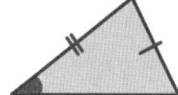 

Part 4_Congruent triangles

Mia's Geometry

4.4 CPCTC

1. CPCTC

Sometimes we need to prove that two segments or two angles are congruent AFTER you show the triangle congruency.

We use triangle congruence and ①_____ to prove that parts of two triangles are congruent.

※ Way to Prove Two Segments or Two Angles are Congruent

1. Prove that the triangles are congruent.

2. State that the two parts are congruent, using the reason ②_____ .
   (Meaning: Corresponding parts of congruent triangles are congruent.)

CPCTC — Corresponding parts of congruent triangles are congruent.

Blank : ① CPCTC   ② CPCTC

EXAMPLE 1. Write a two column proof.

① Given: $\overline{AB} \cong \overline{BC}$, $\overline{AD} \cong \overline{CD}$

Prove: $\angle A \cong \angle C$

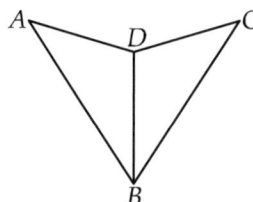

Statements	Reasons

② Given: $\overline{AC}$ and $\overline{DE}$ bisect each other

Prove: $\angle D \cong \angle E$

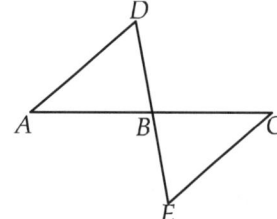

Statements	Reasons

③ Given: $\overline{AB} \cong \overline{AD}$, $\overline{AC} \perp \overline{BD}$

Prove: $\overline{BC} \cong \overline{DC}$

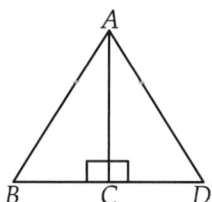

Statements	Reasons

④ Given: $\overline{AB} \parallel \overline{DE}$, $\overline{AC} \cong \overline{EC}$

Prove: $\overline{AB} \cong \overline{ED}$

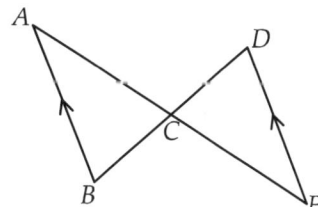

Statements	Reasons

Part 4_Congruent triangles

⑤ Given: $\overline{AC}$ bisects $\overline{BD}$
$\overline{AB} \cong \overline{AD}$
Prove: $\overline{AC} \perp \overline{BD}$

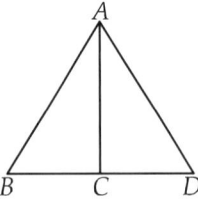

Statements	Reasons

⑥ Given: $\overline{AB} \cong \overline{DC}$, $\overline{AD} \cong \overline{BC}$
Prove: $\overline{AB} \parallel \overline{DC}$

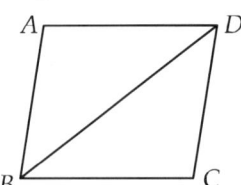

Statements	Reasons

⑦ Given: B is midpoint of $\overline{AC}$
B is midpoint of $\overline{DE}$
Prove: $\overline{AD} \parallel \overline{EC}$

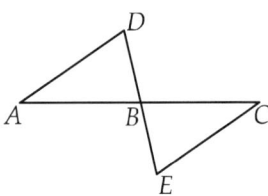

Statements	Reasons

⑧ Given: $\overline{AC} \perp \overline{BD}$, $\overline{AB} \cong \overline{AD}$
Prove: $\overline{AC}$ bisects $\overline{BD}$

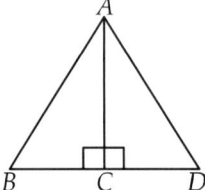

Statements	Reasons

⑨ *Given: $\overline{BE} \cong \overline{DF}$, $\overline{AE} \cong \overline{CF}$
  $\angle 1 \cong \angle 4$
Prove: $\angle FBC \cong \angle EDA$

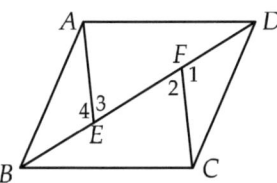

Statements	Reasons

⑩ Given: $\overline{AC} \cong \overline{EC}$,
  $\angle 1 \cong \angle 4$
Prove: $\overline{AD} \cong \overline{EB}$

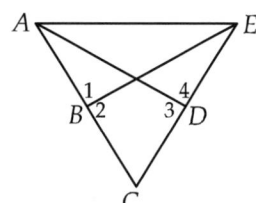

Statements	Reasons

⑪ *Given: M is midpoint of $\overline{BC}$
$\overline{AB} \cong \overline{AC}$

Prove: $\angle 1 \cong \angle 4$

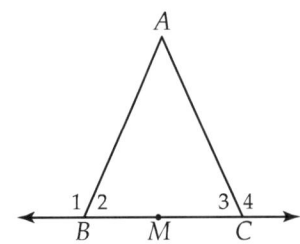

Statements	Reasons

⑫ *Given: $\overline{AB} \cong \overline{AD}$, $\overline{BC} \cong \overline{DC}$

Prove: $\angle 1 \cong \angle 4$

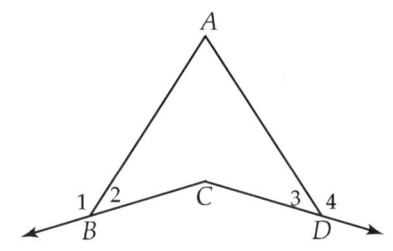

Statements	Reasons

⑬ *Given: $\overline{AB} \perp \overline{BC}, \overline{DC} \perp \overline{BC}$
$\angle 1 \cong \angle 3$, $\overline{AB} \cong \overline{DC}$

Prove: $\overline{BE} \cong \overline{CE}$

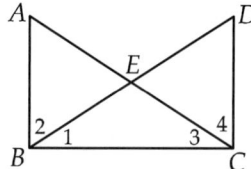

⑭ * Given: $\overline{AD} \perp \overline{DC}, \overline{BC} \perp \overline{DC}$
$\overline{AD} \cong \overline{BC}$

Prove: $\overline{AB} \cong \overline{CD}$

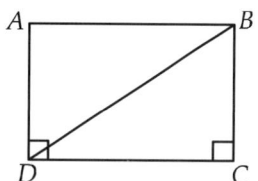

Statements	Reasons

Statements	Reasons

Part 4_Congruent triangles

⑮ * Given: $\overline{AB} \perp \overline{BC}, \overline{DC} \perp \overline{BC}$
$\overline{DE} \perp \overline{EC}, \overline{EC} \cong \overline{AB}$

Prove: $\overline{BC} \cong \overline{ED}$

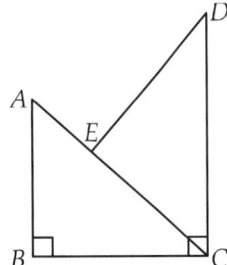

Statements	Reasons

Mia's Geometry
4.5 Isosceles Triangles

1. Isosceles Triangles Theorem

① _____ triangle is a triangle that has at least two congruent sides.

Each part of the Isosceles triangle has a special name.

Two congruent sides are called ② _____.

The third side is called ③ _____.

The angle between the congruent sides is called ④ _____.

Two angles adjacent to the base are called ⑤ _____.

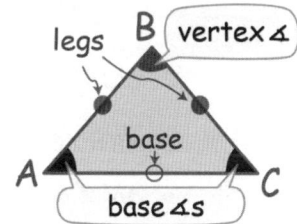

※ Isosceles Triangle Theorem

Isosceles Triangle Theorem
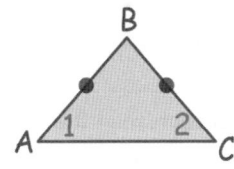 If two sides of a triangle are congruent, then the angles opposite those sides(=base ∠s) are congruent. ex) If $\overline{BA} \cong \overline{BC}$, then ∠2 = ∠1.

☺ Memorizing Tip:

If it start with 'sIdes are congruent...', it is **I**sosceles Triangle Theorem

---

Blank : ① Isosceles ② legs ③ base ④ vertex ∠ ⑤ base ∠s

☺ Proof :

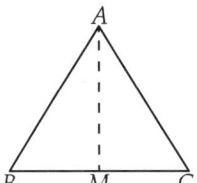

Given: $\overline{AB} \cong \overline{AC}$
Prove: $\angle B \cong \angle C$

Statements	Reasons
1. Draw angle bisector of $\angle A$ and let it $\overline{AM}$.	1. Auxiliary line (Two pts. determine a segment)
2. $\angle MAB \cong \angle MAC$	2. ①_____
3. $\overline{AB} \cong \overline{AC}$	3. Given
4. $\overline{AM} \cong \overline{AM}$	4. ②_____ Property
5. $\triangle ABM \cong \triangle ACM$	5. ③_____
6. $\angle B \cong \angle C$	6. ④_____

※ Converse of Isosceles Triangle Theorem

Converse of Isosceles Triangle Theorem

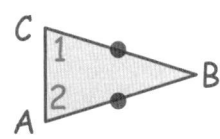

If two base angles of a triangle are congruent, then the sides opposite those angles are congruent.

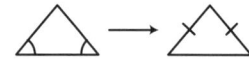

ex) If $\angle 2 = \angle 1$, then $\overline{BA} \cong \overline{BC}$.

Blank : ① Def of ∠ bisector ② reflexive ③ SAS postulate ④ CPCTC

EXAMPLE 1. For the given two congruent angles, name two congruent segments. For the given two congruent segments, name two congruent angles. Name the theorem that justifies your answer.

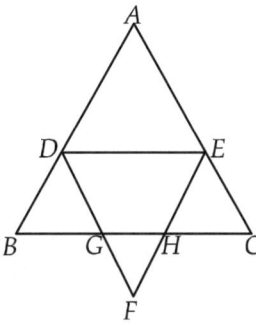

① $\overline{AB} \cong \overline{AC}$

② $\overline{DF} \cong \overline{DE}$

③ $\overline{HE} \cong \overline{HC}$

④ $\overline{EA} \cong \overline{ED}$

⑤ $\angle DFE \cong \angle DEF$

⑥ $\angle FGH \cong \angle GFH$

⑦ $\angle ADE \cong \angle AED$

⑧ $\angle CBA \cong \angle CAB$

EXAMPLE 2. Find the value of the variable(s) in each figure. Figures are not drawn to scale.

①

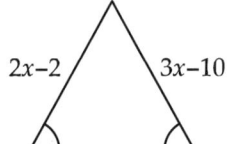

$2x-2$ $3x-10$

②

y

$10-y$

Part 4_Congruent triangles 141

③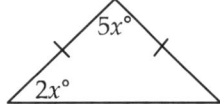

④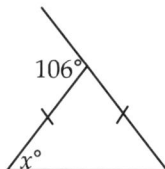

⑤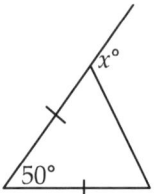

⑥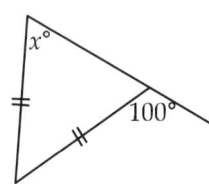

⑦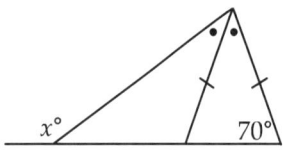

⑧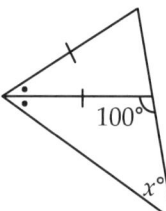

⑨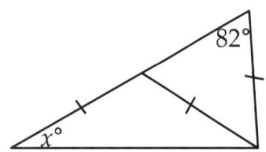

⑩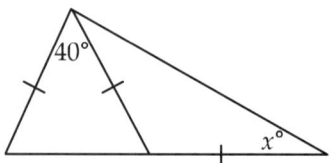

⑪ *
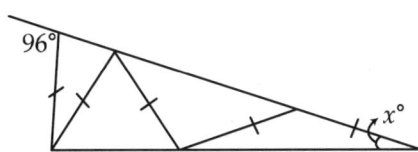

⑫ *
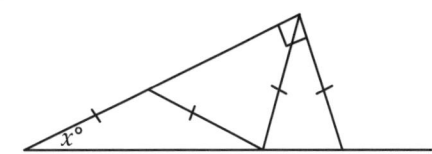

EXAMPLE 3. Write a two column proof.

① Given: $\overline{AB} \cong \overline{BC}$
   Prove: $\angle 1 \cong \angle 4$

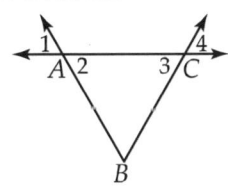

Statements	Reasons

② Given: $\angle C \cong \angle D$, $BC = ED$
   Prove: $\angle 1 \cong \angle 2$

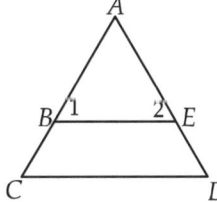

Statements	Reasons

③ Given: $\overline{AB} \cong \overline{AC}$
$\overline{BD}$ bisects $\angle ABC$
$\overline{CD}$ bisects $\angle ACB$
Prove: $\overline{BD} \cong \overline{CD}$

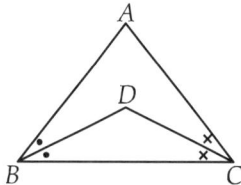

Statements	Reasons

④ Given: $\overline{AB} \cong \overline{AC}$
Prove: $\angle 1 \cong \angle 3$

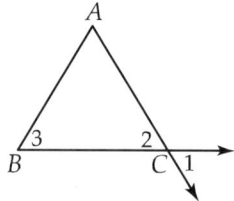

Statements	Reasons

⑤ Given: $\overline{AO} \cong \overline{DO}$, $\angle A \cong \angle D$
Prove: $\angle 1 \cong \angle 2$

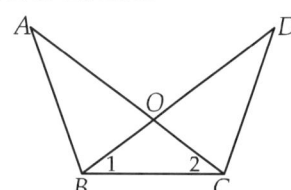

Statements	Reasons

⑥ Given: $\overline{AC} \cong \overline{AD}$, $\overline{CE} \cong \overline{BD}$
Prove: $\overline{AE} \cong \overline{AB}$

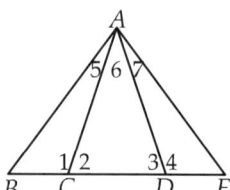

Statements	Reasons

⑦ * Given: ∠1 ≅ ∠2, ∠3 ≅ ∠6

Prove: $\overline{AB} \cong \overline{AE}$

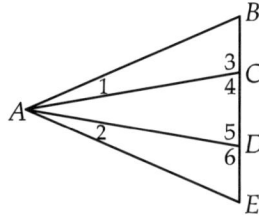

⑧ * Given: ∠2 ≅ ∠3
$\overline{FB} \cong \overline{DC}$, $\overline{FG} \cong \overline{DE}$

Prove: $\overline{AB} \cong \overline{AC}$

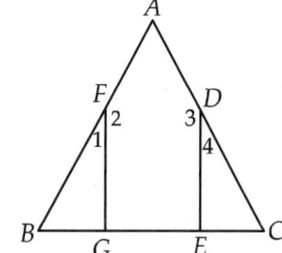

Statements	Reasons

Statements	Reasons

Part 4_Congruent triangles

⑨ * Given: $\overline{AB} \cong \overline{AC}$

E is midpoint of $\overline{AB}$

D is midpoint of $\overline{AC}$

Prove: $\overline{OB} \cong \overline{OC}$

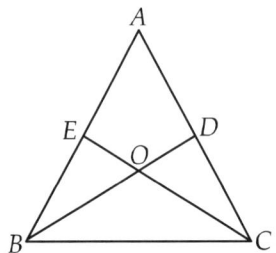

Statements	Reasons

2. Definition of Equilateral Triangles

※ **Definition of Equilateral Triangles**

Definition of Equilateral Triangles

1. A triangle is equilateral if and only if it is equiangular.
2. Each angle of an equilateral triangle measures 60°.

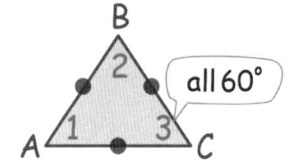

An equilateral triangle is also an isosceles triangle.

146 Mia's Geometry

Mia's Geometry
4.6 Using Congruent Triangles

1. Using Congruent Triangles

Sometimes it is impossible to prove a pair of triangles congruent at once.
Proving OTHER pair of triangles congruent could help you.

EXAMPLE 1. Write a two column proof.

① *Given: $\overline{AO} \cong \overline{DO}$
$\overline{CO} \cong \overline{FO}$
Prove: $\overline{BC} \cong \overline{EF}$

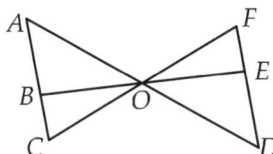

Statements	Reasons

② *Given: F is midpoint of $\overline{AB}$
$\overline{AD} \cong \overline{BC}$, $\angle A \cong \angle B$
$\overline{FE} \perp \overline{DC}$
Prove: $\angle DFE \cong \angle CFE$

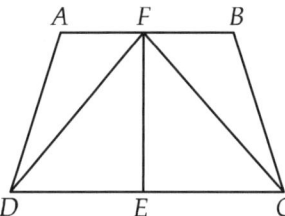

Statements	Reasons

Part 4_Congruent triangles 147

③ *Given: $\overline{AD}$ bisects $\angle BAF$
$\overline{AB} \cong \overline{AF}$, $\overline{BC} \cong \overline{FE}$
$\angle C, \angle E$ are right angles
Prove: $\overline{CD} \cong \overline{ED}$

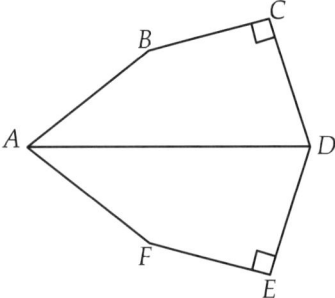

Statements	Reasons

④ *Given: $\overline{AB} \cong \overline{AD}$
$\overline{CB} \cong \overline{CD}$
Prove: $\overline{EB} \cong \overline{ED}$

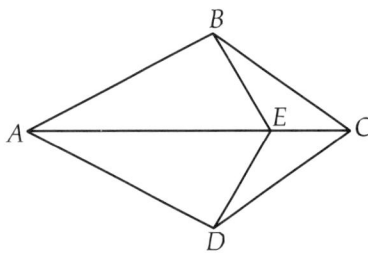

Statements	Reasons

⑤ *Given: $\overline{AB} \cong \overline{CB}, \overline{AE} \cong \overline{CD}$
$\overline{AO} \cong \overline{CO}$
Prove: $\overline{EB} \cong \overline{DB}$

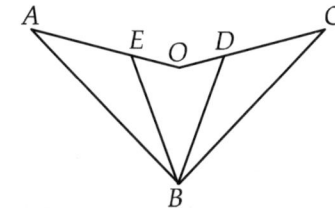

Statements	Reasons

⑥ *Given: $\overline{AC} = \overline{AD}$
$\overline{AB} = \overline{AE}$
Prove: $\overline{OC} = \overline{OD}$

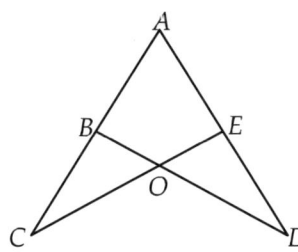

Statements	Reasons

Mia's Geometry

Postulates, Theorems from CH4

*All in One (sorted by Miamath)

To prove that two triangles are congruent..	
SSS Postulate (side-side-side postulate)	
SAS Postulate (side-angle-side postulate)	
ASA Postulate (angle-side-angle postulate)	
AAS Theorem (angle-angle-side theorem)	
HL Theorem (Hypotenuse-Leg theorem, Right △s ONLY)	

CPCTC	Corresponding parts of congruent triangles are congruent
Isosceles Triangle Theorem If two legs of a triangle are congruent, then the base angles are congruent.	
Converse of Isosceles Triangle Theorem If two base angles of a triangle are congruent, then the legs are congruent.	

Part 5
Relationships in Triangles

5.1 Median, Altitude, and Bisectors

5.2 Centers of Triangles

5.3 Midsegment Theorem

5.4 Properties of Inequalities

5.5 Inequalities in One Triangle

5.6 Inequalities in Two Triangles

Postulates or Theorems from Chapter 5

Mia's Geometry

5.1 Median, Altitude, and Bisectors

1. Median, Altitude, and Bisectors

There are four different types of lines (or segments) in a triangle.

※ Median, Altitude, and Bisectors

Definition of Median
 **Median** is a segment from a *vertex* to the ① _____ of the opposite side. ☺ *Median* goes to the *Middle*.

Definition of Altitude
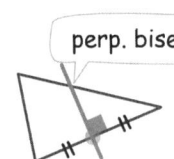 **Altitude** is a segment from a *vertex* that is ② _____ to the opposite side. ☺ **Height** is the length of the altitude.

Definition of Perpendicular bisector
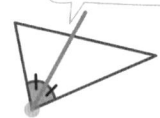 **Perpendicular bisector** is a line or segment that is ③ _____ to the side and passes through its ④ _____ .

Definition of Angle bisector
Angle bisector is a line or segment that divides an angle into two congruent angles

Blank : ① midpoint ② perpendicular ③ perpendicular ④ midpoint

Every triangle has ①_____ medians, altitudes, perp. bisectors, angle bisectors.

EXAMPLE 1. For each triangle, identify the segment of the triangle.

①
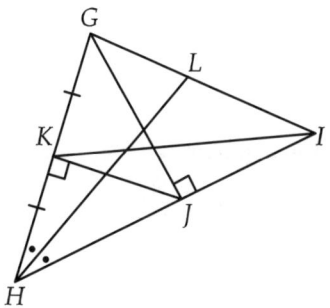

Median : _____

Altitude : _____

Perpendicular bisector : _____

Angle bisector : _____

②
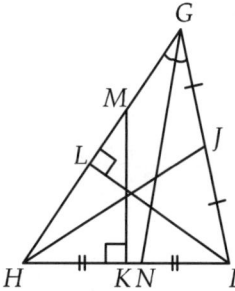

Median : _____

Altitude : _____

Perpendicular bisector : _____

Angle bisector : _____

③
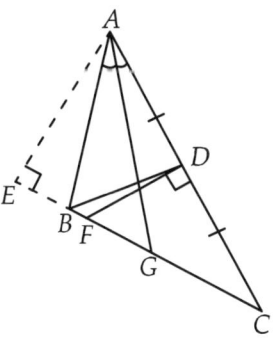

Median : _____

Altitude : _____

Perpendicular bisector : _____

Angle bisector : _____

④
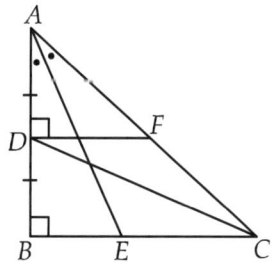

Median : _____

Altitude : _____

Perpendicular bisector : _____

Angle bisector : _____

Blank : ① three

2. Perpendicular Bisector and Angle Bisector Theorem

In geometry, equidistant means "equally distant."

※ Perpendicular Bisector Theorem

Perpendicular Bisector Theorem

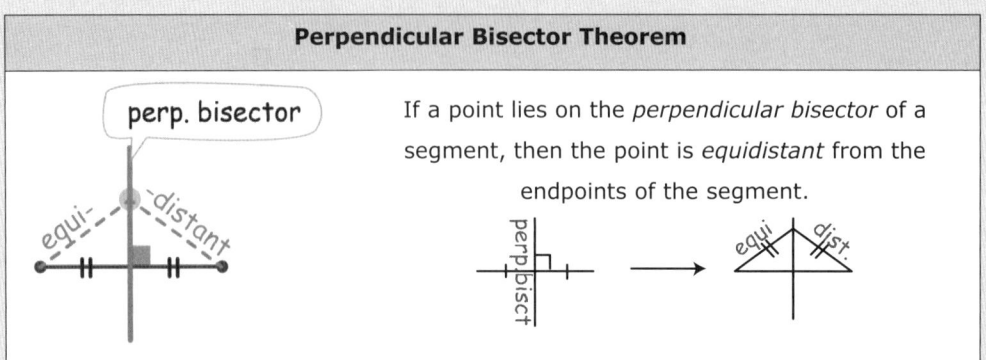

If a point lies on the *perpendicular bisector* of a segment, then the point is *equidistant* from the endpoints of the segment.

Converse of Perpendicular Bisector Theorem

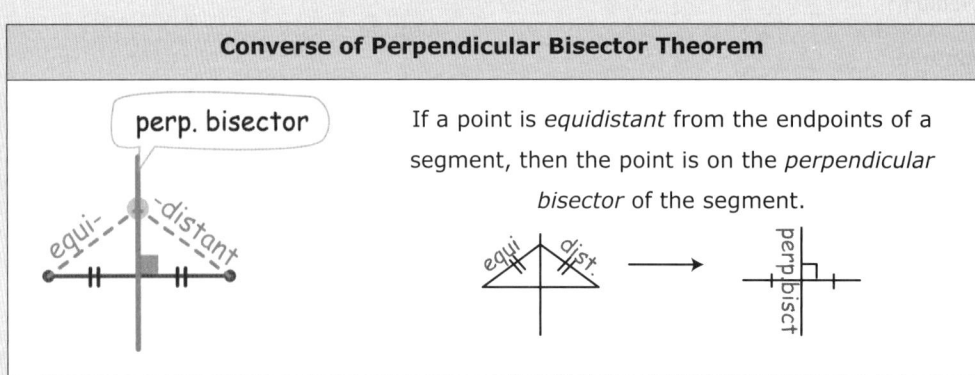

If a point is *equidistant* from the endpoints of a segment, then the point is on the *perpendicular bisector* of the segment.

☺ Proof : Perpendicular Bisector Theorem

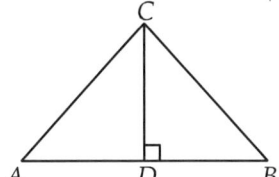

Given: $\overline{CD}$ is ⊥ bisector of $\overline{AB}$
Prove: $\overline{AC} \cong \overline{BC}$

Statements	Reasons
1. $\overline{CD}$ is ⊥ bisector of $\overline{AB}$	1. Given
2. D is midpt of $\overline{AB}$	2. Def of ⊥ bisector
3. $\overline{AD} \cong \overline{BD}$	3. Def of midpt.
4. ∠ADC and ∠BDC are right ∠s	4. Def of ⊥ bisector
5. ∠ADC ≅ ∠BDC	5. All right ∠s are ≅
6. $\overline{CD} \cong \overline{CD}$	6. Reflexive
7. △ADC ≅ △BDC	7. ① _____
8. $\overline{AC} \cong \overline{BC}$	8. ② _____

※ Angle Bisector Theorem

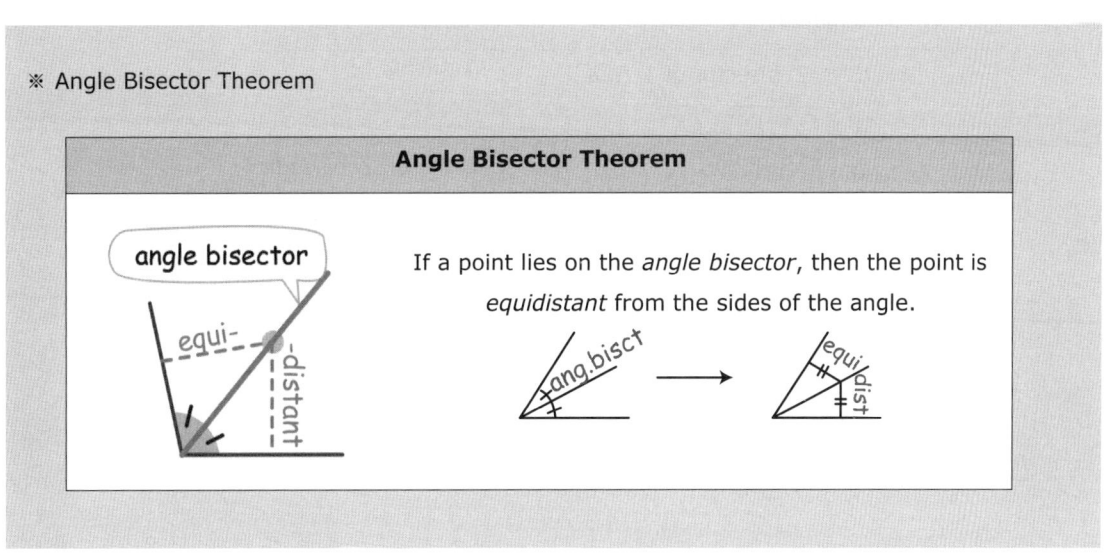

Blank : ① SAS postulate ② CPCTC

Converse of Angle Bisector Theorem

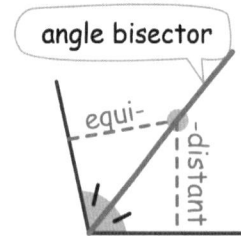

If a point is *equidistant* from the sides of the angle, then the point lies on the *angle bisector*.

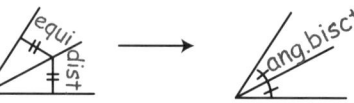

☺ Proof : Angle Bisector Theorem

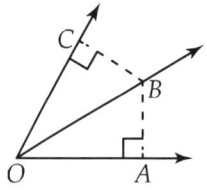

Given: $\overrightarrow{OB}$ is ∠ bisector of ∠AOC
$\overline{AB} \perp \overline{OA}, \overline{BC} \perp \overline{OC}$

Prove: $\overline{AB} \cong \overline{CB}$

Statements	Reasons
1. $\overrightarrow{OB}$ is ∠ bisector of ∠AOC $\overline{AB} \perp \overline{OA}, \overline{BC} \perp \overline{OC}$	1. Given
2. ∠AOB ≅ ∠COB	2. Def of ∠ bisector
3. ∠OAB and ∠OCB are right ∠s	3. Def of ⊥ lines
4. ∠OAB ≅ ∠OCB	4. All right ∠s are ≅
5. $\overline{OB} \cong \overline{OB}$	5. Reflexive
6. △AOB ≅ △COB	6. ① _____
7. $\overline{AB} \cong \overline{CB}$	7. ② _____

Blank : ① AAS theorem   ② CPCTC

EXAMPLE 2. Find the value of x. Name the theorem that justifies your answer.

①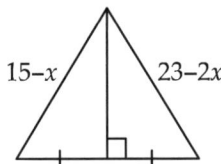

②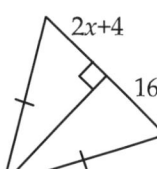

③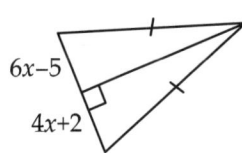

④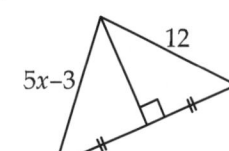

⑤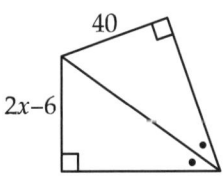

⑥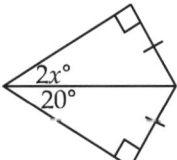

⑦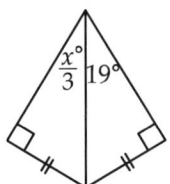

⑧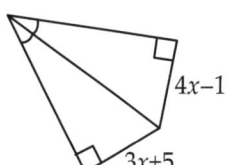

EXAMPLE 3. Write a two column proof.

① Given: $\overline{DA} \cong \overline{DB}$, $\overline{OC} \perp \overline{AB}$

Prove: $\overline{AC} \cong \overline{BC}$

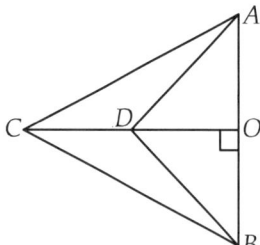

② Given: $\overline{AE}$ is $\perp$ bisector of $\overline{DB}$
$\overline{BE}$ is $\perp$ bisector of $\overline{AC}$
$\angle BAD \cong \angle ABC$

Prove: $\triangle BAD \cong \triangle ABC$

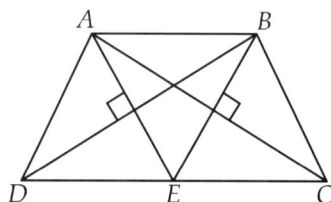

Statements	Reasons

Statements	Reasons

③ Given: △OAB is isosceles △
$\overline{AO}$ bisects $\angle CAB$
$\overline{BO}$ bisects $\angle DBA$

Prove: $\overline{CO} \cong \overline{DO}$

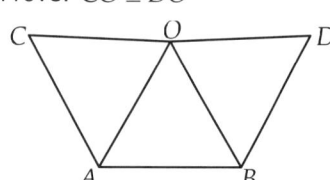

Statements	Reasons

Mia's Geometry
5.2 Centers of Triangles

1. Point of Concurrency

Two or more lines are called ①_____ if there is a common point to all of them.

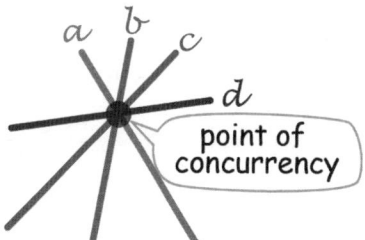

Line a, b, c, d are concurrent.

Point O is point of ②_____

In the previous chapter, we've learned that every triangle has three medians, altitudes, perp. bisector, angle bisector.

2. Circumcircle and Incircle

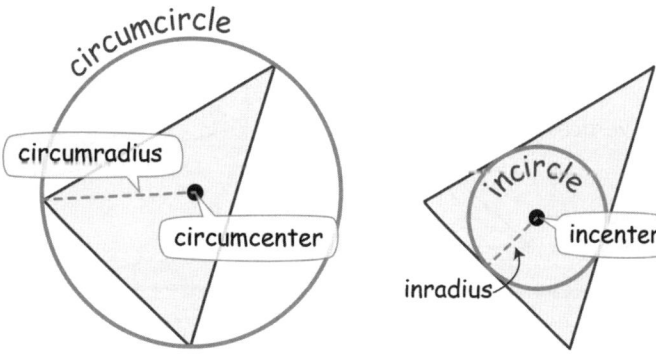

A ③_____ is a circle that passes through all vertices (corner points) of a polygon. ('*circum-*' means 'around')

An ④_____ is a circle that fits the *inside* of a polygon. ('*in-*' means 'inside')

Blank : ① concurrent ② concurrency ③ circumcircle ④ incircle

3. Circumcenter

Where all three perpendicular bisectors intersect is a "①_____"

(the center of a triangle's circumcircle),

, that is equidistant from the three ②_____ of the triangle.

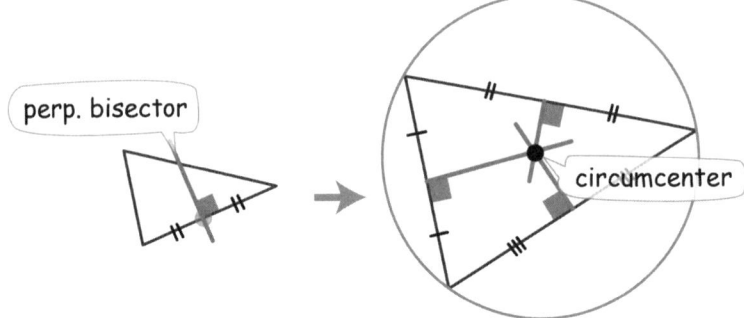

※ Circumcenter Theorem

Circumcenter Theorem
The point of concurrency for the *perpendicular bisectors* of a triangle is called the ③_____ which is *equidistant from the vertices* of the triangle.

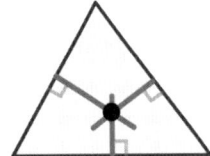 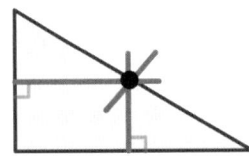 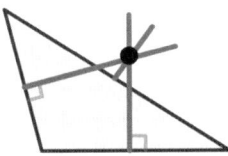

We can notice that the circemcenter is located at;

for acute triangle   for right triangle   for obtuse triangle

: ④_____ the triangle.   : ⑤_____ the triangle.   : ⑥_____ the triangle.

Blank : ① circumcenter   ② vertices   ③ circumcenter   ④ inside   ⑤ on   ⑥ outside

EXAMPLE 1. Point O is the circumcenter of $\triangle ABC$. Find the value of the variable(s) in each figure.

☺ Tip: If a point is circumcenter, then the point is
　　　　　i) on the $\perp$ bisector　　ii) equidistant from the vertices.

①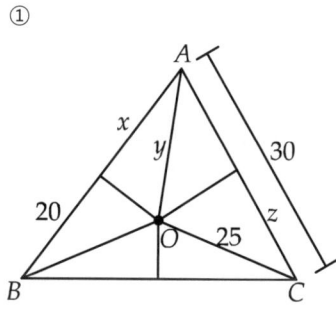

②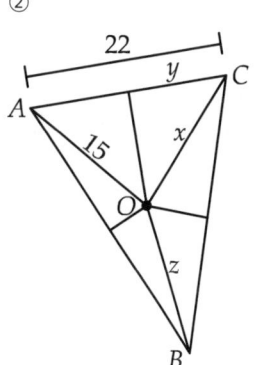

③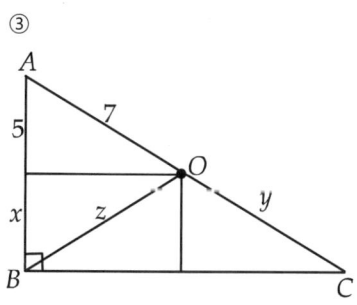

④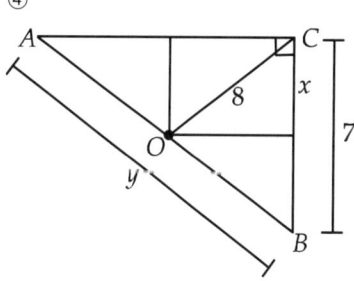

⑤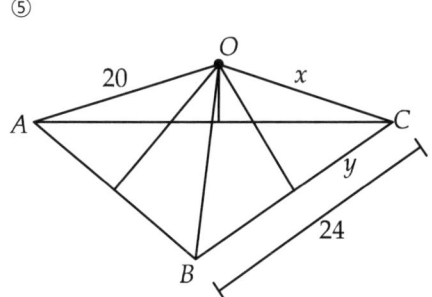

⑥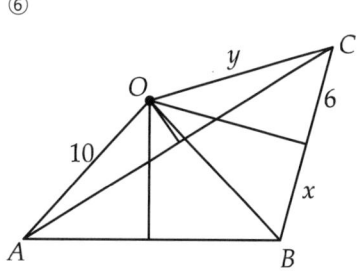

Part 5_Relationships in Triangles　163

⑦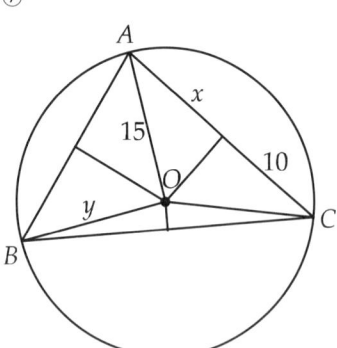

⑧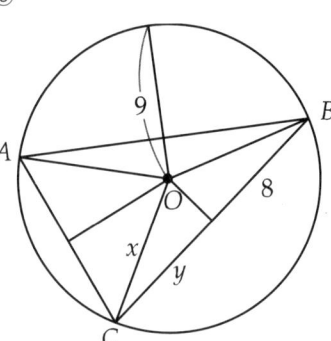

⑨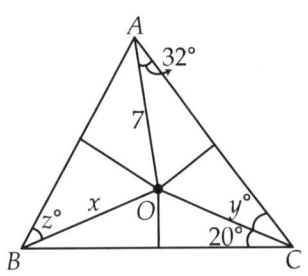

⑩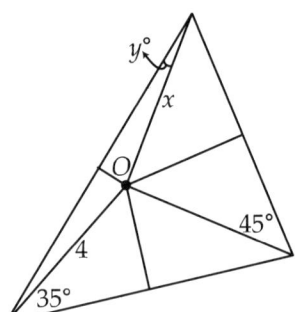

☺ We can notice that the circumcenter of an acute triangle can create three ① _____ triangles.

Blank : ① isosceles

4. Incenter

Where all three angle bisectors intersect is a "①_____"

(the center of a triangle's incircle)

, that is equidistant from the three ②_____ of the triangle.

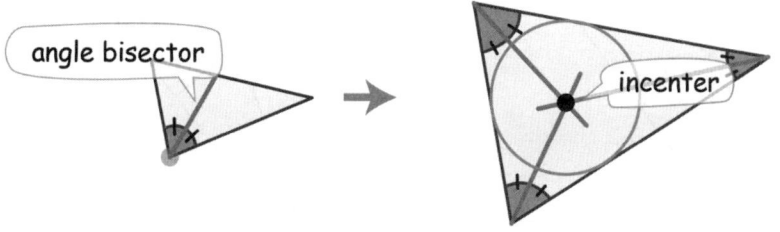

※ Incenter Theorem

Incenter Theorem

The point of concurrency for the *angle bisectors* of a triangle is called the ③_____ which is *equidistant from the sides* of the triangle.

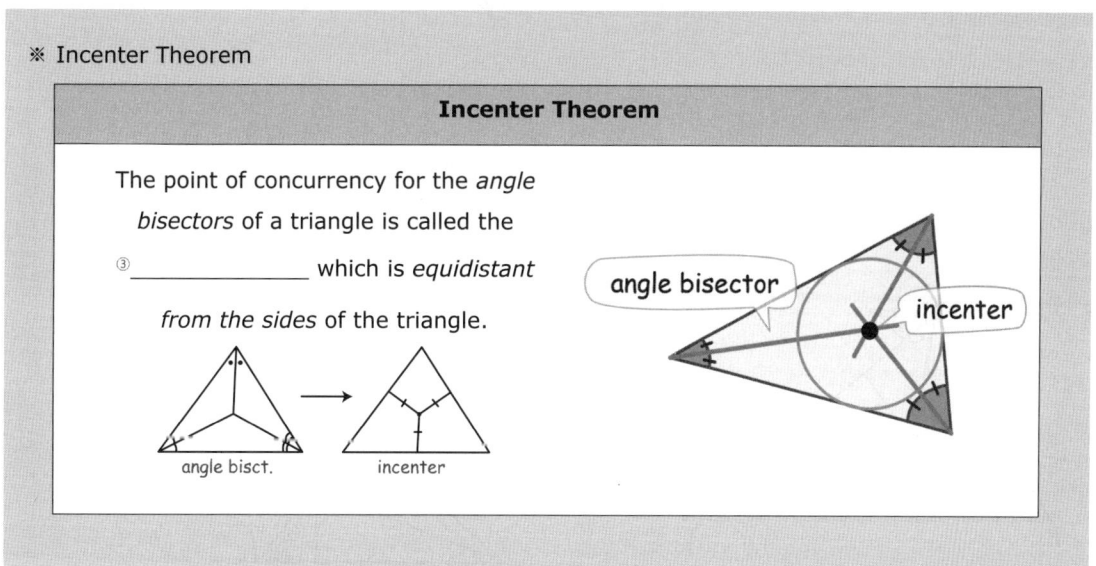

We can notice that the incenter is located at;

for acute triangle   for right triangle   for obtuse triangle

: ④_____ the triangle. : ⑤_____ the triangle. : ⑥_____ the triangle.

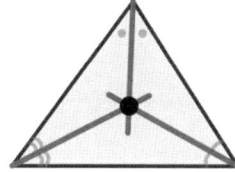 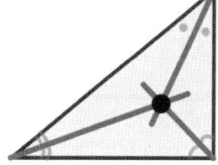 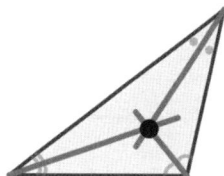

Blank : ① incenter ② sides ③ incenter ④ inside ⑤ inside ⑥ inside

EXAMPLE 2. Point O is the incenter of $\triangle ABC$. Find the value of the variable(s) in each figure.

☺ Tip: If a point is incenter, then the point is
  i) on the ∠ bisector   ii) equidistant from the sides.

①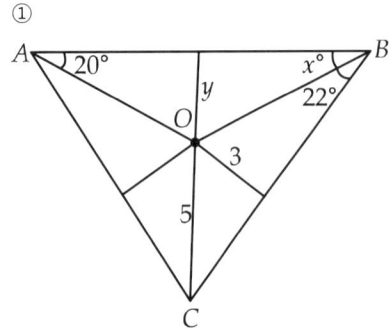

②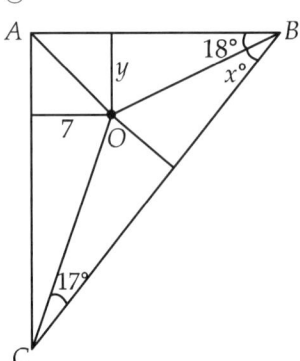

③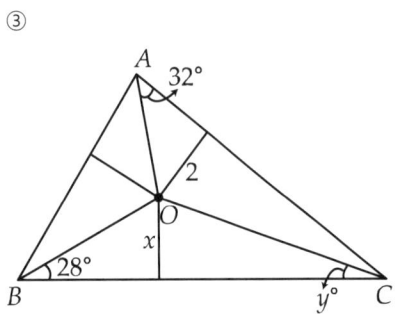

④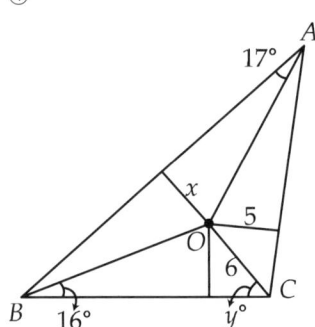

⑤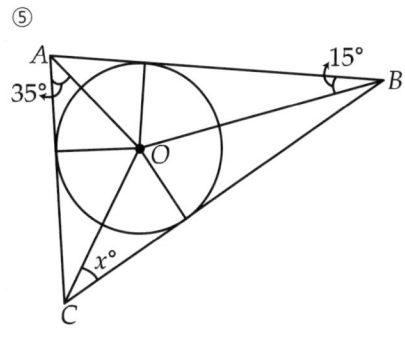

⑥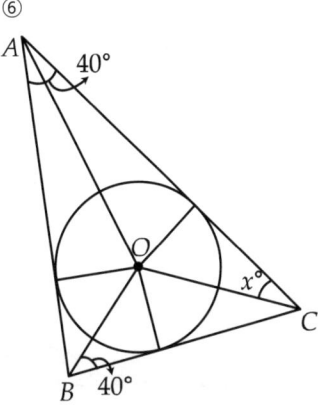

5. Centroid

Where all three medians intersect is a "①_____".

(which is also the "center of mass")

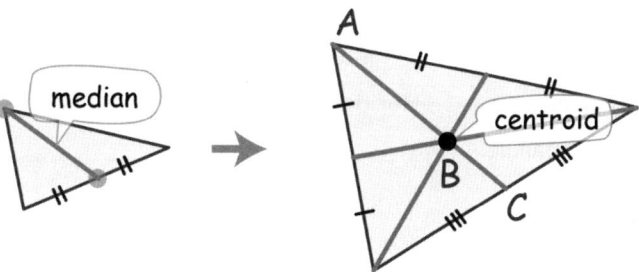

Blank : ① centroid

Centroid is the center of mass of a triangle.
It balances the triangle.

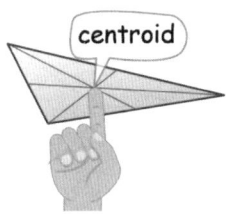

※ Centroid Theorem

Centroid Theorem

The centroid of a triangle is located **two-third** of the distance from a vertex to the midpoint of the side opposite the vertex on a median.

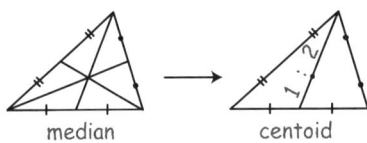
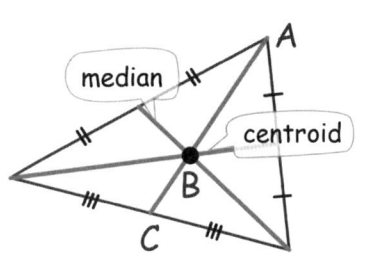

ex) $BC : AB =$ ①_____

☺ longer part is twice the shorter part of the median

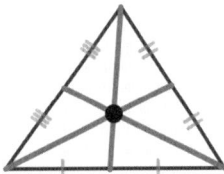
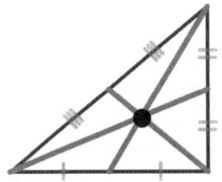
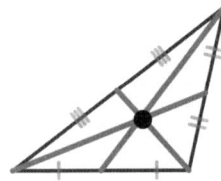

We can notice that the centroid is located at;

for acute triangle   for right triangle   for obtuse triangle
: ②_____ the triangle.   : ③_____ the triangle.   : ④_____ the triangle.

Blank : ① 1 : 2   ② inside   ③ inside   ④ inside

EXAMPLE 3. Point O is the centroid of $\triangle ABC$. Find the value of the variable(s) in each figure.

①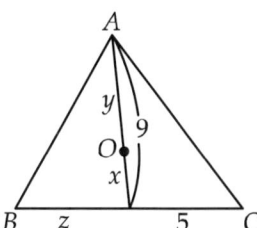

②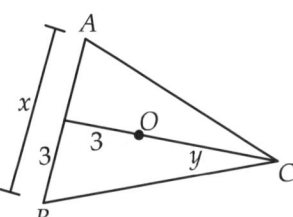

③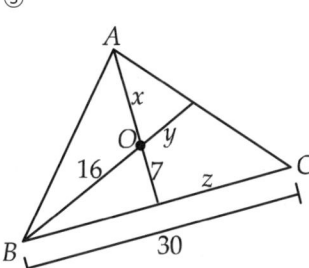

④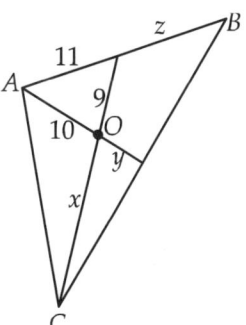

EXAMPLE 4. Point O is the centroid of $\triangle ABC$ and Point M is the centroid of $\triangle OBC$ (not shown). If $AD = 27$, find OM.

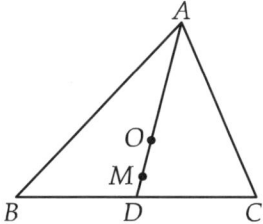

6. Orthocenter

Where all three altitudes intersect is a "①_____".

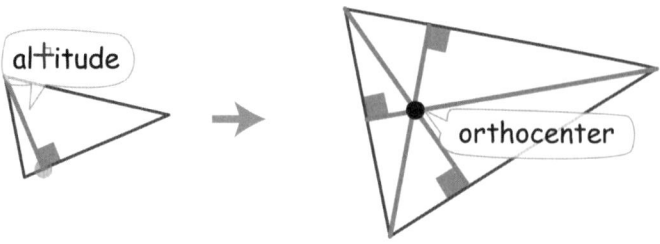

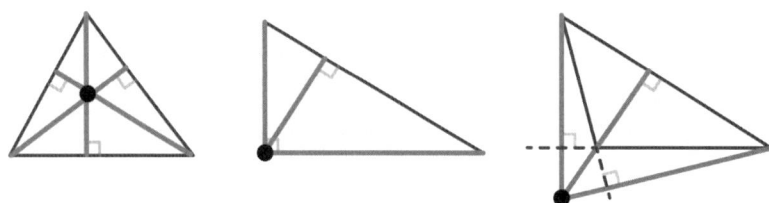

We can notice that the orthocenter is located at;

for acute triangle   for right triangle   for obtuse triangle

: ② _____ the triangle.   : ③ _____ the triangle.   : ④ _____ the triangle.

Blank : ① orthocenter   ② inside   ③ on   ④ outside

* All in One

Centers	Fact	Location
perp. bisector / circumcenter	Equidistant from the ①_____ of the triangle	Acute: ②_____ the △ Right: ③_____ the △ Obtuse: ④_____ the △
angle bisector / incenter	Equidistant from the ⑤_____ of the triangle	Always inside the △
median / centroid	Long part is twice the short part of the median	Always inside the △
altitude / orthocenter		Acute: ⑥_____ the △ Right: ⑦_____ the △ Obtuse: ⑧_____ the △

Blank : ① vertices ② inside ③ on ④ outside ⑤ sides ⑥ inside ⑦ on ⑧ outside

EXAMPLE 5. Name the point of concurrency shown in the figure.

①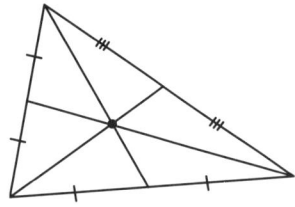

②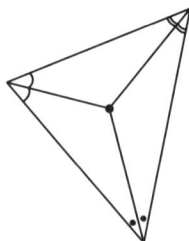

③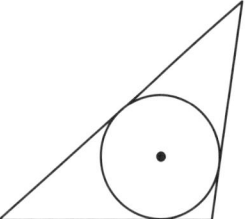

④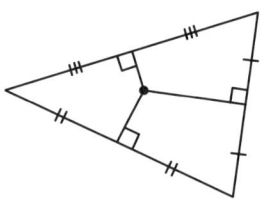

⑤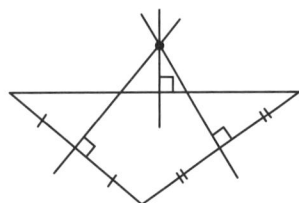

⑥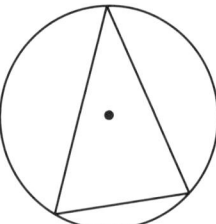

⑦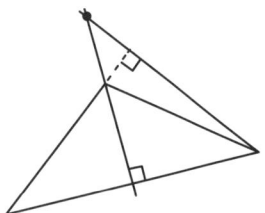

⑧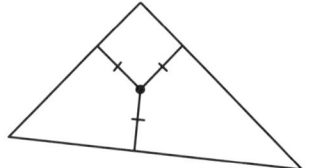

⑨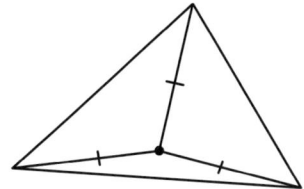

⑩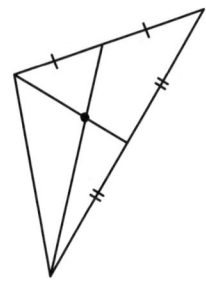

⑪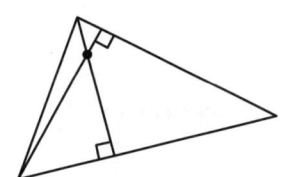

Part 5_Relationships in Triangles

Mia's Geometry

5.3 Midsegment Theorem

1. Midsegment

① _____ is a segment that joins the midpoints of two sides of a triangle. Every triangle has ② _____ midsegments.

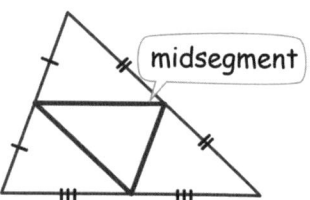

 vs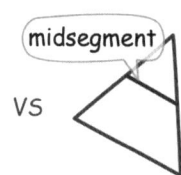

☺ Median goes vertex to midpoint.
   Midsegment goes midpoint to midpoint.

※ Triangle Midsegment Theorem

Triangle Midsegment Theorem
A midsegment of a triangle is ③ _____ to a side of the triangle, and its length is ④ _____ the length of that side. 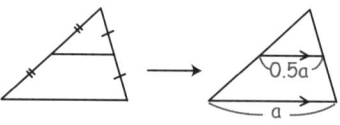   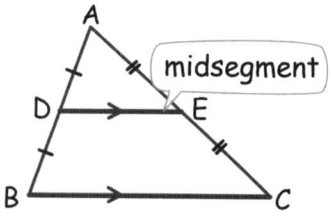 ($\overline{DE} \parallel \overline{BC}$ and $DE = \frac{1}{2} BC$)

Blank : ① Midsegment ② three ③ parallel ④ half

EXAMPLE 1. For the given diagram, Find the value of x, y, or z. The figures are not drawn to scale.

①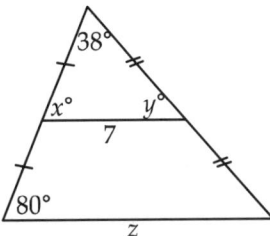

②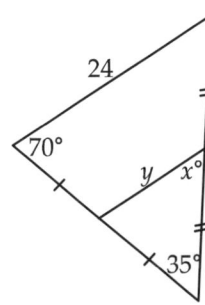

③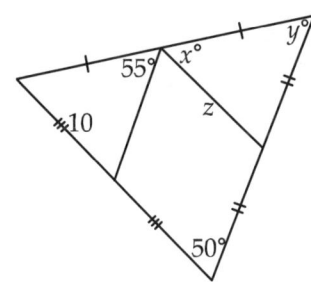

④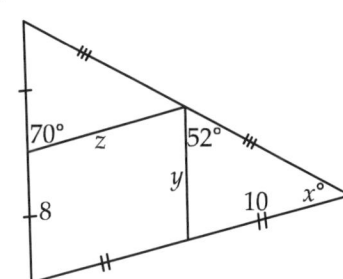

⑤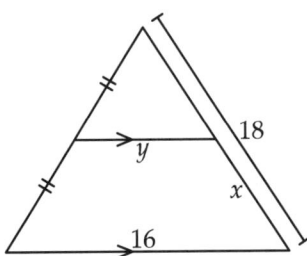

⑥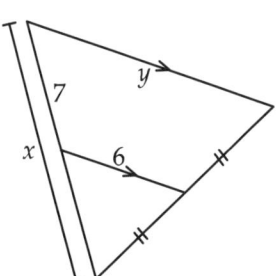

⑦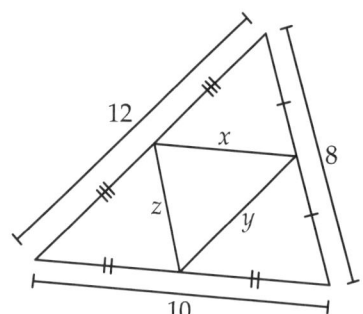

⑧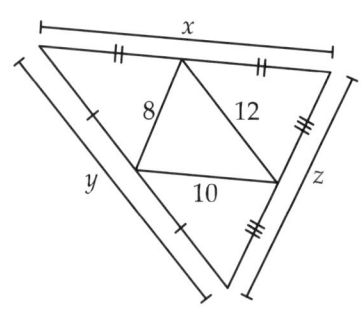

⑨ *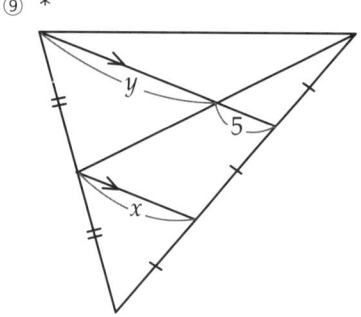

⑩ *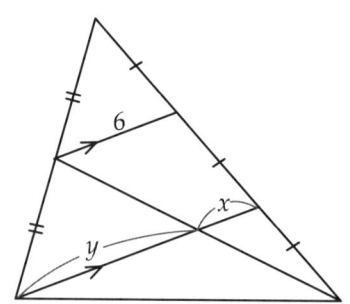

⑪ *O is centroid of △ ABC

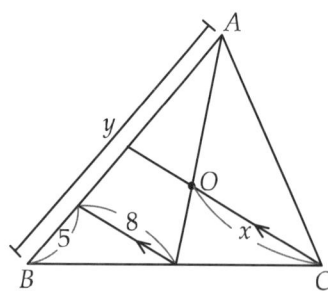

⑫ *O is centroid of △ ABC

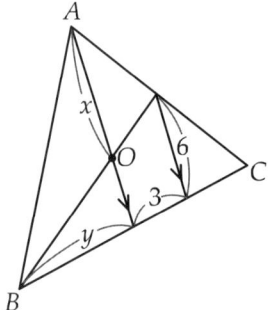

EXAMPLE 2. In the figure, what is EF?

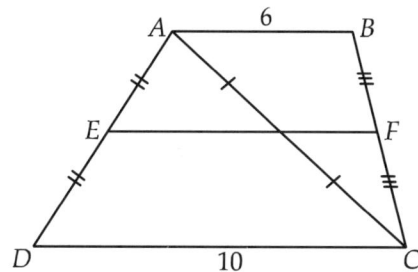

EXAMPLE 3. Point O is the centroid of $\triangle ABC$. If the perimeter of $\triangle ABC$ is 24 cm, what is the perimeter of $\triangle DEF$?

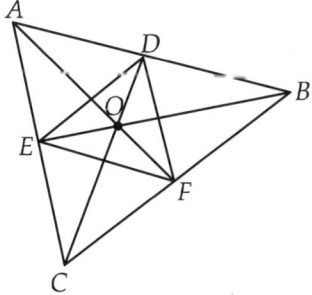

EXAMPLE 4. If the perimeter of △ ABC is 36 cm, what is the perimeter of △ MNO?

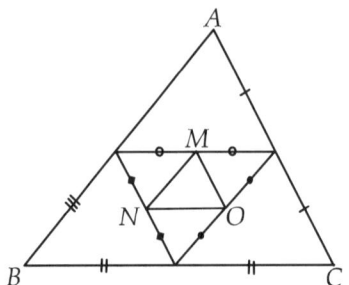

Mia's Geometry

5.4 Properties of Inequalities

1. Properties of Inequalities

※ Properties of Inequalities

Properties of Inequalities
① If $a > b$ and $c \geq d$, then a ①____ $> b \pm d$.
② If $a > b$ and $c > 0$, then $ac > bc$ and $a/c > b/c$.
③ If $a > b$ and $c < 0$, then ac ②__ bc and $a/c < b/c$.
④ If $a > b$ and $b > c$, then ③_____. (Transitive property of inequalities)
⑤ If $a = b + c$ and $c > 0$, then $a > b$.

EXAMPLE 1. Determine whether the statement is true of false.

① If $a > 2$, then $a + 2 > 4$.

② If $a < b$, then $a - 4 < b - 4$.

③ If $c > 4$, then $-c > -4$.

④ If $\dfrac{b}{2} < -4$, then $b > -8$.

⑤ If $x > 6$, then $x > 4$.

⑥ If $x > 17$, then $x > 13$.

Blank : ① ±c   ② <   ③ a > c

⑦ If $a-1>4$, then $a>7$.

⑧ If $a+2>8$, then $a>7$.

⑨ If $x>y$ and $y>20$, then $x>17$.

⑩ If $a>b$ and $a>c$, then $b>c$.

⑪ If $a>b$ and $c>d$, then $a+b>c+d$.

⑫ If $a>b$ and $c>d$, then $a+c>b+d$.

⑬ If $a>b$ and $c=d$, then $a+c>b+d$

⑭ If $a+b=c$ and $b>0$, then $a>c$

⑮ If $a=b+4$, then $a>b$.

⑯ If $x+y=z$ and $x>r$, then $r+y<z$.

EXAMPLE 2. Determine whether the statements can be deduced from the given figure.

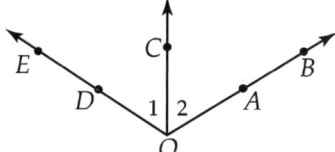

① $m\angle 1 + m\angle 2 = m\angle AOD$ ② $AO + AB = OB$

③ $OA > AB$ ④ $OA < OB$

⑤ $m\angle AOD > m\angle 2$ ⑥ $m\angle 1 < m\angle AOD$

⑦ $AB > ED$

EXAMPLE 3. Write a two column proof.

① Given: $OA < OC$, $OB < OD$
   Prove: $AB < CD$

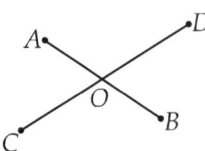

Statements	Reasons

② Given: $AC < BD$
   Prove: $AB < CD$

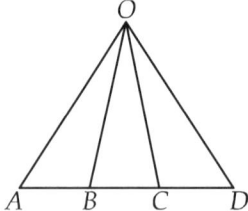

Statements	Reasons

③ Given: $\angle 1$ and $\angle 2$ are vertical angles
   Prove: $m\angle AOB > m\angle 2$

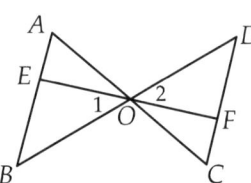

Statements	Reasons

④ Given: $m\angle AOB = m\angle DOC$
   Prove: $m\angle AOC > m\angle DOC$

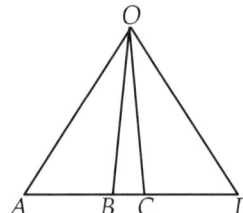

Statements	Reasons

2. Exterior Angle Inequality Theorem

※ Exterior Angle Inequality Theorem

Exterior Angle Inequality Theorem

The measure of any exterior angle of a triangle is greater than the remote interior angles.

ex) $m\angle A$ ① ___ $m\angle B$, $m\angle A$ ② ___ $m\angle C$

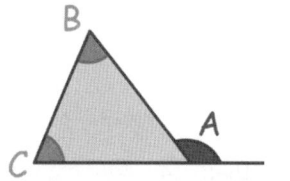

☺ Tip : Exterior Angle Inequality Theorem VS Exterior Angle Theorem

Exterior Angle Inequality Theorem : $m\angle A$ ③ _____

Exterior Angle Theorem : $m\angle A$ ④ _____

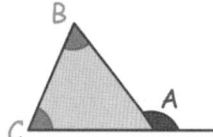

EXAMPLE 4.   Determine which angle has the greatest measure.

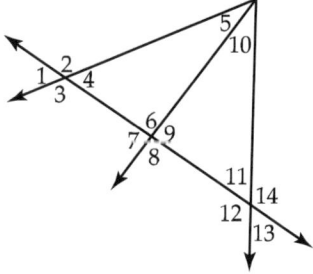

① ∠2, ∠5, ∠6

② ∠4, ∠5, ∠7

③ ∠6, ∠10, ∠11

④ ∠9, ∠10, ∠14

⑤ ∠9, ∠10, ∠12

⑥ ∠8, ∠10, ∠11

Blank : ① >   ② >   ③ > $m\angle B$ ④ = $m\angle B + m\angle C$

Part 5_Relationships in Triangles   183

EXAMPLE 5.   List *all* angles whose measures are;

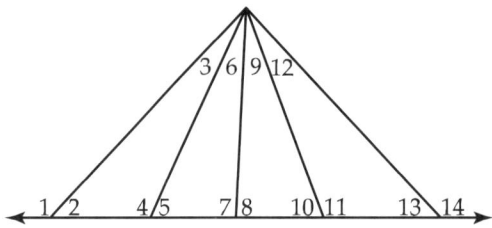

① less than ∠4

② less than ∠10

③ less than ∠8

④ less than ∠11

⑤ greater than ∠8

⑥ greater than ∠9

⑦ greater than ∠6

⑧ greater than ∠10

EXAMPLE 6. Write a two column proof.

① Given: ∠3 and ∠4 are vertical angles
Prove: $m\angle 1 < m\angle 4$

② Given: $\overline{AB} \perp \overline{BC}$
Prove: $m\angle ACD > 90°$

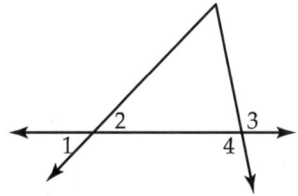

Statements	Reasons

Statements	Reasons

Mia's Geometry
5.5 Inequalities in One Triangle

1. Angle-Side Relationships Theorem

※ Angle-Side Relationships Theorem

Angle-Side Relationships Theorem

In a triangle, the side opposite the larger angle is the longer side, and vice versa.

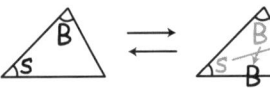 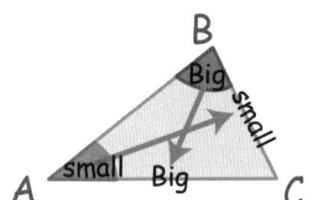

ex) If $\angle A < \angle B$, then $a < b$.

If $a < b$, then $\angle A < \angle B$.

☺ Proof :

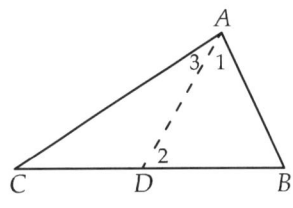

Given: $CB > AB$

Prove: $m\angle A > m\angle C$

Statements	Reasons
1. Draw segment $\overline{AD}$ with point D such that $AB = DB$	1. Auxiliary line
2. $m\angle 1 = m\angle 2$	2. ① _____
3. $m\angle A = m\angle 1 + m\angle 3$	3. ② _____
4. $m\angle A > m\angle 1$	4. ③ _____
5. $m\angle A > m\angle 2$	5. ④ _____
6. $m\angle 2 > m\angle C$	6. ⑤ _____
7. $m\angle A > m\angle C$	7. ⑥ _____

Blank : ① Isos. △ thm. ② ∠ add. post ③ Property of ineq. ④ Substitution prop. ⑤ Ext ∠ ineq. thm ⑥ Property of ineq.

EXAMPLE 1. List the angles A to C in order from least to greatest measure. Figures are not drawn to scale.

①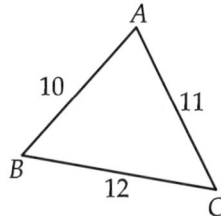

②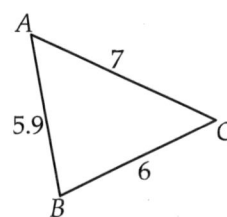

③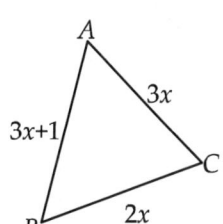

④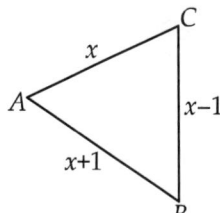

EXAMPLE 2. List the sides a to e in order from least to greatest measure. Figures are not drawn to scale.

①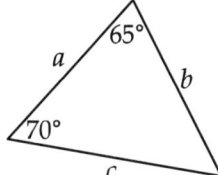

②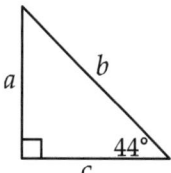

③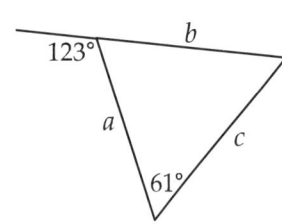

④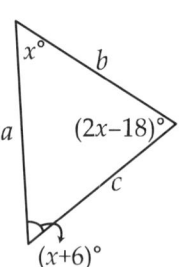

⑤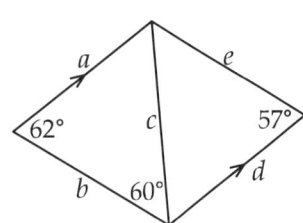

⑥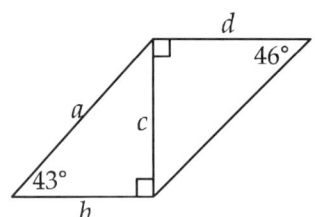

⑦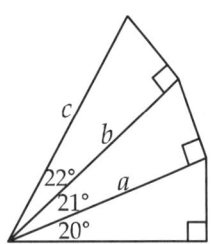

2. The Triangle Inequality Theorem

※ Triangle Inequality Theorem

Triangle Inequality Theorem

The sum of the lengths of any two sides of a triangle is greater than the length of the third side.

ex) $a + c > b$

① _____ $> c$

② _____ $> a$

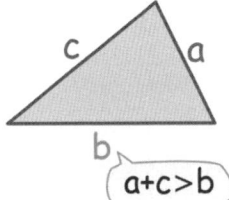

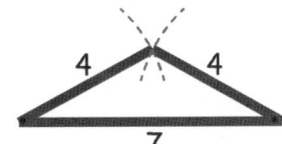

Side 4, 4, 7 form a triangle

because ③ _____ .

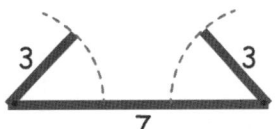

Side 3, 3, 7 doesn't form a triangle,

because ④ _____ .

EXAMPLE 3. Determine whether the given measures can be the lengths of the sides of a triangle.

☺ Tip : We usually check only if
(sum of other two sides) > (longest side)

① 4, 6, 9

② 8, 10, 20

③ 12, 12, 24

④ 6, 7, 13

⑤ 13, 17, 31

⑥ 15, 17, 31

Blank : ① $a + b$ ② $b + c$ ③ $4 + 4 > 7$ ④ $3 + 3 < 7$

EXAMPLE 4. Write a two column proof.

① Given: $\angle 1 \cong \angle 2$
   Prove: $AB + AC > CD$

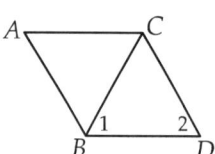

Statements	Reasons

② Given: $AB = AC$
   Prove: $AD + AB > CD$

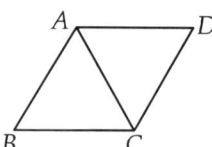

Statements	Reasons

③ Given: $BE = ED$
   Prove: $AB + AC > CD$

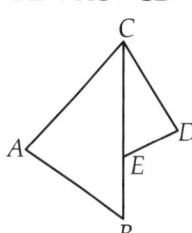

Statements	Reasons

④ Given: M is midpoint of $\overline{AD}$
   Prove: $MD + BM > AB$

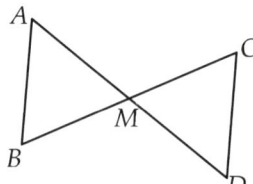

Statements	Reasons

⑤ *Given: $\overline{PS} \parallel \overline{QR}$, $\angle P \cong \angle R$
   Prove: $PS + SR > QS$

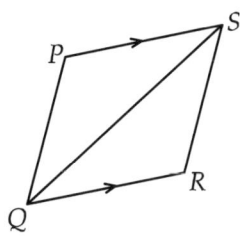

Statements	Reasons

⑥ *Given: $\overline{JM}$ bisects $\angle KJL$
   $\angle JMK \cong \angle JML$
   Prove: $JL < JM + MK$

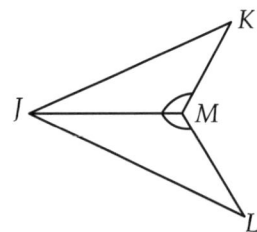

Statements	Reasons

Mia's Geometry
5.6 Inequalities in Two Triangles

1. SAS Inequality Theorem

The next theorems compare two triangles.

Suppose you take two sticks, hinge them at a common end, and attach a rubber band at the other ends.
When comparing two triangles with two pairs of congruent sides, you can see that the triangle with the larger angle between those sides has the larger third side.

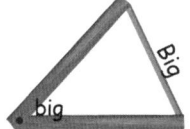

※ SAS Inequality Theorem (Hinge Theorem)

SAS Inequality Theorem (Hinge Theorem)

If $AB = XY$, $AC = XZ$,

and $m\angle A < m\angle X$, then $BC < YZ$.

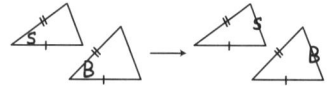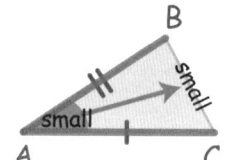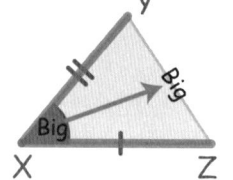

2. SSS Inequality Theorem

※ SSS Inequality Theorem

SSS Inequality Theorem

If $AB = XY$, $AC = XZ$,

and $BC < YZ$, then $m\angle A < m\angle X$.

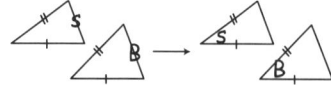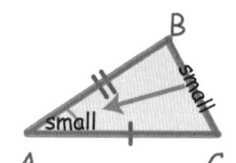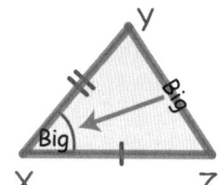

☺ Remember:

Using SAS Inequality Theorem, we compare ①_____

Using SSS Inequality Theorem, we compare ②_____

EXAMPLE 1. What inequality can we deduce from the figure? Name the theorem that supports your answer.

①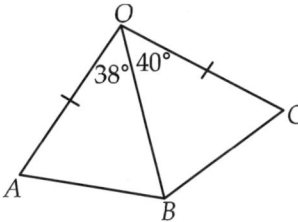

②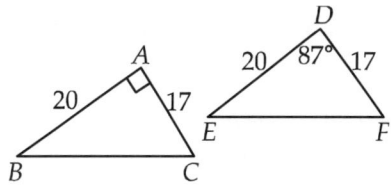

③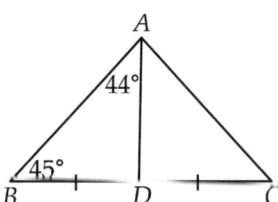

④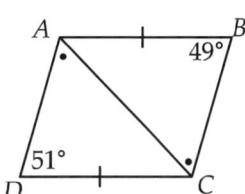

⑤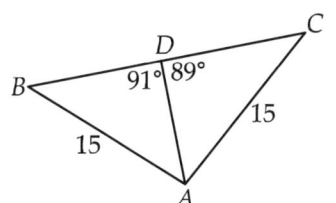

⑥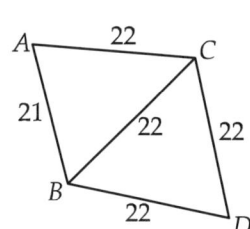

Blank : ① sides   ② angles

⑦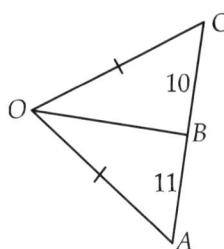

⑧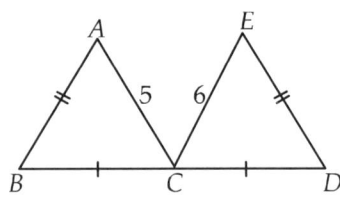

⑨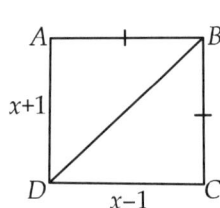

EXAMPLE 2. Complete the statement with > or <. Name the theorem that supports your answer.

① OA ___ OC
OA ___ 10
$OA + OB$ ___ 10

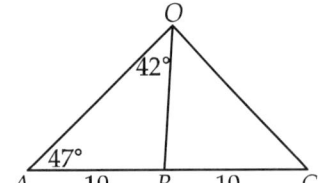

② AB ___ DE
$m\angle BOC$ ___ $m\angle DOC$
AB ___ 24

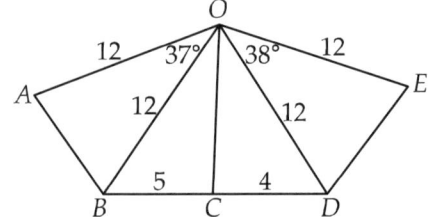

③ $m\angle AOB$ ___ $m\angle COD$

  $m\angle BOC$ ___ $m\angle BCE$

  $m\angle ABO$ ___ $m\angle OAB$

④ $m\angle AOB$ ___ $m\angle BOC$

  $m\angle A$ ___ $m\angle AOB$

  $m\angle A$ ___ $m\angle AOP$

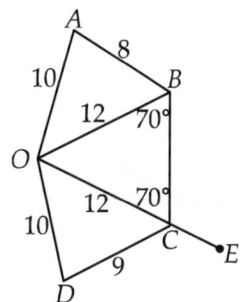
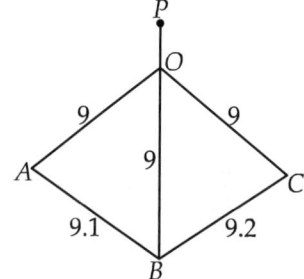

EXAMPLE 3. Write a two column proof.

① Given: $AB = DC$
   $m\angle 1 < m\angle 2$
   Prove: $AD < BC$

② Given: $AB = AD$
   $BC > CD$
   Prove: $m\angle 1 > m\angle 2$

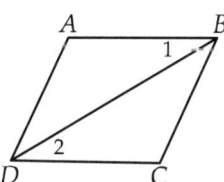
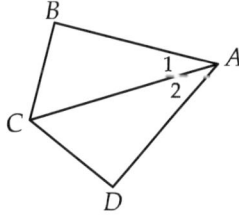

Statements	Reasons

Statements	Reasons

③ Given: D is midpoint of $\overline{EC}$
   $m\angle 1 = m\angle 2$
   $AE < BC$
   Prove: $m\angle 3 < m\angle 4$

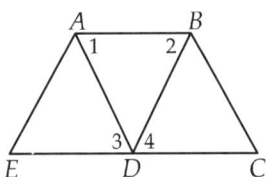

Statements	Reasons

④ Given: $m\angle 3 = m\angle 4$
   $m\angle 1 > m\angle 2$
   Prove: $BD > CD$

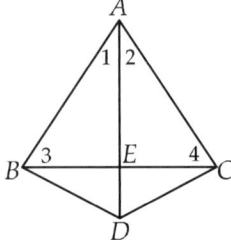

Statements	Reasons

⑤ *Given: $m\angle 1 < m\angle 2$
   $AD = BE, DC = EC$
   Prove: $m\angle 3 > m\angle 4$

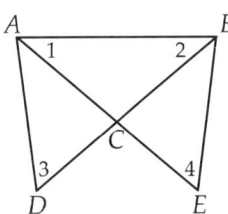

Statements	Reasons

⑥ Given: $AB = CD$
   Prove: $AD < BC$

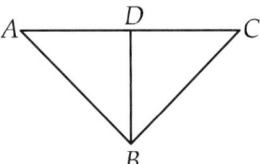

Statements	Reasons

196 Mia's Geometry

⑦ *Given: $m\angle B = m\angle ACB$
$AC = DC$

Prove: $CB > AD$

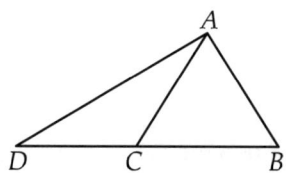

Statements	Reasons

Mia's Geometry

Postulates, Theorems from CH5

*All in One (sorted by Miamath)

About perpendicular bisector and angle bisector..	
Perpendicular Bisector Theorem If a point lies on the *perpendicular bisector* of a segment, then the point is *equidistant* from the endpoints of the segment.	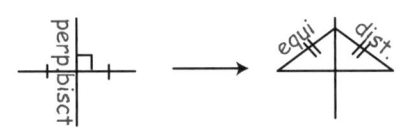
Converse of Perpendicular Bisector Theorem If a point is *equidistant* from the endpoints of a segment, then the point is on the *perpendicular bisector* of the segment.	
Angle Bisector Theorem If a point lies on the *angle bisector*, then the point is *equidistant* from the sides of the angle.	
Converse of Angle Bisector Theorem If a point is *equidistant* from the sides of the angle, then the point lies on the *angle bisector*.	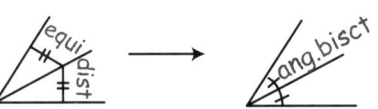

About centers of triangle..

Circumcenter Theorem
The point of concurrency for the *perpendicular bisectors* of a triangle is called the circumcenter which is *equidistant from the vertices* of the triangle.

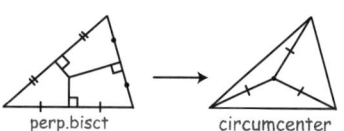
perp.bisct → circumcenter

Incenter Theorem
The point of concurrency for the *angle bisectors* of a triangle is called the incenter which is *equidistant from the sides* of the triangle.

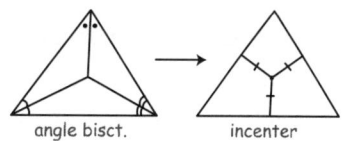
angle bisct. → incenter

Centroid Theorem
The centroid of a triangle is located **two-third** of the distance from a vertex to the midpoint of the side opposite the vertex on a median.

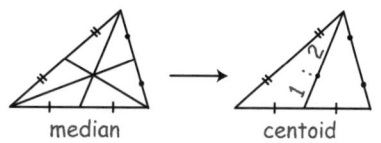
median → centoid

Triangle Midsegment Theorem
A midsegment of a triangle is parallel to a side of the triangle, and its length is half the length of that side.

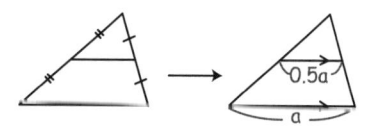

About inequalities..

Properties of Inequalities

①   If $a > b$ and $c \geq d$. then $a \pm c > b \pm d$.

②   If $a > b$ and $c > 0$. then $ac > bc$ and $a/c > b/c$.

③   If $a > b$ and $c < 0$, then $ac < bc$ and $a/c < b/c$.

④   If $a > b$ and $b > c$, then $a > c$.

⑤   If $a = b + c$ and $c > 0$. then $a > b$.

About triangle inequalities..	
Exterior Angle Inequality Theorem The measure of any exterior angle of a triangle is greater than the remote interior angles.	∠3 > ∠1, ∠3 > ∠2
Angle-Side Relationships Theorem In a triangle, the side opposite the larger angle is the longer side, and vice versa.	
Triangle Inequality Theorem The sum of the lengths of any two sides of a triangle is greater than the length of the third side.	$a + b > c$
SAS Inequality Theorem (Hinge Theorem) If $AB = XY$, $AC = XZ$, and $m\angle A < m\angle X$, then $BC < YZ$.	
SSS Inequality Theorem If $AB = XY$, $AC = XZ$, and $BC < YZ$, then $m\angle A < m\angle X$.	

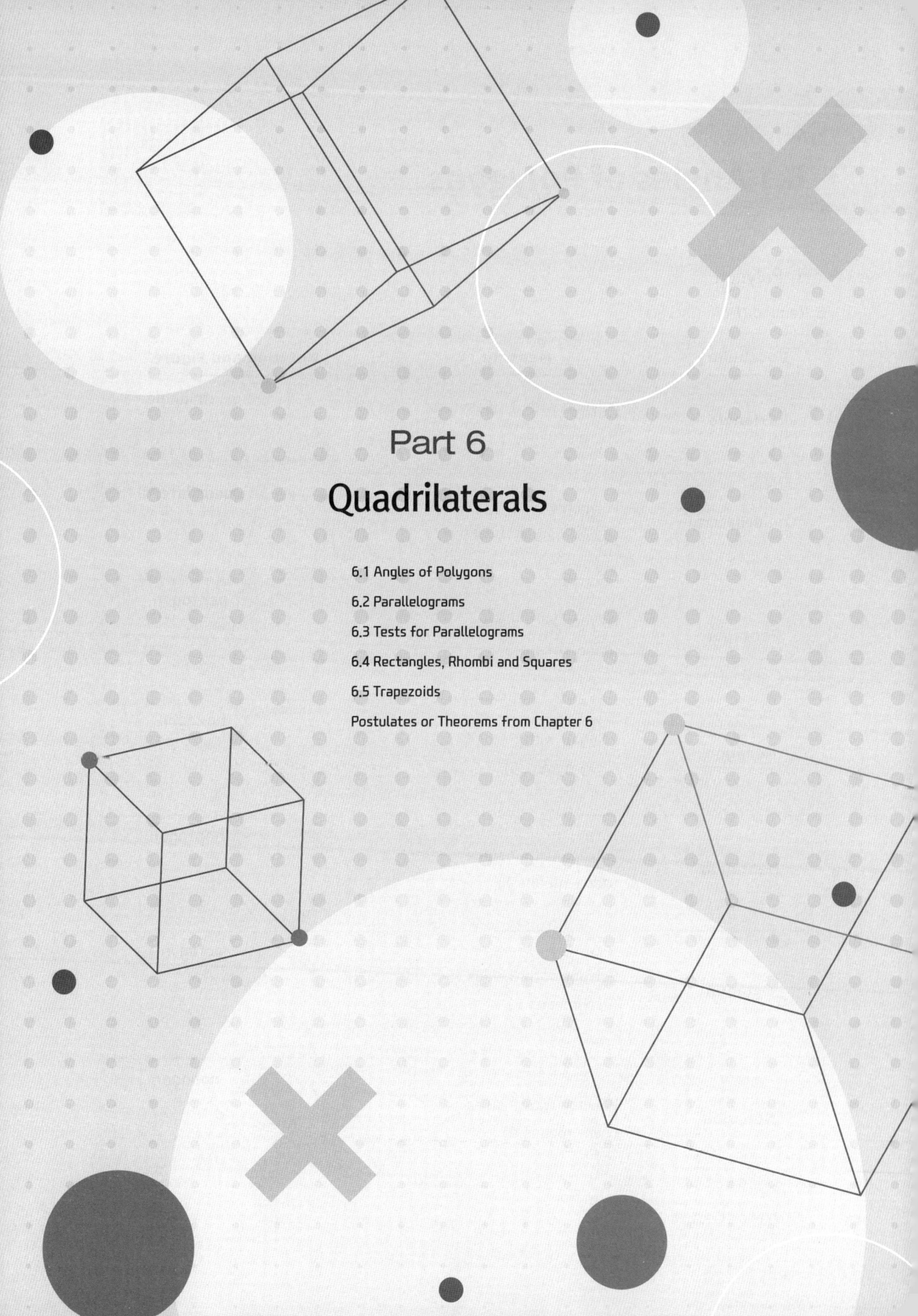

Part 6
Quadrilaterals

6.1 Angles of Polygons

6.2 Parallelograms

6.3 Tests for Parallelograms

6.4 Rectangles, Rhombi and Squares

6.5 Trapezoids

Postulates or Theorems from Chapter 6

Mia's Geometry
6.1 Angles of Polygons

1. Polygon

☺ Remind (from Ch 1.4)

Vocabulary	Meaning	Notation and Figure
Triangle	Polygon with 3 sides (*tri-* means 3)	triangle
Quadrilateral	Polygon with 4 sides (*quad-* means 4)	quadrilateral
Pentagon	Polygon with 5 sides (*pent-* means 5)	pentagon
Hexagon	Polygon with 6 sides (*hex-* means 6)	hexagon
Heptagon	Polygon with 7 sides (*hept-* means 7)	heptagon
Octagon	Polygon with 8 sides (*oct-* means 8)	octagon
Nonagon	Polygon with 9 sides (*non-* means 9)	nonagon

| **Decagon** | Polygon with 10 sides (*dec-* means 10) | 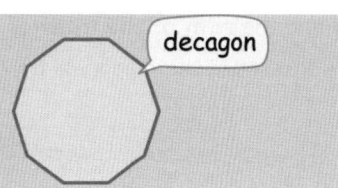 |

A **regular** polygon has all angles equal and all sides equal.

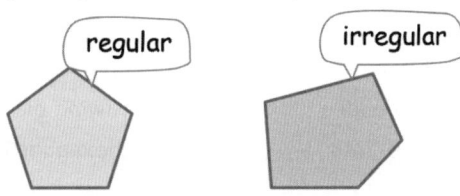

A **convex** polygon has all interior angles less than 180° (all vertices pointing outwards from the center).

2. Sum of Measures of Interior Angles

① _____ angle is an angle inside a polygon.

② _____ angle is the angle between any side of a polygon, and a line extended from the next side.

We know that the sum of the interior angle of a triangle is ③ _____.
(Triangle Sum Theorem)

Blank : ① Interior   ② Exterior   ③ 180°

To find the **sum of the interior angles** of **polygon with n sides,** we draw all of the diagonals from one vertex.

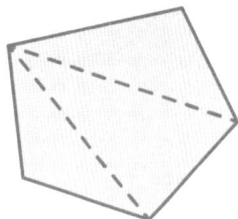 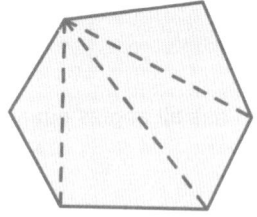

Drawing diagonals divides a pentagon(5 sides) into ① _____ triangles.

The sum of the angles are ② _____.

Drawing diagonals divides hexagon(6 sides) into ③ _____ triangles.

The sum of the angles are ④ _____.

In general, sum of the angles in any **polygon with n sides** is ⑤ _____.

※ Interior Angle Sum Theorem

Interior Angle Sum Theorem
If a convex polygon has n sides, then the sum of the measures of its interior angles is $$(n-2)\,180°$$ 

Blank : ① 3   ② 3(180°) = 540°   ③ 4   ④ 4(180°) = 720°   ⑤ (n − 2) 180°

3. Sum of Measures of Exterior Angles

We can observe that when we join all the exterior angles together, we form a complete angle of 360°.

So, all the Exterior Angles of a polygon add up to ① _____.

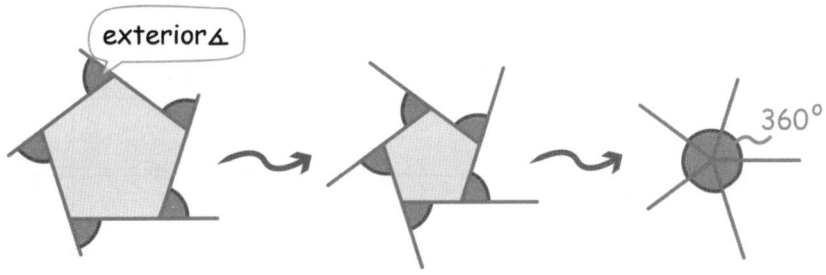

※ Exterior Angle Sum Theorem

Exterior Angle Sum Theorem

If a polygon is convex, then the sum of the measures of the exterior angles, one at each vertex, is

360°.

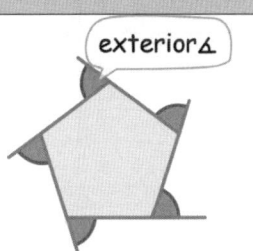

Blank : ① 360°

EXAMPLE 1. Complete the table for regular polygon. You may use calculator for simple calculations. Round to the nearest tenth if needed.

☺ Measure of EACH int. ∠ of regular polygon = ① _____

Measure of EACH ext. ∠ of regular polygon = ② _____

	Number of sides	Int. ∠ Sum	Ext. ∠ Sum	Measure of each int. ∠	Measure of each ext. ∠
①	6				
②	10				
③		900			
④		1080			
⑤				150	
⑥				165	
⑦					10
⑧					20

EXAMPLE 2. Fill in the blanks.

① $x + y = $ _____   ② $x - y = $ _____

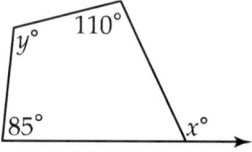

Blank : ① $\dfrac{(n-2)180°}{n}$ ② $\dfrac{360°}{n}$

③ $y - x =$ _____

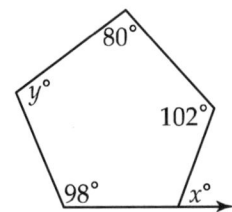

④ $x + y + z =$ _____

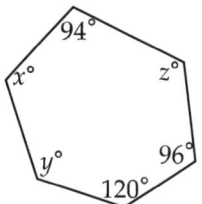

⑤ $x - y =$ _____

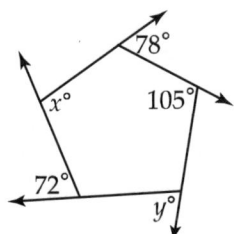

⑥ $x + y =$ _____

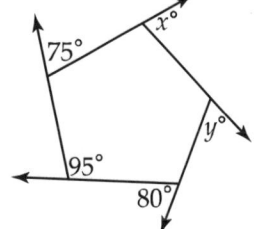

⑦ $x =$ _____

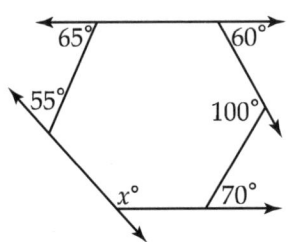

⑧ $x =$ _____

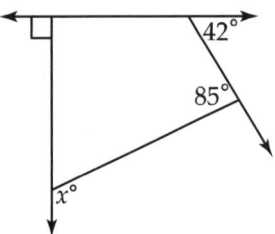

EXAMPLE 3. Two sides of a regular pentagon are extended as shown in the figure. What is the value of x?

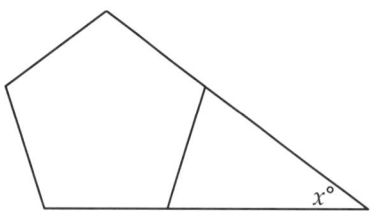

EXAMPLE 4. * What is $m\angle 1 + m\angle 2 + m\angle 3 + \cdots + m\angle 10$?

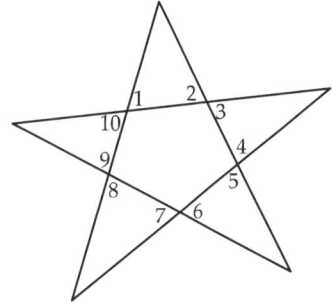

EXAMPLE 5. * What is $m\angle 1 + m\angle 2 + m\angle 3 + m\angle 4 + m\angle 5$?

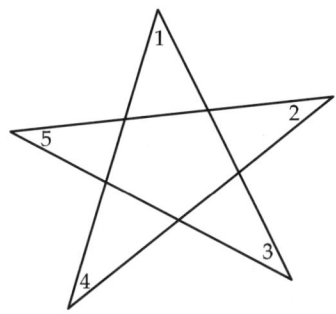

EXAMPLE 6. * What is $m\angle 1 + m\angle 2 + m\angle 3 + m\angle 4 + m\angle 5 + m\angle 6$?

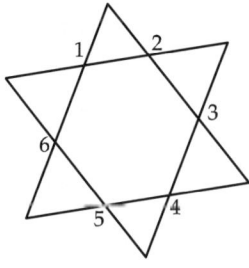

Mia's Geometry
6.2 Parallelograms

1. Parallelograms

※ Definition of Parallelogram

Definition of Parallelogram
ABCD is a parallelogram if and only if both pairs of opposite sides are parallel. 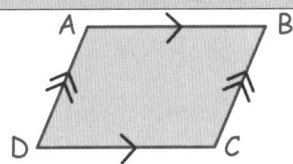

※ Theorems about Parallelogram

	Theorem	
If $ABCD$ is a parallelogram,	then the opposite ①_____ are congruent. ($\square$ → opp. sides ≅.)	$\overline{AB} \cong \overline{DC}$ and $\overline{AD} \cong \overline{BC}$
	then the opposite ②_____ are congruent. ($\square$ → opp. ∠s ≅.)	$\angle A \cong \angle C$ and $\angle B \cong \angle D$
	then the diagonals ③_____ each other. ($\square$ → diag. bisct.)	$AP = PC$ and $BP = PD$

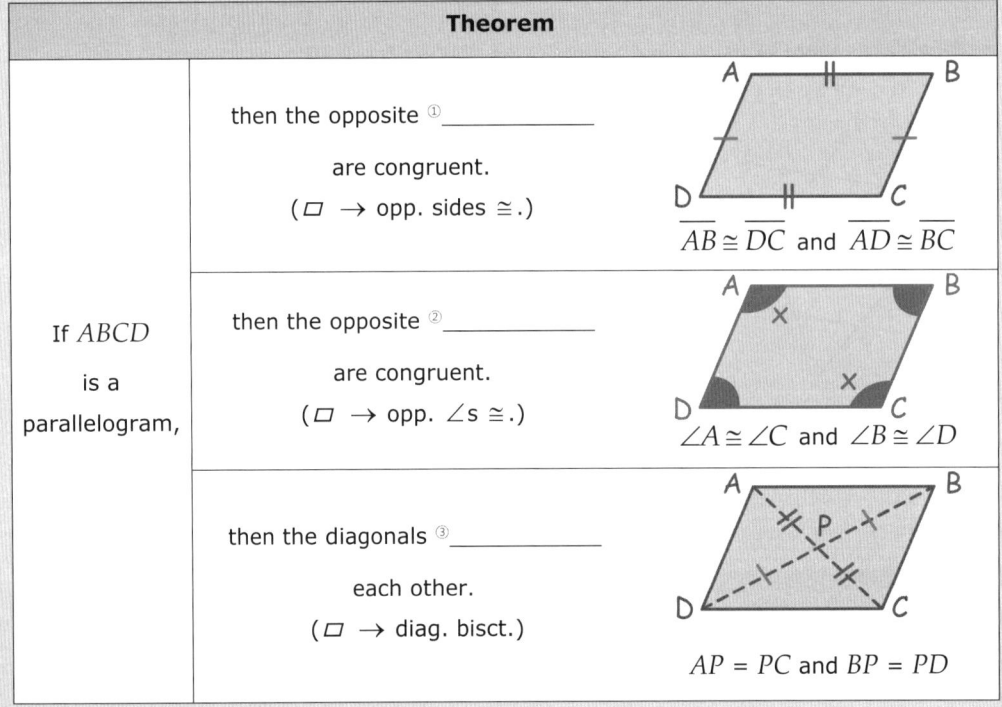

($\square$ means parallelogram in this book)

Blank : ① sides ② angles ③ bisect

☺ Memorizing Tip

Definition :

Theorem :

☺ Proof : ▱ → diag. bist.

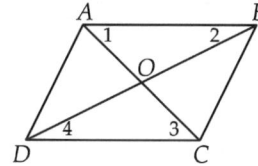

Given: ▱ $ABCD$

Prove: $AO = CO, DO = BO$

Statements	Reasons
1. ▱ $ABCD$	1. Given
2. $\overline{AB} \parallel \overline{CD}$	2. ① _____
3. $\angle 1 \cong \angle 3$, $\angle 2 \cong \angle 4$	3. ② _____
4. $\overline{AB} \cong \overline{CD}$	4. ③ _____
5. $\triangle ABO \cong \triangle CDO$	5. ④ _____
6. $AO = CO, DO = BO$	6. CPCTC

Blank : ① Def. of ▱   ② ∥→Alternate int. ∠s are ≅   ③ ▱ → opp. sides are ≅   ④ ASA post.

EXAMPLE 1. For ▱ABCD and ▱MNOP, name the definition, theorem, or postulate that justifies the given statements.

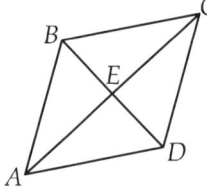
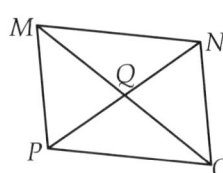

① $BE = ED$

② $MQ = \frac{1}{2}MO$

③ $\overline{AB} \parallel \overline{CD}$

④ $\overline{MN} \parallel \overline{PO}$

⑤ $\overline{AB} \cong \overline{DC}$

⑥ $\angle NMP \cong \angle PON$

⑦ $m\angle BAD = m\angle DCB$

⑧ $\angle MNO, \angle PON$ are supplementary

⑨ $\angle BAC \cong \angle DCA$

⑩ $MP = NO$

EXAMPLE 2. For the given parallelogram, find the value of the variable(s) in each figure.

①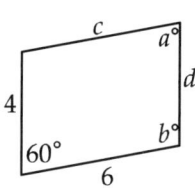

②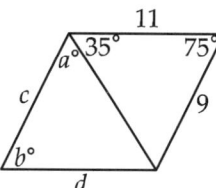

③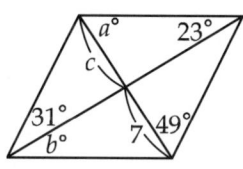

④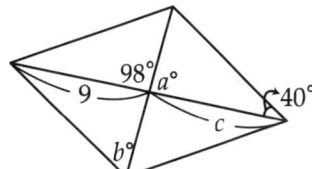

⑤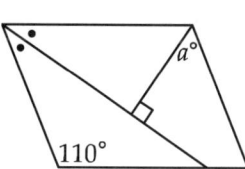

⑥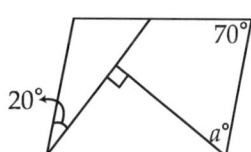

⑦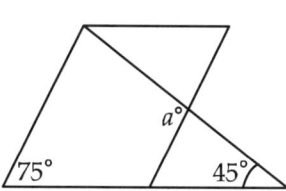

⑧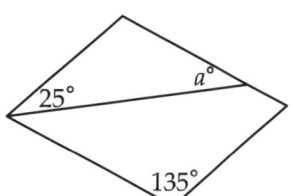

EXAMPLE 3. Write a two column proof.

① Given: ▱ABCD, ▱DEFG

Prove: ∠B ≅ ∠F

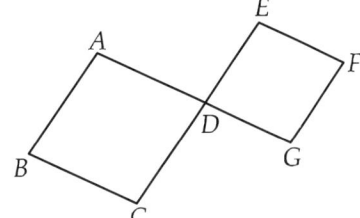

② Given: ▱ABCD, ▱CDEF

Prove: $\overline{AB} \cong \overline{EF}$

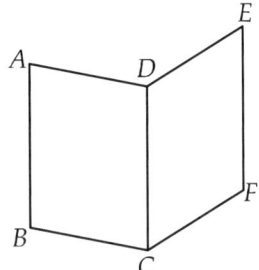

Statements	Reasons

Statements	Reasons

③ Given: ▱ABCD, $\overline{BE}$ bisects ∠ABC

Prove: $\overline{FD} \cong \overline{ED}$

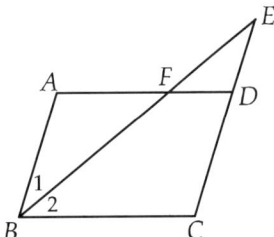

④ Given: ▱ABCD, $\overline{AD} \cong \overline{DE}$

Prove: ∠B ≅ ∠E

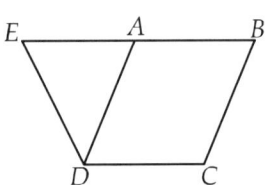

Statements	Reasons

Statements	Reasons

⑤ Given: ▱ABCD, $\overleftrightarrow{MN}$ passes point O
Prove: $\overline{MO} \cong \overline{NO}$

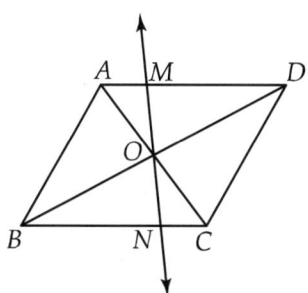

Statements	Reasons

⑥ Given: ▱ABCD
Prove: $\overline{MO} \cong \overline{NO}$

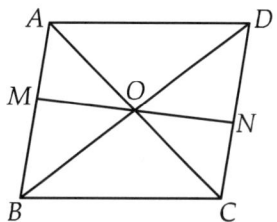

Statements	Reasons

⑦ *Given: ▱ ABCD

$\overline{EB} \perp \overline{ED}$, $\overline{FD} \perp \overline{FB}$

Prove: ∠EDA ≅ ∠FBC

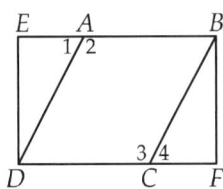

Statements	Reasons

⑧ *Given: ▱ ABCD

A, B, D are midpoints of

$\overline{EF}, \overline{FC}, \overline{EC}$ respectively

Prove: △FAB ≅ △AED

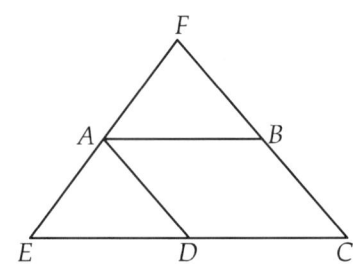

Statements	Reasons

216 Mia's Geometry

⑨ *Given: ▱ABCD

M is midpoint of $\overline{AD}$

Prove: $\overline{MO} \parallel \overline{DC}$

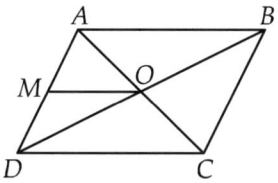

Statements	Reasons

Part 6_Quadrilaterals

Mia's Geometry

6.3 Tests for Parallelograms

1. Conditions for a Parallelogram

When we have a quadrilateral, let's try to prove it whether it is a parallelogram or not!

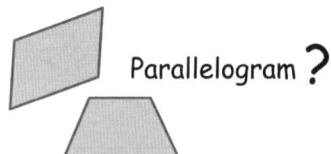 Parallelogram?

※ Definition of Parallelogram

Definition of Parallelogram	
$ABCD$ is a parallelogram if and only if both pairs of opposite sides are parallel.	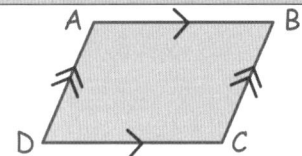

※ Theorems about Parallelogram

Theorem		
If both pairs of opposite ①_____ are congruent, (Opp. sides ≅ → ▱)		then $ABCD$ is a **parallelogram**.
If both pairs of opposite ②_____ are congruent, (Opp. ∠s ≅ → ▱)		
If the diagonals ③_____ each other, (Diag. bisct. → ▱)		
If one pair of opposite sides is both congruent and ④_____, (One pair sides ≅ and ∥ → ▱)	$\overline{AB} \cong \overline{DC}$ and $\overline{AB} \parallel \overline{DC}$	

☺ Memorizing Tip:

Definition :

Theorem :

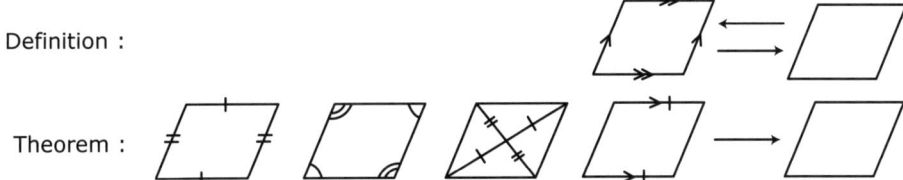

EXAMPLE 1. Determine whether the quadrilateral must be a parallelogram. If the answer is yes, state the definition or theorem that applies.

①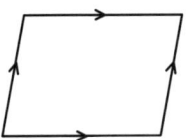

②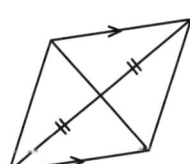

③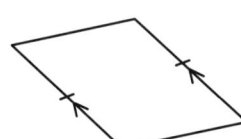

④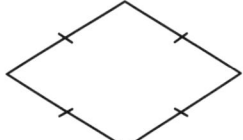

Blank : ① sides   ② angles   ③ bisect   ④ parallel

⑤ 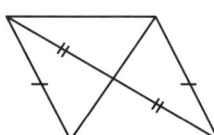   ⑥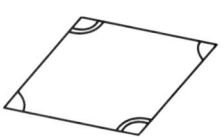

⑦ 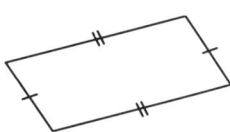   ⑧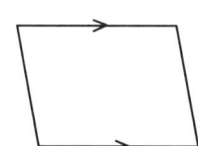

⑨ 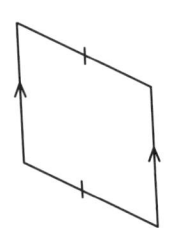   ⑩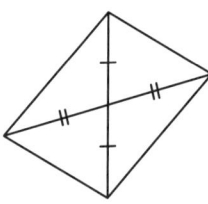

⑪ 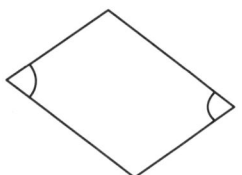   ⑫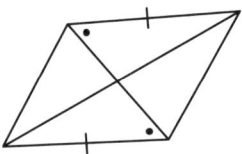

EXAMPLE 2. Write a two column proof.

① Given: ▱ ABCD

∠FDB ≅ ∠EBD

Prove: FBED is ▱

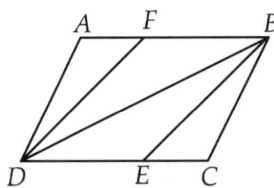

Statements	Reasons

② Given: ▱ ABCD

▱ BEFC

Prove: AEFD is ▱

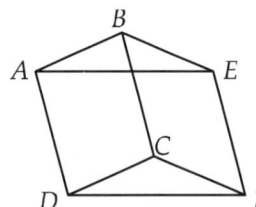

Statements	Reasons

③ Given: ▱ ABCD

$\overline{AF} \cong \overline{CE}$

Prove: FBED is ▱

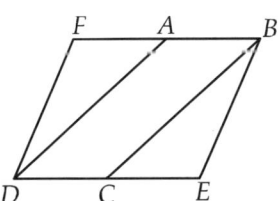

Statements	Reasons

④ Given: ▱ ABCD

$\overline{AE} \cong \overline{FC}$

Prove: AECF is ▱

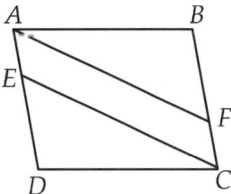

Statements	Reasons

Part 6_Quadrilaterals

⑤ Given: ▱ABCD, $\overline{AE}$ bisects $\overline{BC}$

F is midpoint of $\overline{AE}$

Prove: ACEB is ▱

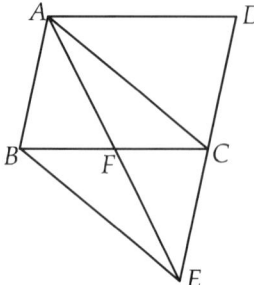

⑥ Given: ▱ABCD

Points E, F, G, H is midpoint of

$\overline{AO}, \overline{BO}, \overline{CO}, \overline{DO}$ respectively

Prove: EFGH is ▱

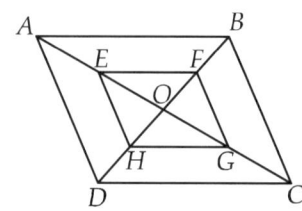

Statements	Reasons

Statements	Reasons

⑦ Given: ▱ABCD, $\overline{AM} \parallel \overline{CN}$

Prove: AMCN is ▱

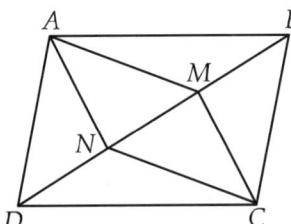

⑧ *Given: ▱ABCD, $\overline{AC} \perp \overline{DE}, \overline{AC} \perp \overline{BF}$

Prove: BEDF is ▱

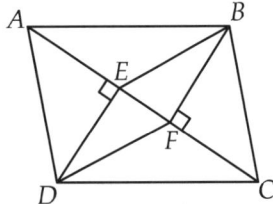

Statements	Reasons

Statements	Reasons

⑨ Given: ▱ ABCD

$\overline{AE} \cong \overline{EF} \cong \overline{FC}$

Prove: DEBF is ▱

(Draw auxiliary line $\overline{BD}$ with intersection point O with $\overline{AC}$)

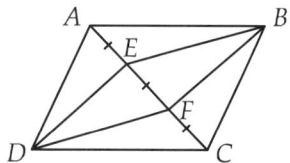

Statements	Reasons

Mia's Geometry
6.4 Rectangles, Rhombi and Squares

1. Special Parallelograms

In this section you will study the properties of special parallelograms:

Rectangle, rhombus, and square.

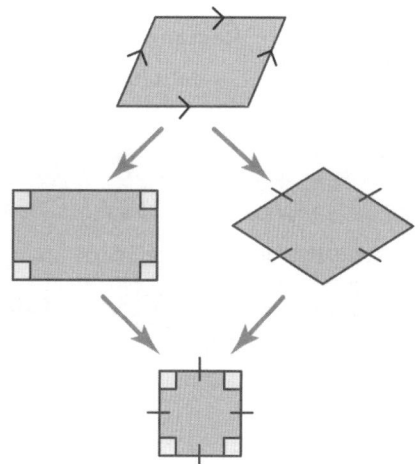

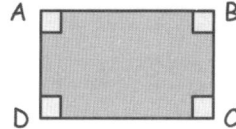

Rectangle is a parallelogram with four ①_____ _____.

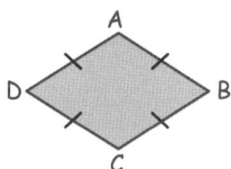

Rhombus is a parallelogram with four ②_____ _____.

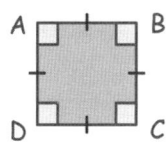

Square is a parallelogram with four ③_____ _____ and four ④_____ _____.

Blank : ① right angles   ② congruent sides   ③ right angles   ④ congruent sides

Part 6_Quadrilaterals   225

2. Properties of Rectangles

※ Definition of Rectangle

Definition of Rectangle
Rectangle is a parallelogram with four right angles.

※ Properties of Rectangle

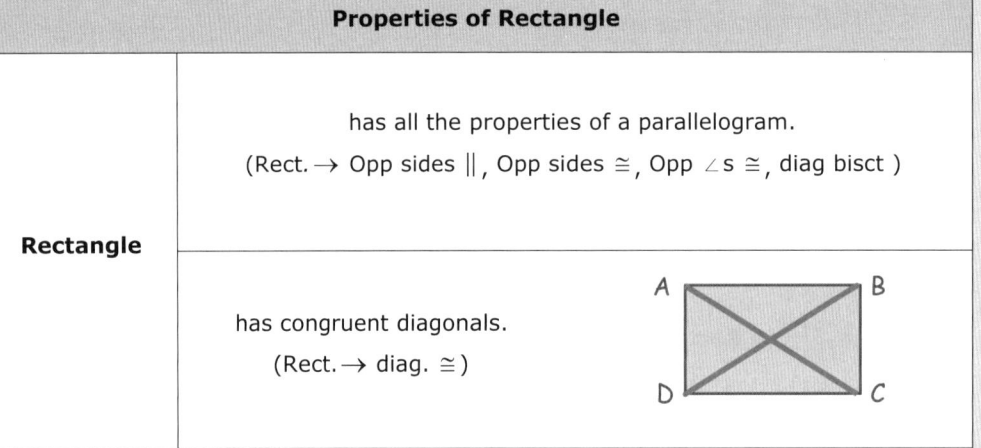

Properties of Rectangle	
Rectangle	has all the properties of a parallelogram. (Rect. → Opp sides ∥, Opp sides ≅, Opp ∠s ≅, diag bisct)
	has congruent diagonals. (Rect. → diag. ≅)

- Every rectangle is a parallelogram.

EXAMPLE 1. $ABCD$ and $FGHI$ are rectangles. Can we conclude the following statement? If yes, state the definition or theorem that applies.

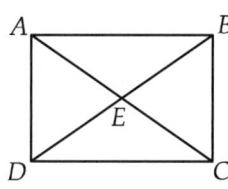
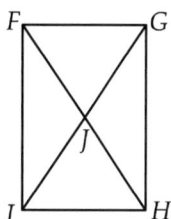

① $\overline{AB} \parallel \overline{CD}$

② $\overline{FJ} \cong \overline{HJ}$

③ $\overline{AE} \cong \overline{CE}$

④ $\overline{FG} \cong \overline{GH}$

⑤ $m\angle A = 90°$

⑥ $m\angle IHG = 90°$

⑦ $\overline{BD} \cong \overline{AC}$

⑧ $\overline{FH} \cong \overline{IG}$

⑨ $\overline{AC} \perp \overline{DB}$

⑩ $m\angle GFH \cong m\angle IFH$

EXAMPLE 2. For the given rectangles, find the value of the variable(s) in each figure.

①
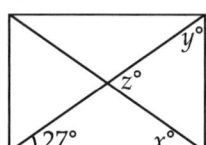

②
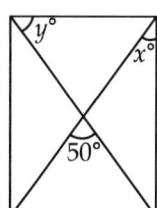

③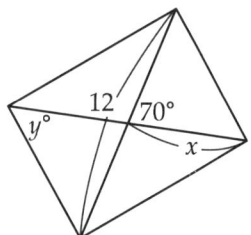

④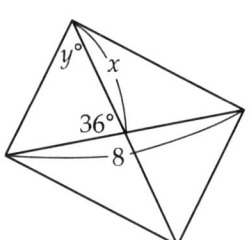

EXAMPLE 3. Write a two column proof.

① Given: $ABCD$ is a rectangle

  Prove: $\angle 1 \cong \angle 2$

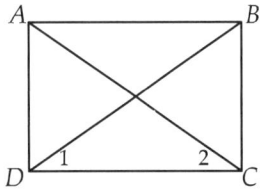

Statements	Reasons

② Given: $ABCD$ is a rectangle

  E is midpoint of $\overline{DC}$

  Prove: $\overline{AE} \cong \overline{BE}$

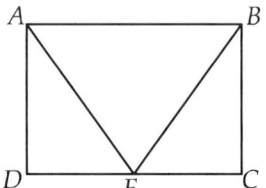

Statements	Reasons

228 Mia's Geometry

③ Given: *ABCD* is a rectangle

   BCED is a parallelogram

   Prove: ∠*CAD* ≅ ∠*CED*

④ Given: *ABCD* is a rectangle

   AE = *BF*

   Prove: $\overline{EG} \cong \overline{FG}$

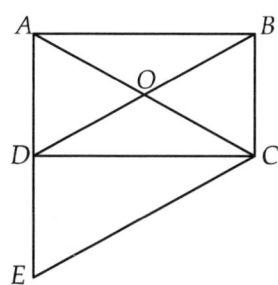
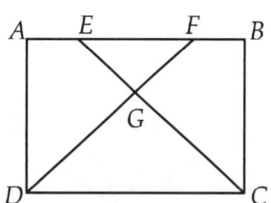

Statements	Reasons

Statements	Reasons

⑤ Given: $ABCD$ is a rectangle
$\overline{DG} \cong \overline{CG}$
Prove: $\overline{AG} \cong \overline{BG}$

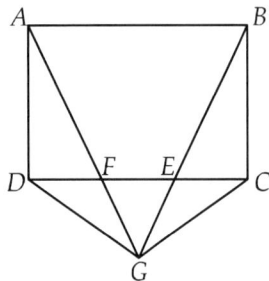

Statements	Reasons

3. Properties of Rhombi

※ Definition of Rhombus

Definition of Rhombus
Rhombus is a parallelogram with four congruent sides. 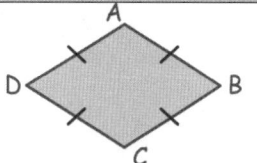

※ Properties of Rhombus

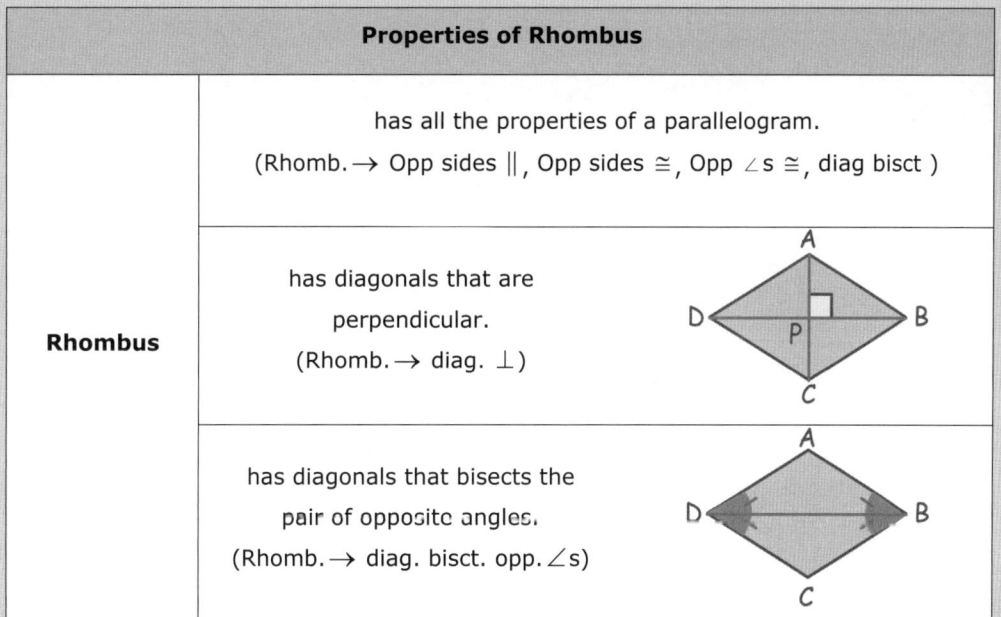

	Properties of Rhombus
Rhombus	has all the properties of a parallelogram. (Rhomb. → Opp sides ∥, Opp sides ≅, Opp ∠s ≅, diag bisct)
	has diagonals that are perpendicular. (Rhomb. → diag. ⊥)
	has diagonals that bisects the pair of opposite angles. (Rhomb. → diag. bisct. opp. ∠s)

- Every rhombus is a parallelogram.
- Plural of rhombus is rhombi.

☺ Tip: Rectangle VS Rhombus

Rectangle : diagonals are ① _____

Rhombus : diagonals are ② _____ and ③ _____

Blank : ① congruent (≅)　② perpendicular (⊥)　③ bisect opposite angles

EXAMPLE 4. *ABCD* and *FGHI* are rhombi. Can we conclude the following statement? If yes, state the definition or theorem that applies.

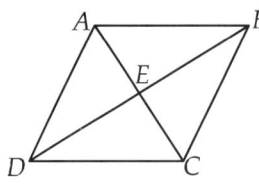
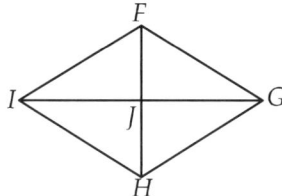

① $\overline{AC} \perp \overline{BE}$

② $\overline{FJ} \cong \overline{HJ}$

③ $\overline{AB} \cong \overline{BC}$

④ $\overline{IG} \cong \overline{FH}$

⑤ $\angle ADE \cong \angle CDE$

⑥ $m\angle IHJ = m\angle GHJ$

⑦ $\angle EDC \cong \angle ECD$

⑧ $\overline{FJ} \perp \overline{JG}$

⑨ $\overline{AC} \cong \overline{DB}$

⑩ $\overline{IF} \cong \overline{FG}$

EXAMPLE 5. For the given rhombus, find the value of the variable(s) in each figure.

①
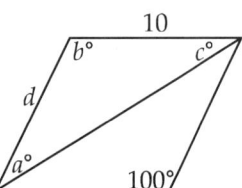

②

232 Mia's Geometry

③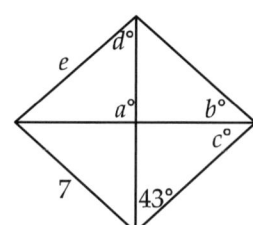

④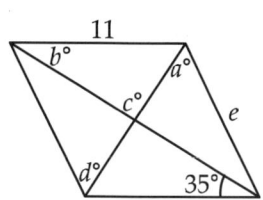

EXAMPLE 6. Write a two column proof.

① Given: $ABCD$ is a rhombus.

Prove: $\triangle BAO \cong \triangle DAO$

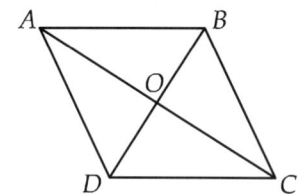

Statements	Reasons

② Given: $ABCD$ is a rhombus.

Prove: $\angle 1$ and $\angle 2$ are complementary.

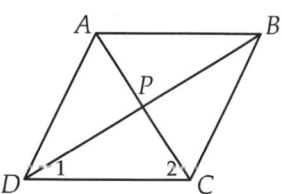

Statements	Reasons

③ Given: *ABCD* is a rhombus.
  ∠ADP ≅ ∠ABQ
Prove: $\overline{CP} \cong \overline{CQ}$

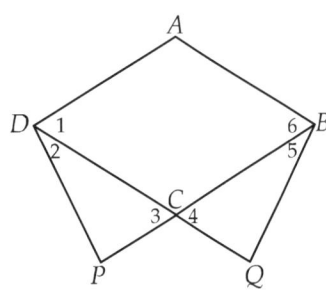

Statements	Reasons

④ Given: *ABCD* is a rhombus.
  $\overline{DP} \cong \overline{BP}$
Prove: ∠DCP ≅ ∠BCP

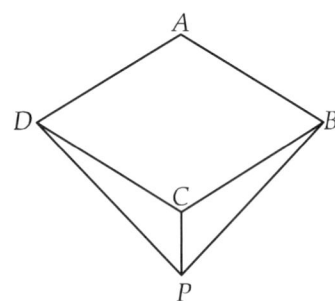

Statements	Reasons

⑤ Given: *ABCD* is a rhombus.
F is the midpoint of $\overline{AE}$
Prove: $\overline{AD} \cong \overline{CE}$

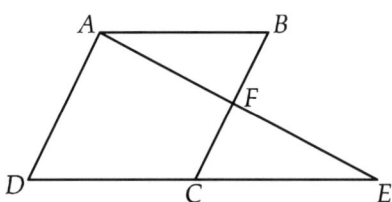

⑥ Given: *ABCD* is a rhombus.
Prove: △ *APC* is isosceles.

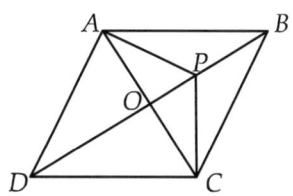

Statements	Reasons

Statements	Reasons

4. Properties of Squares

※ Definition of Square

Definition of Square
Square is a parallelogram with four right angles and four congruent sides. 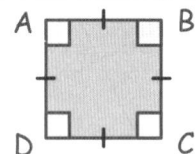

※ Properties of Square

Properties of Square		
Square	has all the properties of a parallelogram. (Square → Opp sides ∥, Opp sides ≅, Opp ∠s ≅, diag bisct)	
	has diagonals that are both congruent and perpendicular. (Square → diag. ≅ and ⊥)	
	has diagonals that bisects the pair of opposite angles. (Square → diag. bist. opp. ∠s)	

- Every square is a ① _____ , _____ , _____ .

Blank : ① rectangle, rhombus, square

EXAMPLE 7. Check marks in the appropriate spaces.

	parallelogram	rectangle	rhombus	square
Two pairs of opposite sides are parallel.				
Opposite sides are congruent.				
Opposite angles are congruent.				
The quadrilateral is equilateral				
The quadrilateral is equiangular (right $\angle$).				
The diagonals bisect each other.				
The diagonals are congruent.				
The diagonals are perpendicular				
The diagonal bisects the pair of opposite angles.				

Mia's Geometry

6.5 Trapezoids

1. Trapezoids

Trapezoid is a quadrilateral that one pair of opposite sides is ①_____.

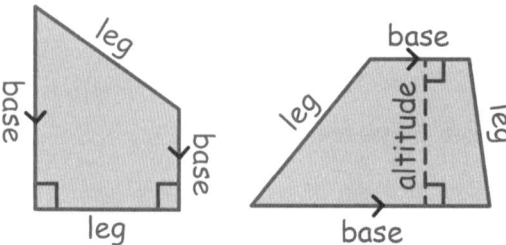

The parallel sides are the "②_____"

The other two sides are the "③_____"

The distance (at right angles) from one base to the other is called the "④_____"

2. Isosceles Trapezoid

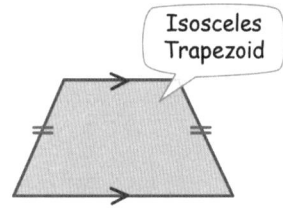

Isosceles trapezoid is a quadrilateral that the one pair of sides is ⑤_____ and sides that aren't parallel are ⑥_____.

※ Definition of Isosceles Trapezoids

Definition of Isosceles Trapezoid
Isosceles Trapezoid is a quadrilateral with one pair of parallel sides and congruent non-parallel sides. 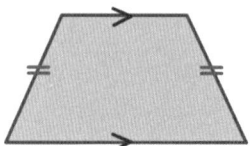

Blank : ① parallel ② bases ③ legs ④ altitude ⑤ parallel ⑥ congruent

※ Properties of Isosceles Trapezoid

Properties of Isosceles Trapezoid		
Isosceles trapezoid	has ① _____ base angles. (Isos. Trap. → base ∠s ≅)	base angles $\angle A \cong \angle B$ and $\angle D \cong \angle C$
	has ② _____ diagonals. (Isos. Trap. → diag. ≅)	$\overline{AC} \cong \overline{DB}$

EXAMPLE 1. ABCD and EFGH are isosceles trapezoids. Can we conclude the following statement? If yes, state the definition or theorem that applies.

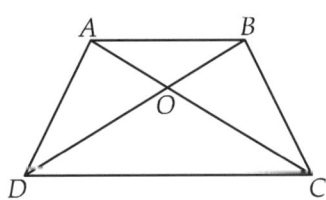
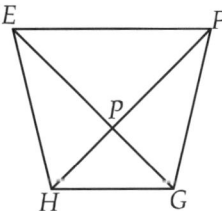

① $\overline{AD} \cong \overline{BC}$

② $\overline{EF} \cong \overline{HG}$

③ $\overline{AC} \cong \overline{BD}$

④ $\overline{EH} \cong \overline{FG}$

⑤ $\angle BAD \cong \angle ABC$

⑥ $\overline{EG} \perp \overline{FH}$

Blank : ① congruent   ② congruent

⑦ ∠ADC ≅ ∠CBA

⑧ $\overline{EG} \cong \overline{FH}$

⑨ $\overline{AB} \parallel \overline{DC}$

⑩ m∠EHG = m∠FGH

EXAMPLE 2. Write a two column proof.

① Given: Isosceles trap. ABCD

Prove: ∠B and ∠D are supplementary.

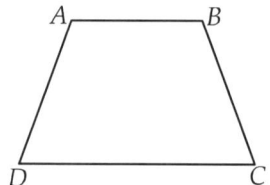

Statements	Reasons

② Given: Isosceles trap. ABCD

$\overline{DC} \cong \overline{DE}$

Prove: ABED is parallelogram.

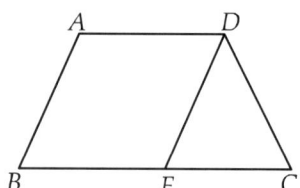

Statements	Reasons

③ Given: Isosceles trap. *ABCD*

Prove: ∠*DAC* ≅ ∠*CBD*

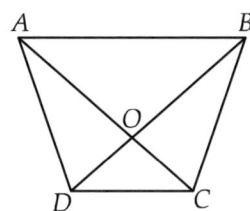

Statements	Reasons

④ Given: Isosceles trap. *ABCD*

Prove: △ *ABO* is isosceles.

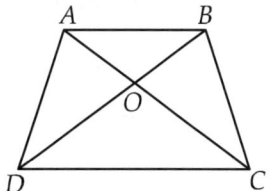

Statements	Reasons

⑤ Given: Isosceles trap. $ABCD$
$\angle ADP \cong \angle BCP$

Prove: $\triangle DPC$ is isosceles.

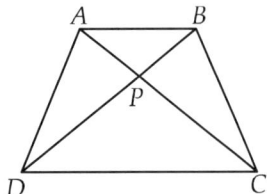

Statements	Reasons

3. Midsegment of Trapezoid

☺ Remind:

Triangle Midsegment Theorem:

A midsegment of a triangle is ①_____ to a side of the triangle, and its length is ②_____ the length of that side.

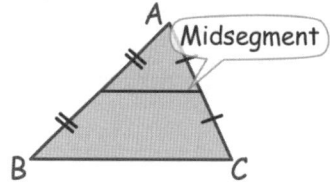

Midsegment of a trapezoid is the segment that joins the midpoints of the legs.

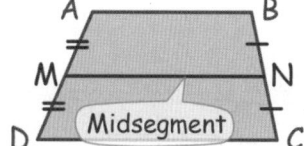

※ Trapezoid Midsegment Theorem

Trapezoid Midsegment Theorem
Trapezoid Midsegment is ③_____ to each base, and its length is ④_____ the sum of the lengths of the bases.   ex) $\overline{MN} \parallel \overline{AB}, \overline{MN} \parallel \overline{DC}$ and $MN = \frac{1}{2}(AB+DC)$ 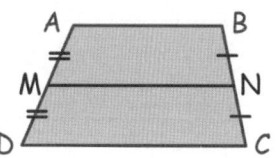

EXAMPLE 3. Each diagram shows a trapezoid and its midsegment. Find the value of the variable(s) in each figure.

①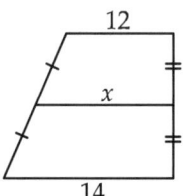

②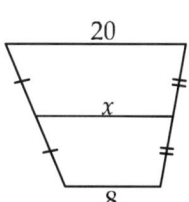

Blank : ① parallel ② half ③ parallel ④ half

③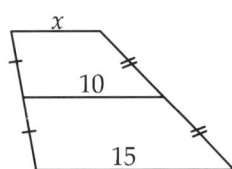

④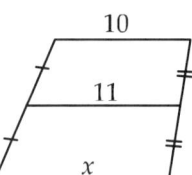

⑤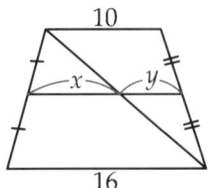

⑥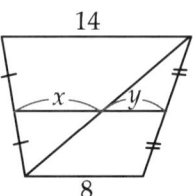

⑦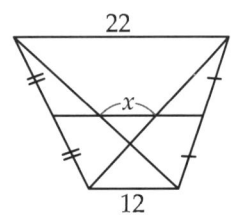

⑧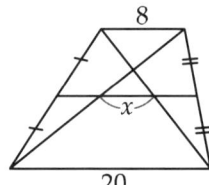

4. Quadrilateral Family Tree

Quadrilateral definitions are **inclusive**.

Some types are also included in the definition of other types!

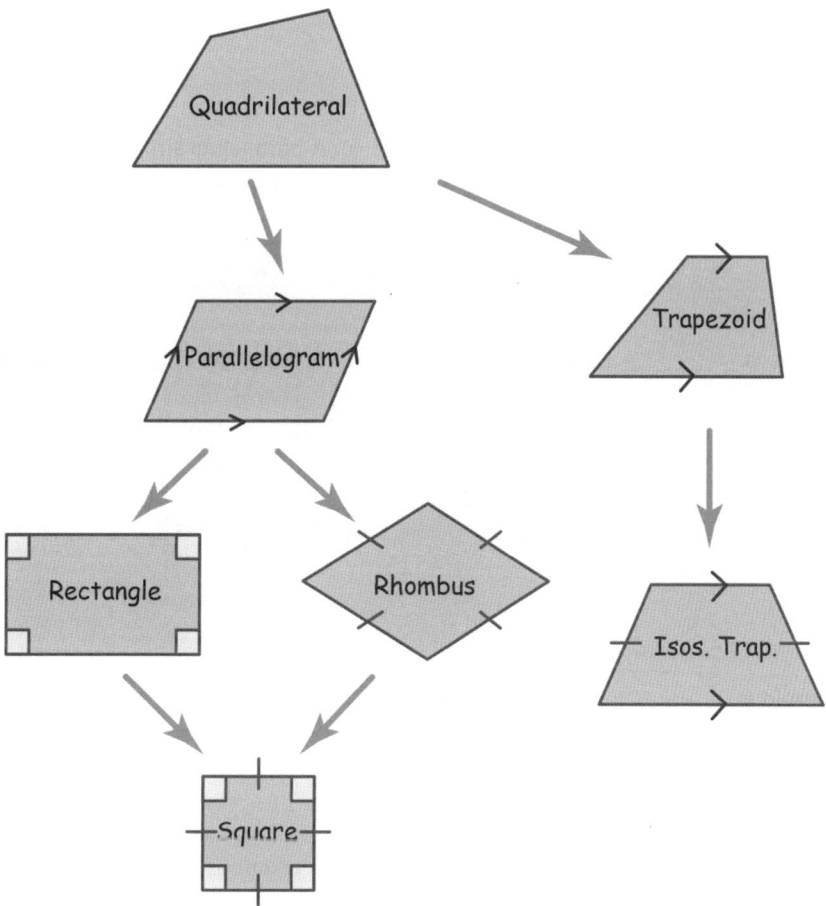

EXAMPLE 4. Let's make a Venn Diagram of it. Add the appropriate labels for *A, B, C,* and *D*.

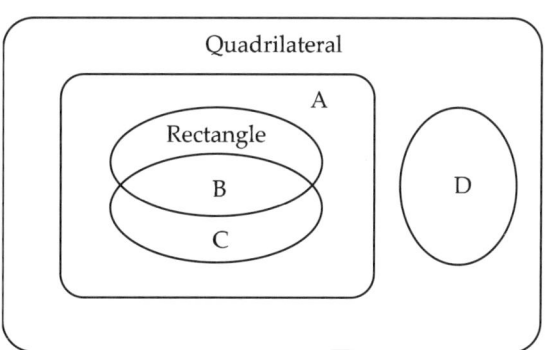

EXAMPLE 5. Fill in the blanks with *always, sometimes*, or *never* to make each statement true.

① A rhombus is _____ a parallelogram.

② A rectangle is _____ a trapezoid.

③ A square is _____ a quadrilateral.

④ A parallelogram is _____ a quadrilateral.

⑤ A rhombus is _____ a square.

⑥ A rectangle is _____ a square.

⑦ A trapezoid is _____ isosceles.

⑧ A rectangle is _____ a rhombus.

⑨ A trapezoid is _____ a parallelogram.

⑩ A square is _____ a rectangle.

⑪ A rectangle _____ has four right angles.

⑫ A rhombus _____ has four right angles.

⑬ A parallelogram is _____ equilateral.

⑭ A trapezoid is _____ equilateral.

Mia's Geometry
Postulates, Theorems from CH6

*All in One (sorted by Miamath)

About perpendicular bisector and angle bisector..
Interior Angle Sum Theorem If a convex polygon has n sides, then the sum of the measures of its interior angles is (n-2)180°.
Exterior Angle Sum Theorem If a polygon is convex, then the sum of the measures of the exterior angles is 360°.

If a parallelogram is given..	
Definition of Parallelogram $ABCD$ is a parallelogram if and only if both pairs of opposite sides are parallel.	
Theorems about Parallelogram If $ABCD$ is a parallelogram, ① then the opposite sides are congruent. ($\square$ → opp. sides $\cong$.) ② then the opposite angles are congruent. ($\square$ → opp. ∠s $\cong$.) ③ then the diagonals bisect each other. ($\square$ → diag. bist.)	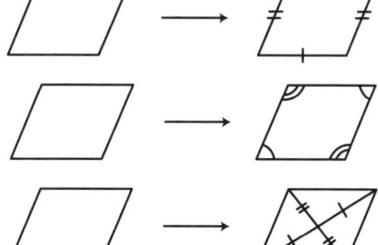

To prove that it is a parallelogram..	
Definition of Parallelogram $ABCD$ is a parallelogram if and only if both pairs of opposite sides are parallel.	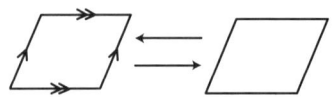
Theorems about Parallelogram ① If both pairs of opposite sides are congruent, (Opp. sides $\cong$ → $\square$) ② If both pairs of opposite angles are congruent, (Opp. ∠s $\cong$ → $\square$) ③ If the diagonals bisect each other, (Diag. bisct. → $\square$) ④ If one pair of opposite sides is both congruent and parallel, (One pair sides $\cong$ and ∥ → $\square$) then $ABCD$ is a parallelogram.	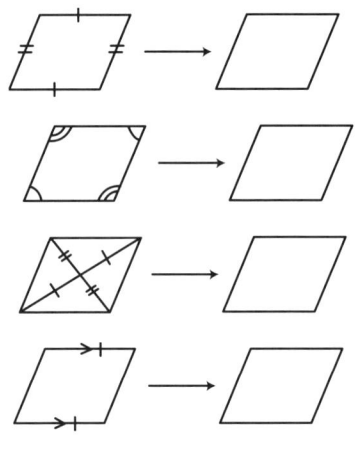

If a rectangle is given..

Definition of Rectangle
Rectangle is a parallelogram with four right angles.

Properties of Rectangle
① Rectangle has all the properties of parallelogram.

(Rect. → Opp sides ∥, Opp sides ≅, Opp ∠s ≅, diag bisct)

② Rectangle has congruent diagonals.

(Rect. → diag. ≅)

If a rhombus is given..

Definition of Rhombus
Rhombus is a parallelogram with four congruent sides.

Properties of Rhombus
① Rhombus has all the properties of parallelogram.

(Rhomb. → Opp sides ∥, Opp sides ≅, Opp ∠s ≅, diag bisct)

② Rhombus has diagonals that are perpendicular.

(Rhomb. → diag. ⊥)

③ Rhombus has diagonals that bisects the pair of opposite angles.

(Rhomb. → diag. bisct. opp. ∠s)

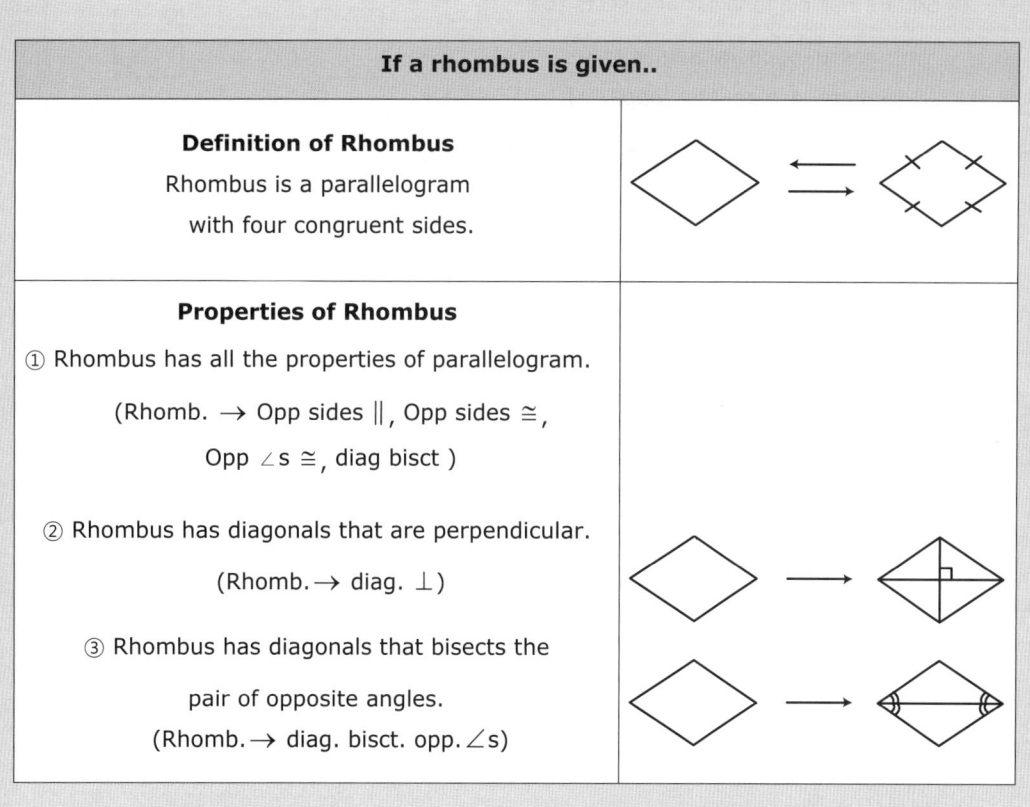

If a square is given..	
Definition of Square Square is a parallelogram with four right angles and four congruent sides.	
Properties of Square ① Square has all the properties of a parallelogram. (Square → Opp sides ∥, Opp sides ≅, Opp ∠s ≅, diag bisct) ② Square has diagonals that are both congruent and perpendicular. (Square → diag. ≅ and ⊥) ③ Square has diagonals that bisects the pair of opposite angles. (Square → diag. bist. opp. ∠s)	

If an isosceles trapezoid is given..	
Definition of Isosceles Trapezoids Isosceles Trapezoid is a quadrilateral with one pair of parallel side and congruent nonparallel side.	
Properties of Isosceles Trapezoids ① Isosceles trapezoid has congruent base angles. (Isos. Trap. → base ∠s ≅) ② Isosceles trapezoid has congruent diagonals. (Isos. Trap. → diag. ≅)	

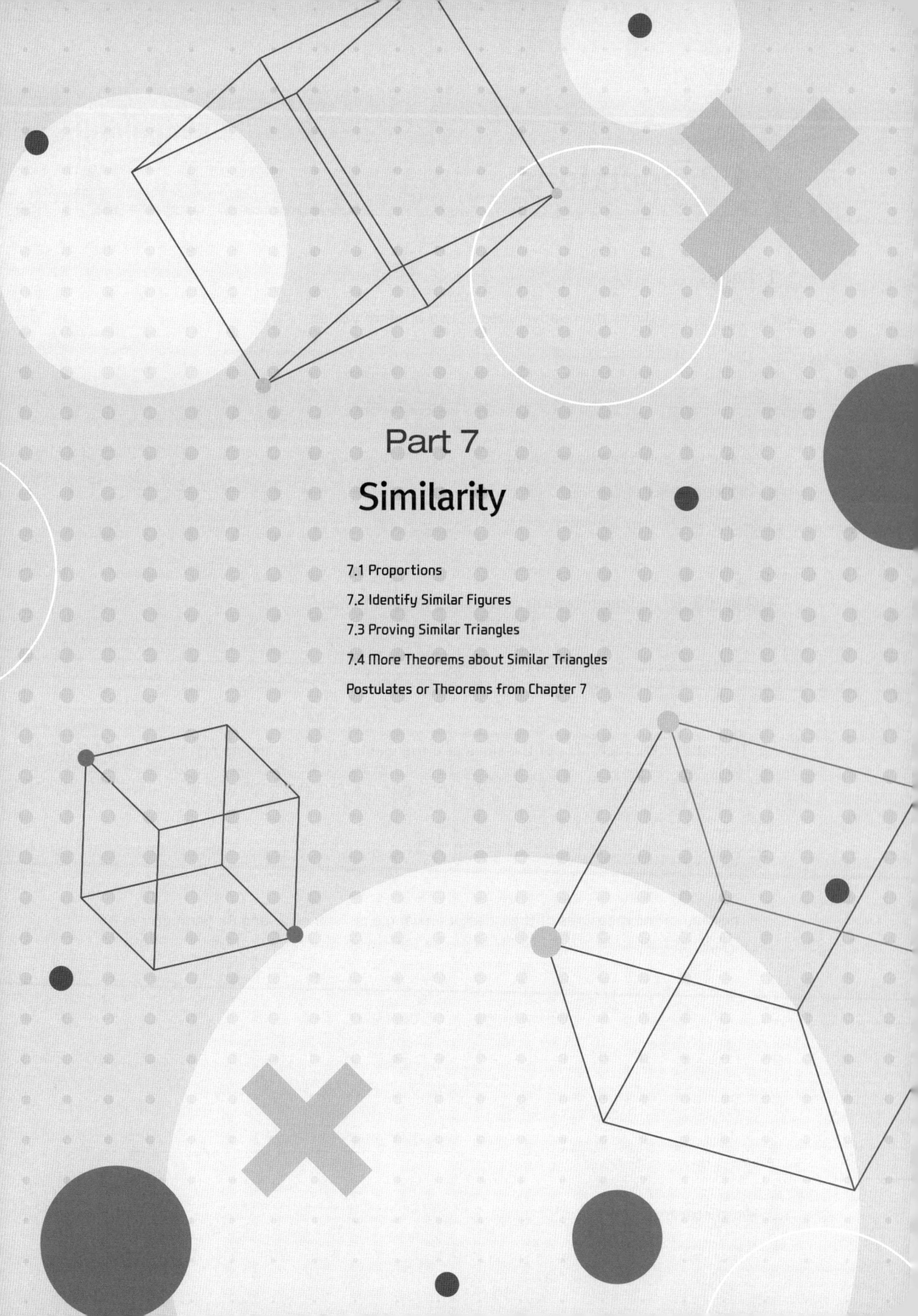

Part 7
Similarity

7.1 Proportions
7.2 Identify Similar Figures
7.3 Proving Similar Triangles
7.4 More Theorems about Similar Triangles
Postulates or Theorems from Chapter 7

Mia's Geometry

7.1 Proportions

1. Ratios

A ①_____ shows the relative sizes of two or more values.

※ **Ratio**

Ratio of a and b can be shown in different ways :

Ratio
$$a:b = \frac{a}{b} = a \text{ to } b$$

EXAMPLE 1. Find the measures of the sides of each triangle.

☺ When two things are in ratio 2 : 3 , let ②_____.

① The ratio of the measures of the sides of a triangle is 3 : 4 : 6, and its perimeter is 104 feet.

② The ratio of the measures of the sides of a triangle is 7 : 9 : 12, and its perimeter is 84 inches.

Blank : ① ratio ② 2x, 3x

EXAMPLE 2. Find the measures of the angles.

① The ratio of the meaxures of two complementary angles is 3 : 2

② The ratio of the meaxures of two supplementary angles is 2 : 7.

③ The measure of the angles of a triangle are in the ratio 4:5:6.

2. Proportions

※ **Proportions**

Proportions say that two ratios are equal. $\dfrac{a}{b} = \dfrac{c}{d}$

We can write a proportion as; $\dfrac{a}{b} = \dfrac{c}{d}$ or $a:b=c:d$.

a and d are called the ①_____ since it is at the *end* or proportion.

b and c are called the ②_____ since it is in the *middle* or proportion.

For $\dfrac{a}{b} = \dfrac{c}{d}$, if we multiply both sides by bd,

$$\dfrac{a}{b} \cdot \boxed{\text{③}} = \dfrac{c}{d} \cdot \boxed{\text{④}} \Rightarrow \boxed{\text{⑤}} = bc$$

We will get the property called the **means-extremes property** (=cross product property).

Blank : ① extremes   ② means   ③ bd   ④ bd   ⑤ ad

※ Means-extremes property

Means-extremes property (=Cross Product Property)

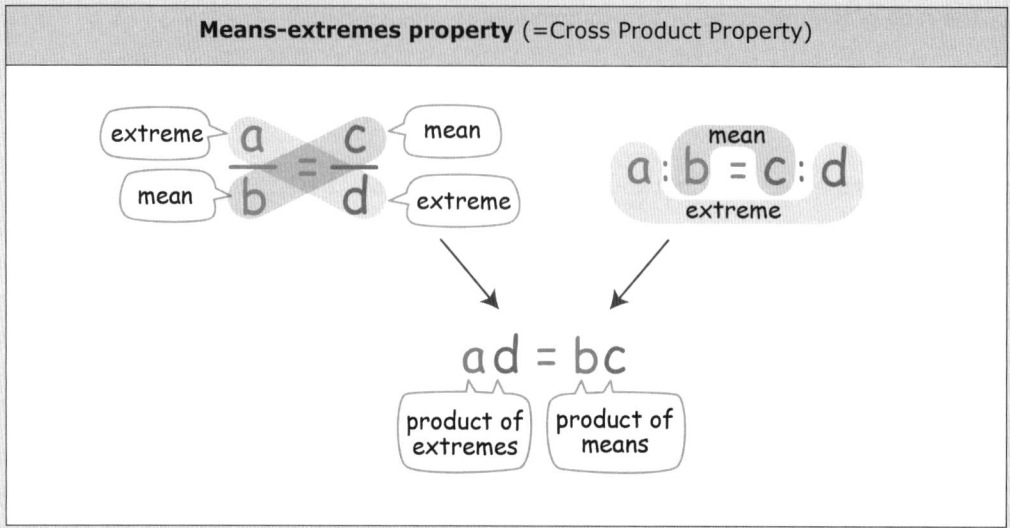

※ Properties of Proportions

Properties of Proportions

If $\dfrac{a}{b} = \dfrac{c}{d}$, then

① You can do cross multiplication ; $ad = bc$

② You can change the means ; $\dfrac{a}{c} = \dfrac{b}{d}$.

③ You can take reciprocals on both sides ; $\dfrac{b}{a} = \dfrac{d}{c}$.

④ You can add 1 to both sides ; $\dfrac{a+b}{b} = \dfrac{c+d}{d}$

EXAMPLE 3. Complete each statement.

① If $\dfrac{x}{5} = \dfrac{y}{2}$, then $\dfrac{x}{y} = \dfrac{\boxed{}}{\boxed{}}$

② If $\dfrac{m}{7} = \dfrac{10}{n}$, then $\dfrac{m}{10} = \dfrac{\boxed{}}{\boxed{}}$

③ If $9m = 4n$, then $\dfrac{m}{n} = \dfrac{\boxed{}}{\boxed{}}$

④ If $x = 2y$, then $\dfrac{x}{y} = \dfrac{\boxed{}}{\boxed{}}$

⑤ If $\dfrac{3}{t} = \dfrac{11}{r}$, then $\dfrac{t}{r} = \dfrac{\boxed{}}{\boxed{}}$

⑥ If $\dfrac{11}{b} = \dfrac{13}{c}$, then $\dfrac{b}{c} = \dfrac{\boxed{}}{\boxed{}}$

⑦ If $\dfrac{a+4}{4} = \dfrac{b+5}{5}$, then $\dfrac{a}{4} = \dfrac{\boxed{}}{\boxed{}}$

⑧ If $\dfrac{t+2}{2} = \dfrac{r+3}{3}$, then $\dfrac{t}{2} = \dfrac{\boxed{}}{\boxed{}}$

EXAMPLE 4. Solve each proportion.

① $\dfrac{3}{x} = \dfrac{6}{10}$

② $\dfrac{4}{x} = \dfrac{2}{5}$

③ $\dfrac{x-1}{x+3} = \dfrac{3}{4}$

④ $\dfrac{4}{5} = \dfrac{x-1}{x+4}$

⑤ $\dfrac{2}{x} = \dfrac{x}{5x-12}$

⑥ $\dfrac{x-3}{x} = \dfrac{8}{x+3}$

⑦ $\dfrac{x-6}{x-7} = \dfrac{x-4}{x-2}$

⑧ $\dfrac{x-6}{x+6} = \dfrac{x-1}{x+7}$

Mia's Geometry

7.2 Identify Similar Figures

1. Similar Polygons

When two polygons have *same shape* and *same size*, we say two polygons are ①_____.

When two polygons have *same shape* but *different size*, we say two polygons are ②_____.

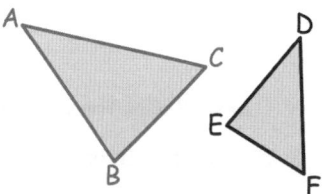

We use the symbol ③_____ which means *same shape*.

※ Similar Polygons

Two Polygons are **similar** if the polygons have the **same shape** but **differenct size**.

When two polygons are similar:

Corresponding angles are ④_____ and

corresponding sides are ⑤_____.

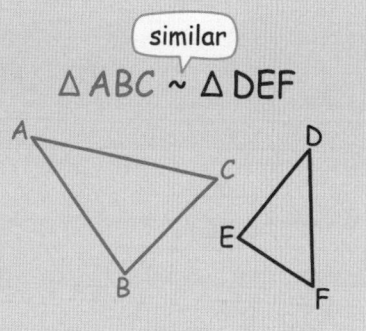

△ABC ~ △DEF

The **similarity ratio** (= scale ratio) is the ratio of the lengths of corresponding sides.

ex) For △ABC and △DEF,

∠A ≅ ⑥____, ∠B ≅ ⑦____, ∠C ≅ ∠F

$\dfrac{9}{6} = \dfrac{⑧}{4} = \dfrac{12}{⑨} \Rightarrow \dfrac{AB}{⑩} = \dfrac{⑪}{EF} = \dfrac{CA}{FD}$.

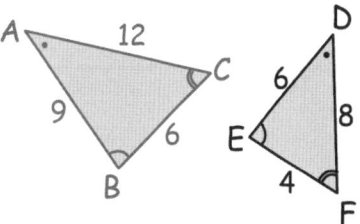

Blank : ① congruent ② similar ③ ~ ④ congruent ⑤ proportional ⑥ D ⑦ E ⑧ 6 ⑨ 8 ⑩ DE ⑪ BC

Since the corresponding angles are ①_____ and corresponding sides are ②_____,

we can write as; ③_____

The similarity ratio (= scale ratio) will be ④_____.

EXAMPLE 1. The given figures are similar. △OPQ, △RST, △UVW, and △XYZ is not shown. Complete each statement.

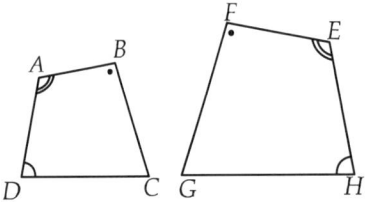

△OPQ ~ △RST   △UVW ~ △XYZ

① ∠C ≅ ☐

② ∠K ≅ ☐

③ $\dfrac{AB}{BC}$ = ☐

④ $\dfrac{JI}{JK}$ = ☐

⑤ ∠P ≅ ☐

⑥ ∠W ≅ ☐

⑦ $\dfrac{PQ}{QO}$ = ☐

⑧ $\dfrac{UV}{UW}$ = ☐

Blank : ① congruent   ② proportional   ③ △ABC ~ △DEF   ④ 3 : 2 or $\dfrac{3}{2}$

EXAMPLE 2. Two similar polygons are shown. Write the similarity statement and find the value of the variable(s) in each figure.

①

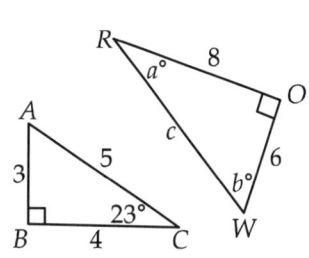

②

③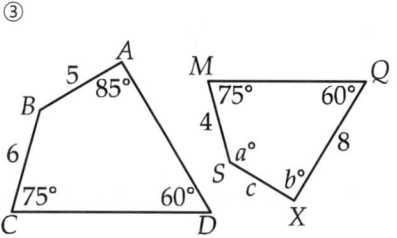

④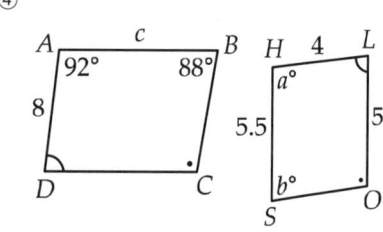

⑤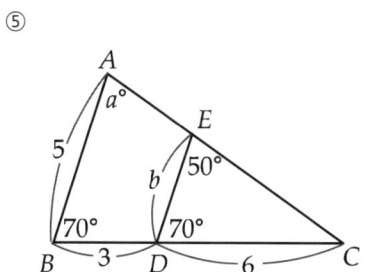

⑥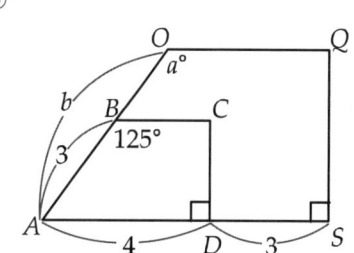

EXAMPLE 3. Fill in the blanks with *always, sometimes,* or *never* to make each statement true.

① Two isosceles triangles are _____ similar.

② Two rectangles are _____ similar.

③ Two equilateral triangles are _____ similar.

④ Two squares are _____ similar.

⑤ Two right triangles are _____ similar.

⑥ Two rhombi are _____ similar.

⑦ Two regular pentagons are _____ similar.

⑧ Two regular polygons are _____ similar.

⑨ An isosceles triangle and a scalene triangle are _____ similar.

⑩ An right triangle and a scalene triangle are _____ similar

⑪ Two similar triangles are _____ congruent.

⑫ Two equilateral triangles are _____ congruent..

⑬ Two isosceles right triangles are _____ similar.

⑭ Two congruent polygons are _____ similar.

⑮ Two isosceles right triangles are _____ congruent.

Mia's Geometry

7.3 Proving Similar Triangles

1. Identify Similar Triangles

To prove that two triangles are similar, we need to show that they satisfy one of these postulates or theorems.

※ Postulates and Theorems for Similar Triangles

AA Similarity Postulate

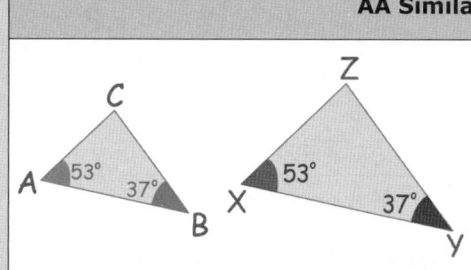

If $\angle A \cong \angle X$ and $\angle B \cong \angle Y$,

then $\triangle ABC \sim \triangle XYZ$.

SSS Similarity Theorem

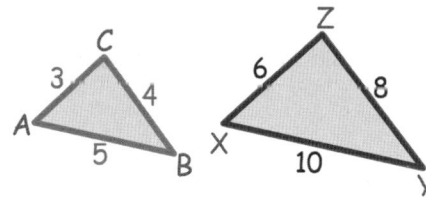

If $\dfrac{AB}{XY} = \dfrac{BC}{YZ} = \dfrac{CA}{ZX}$,

then $\triangle ABC \sim \triangle XYZ$.

SAS Similarity Theorem

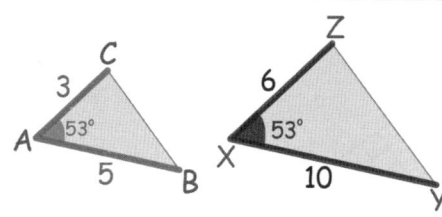

If $\dfrac{AB}{XY} = \dfrac{CA}{ZX}$ and $\angle A \cong \angle X$,

then $\triangle ABC \sim \triangle XYZ$.

Part 7_Similarity 261

☺ Memorizing Tip:

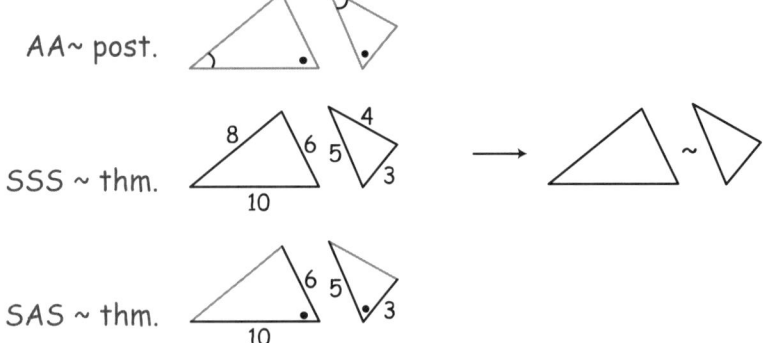

☺ Memorizing Tip: Congruent △ VS Similar △

Congruent △	Similar △
SSS, SAS, ASA postulate	AA ~ postulate
AAS, HL theorem	SSS ~, SAS ~ theorem

EXAMPLE 1. Determine whether each pair of triangles is similar. Name the theorem or postulate that justifies the given statements.

① ②

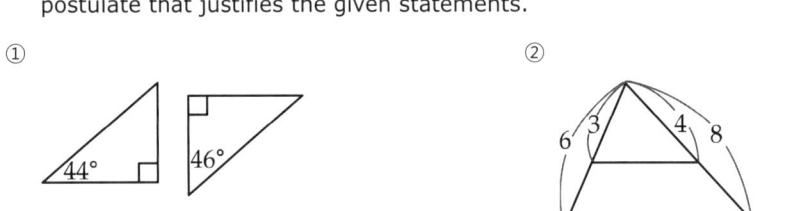

③ ④

⑤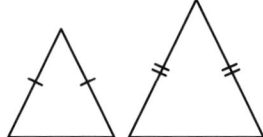

⑥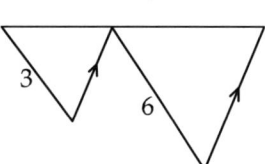

⑦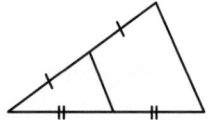

⑧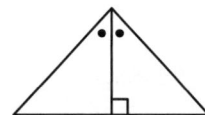

⑨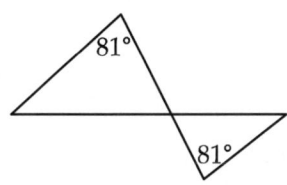

⑩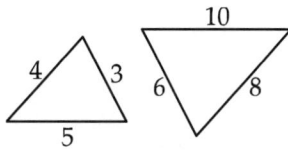

⑪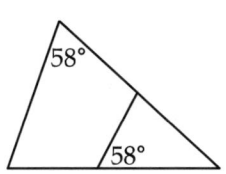

⑫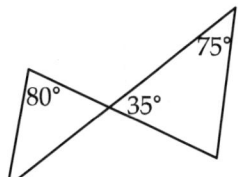

Part 7_Similarity   263

EXAMPLE 2. Write a two column proof.

① Given: ▱ ABCD

Prove: △ABF ~ △ECF

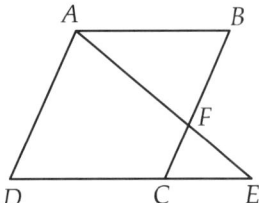

Statements	Reasons

② Given: ∠ADE ≅ ∠ABC

Prove: △ADE ~ △ABC

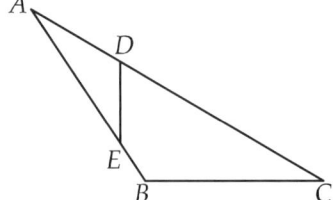

Statements	Reasons

③ Given: $\overline{AB} \perp \overline{BF}, \overline{DF} \perp \overline{BF}$

∠1 ≅ ∠4

Prove: △ABC ~ △DFE

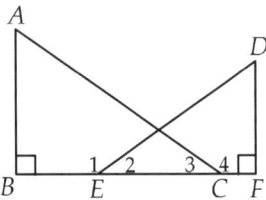

Statements	Reasons

④ Given: ▱ ABCD

, $\overline{AB} \perp \overline{ED}, \overline{FG} \perp \overline{BC}$

Prove: △AED ~ △CGF

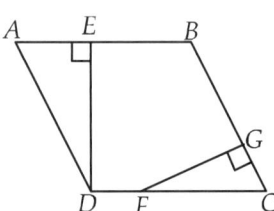

Statements	Reasons

⑤ Given: D is midpoint of $\overline{AB}$
   E is midpoint of $\overline{AC}$

Prove: $\triangle ABC \sim \triangle ADE$

⑥ Given: $\overline{AB} \cong \overline{AC}$
   $\square AEDF$

Prove: $\triangle DEB \sim \triangle DFC$

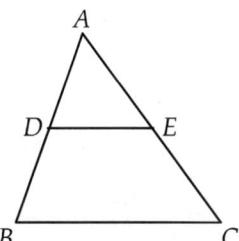
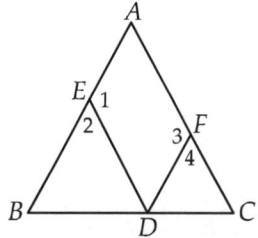

Statements	Reasons

Statements	Reasons

Part 7_Similarity 265

⑦ *Given: $\overline{AB} \cong \overline{AC}$,
   $\overline{DE} \perp \overline{BC}, \overline{DE} \parallel \overline{FG}$
   Prove: △DEB ~ △FGC

⑧ Given: $\overline{BC}$ bisects ∠ACD
   $AC \cdot CE = DC \cdot BC$
   Prove: △ABC ~ △DEC

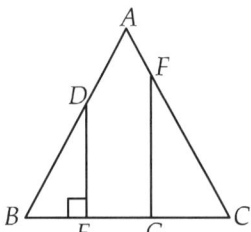
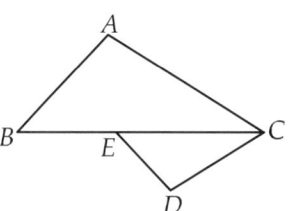

Statements	Reasons

Statements	Reasons

⑨ * Given: E is midpoint of $\overline{AB}$
   D is midpoint of $\overline{AC}$
   F is midpoint of $\overline{BC}$
Prove: $\triangle ABC \sim \triangle EDF$

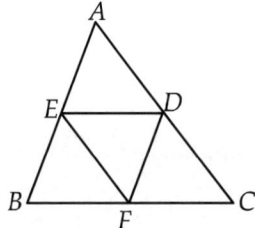

Statements	Reasons

2. CSSTP or CASTC

For congruent triangles, we had CPCTC.
But for similar triangles, we have CSSTP or CASTC.

We use similar triangles and CSSTP or CASTC
to prove that the *angles* are ①_____ or *sides* are ②_____.

※ Way to Prove Sides are Proportional

1. Prove that the triangles are similar.
2. State that the **sides** are **proportional**,
   using the reason ③_____ .
   (Meaning: Corresponding sides of similar triangles are proportional.)

CSSTP
Corresponding sides of similar triangles are proportional.
(or 'Corres. sides are prop. in ~ △')

※ Way to Prove Angles are Congruent

1. Prove that the triangles are similar.
2. State that the **angles** are **congruent**,
   using the reason ④_____ .
   (Meaning: Corresponding angles of similar triangles are congruent.)

CASTC
Corresponding angles of similar triangles are congruent.
(or 'Corres. ∠s are ≅ in ~ △')

Blank : ① congruent   ② proportional   ③ 'CSSTP' or 'Corres. sides are prop. in ~ △'
④ 'CASTC' or 'Corres. ∠s are ≅ in ~ △'

EXAMPLE 3. Write a two column proof.

① Given: $\dfrac{AB}{AD} = \dfrac{AC}{AE}$

Prove: $\overline{DE} \parallel \overline{BC}$

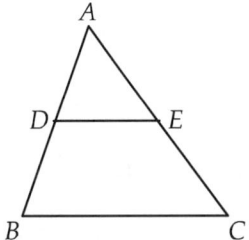

Statements	Reasons

② Given: $\dfrac{AC}{EC} = \dfrac{BC}{DC}$

Prove: $\overline{AB} \parallel \overline{DE}$

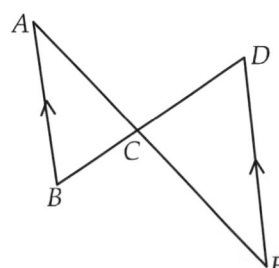

Statements	Reasons

③ Given: $\dfrac{AC}{AB} = \dfrac{AB}{AD} = \dfrac{BC}{DB}$

Prove: $\angle C \cong \angle DBA$

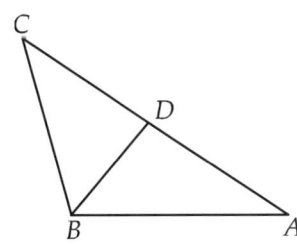

Statements	Reasons

④ Given: $\dfrac{AB}{CD} = \dfrac{BC}{DE} = \dfrac{CA}{EC}$

Prove: $\overline{BC} \parallel \overline{DE}$

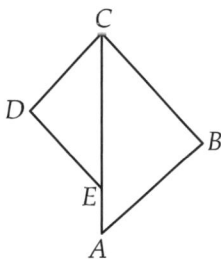

Statements	Reasons

Part 7_Similarity 269

⑤ Given: $\overline{AB} \perp \overline{BC}, \overline{AD} \perp \overline{DB}$

Prove: $AB^2 = AD \cdot AC$

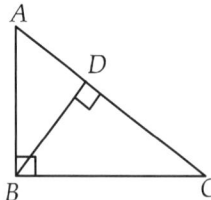

⑥ Given: $\overline{ED} \parallel \overline{BC}$

Prove: $\dfrac{EF}{BG} = \dfrac{FD}{GC}$

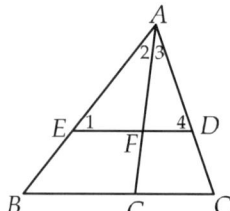

Statements	Reasons

Statements	Reasons

⑦ * Given: $\overline{AB} \perp \overline{BC}, \overline{DC} \perp \overline{BC}$
$\overline{DE} \perp \overline{AC}$

Prove: $\dfrac{AB}{CE} = \dfrac{BC}{ED}$

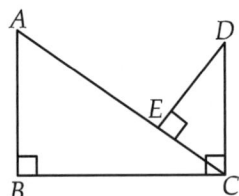

⑧ * Given: $ABCD$ is trapezoid

Prove: $\dfrac{AE}{CE} = \dfrac{BE}{DE}$

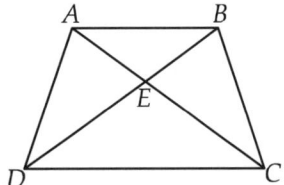

Statements	Reasons

Statements	Reasons

EXAMPLE 4. Two similar triangles are given. Find the value of the variable(s) in each figure. The figures are not drawn to scale.

①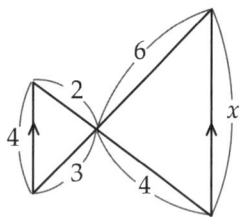

②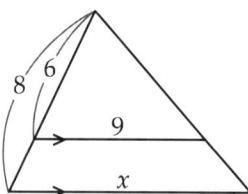

③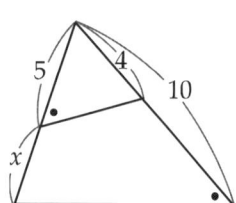

④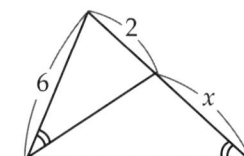

⑤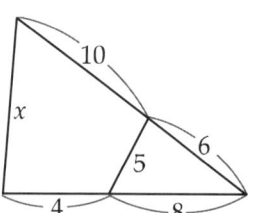

⑥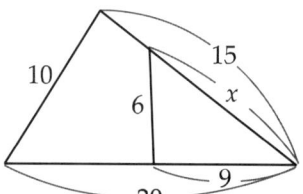

⑦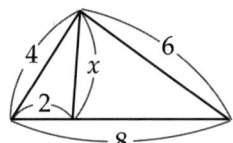

⑧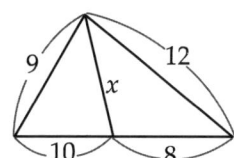

⑨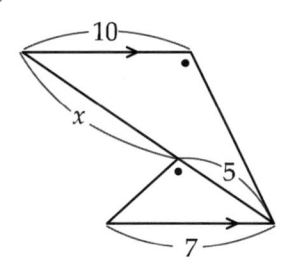

⑩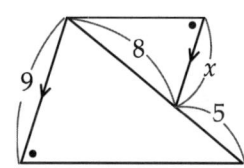

⑪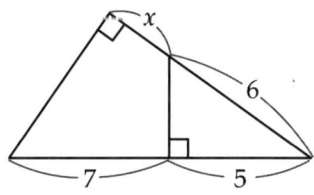

⑫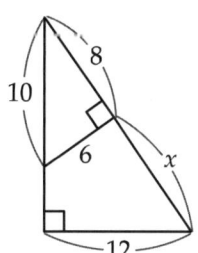

EXAMPLE 5. ABCD is a rhombus, find the value of x.

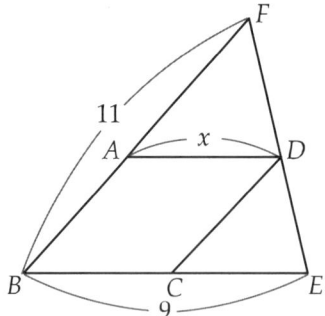

EXAMPLE 6. * Find the value of x and y.

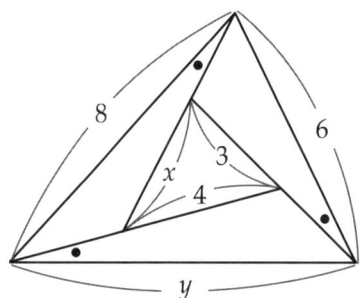

Mia's Geometry

7.4 More Theorems about Similar Triangles

1. The Side Splitter Theorem

Side Splitter Theorem says that if a line parallel to one side of a triangle intersects the other two sides, then it divides those sides proportionally.

※ Side Splitter Theorem

Side Splitter Theorem (Triangle Proportionality Theorem)

For triangle ABC, if $\overline{PQ} \parallel \overline{BC}$, then

$$\frac{AP}{PB} = \frac{AQ}{QC}$$

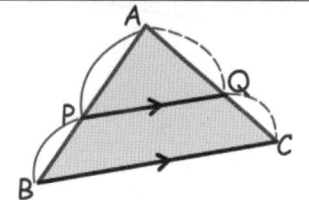

☺ Proof : Side Splitter Theorem

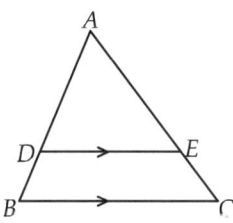

Given: $\overline{BC} \parallel \overline{DE}$

Prove: $\dfrac{AD}{DB} = \dfrac{AE}{EC}$

Statements	Reasons
1. $\overline{BC} \parallel \overline{DE}$	1. Given
2. $\angle A \cong \angle A$	2. Reflexive
3. $\angle ADE \cong \angle B$	3. $\parallel \to$ corresp. $\angle$s are $\cong$
4. $\triangle ABC \sim \triangle ADE$	4. ① _____
5. $\dfrac{AB}{AD} = \dfrac{AC}{AE}$	5. ② _____
6. $AB = AD + DB$, $AC = AE + EC$	6. Seg. add. post
7. ③ _____	7. Substitution
8. $\dfrac{AD}{DB} = \dfrac{AE}{EC}$	8. ④ _____

Blank : ① AA~ post.   ② Corres. sides are prop. in ~ △   ③ $\dfrac{AD+DB}{AD} = \dfrac{AE+EC}{AE}$ ④ properties of proportions

Side Splitter Theorem can also create other proportions;

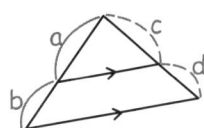
$\dfrac{a}{b} = \dfrac{c}{d}$ $\dfrac{\text{upper left}}{\text{lower left}} = \dfrac{\text{upper right}}{\text{lower right}}$

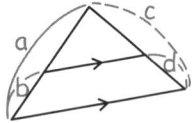
$\dfrac{a}{b} = \dfrac{c}{d}$ $\dfrac{\text{whole left}}{\text{lower left}} = \dfrac{\text{whole right}}{\text{lower right}}$

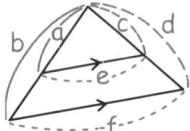
$\dfrac{a}{b} = \dfrac{c}{d} = \dfrac{e}{f}$ $\dfrac{\text{upper left}}{\text{whole left}} = \dfrac{\text{upper right}}{\text{whole right}} = \dfrac{\text{upper parallel}}{\text{lower parallel}}$

(similar triangle)

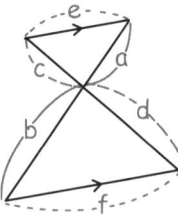
$\dfrac{a}{b} = \dfrac{c}{d} = \dfrac{e}{f}$ $\dfrac{\text{upper right}}{\text{lower left}} = \dfrac{\text{upper left}}{\text{lower right}} = \dfrac{\text{upper parallel}}{\text{lower parallel}}$

(similar triangle)

EXAMPLE 1. Find the value of the variable(s) in each figure. The figures are not drawn to scale.

①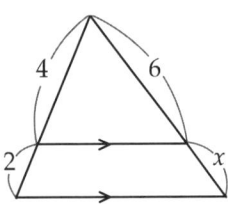

②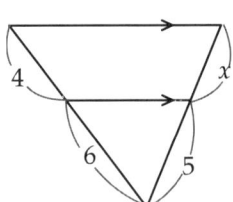

③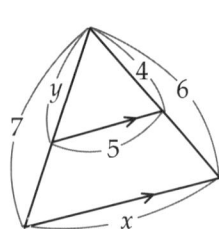

④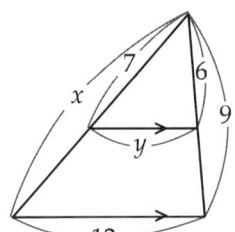

276 Mia's Geometry

⑤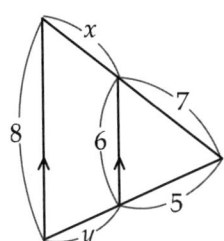

⑥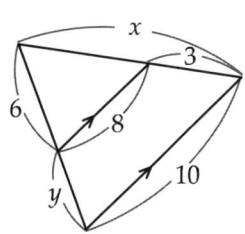

⑦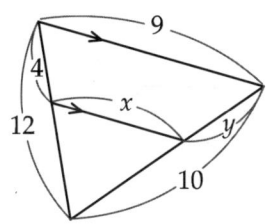

⑧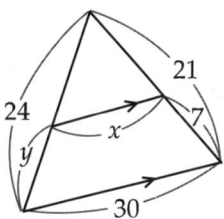

⑨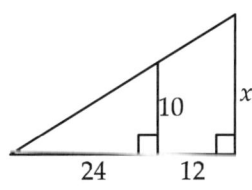

⑩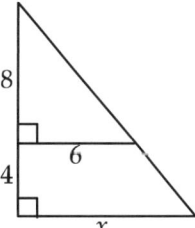

⑪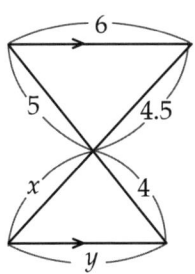

⑫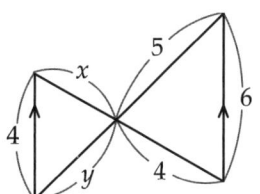

⑬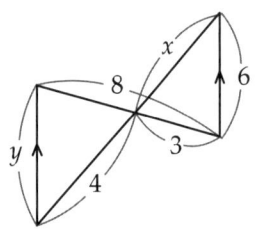

⑭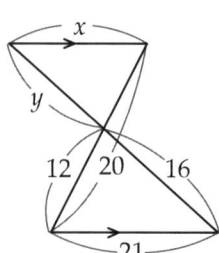

⑮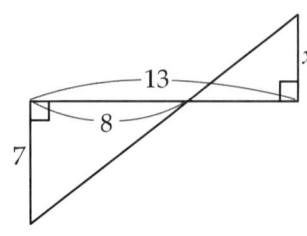

⑯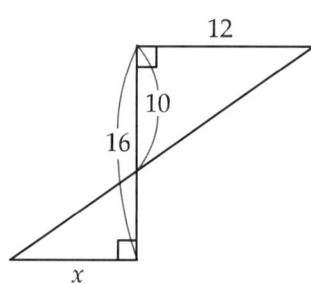

⑰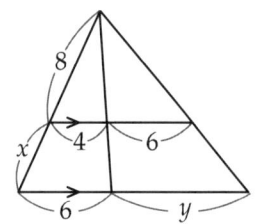

⑱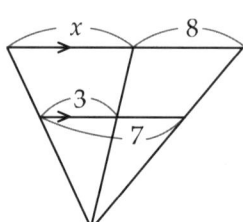

2. Three Parallel Lines Theorem

We can extend the idea of 'Side Splitter Theorem' to the case of multiple parallel lines.

※ Three Parallel Lines Theorem

Three Parallel Lines Theorem

If three parallel lines intersect two transversals, then

$$\frac{AB}{BC} = \frac{DE}{EF}$$

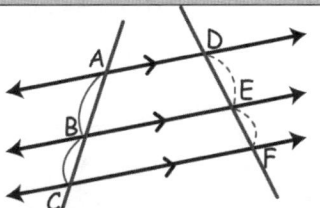

☺ Memorizing Tip:

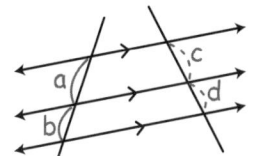 ⟶ $\dfrac{a}{b} = \dfrac{c}{d}$

EXAMPLE 2. Find the value of the variable(s) in each figure. The figures are not drawn to scale.

①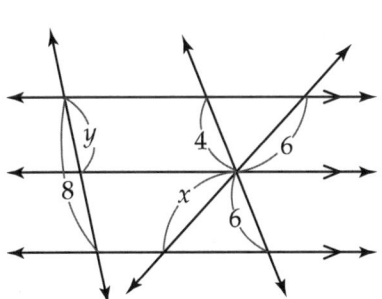

②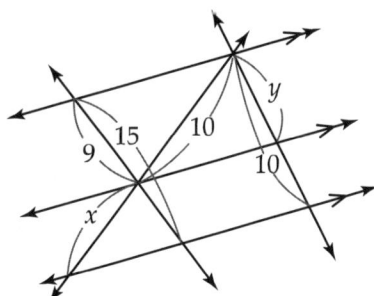

③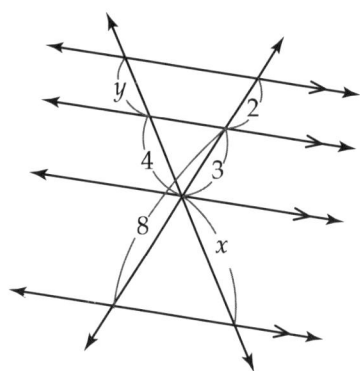

④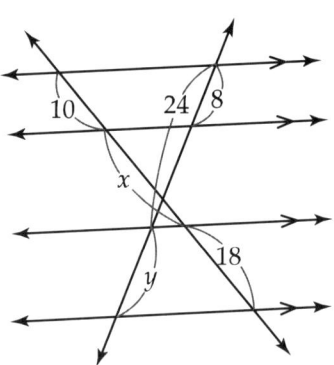

3. Angle Bisector Proportion Theorem

※ Angle Bisector Proportion Theorem

Angle Bisector Proportion Theorem
For triangle ABC, if $\overline{AD}$ bisects the angle BAC $$\frac{AB}{BD} = \frac{AC}{DC}$$ 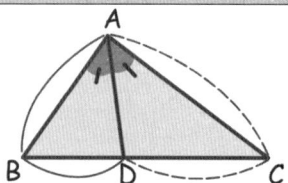

☺ Proof : Angle Bisector Proportion Theorem

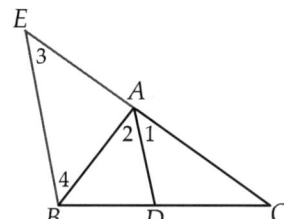

Given: $\overline{AD}$ bisects $\angle BAC$

Prove: $\dfrac{AB}{BD} = \dfrac{AC}{CD}$

Statements	Reasons
1. Draw $\overline{BE}$ such that $\overline{BE} \parallel \overline{DA}$	1. Auxiliary line
2. $\overline{AD}$ bisects $\angle BAC$	2. Given
3. $\angle 1 \cong \angle 2$	3. Def of $\angle$ bisector
4. $\angle 1 \cong \angle 3$	4. $\parallel \rightarrow$ corresp. $\angle$s are $\cong$
5. $\angle 2 \cong \angle 4$	5. $\parallel \rightarrow$ alt int. $\angle$s are $\cong$
6. $\angle 3 \cong \angle 4$	6. Substitution
7. $AE = AB$	7. ① _____
8. $\dfrac{CA}{AE} = \dfrac{CD}{DB}$	8. ② _____
9. ③ _____	9. Substitution
10. $\dfrac{AB}{BD} = \dfrac{AC}{CD}$	10. Property of proportion

☺ Memorizing Tip:

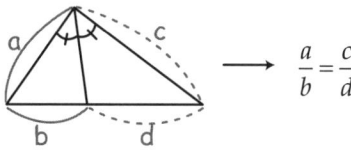

$\dfrac{a}{b} = \dfrac{c}{d}$

Blank : ① Conv. isos. △ thm.   ② side splitter thm.   ③ $\dfrac{CA}{AB} = \dfrac{CD}{DB}$

EXAMPLE 3. Find the value of the variable(s) in each figure. The figures are not drawn to scale.

①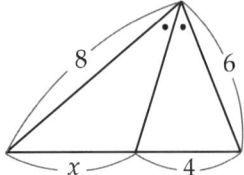

②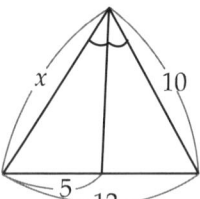

③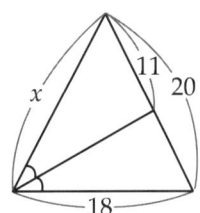

④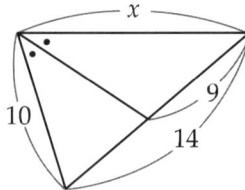

⑤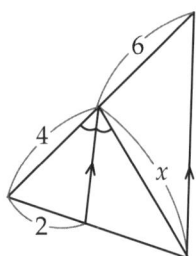

⑥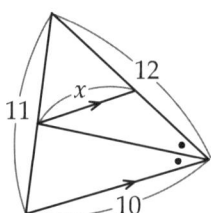

⑦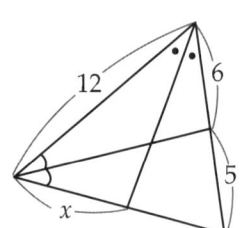

Mia's Geometry

Postulates, Theorems from CH7

*All in One (sorted by Miamath)

About proportions..
Properties of Proportions
If $\dfrac{a}{b}=\dfrac{c}{d}$, then   ① You can do cross multiplication ; $ad = bc$ (Cross product property).   ② You can change the means ; $\dfrac{a}{c}=\dfrac{b}{d}$.   ③ You can take reciprocals on both sides ; $\dfrac{b}{a}=\dfrac{d}{c}$.   ④ You can add 1 to both sides ; $\dfrac{a+b}{b}=\dfrac{c+d}{d}$

To prove that two triangles are similar..	
AA Similarity Postulate	
SSS Similarity Theorem	
SAS Similarity Theorem	

Part 7_Similarity

CSSTP	Corresponding sides of similar triangles are proportional.
CASTC	Corresponding angles of similar triangles are congruent.

Theorems about Similar Triangles

$$\frac{a}{b} = \frac{c}{d} = \frac{e}{f}$$

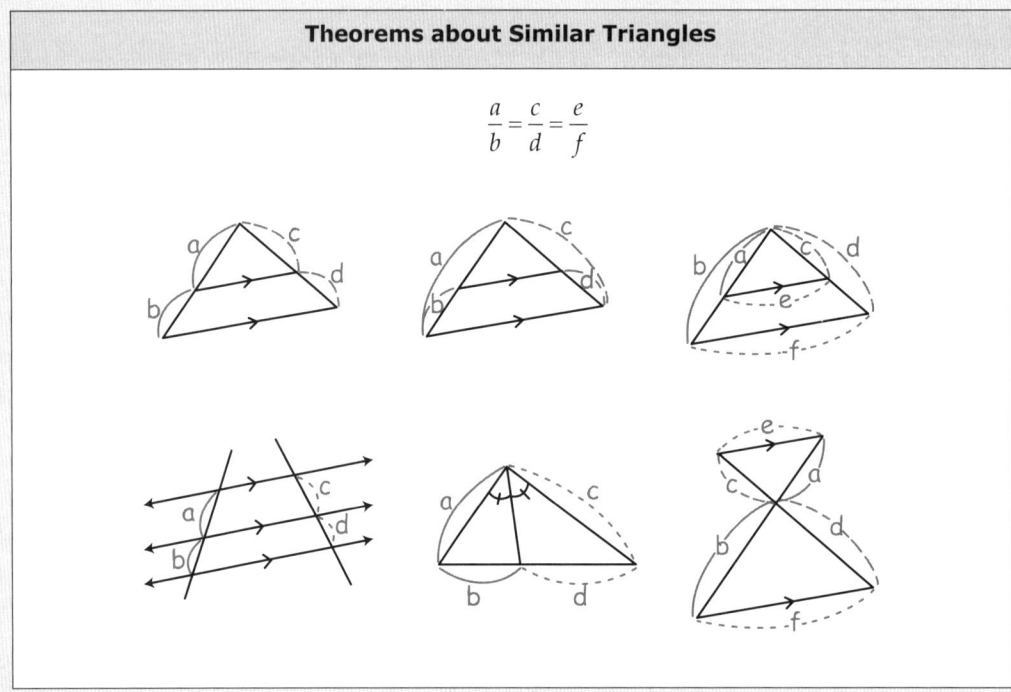

Part 8
Right Triangles and Trigonometry

8.1 Right Triangle Similarity

8.2 The Pythagorean Theorem

8.3 Special Right Triangles

8.4 Trigonometry of Right Triangles

8.5 Angle of elevation or depression

Mia's Geometry

8.1 Right Triangle Similarity

1. Right triangle Similarity

The altitude to the hypotenuse of a right triangle divides the triangle into two ①_____ triangles.

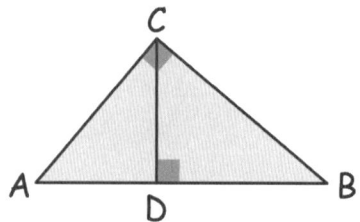

△ABC ~ △ACD ~ △CBD

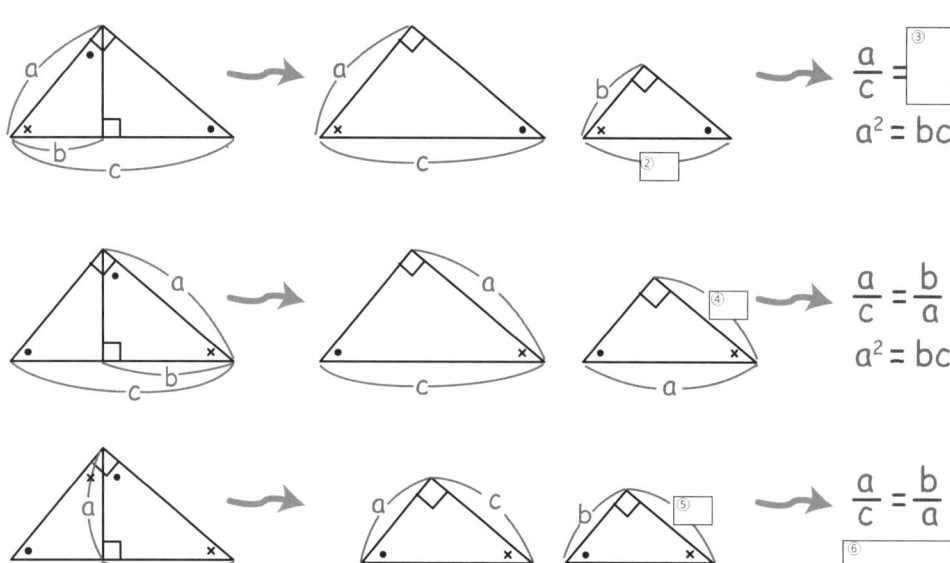

※ Similarity in Right Triangle

The altitude of a right triangle divides the triangle into two similar triangles.

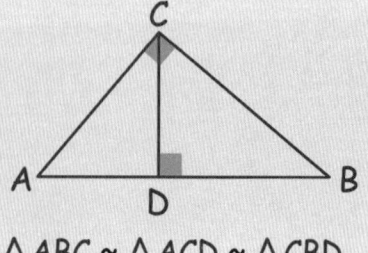

△ABC ~ △ACD ~ △CBD

Blank : ① similar   ② a   ③ $\dfrac{b}{a}$ ④ b   ⑤ a   ⑥ $a^2 = bc$

286 Mia's Geometry

Using the proportional corresponding sides, we can have ;

※ Formula for Right triangle inside a right triangle (1)

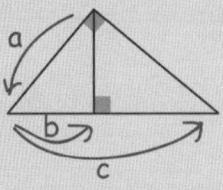 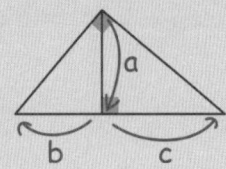 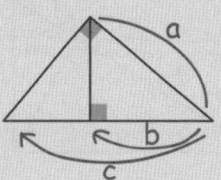

$a^2 = bc$ $a^2 = bc$ $a^2 = bc$

EXAMPLE 1. Find the value of the variable(s) in each figure. The figures are not drawn to scale.

①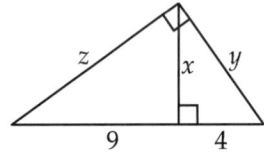

②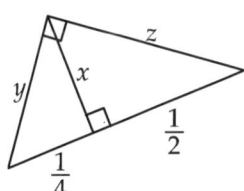

③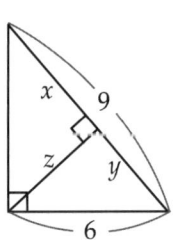

④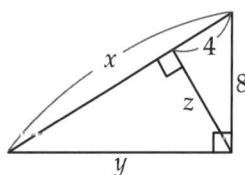

⑤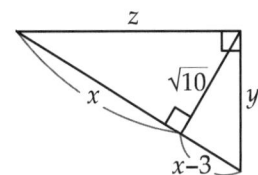

⑥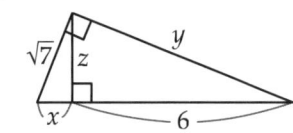

EXAMPLE 2. For the figure, What is the value of xyz?

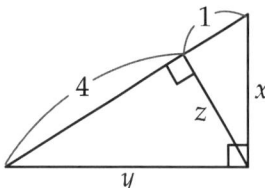

2. Finding length of Altitude of Right Triangle

We already know that the area of a triangle is

$\dfrac{1}{2}$(base)(height).

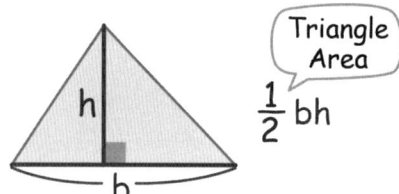

When we have a right triangle inside a right triangle, the area of a triangle can be;

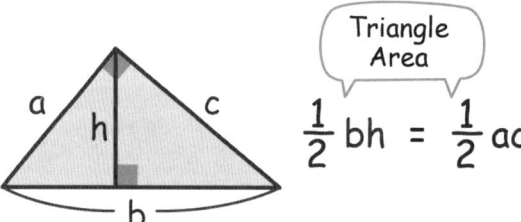

※ Formula for Right triangle inside a right triangle (2)

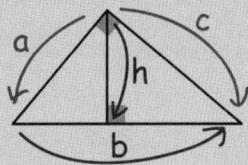

$$ac = bh$$

EXAMPLE 3. Find the value of the variable(s) in each figure. The figures are not drawn to scale.

①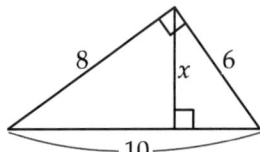

②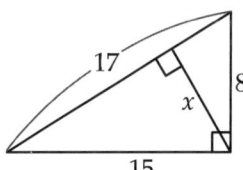

③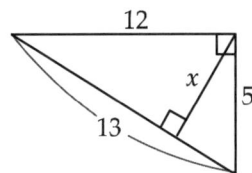

④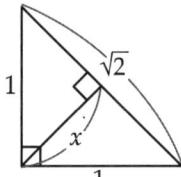

EXAMPLE 4.   * If the figure, △ ABC, △AHD and △ADC are right triangles where $BD = 8$, $CD = 2$. If M is the circumcenter of △ABC, then what is DH?

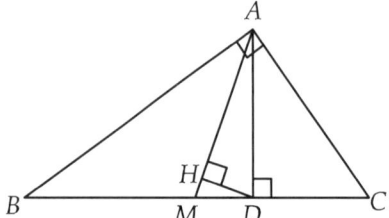

Mia's Geometry

8.2 The Pythagorean Theorem

1. Pythagorean Theorem

☺ Reminder:

When we have a right triangle;

The perpendicular sides are called ①_____

The longest side, opposite the right angle, is called

②_____.

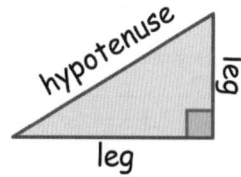

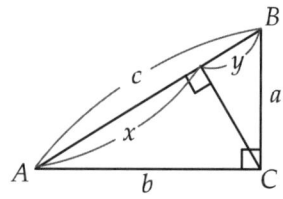

In a right triangle ABC, we've learned that

$$a^2 = ③_____ \text{ and } b^2 = ④_____.$$

Add the two equations and then substitute $c = ⑤\_\_\_\_\_ + ⑥\_\_\_\_\_$;

$$a^2 + b^2 = ⑦\_\_\_\_ + ⑧\_\_\_\_ = c(⑨_____) = ⑩\_\_\_\_\_$$

※ Pythagorean Theorem

Pythagorean Theorem
If a triangle is a right triangle, then the square of the hypotenuse is equal to the sum of the squares of the legs.   → (hypotenuse)² = (leg1)² + (leg2)²   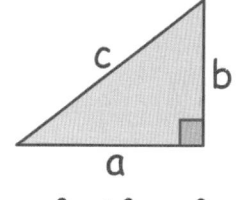 $a^2 + b^2 = c^2$

Blank : ① legs   ② hypotenuse   ③ yc   ④ xc   ⑤ x   ⑥ y   ⑦ yc   ⑧ xc   ⑨ y + x   ⑩ c^2

EXAMPLE 1. Find the value of x.

> ☺ Tip:
> $$hypotenuse = \sqrt{(leg1)^2 + (leg2)^2}$$
> $$leg = \sqrt{(hypotenuse)^2 - (other\ leg)^2}$$

①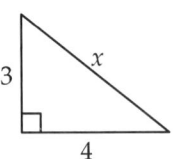

②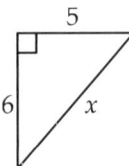

③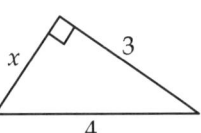

④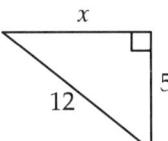

⑤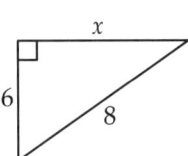

⑥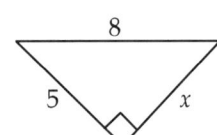

⑦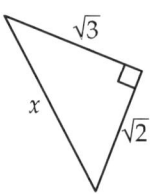

⑧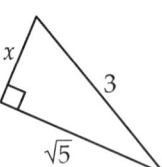

⑨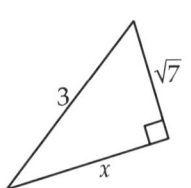

292   Mia's Geometry

2. Pythagorean Triples

A "Pythagorean ①_____" is a set of positive integers that fits the Pythagorean theorem.

ex)

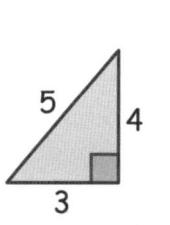 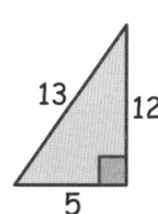 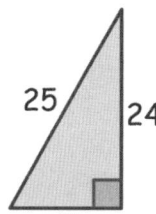 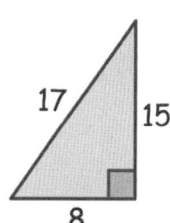

3:4:5,   5:12:13,   7:24:25,   8:15:17, ...

☺ Remember: The biggest number is the hypotenuse.

EXAMPLE 2. Find the value of x. Use the Pythagorean triples.

①
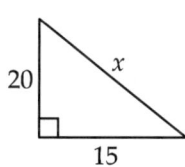

②
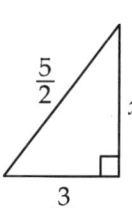

③
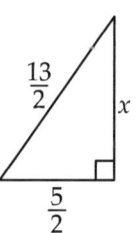

④
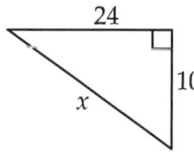

⑤
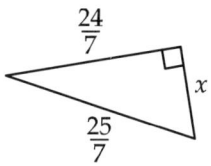

⑥
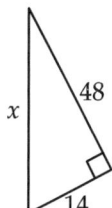

Blank : ① triple

⑦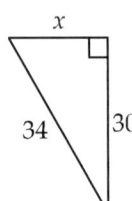

⑧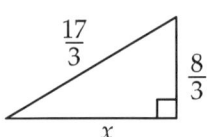

EXAMPLE 3. Find the value of the variable(s) in each figure. The figures are not drawn to scale.

①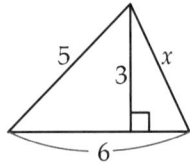

②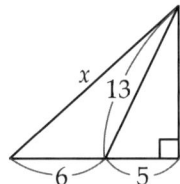

③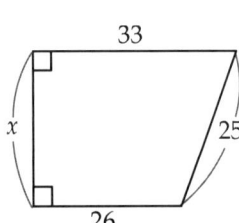

④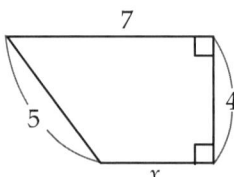

⑤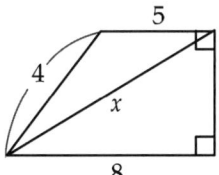

⑥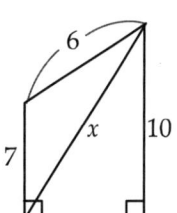

⑦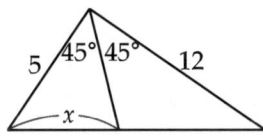

⑧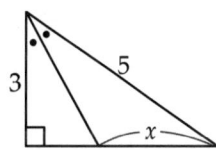

⑨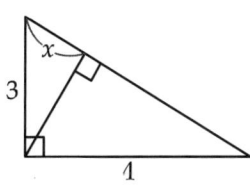

⑩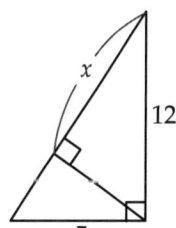

⑪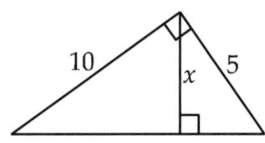

⑫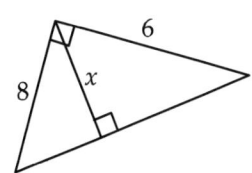

⑬ *
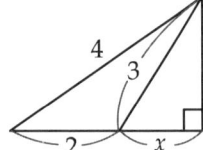

⑭ *
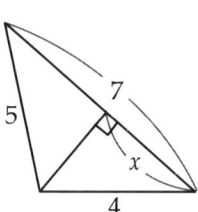

⑮ *
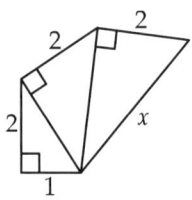

⑯ *
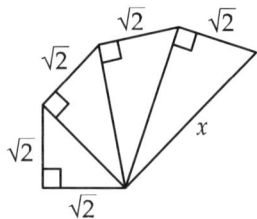

⑰ *
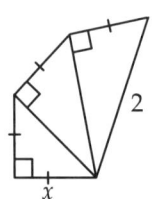

EXAMPLE 4. * Find the value of x.

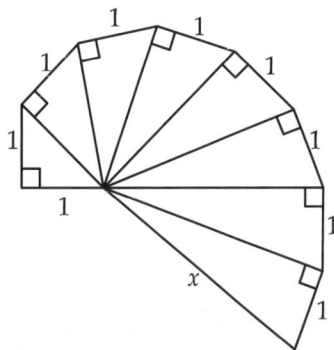

EXAMPLE 5. * Find the value of x.

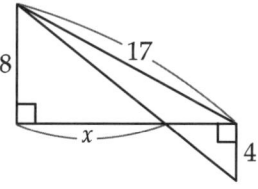

3. Pythagorean Theorem and Triangles

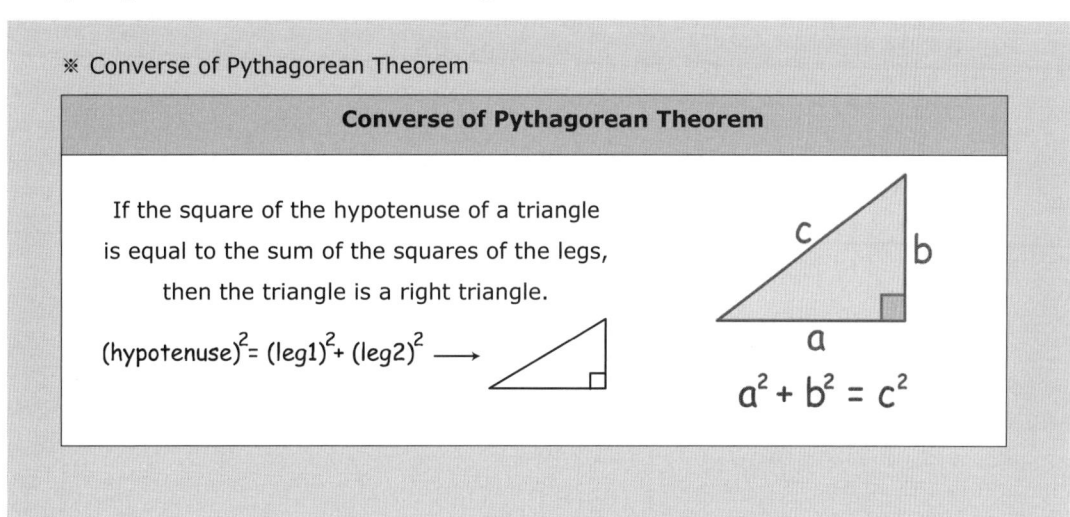

If we expand the idea of Converse of Pythagorean Theorem;

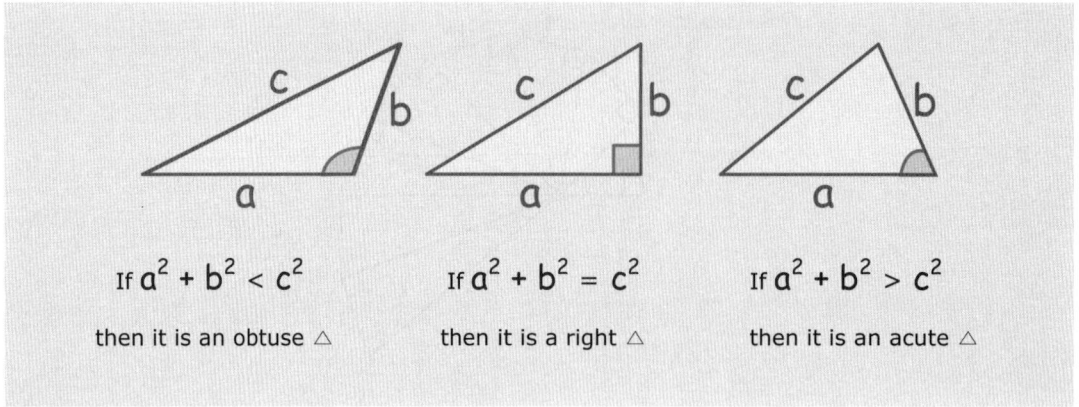

EXAMPLE 6. The lengths of the sides of a triangle are given. Classify each triangle as acute, right, or obtuse.

① 4, 5, 6

② 8, 14, 10

③ $\sqrt{8}$, 5, $\sqrt{14}$

④ 4, 3, , $2\sqrt{3}$

⑤ 0.6, 0.4, 0.3

⑥ 0.6, 0.8, 1

Mia's Geometry
8.3 Special Right Triangles

1. Special Right Triangle

For **45°-45°-90°** right triangle and **30°-60°-90°** right triangle, the sides have a special ratio.

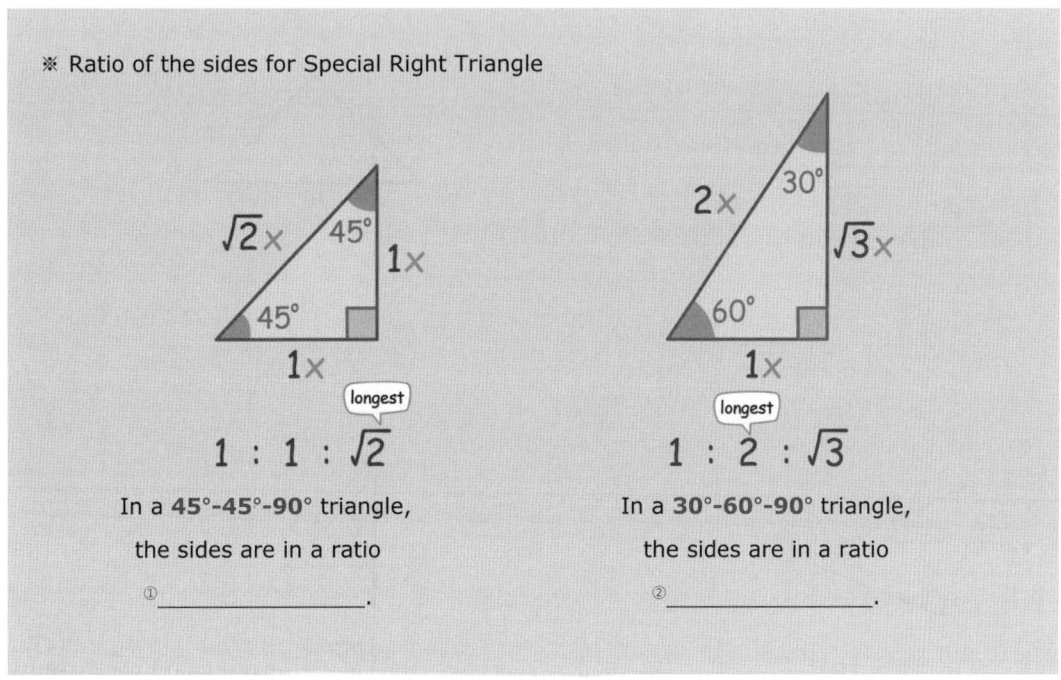

※ Ratio of the sides for Special Right Triangle

In a **45°-45°-90°** triangle, the sides are in a ratio ① _____.

In a **30°-60°-90°** triangle, the sides are in a ratio ② _____.

EXAMPLE 1. Find the value of each variable.

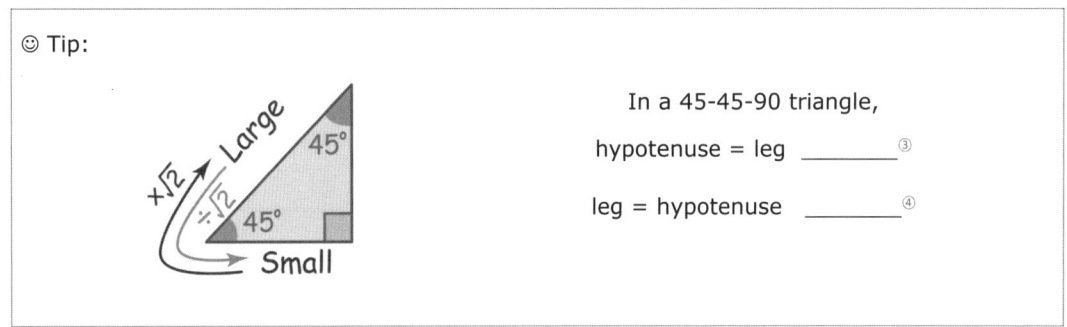

☺ Tip:

In a 45-45-90 triangle,

hypotenuse = leg _____ ③

leg = hypotenuse _____ ④

Blank : ① $1 : 1 : \sqrt{2}$ ($\sqrt{2}$ is the hypotenuse)   ② $1 : 2 : \sqrt{3}$ (2 is the hypotenuse)   ③ $\times \sqrt{2}$ ④ $\div \sqrt{2}$

①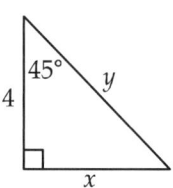

②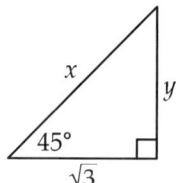

③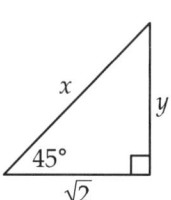

④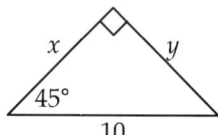

⑤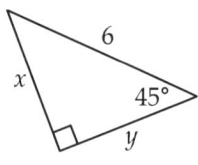

⑥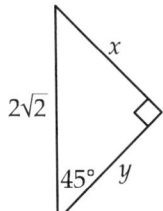

⑦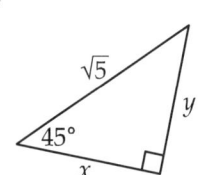

EXAMPLE 2. Find the value of each variable.

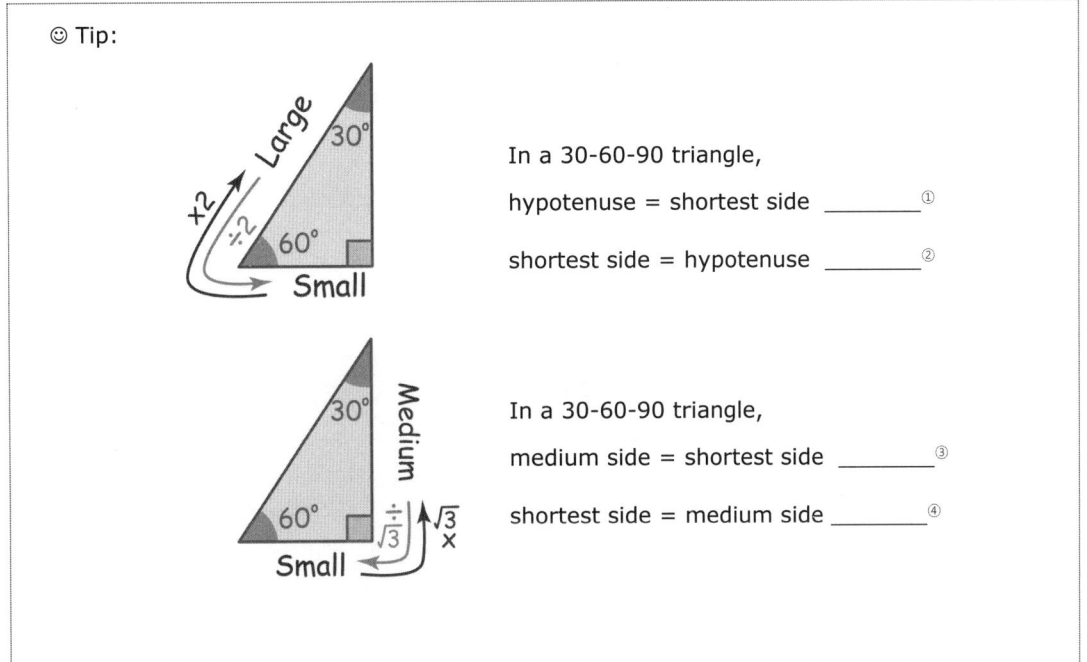

In a 30-60-90 triangle,

hypotenuse = shortest side _____ ①

shortest side = hypotenuse _____ ②

In a 30-60-90 triangle,

medium side = shortest side _____ ③

shortest side = medium side _____ ④

①

②

③

④

Blank : ① ×2   ② ÷2   ③ ×$\sqrt{3}$ ④ ÷$\sqrt{3}$

⑤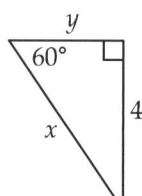

⑥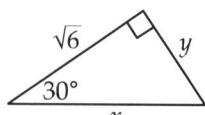

⑦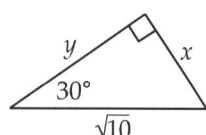

EXAMPLE 3. Find the value of each variable.

①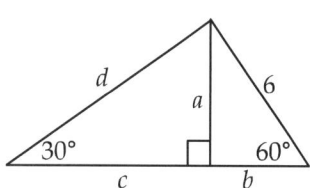

②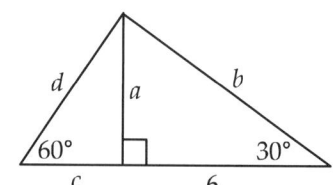

③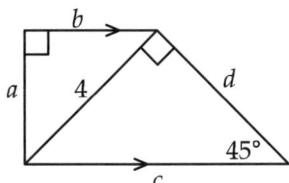

④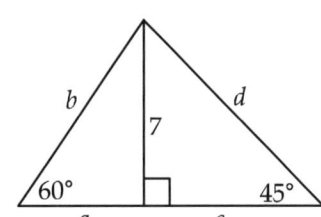

⑤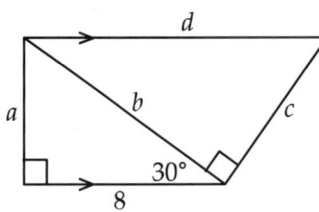

⑥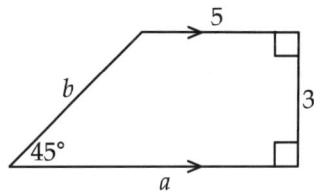

EXAMPLE 4. Find the value of each variable.

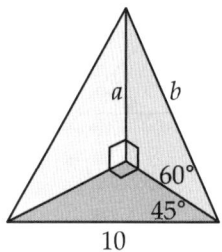

EXAMPLE 5.* Find the OD.

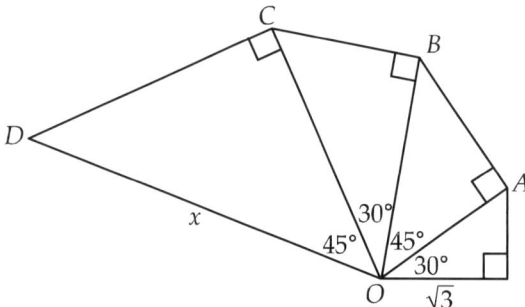

Mia's Geometry
8.4 Trigonometry of Right Triangles

1. Radian Measure

We can measure *the size of the angle* by using *two units*, ①_____ and ②_____.

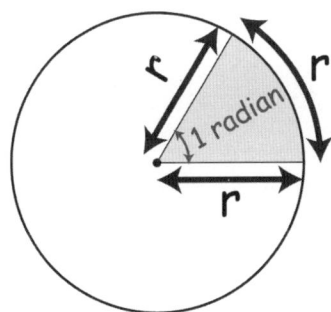

'Radian' is the angle made by taking the ③_____ and **wrapping it along the edge** of a circle

※ Facts about Radian and Degree

① *1 Radian* is about 57.2958°.

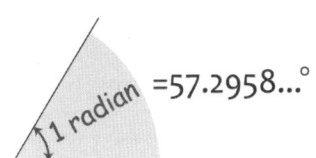

② The unit of *degree* is '°'.

The unit of *radian* is ④_____ or ⑤_____.

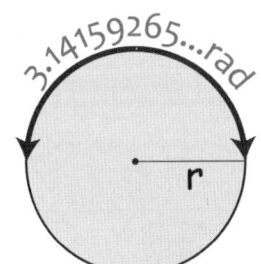

③ There are ⑥_____ *radians* in a half circle

And also ⑦_____° in a half circle

So, ⑧_____ = ⑨_____°

※ Radian and Degree

$$180° = \pi \text{ (rad)}$$

Blank : ① degree   ② radian   ③ radius   ④ rad   ⑤ none   ⑥ π   ⑦ 180   ⑧ π   ⑨ 180

2. Converting Angles

EXAMPLE 1. Convert degrees into radians, and radians into degrees.

☺ Tip:

Converting Degree → Radian

$$\text{Degree}° \times \frac{\pi}{180°}$$

(do not want)

Converting Radian → Degree

$$\text{Radian} \times \frac{180°}{\pi}$$

(want)

① $90°$

② $100°$

③ $120°$

④ $150°$

⑤ $\dfrac{\pi}{3}$

⑥ $\dfrac{5\pi}{3}$

⑦ $\dfrac{4\pi}{3}$

⑧ $\dfrac{\pi}{12}$

⑨ $\dfrac{2}{3}$

⑩ 7

☺ Memorize!

Degrees	$0°$	$30°$	$45°$	$60°$	$90°$	$180°$	$270°$	$360°$
Radians	①	②	③	④	⑤	⑥	⑦	⑧

Blank : ① 0 ② $\dfrac{\pi}{6}$ ③ $\dfrac{\pi}{4}$ ④ $\dfrac{\pi}{3}$ ⑤ $\dfrac{\pi}{2}$ ⑥ π ⑦ $\dfrac{3\pi}{2}$ ⑧ 2π

3. Trigonometry of Right Triangle

A **right triangle with acute angle** θ has names for each side:

① _____ side is adjacent to the angle θ,

② _____ side is opposite the angle θ,

and the longest side is the ③ _____.

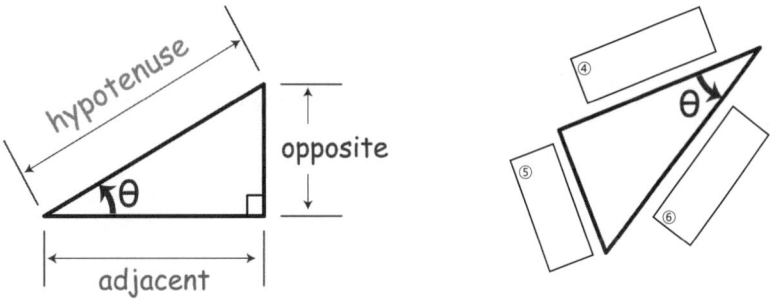

There are **three trigonometric ratios**

which tells you the ⑦ _____ of the ⑧ _____ of a right triangle.

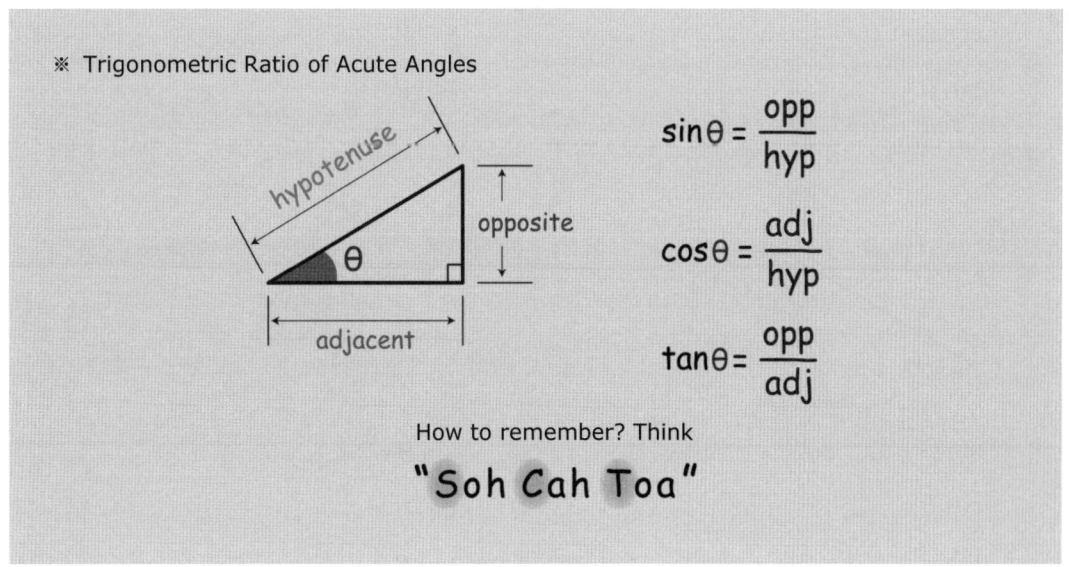

Blank : ① adjacent ② opposite ③ hypotenuse ④ adjacent ⑤ opposite ⑥ hypotenuse ⑦ ratio ⑧ two sides

EXAMPLE 2. Find the exact values of the given trigonometric ratios of the angle θ in the triangle.

①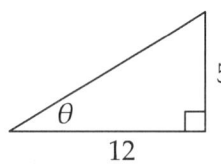

sin θ =

cos θ =

tan θ =

②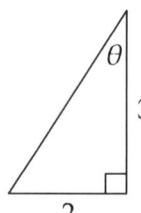

sin θ =

cos θ =

tan θ =

③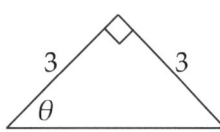

sin θ =

cos θ =

tan θ =

④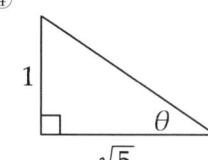

sin θ =

cos θ =

tan θ =

⑤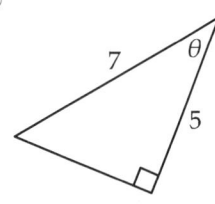

sin θ =

cos θ =

tan θ =

⑥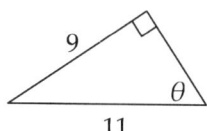

sin θ =

cos θ =

tan θ =

EXAMPLE 3. Express x and y in terms of $\sin\theta$, $\cos\theta$, or $\tan\theta$.

①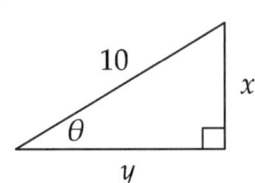

②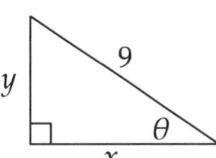

③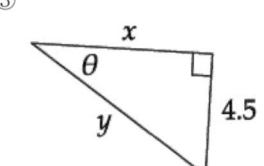

④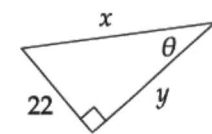

4. Special values of the trigonometric ratio

We already know that the ratios of the sides of **45°-45°-90°** right triangle and **30°-60°-90°** right triangle are ①_____ and ②_____ respectively.

Using these ratios we can calculate the sine, cosine, and tangent of 30°, 45°, 60°.

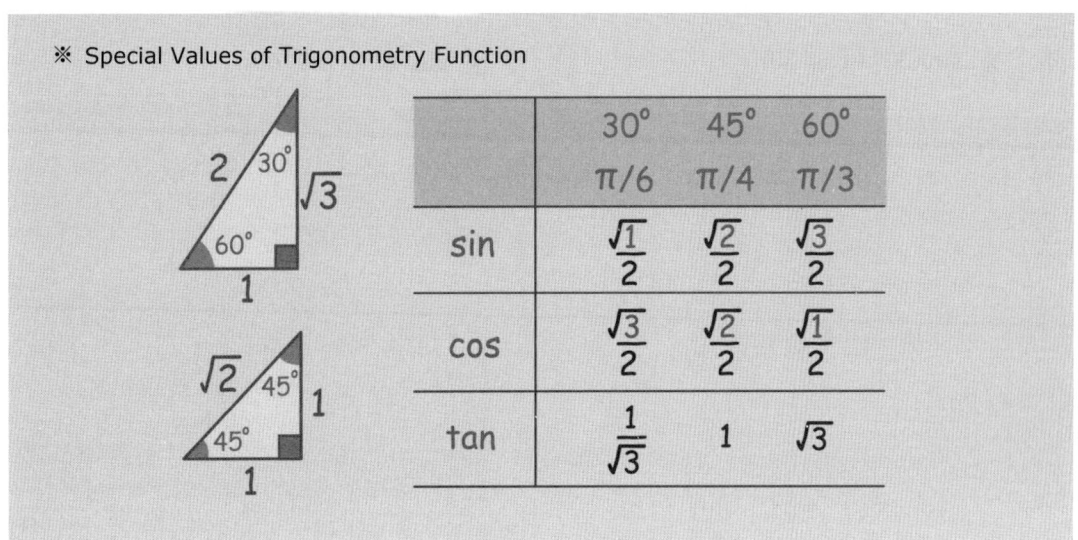

※ Special Values of Trigonometry Function

	30° $\pi/6$	45° $\pi/4$	60° $\pi/3$
sin	$\dfrac{\sqrt{1}}{2}$	$\dfrac{\sqrt{2}}{2}$	$\dfrac{\sqrt{3}}{2}$
cos	$\dfrac{\sqrt{3}}{2}$	$\dfrac{\sqrt{2}}{2}$	$\dfrac{\sqrt{1}}{2}$
tan	$\dfrac{1}{\sqrt{3}}$	1	$\sqrt{3}$

Blank : ① $1 : 1 : \sqrt{2}$ ($\sqrt{2}$ is the hypotenuse)   ② $1 : 2 : \sqrt{3}$ (2 is the hypotenuse)

EXAMPLE 4. Memorize the table and then find the trig ratio.

① $\sin 60°$ ② $\sin 45°$

③ $\cos 45°$ ④ $\cos 30°$

⑤ $\tan \dfrac{\pi}{3}$ ⑥ $\tan \dfrac{\pi}{4}$

⑦ $\cos \dfrac{\pi}{3}$ ⑧ $\sin \dfrac{\pi}{6}$

⑨ $\sin \dfrac{\pi}{4}$ ⑩ $\cos \dfrac{\pi}{3}$

⑪ $\sin 45° \cos 60° + \cos 45° \sin 60°$ ⑫ $\cos 30° \cos 60° - \sin 30° \sin 60°$

⑬ $\sin^2 30° + \cos^2 30°$ ⑭ $\sin^2 60° + \cos^2 60°$

Mia's Geometry
8.5 Angle of elevation or depression

1. Angle of Elevation and Depression

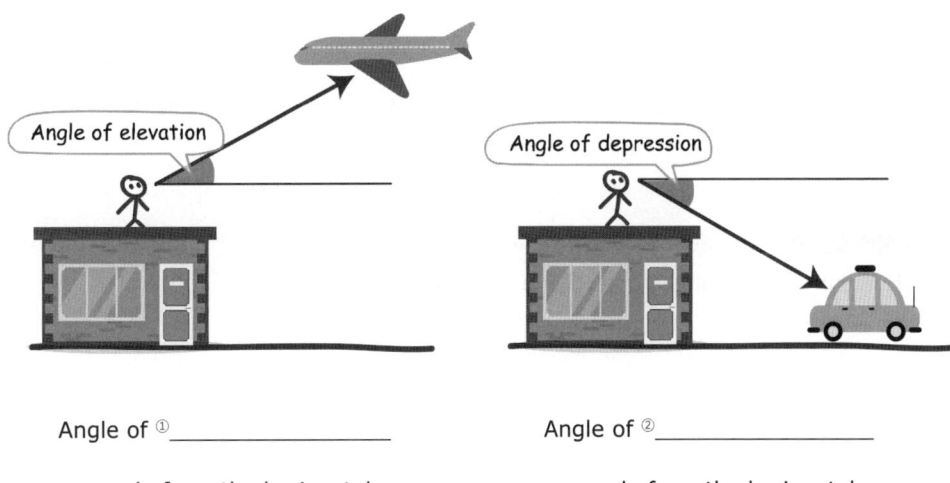

Angle of ①_____

: angle from the horizontal
upward to an object.

Angle of ②_____

: angle from the horizontal
downward to an object.

EXAMPLE 1. A giant redwood tree casts a shadow 200 ft long. Find the height of the tree if the angle of elevation of the sun is 57.6°.

Blank : ① elevation   ② depression

EXAMPLE 2. An airplane is flying at a height of 2 miles above level ground. The angle of depression from the plane to the foot of the tree is 15°. What is the distance the plane must fly to be directly above the tree?

EXAMPLE 3. A 25ft ladder is leaning against a building making 35° angle with the ground. How far up the building does the ladder touch?

EXAMPLE 4. Jay is standing 100 feet from the base of a tree, as shown in the figure. He measures the angle of elevation from the top of his head to the top of the tree to be 37°. If Jay is 6 feet tall, how tall is the tree?

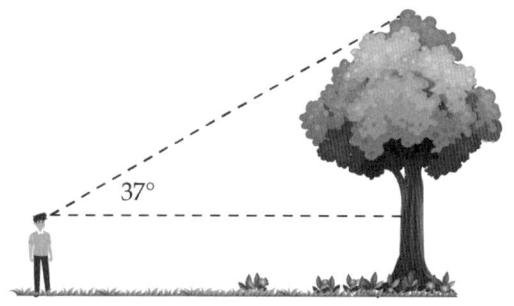

EXAMPLE 5. Two motorists are driving cars on the highway on opposite sides of a plane, and the angle of depression to one car is 46° and to the other is 52°. If the plane is flying at an elevation of 5000 ft directly above the highway, how far apart are the cars?

EXAMPLE 6. From a point on the ground 500 ft from the base of a building, an observer finds that the angle of elevation to the top of the building is 32° and that the angle of elevation to the top of a flagpole atop the building is 36°. Find the length of the flagpole.

2. Inverse Trig Function

※ Inverse Trigonometry function

The Sine function takes an ①_____ and gives us the ②_____.

Inverse Sine **sin⁻¹**(= **arcsin**) takes the ③_____ and gives us the ④_____.

$$\sin(30°) = \frac{1}{2} \quad \rightleftarrows \quad 30° = \sin^{-1}\left(\frac{1}{2}\right)$$
$$30° = \arcsin\left(\frac{1}{2}\right)$$

(Inverse Trig)

EXAMPLE 7. Find the measure of the indicated angle to the nearest degree.

①
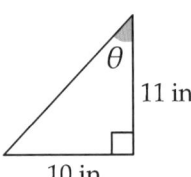
11 in
10 in

②
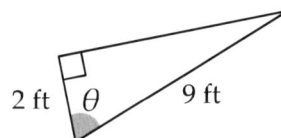
2 ft   9 ft

③
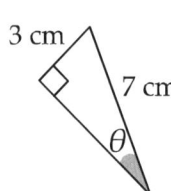
3 cm
7 cm

④
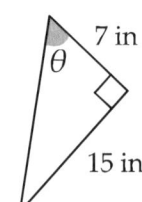
7 in
15 in

Blank : ① angle   ② ratio   ③ ratio   ④ angle

EXAMPLE 8. A 40-ft ladder leans against a building. If the base of the ladder is 12 ft from the base of the building, what is the angle formed by the ladder and the building?

EXAMPLE 9. Joshua observes a boat in the sea below him from a point 6 ft above a 45 ft cliff. He has been told that the distance from the boat to the base of the cliff is 60 ft. What is the angle of depression, in degrees, from Joshua to the boat?

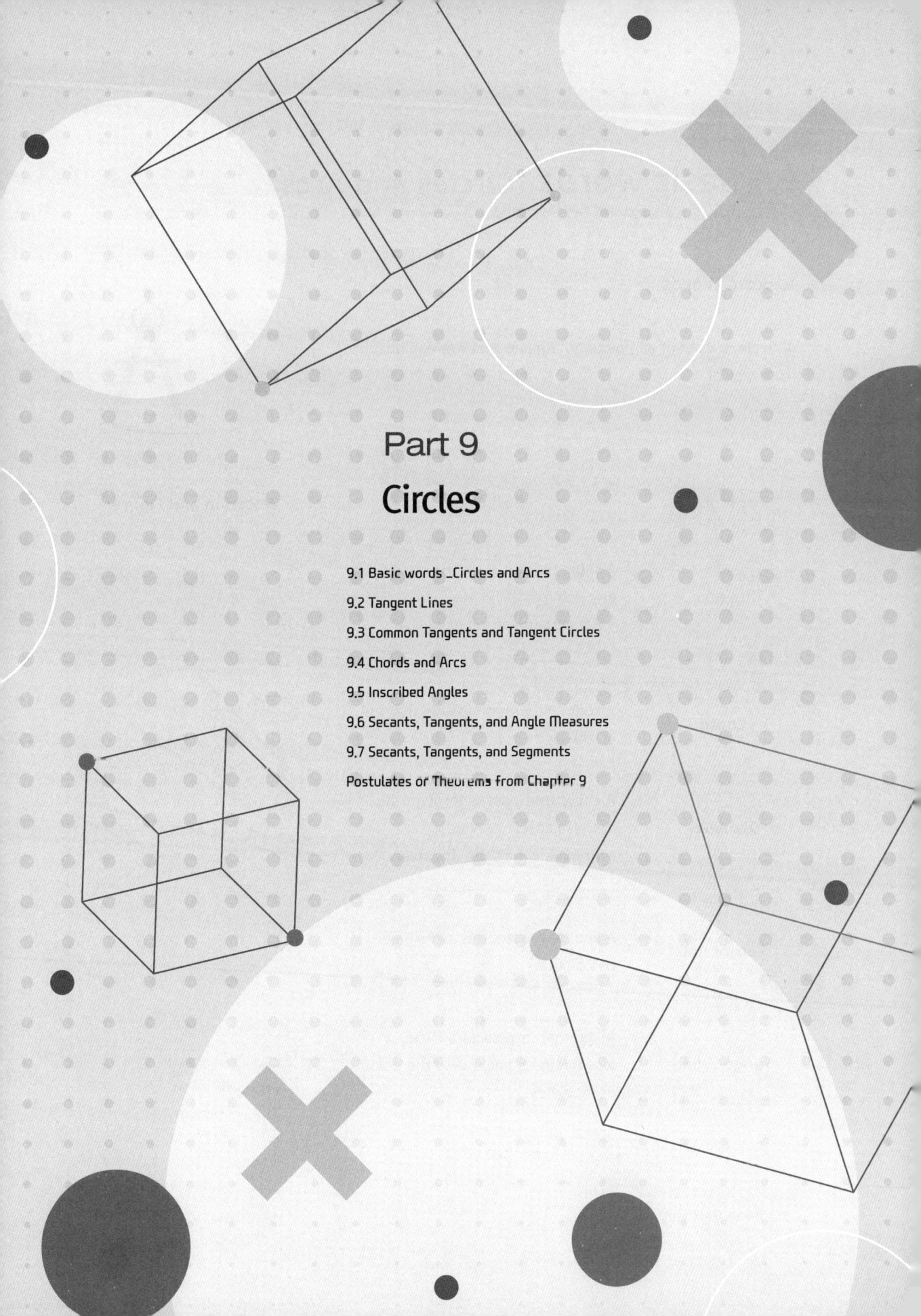

Part 9
Circles

9.1 Basic words _Circles and Arcs
9.2 Tangent Lines
9.3 Common Tangents and Tangent Circles
9.4 Chords and Arcs
9.5 Inscribed Angles
9.6 Secants, Tangents, and Angle Measures
9.7 Secants, Tangents, and Segments
Postulates or Theorems from Chapter 9

Mia's Geometry
9.1 Basic words _Circles and Arcs

1. Basic Words

A **circle** is a set of all points on a plane that are equidistance from a point.

Vocabulary	Definition	Notation and Figure
Radius	A segment that joins the center to any point of the circle • 'Radii' is the plural of radius.	
Chord	A segment with endpoints that lie on the circle	
Diameter	A chord that passes through the circle's center. • A radius is half the diameter.	
Secant line	A line that intersects a circle at two points.	
Tangent line	A line that intersects a circle at exactly one point, called the point of tangency.	

Vocabulary	Definition	Notation and Figure
Concentric circles	Coplanar circles with the same ①_____.	Concentric
Congruent circles	Circles that have congruent ②_____.	Congruent
Tangent circles	Two coplanar circles that intersect at exactly one point	Tangent
Inscribed polygon	A polygon is ③_____ in a circle if all vertices of the polygon lie on the circle.	Inscribed polygon Inscribed polygon Circumscribed Circle
Circumscribed polygon	A polygon is ④_____ about a circle if each side of the polygon is tangent to the circle	Circumscribed polygon Circumscribed polygon Inscribed Circle

Blank : ① center ② radii ③ inscribed ④ circumscribed

2. Angles and Arcs

Vocabulary	Definition	Notation and Figure
Sector	Portion of a circle made by two radii and arc.	
Central angle	An angle whose vertex is at the center of a circle and the sides are the radii. (Angle inside the sector)	central angle, sector, 70°, A, O, B, Arc
Circumference	Distance around its edge of the circle (Circle's perimeter)	
Arc	Part of the circumference of a circle. ex) $\overarc{AB}$	
Arc measure	How many degrees does the arc take up on the circle. • Measured in degrees • Measure of arc $\overarc{AB}$ = ① _____ = $m\angle AOB$ = Central angle	Arc measure 70°, A, O, B, C, 40°, D Central angle, Arc measure $m\angle AOB = m\overarc{AB} = 70°$
Arc length	How long is the arc • Measured in ft, in, cm, m etc.	
Minor arc	An arc with a degree measure less than 180° ex) $\overarc{AB}$	A, minor arc, B, O, major arc, C
Major arc	An arc with a degree measure greater than 180° ex) $\overarc{ACB}$	
Semicircle	An arc with a degree measure of 180° ex) $\overarc{ABC}$	

Blank : ① $m\overarc{AB}$

Vocabulary Check True or false?

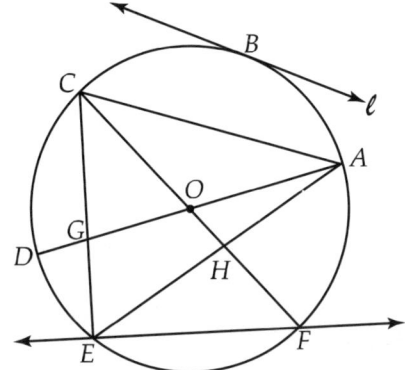

① $\overline{CH}$ is a chord.

② $AO = DO$

③ $OC = 2CF$

④ $\overleftrightarrow{EF}$ is a chord.

⑤ Line l is a tangent line.

⑥ $m\overset{\frown}{AF}$ means the length of arc $\overset{\frown}{AF}$

⑦ $m\angle COD = m\overset{\frown}{CD}$

⑧ $m\angle DAE = m\overset{\frown}{DE}$

⑨ $\overset{\frown}{AC}$ is a major arc.

⑩ $\overset{\frown}{EF}$ is a minor arc.

⑪ $\overset{\frown}{ACD}$ is a semicircle.

⑫ $\triangle ACE$ is circumscribed about a circle.

Mia's Geometry
9.2 Tangent Lines

1. Tangent Lines

A **tangent** to a circle is a line, segment, or ray that intersects the circle in exactly one point.
(It ①_____ the circle.)

The **point of tangency** is the point where a circle and a tangent intersect.

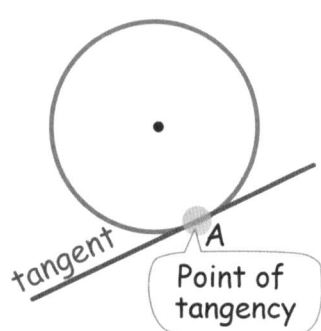

※ Tangent radius Theorem

Tangent radius Theorem

If a line is tangent to a circle, then the line is perpendicular to the radius.

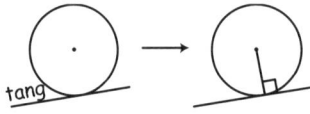
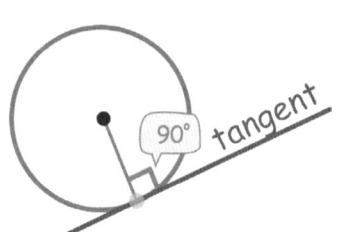

Converse of Tangent radius Theorem

If a line is perpendicular to a radius of a circle at its endpoint on the circle, then the line is a tangent to the circle.

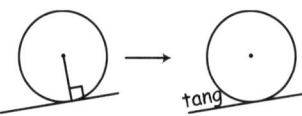
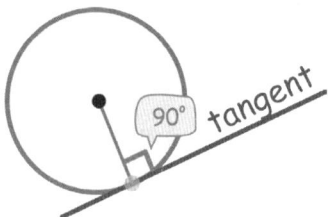

Blank : ① touches

※ Two tangents Theorem

Two tangents Theorem

The two tangents to a circle from a point outside the circle are ①_____.

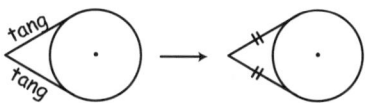
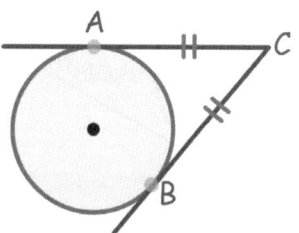

☺ Proof : Two tangents Theorem

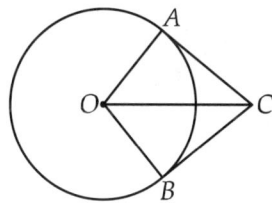

Given: $\overline{AC}$ and $\overline{BC}$ are tangent lines

Prove: $\overline{AC} \cong \overline{BC}$

Statements	Reasons
1. $\overline{AC}$ and $\overline{BC}$ are tangent lines	1. Given
2. $\overline{OA} \perp \overline{AC}, \overline{OB} \perp \overline{BC}$,	2. ② _____
3. $\angle OAC$, $\angle OBC$ are right $\angle$s	3. Definition of $\perp$ lines
4. $\triangle OAC$, $\triangle OBC$ are right $\triangle$s	4. Definition of right $\triangle$s
5. ③ _____	5. All radii are $\cong$ in ⊙
6. ④ _____	6. Reflexive Property
7. $\triangle OAC \cong \triangle OBC$	7. ⑤ _____
8. $\overline{AC} \cong \overline{BC}$	8. ⑥ _____

Blank : ① congruent ② tangent radius thm. ③ $\overline{OA} \cong \overline{OB}$ ④ $\overline{OC} \cong \overline{OC}$ ⑤ HL thm. ⑥ CPCTC

EXAMPLE 1. Find the value of the variable(s) in each figure. The figures are not drawn to scale.

①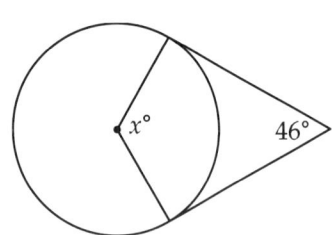

②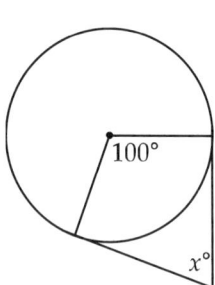

③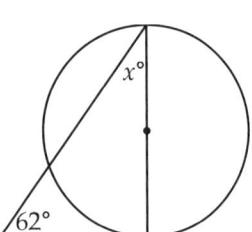

④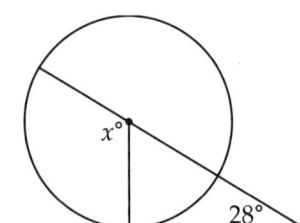

⑤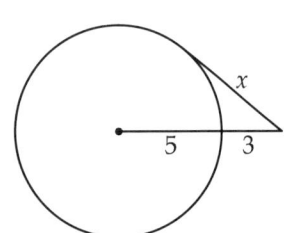

⑥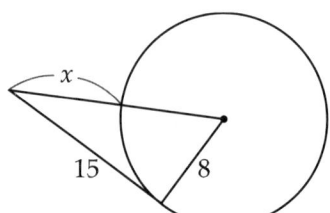

⑦ *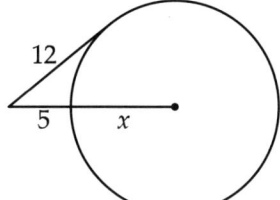

⑧ *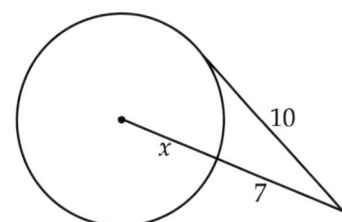

⑨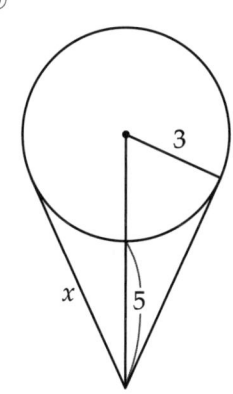

EXAMPLE 2. The figure shows tangent lines and tangent circles. Find x.

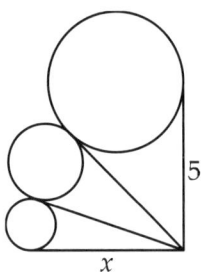

EXAMPLE 3. The figure shows two concentric circles. Find AB.

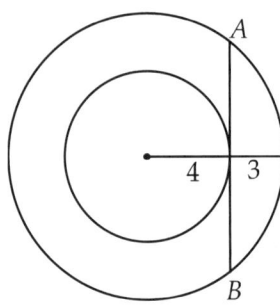

EXAMPLE 4. Find x.

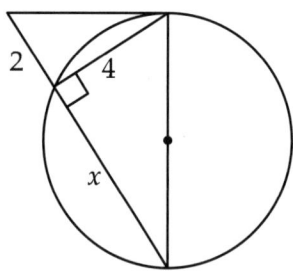

EXAMPLE 5. For the figure, $\overline{AB} \perp \overline{OE}$, $AB = 8$, $m\angle AOB = 120°$. What is DE?

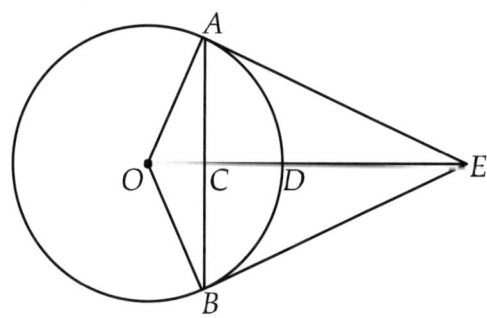

2. Circumscribed Polygon

A polygon is circumscribed about a circle if every side of the polygon is ①_____ to the circle.

※ Facts about Circumscribed Polygon (1)

When a triangle is circumscribed about a circle, then
(when the circle is an incircle)

AE = AD, BE = BF, and CF = CD.

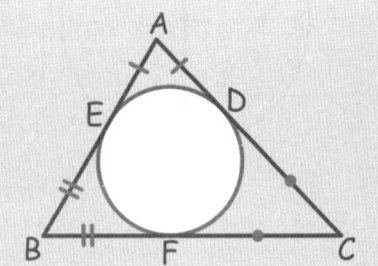

※ Facts about Circumscribed Polygon (2)

When a quadrilateral is circumscribed about a circle,

then AB + CD = AD + BC.

The perimeter of ▱ABCD = 2(AB + CD)

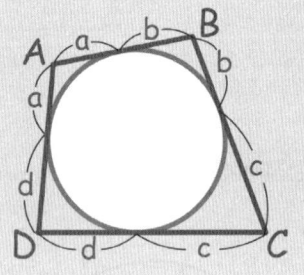

☺ Proof:

$$AB + DC = (②\_\_\_ + b) + (d + ③\_\_\_) = (a + d) + (④\_\_\_ + c) = AD + BC$$

※ Facts about Circumscribed Polygon (3)

The perimeter of △ABC =

AB + BC + CA = 2AD = 2AE

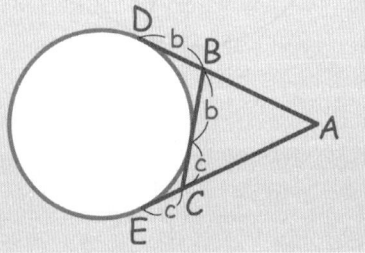

☺ Proof:

$$AB + BC + CA = AB + (⑤\_\_\_ + c) + CA = (AB + ⑥\_\_\_) + (c + CA)$$
$$= AD + AE = 2AD$$

Blank : ① tangent ② a ③ c ④ b ⑤ b ⑥ b

EXAMPLE 6. Find the perimeter of triangle ABC or quadrilateral ABCD.

① Perimeter of △ABC

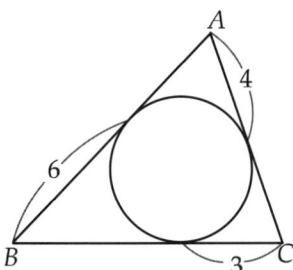

② Perimeter of △ABC

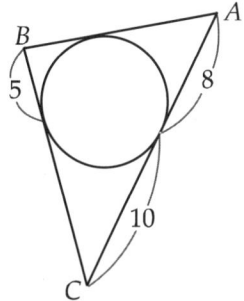

③ Perimeter of △ABC

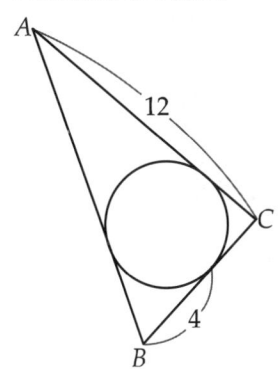

④ Perimeter of △ABC

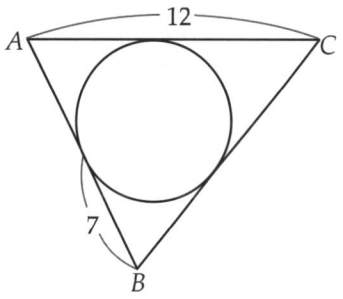

⑤ Perimeter of □ABCD

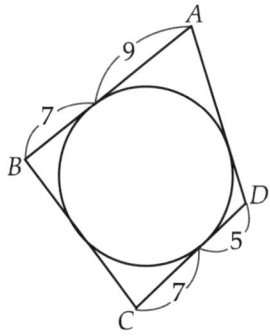

⑥ Perimeter of □ABCD

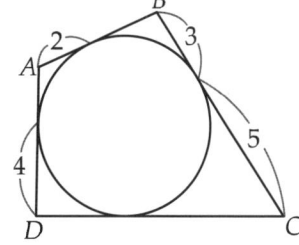

⑦ Perimeter of □ABCD

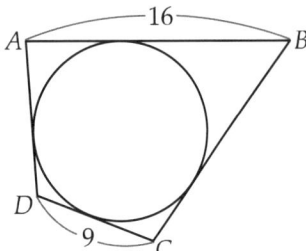

⑧ Perimeter of □ABCD

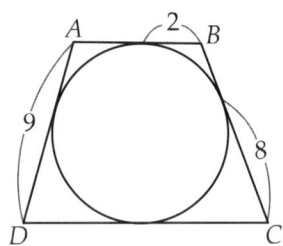

⑨ Perimeter of □ABCD

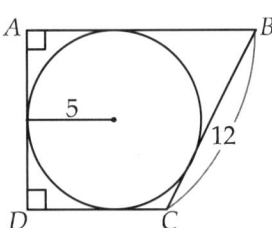

⑩ Perimeter of □ABCD

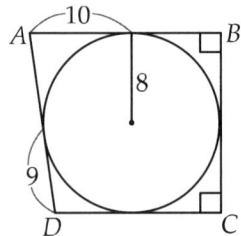

⑪ Perimeter of △ABC

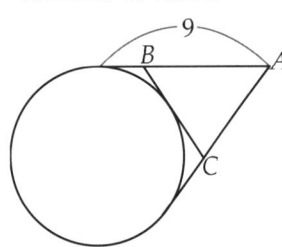

⑫ Perimeter of △ABC

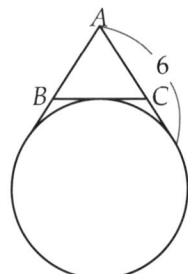

⑬ *Perimeter of □ABCD

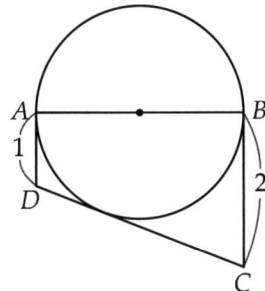

⑭ *Perimeter of □ABCD

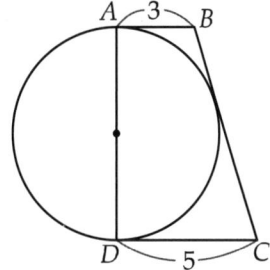

EXAMPLE 7. Triangle ABC is circumscribed about a circle. If $AB = 8$, $AC = 6$, $BC = 11$. What is x?

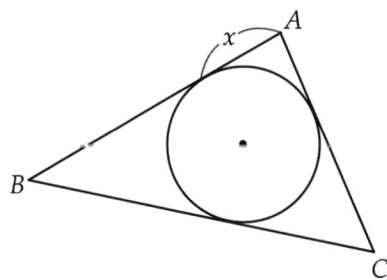

EXAMPLE 8. A right triangle is circumscribed about a circle. What is the length of the radius of the circle?

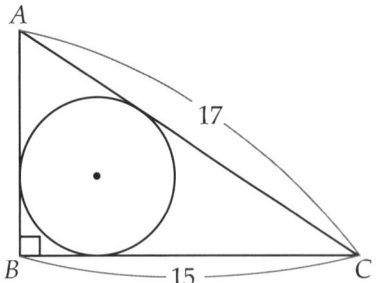

EXAMPLE 9. A right triangle is circumscribed about a circle. What is x?

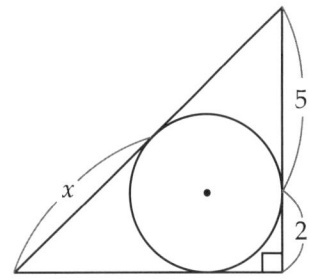

Mia's Geometry

9.3 Common Tangents and Tangent Circles

1. Common tangent

Common tangent is a line or segment that touches two circles at exactly one point each.
We have two different common tangents;

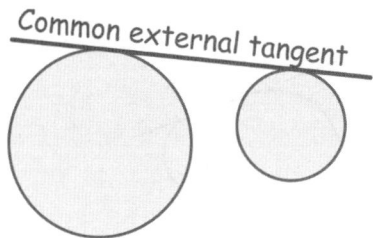

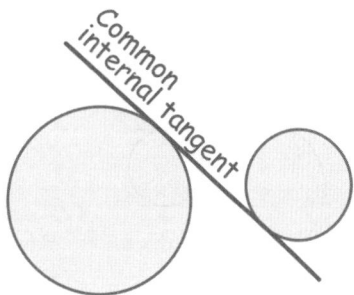

Common external tangent:
A tangent that does not pass between the two circles.

Common internal tangent:
A tangent that passes between the two circles.

2. Tangent circles

Tangent circles are two coplanar circles that intersect at exactly one point.

We have two different tangent circles;

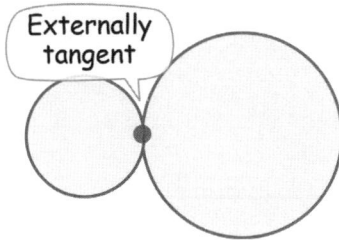

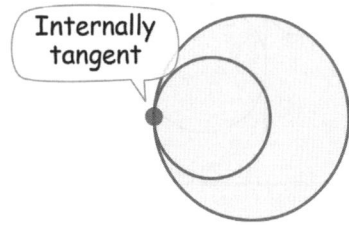

External tangent Circles:
Circles touch at one point, and one circle is outside the other.

Internal tangent Circles:
Circles touch at one point, and one circle is inside the other.

EXAMPLE 1. (i) Tell whether the circles are externally tangent, internally tangent, or not tangent.
(ii) Tell whether the line is a common external tangent, common internal tangent, or neither.

①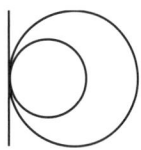

②

③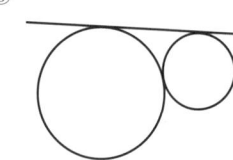

④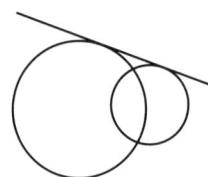

⑤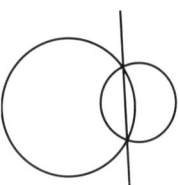

⑥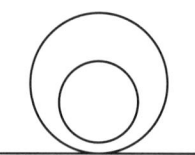

⑦

※ Facts about Common Tangents (1)

The Pythagorean theorem can be used to calculate the length of a common tangent between two circles.

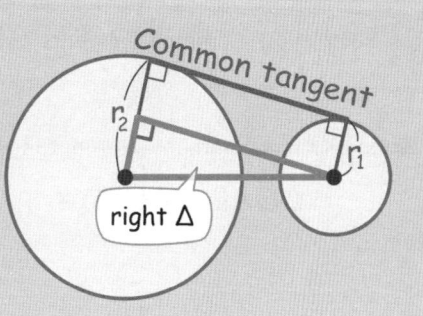

※ Facts about Common Tangents (2)

When $\overline{BD}$ is a common internal tangent;

△OBA ~ △ODC

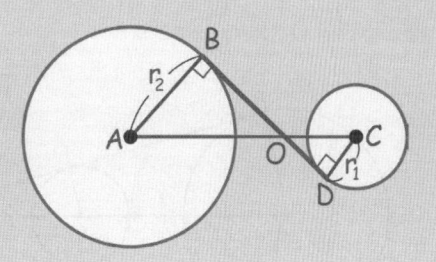

☺ Proof :

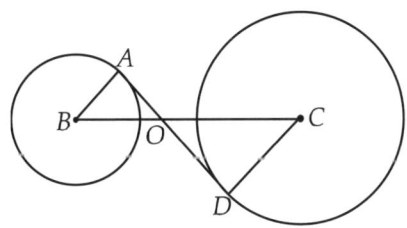

Given: $\overline{AD}$ is common internal tangent

Prove: △OBA ~ △ODC

Statements	Reasons
1. $\overline{AD}$ is common internal tangent	1. Given
2. $\overline{AB} \perp \overline{AD}, \overline{CD} \perp \overline{AD}$	2. ① _____
3. ∠BAO, ∠CDO are right ∠s	3. Definition of right triangle
4. ∠BAO ≅ ∠CDO	4. All right ∠s are ≅
5. ② _____	5. Vertical ∠s theorem
6. △OBA ~ △ODC	6. ③ _____

Blank : ① tangent radius thm.　② ∠AOB ≅ ∠DOC　③ AA ~ post.

※ Facts about Common Tangents (3)

When $\overline{BO}$ is a common external tangent;

$$\triangle OAB \sim \triangle OCD$$

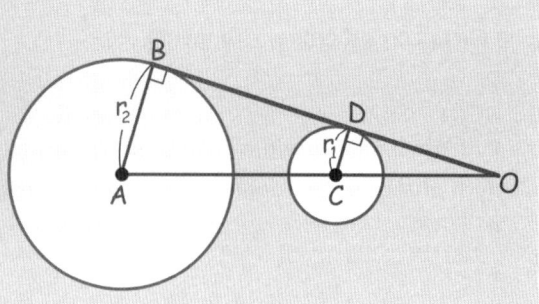

☺ Proof :

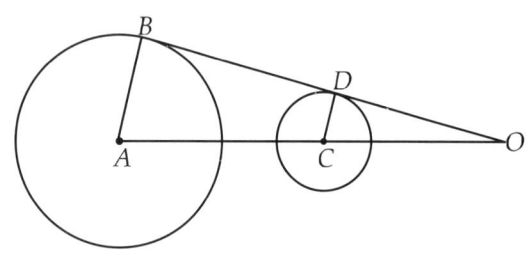

Given: $\overline{OB}$ is common external tangent

Prove: $\triangle OAB \sim \triangle OCD$

Statements	Reasons
1. $\overline{OB}$ is common external tangent	1. Given
2. $\overline{AB} \perp \overline{OB}, \overline{CD} \perp \overline{OB}$	2. ① _____
3. $\angle ABO$, $\angle CDO$ are right $\angle$s	3. Definition of right triangle
4. $\angle ABO \cong \angle CDO$	4. All right $\angle$s are $\cong$
5. ② _____	5. Reflexive property
6. $\triangle OAB \sim \triangle OCD$	6. ③ _____

Blank : ① tangent radius thm.   ② $\angle O \cong \angle O$ ③ AA ~ post.

EXAMPLE 2. Find the value of the variable(s) in each figure. The figures are not drawn to scale.

①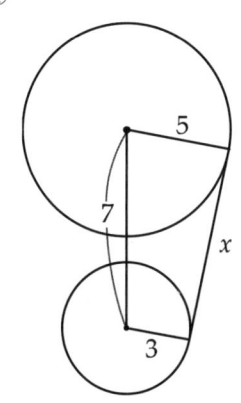

②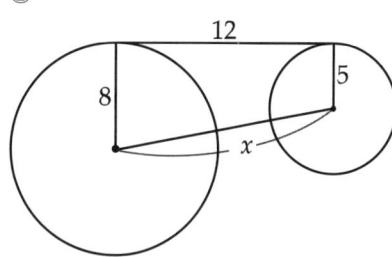

③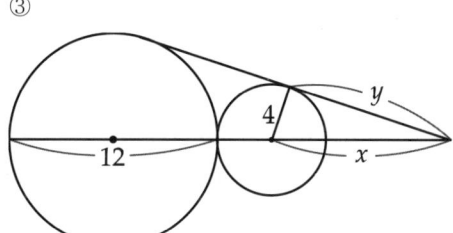

④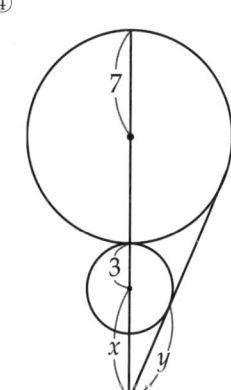

⑤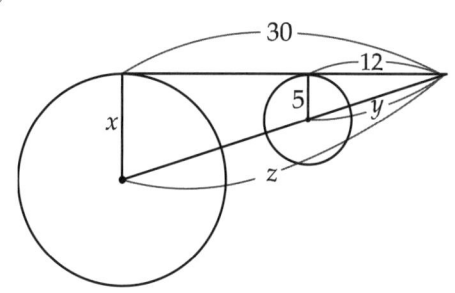

⑥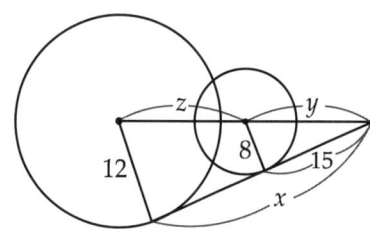

⑦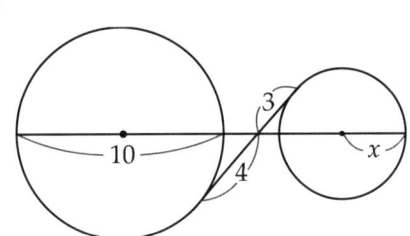

⑧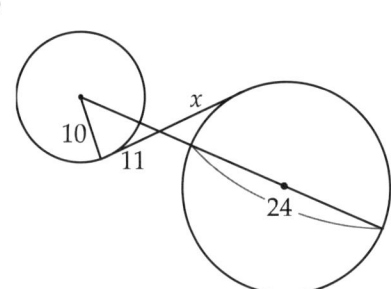

EXAMPLE 3. Three tangent circles are given as shown. If $AB = 8$, $AC = 11$, $BC = 13$. What are the radii of each circle?

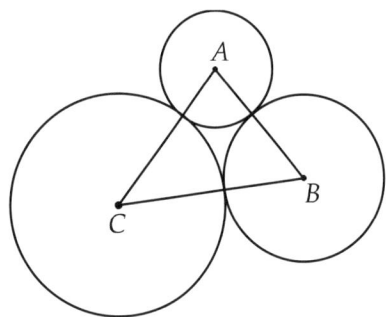

EXAMPLE 4. * Three tangent circles are inscribed in a square as shown. If the radii of all the circles are 5 cm, what is the length of side of the square?

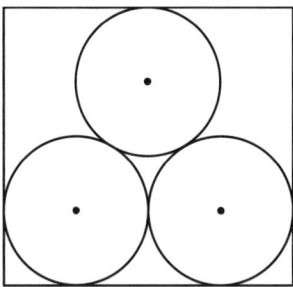

EXAMPLE 5. * Three tangent circles are inscribed in an equilateral triangle. If the radii of all the circles are 5 cm, what is the length of one side of the equilateral triangle?

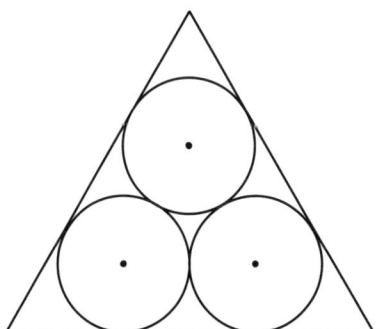

EXAMPLE 6. * Two circles and a common external tangent line l is given as shown. If $AB = 2$, $CD = 4$, and $EF = 8$, then what are the radii of each circle?

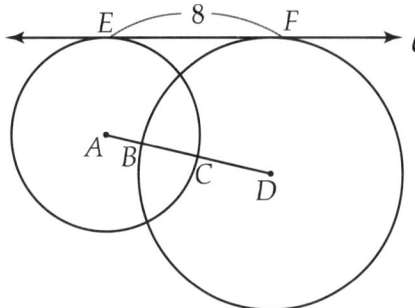

EXAMPLE 7. * Two tangent circles are given as shown. If the radii of the circles are 1cm and 2cm, respectively, what is DO?

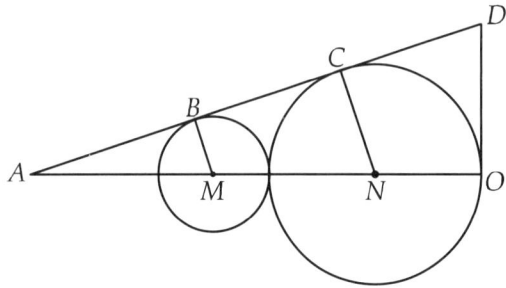

Mia's Geometry

9.4 Chords and Arcs

1. Basic Theorems about Circle and Arc

※ Radius Congruence Property

All radii are ≅ in ⊙.

All radii of a circle are congruent.

ex) In ⊙O, $\overline{OA} \cong \overline{OB} \cong \overline{OC}$.

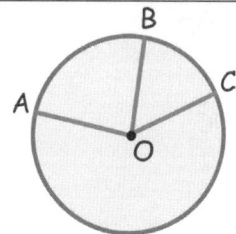

※ Arc Addition Postulate

Arc Addition Postulate

The measure of an arc formed by two adjacent arcs is the sum of the measures of the two arcs.

ex) $m\overparen{AB} + m\overparen{BC} = m\overparen{ABC}$.

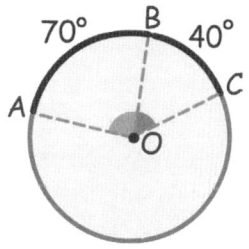

※ Congruent Arcs Theorem

Congruent Arcs Theorem (≅ arcs ⇄ ≅ central ∠s)

Within a circle or in congruent circles, two arcs are congruent if and only if their central angles are congruent.

ex) If ∠1 ≅ ∠2, then $\overparen{AB} \cong \overparen{CD}$.

If $\overparen{AB} \cong \overparen{CD}$, then ∠1 ≅ ∠2.

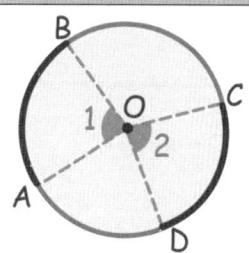

Part 9_Circles 341

EXAMPLE 1. Find the following.

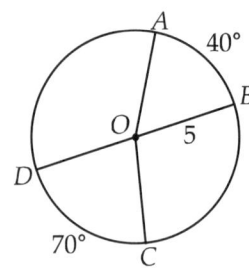

① OA ② BD

③ $m\widehat{AB}$ ④ $m\widehat{BC}$

⑤ $m\angle AOD$ ⑥ $m\angle COD$

⑦ $m\widehat{ADC}$ ⑧ $m\widehat{ABC}$

⑨ $m\widehat{BDA}$ ⑩ $m\widehat{DBC}$

EXAMPLE 2. True or False?

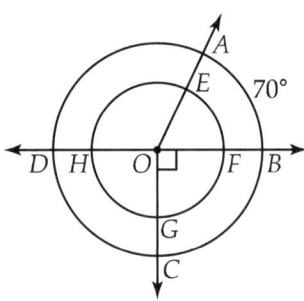

① $m\widehat{EF} = 90°$ ② $\widehat{ABC} \cong \widehat{EFG}$

③ $m\angle AOD = 110°$ ④ $m\widehat{AB} = m\widehat{EF}$

⑤ $\widehat{AB} \cong \widehat{EF}$ ⑥ $m\widehat{EH} = 110°$

⑦ $m\widehat{AD} = m\widehat{EH}$ ⑧ $\widehat{BC} \cong \widehat{DC}$

⑨ $\widehat{FG} \cong \widehat{HG}$ ⑩ $m\angle BOC = 90°$

2. Chord and Arc Congruence Theorem

※ Chord and Arc Congruence Theorem

Chord and Arc Congruence Theorem ($\cong$ arcs $\rightleftarrows$ $\cong$ chords)

Within a circle or in congruent circles, two chords are congruent if and only if their corresponding arcs are congruent."

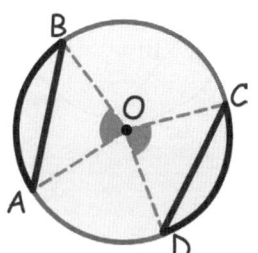

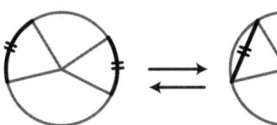

ex) If $\widehat{AB} \cong \widehat{CD}$ then $\overline{AB} \cong \overline{CD}$.

If $\overline{AB} \cong \overline{CD}$ then $\widehat{AB} \cong \widehat{CD}$.

☺ Proof :

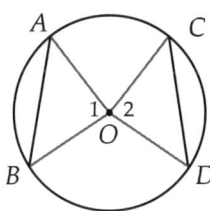

Given: $\widehat{AB} \cong \widehat{CD}$

Prove: $\overline{AB} \cong \overline{CD}$

Statements	Reasons
1. $\widehat{AB} \cong \widehat{CD}$	1. Given
2. $\angle 1 \cong \angle 2$	2. $\cong$ arcs $\rightarrow$ $\cong$ central $\angle$s
3. $\overline{AO} \cong \overline{CO}, \overline{BO} \cong \overline{DO}$	3. ① _____
4. $\triangle OAB \cong \triangle OCD$	4. SAS postulate
5. $\overline{AB} \cong \overline{CD}$	5. CPCTC

Blank : ① All radii are $\cong$ in ⊙

EXAMPLE 3. Find the value of the variable(s) in each figure. The figures are not drawn to scale.

①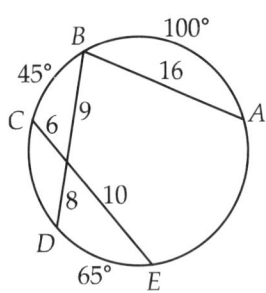

$m\widehat{CD} =$ _____

$m\widehat{AE} =$ _____

②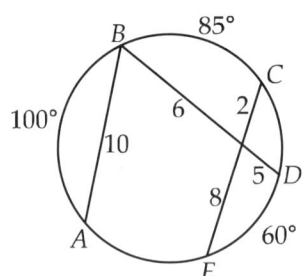

$m\widehat{CD} =$ _____

$m\widehat{AE} =$ _____

③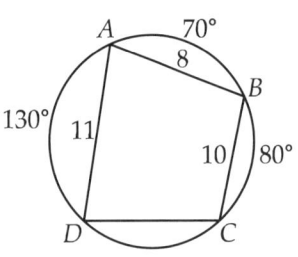

$m\widehat{CD} =$ _____

$CD =$ _____

④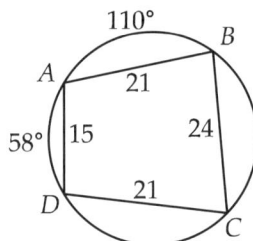

$m\widehat{BC} =$ _____

⑤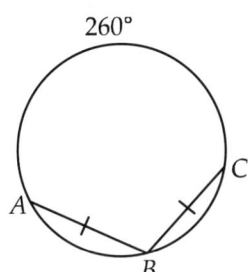

⑥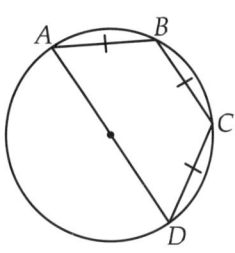

$m\widehat{AB} =$ _____

$m\widehat{AB} =$ _____

EXAMPLE 4.   * Write a two column proof.

> ☺ Tip: Use the reason;
> All radii are ≅ in ⊙
> Arc Addition Postulate
> ≅ arcs ⇄ ≅ chords

① *Given: $\overline{AB} \parallel \overline{DC}$

  Prove: $ABCD$ is parallelogram

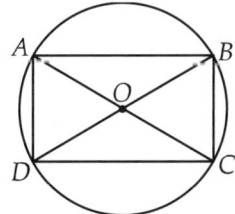

② *Given: Circle O

  Prove: $\angle 1 \cong \angle 4$

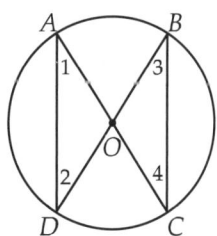

Statements	Reasons

Statements	Reasons

③ *Given: $\angle B \cong \angle C$

Prove: $\overset{\frown}{AB} \cong \overset{\frown}{AC}$

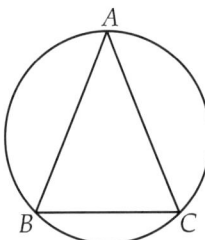

Statements	Reasons

④ *Given: $\overset{\frown}{AB} \cong \overset{\frown}{AC}$

Prove: $\angle B \cong \angle C$

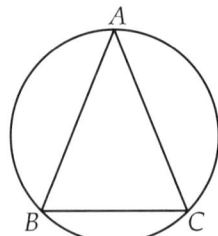

Statements	Reasons

⑤ *Given: $m\overset{\frown}{AC} = m\overset{\frown}{BD}$

Prove: $m\overset{\frown}{AB} = m\overset{\frown}{CD}$

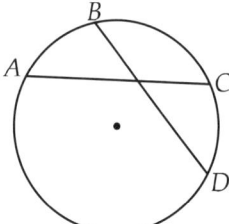

Statements	Reasons

⑥ *Given: $m\overset{\frown}{AB} = m\overset{\frown}{CD}$

Prove: $m\overset{\frown}{AC} = m\overset{\frown}{BD}$

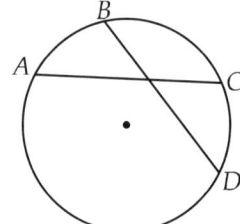

Statements	Reasons

3. Perpendicular Diameter Theorem

※ Perpendicular Diameter Theorem

Perpendicular Diameter Theorem (⊥ to chord → bisect the chord)

If a diameter of a circle is perpendicular to a chord, then the diameter bisects the chord.

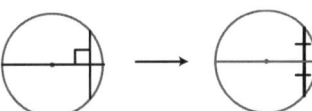

ex) If $\overline{AB} \perp \overline{CD}$ then $\overline{CE} \cong \overline{DE}$.

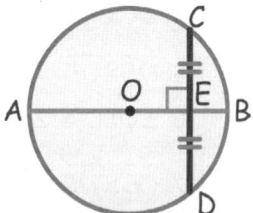

Converse of Perpendicular Diameter Theorem (bisect the chord → ⊥ to chord)

If a diameter bisects a chord, then the diameter is perpendicular to the chord.

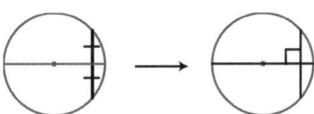

ex) If $\overline{CE} \cong \overline{DE}$ then $\overline{AB} \perp \overline{CD}$.

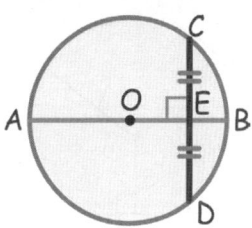

☺ Proof :

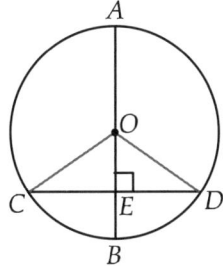

Given: $\overline{AB} \perp \overline{CD}$

Prove: $\overline{CE} \cong \overline{DE}$

Statements	Reasons
1. $\overline{AB} \perp \overline{CD}$	1. Given
2. $\angle OEC$, $\angle OED$ are right $\angle$s	2. Definition of $\perp$ lines
3. $\triangle OEC$, $\triangle OED$ are right $\triangle$s	3. Definition of right $\triangle$s
4. $\overline{OC} \cong \overline{OD}$	4. ①_____
5. $\overline{OE} \cong \overline{OE}$	5. Reflexive property
6. $\triangle OEC \cong \triangle OED$	6. ②_____
7. $\overline{CE} \cong \overline{DE}$	7. CPCTC

EXAMPLE 5. Find the value of the variable(s) in each figure.

①
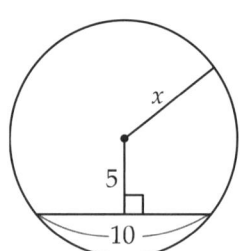

②
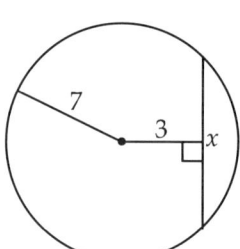

③
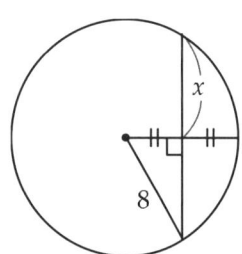

④
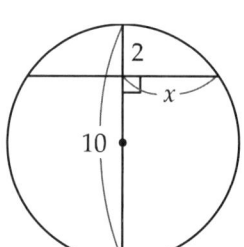

Blank : ① All radii are $\cong$ in $\odot$ ② HL thm.

⑤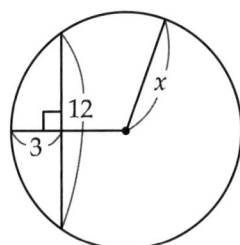

⑥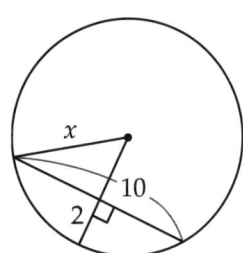

⑦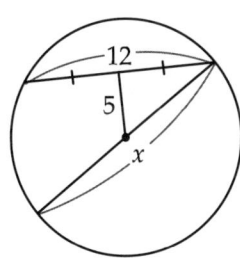

⑧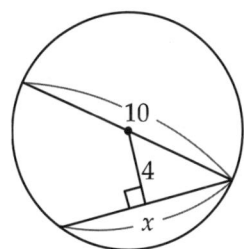

⑨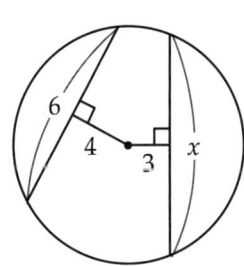

⑩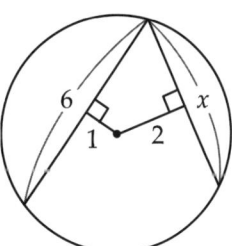

⑪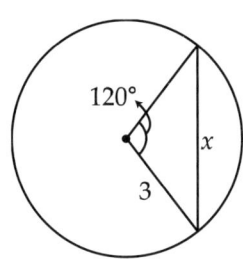

⑫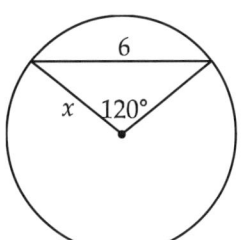

EXAMPLE 6. $AB = 16$cm, $CD = 30$cm and the radius of the circle is 17cm. Find the distance between the parallel chords.

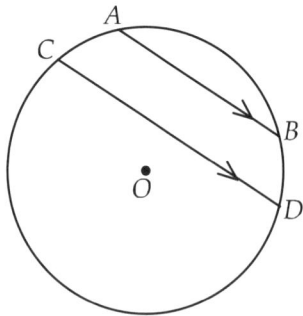

EXAMPLE 7. Two concentric circles with radii 17 cm and 10cm are given. If $CD = 12$cm, then what is AB?

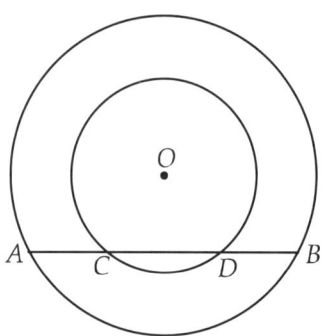

EXAMPLE 8. Two circles pass through each other's centers as shown. If the radius of one circle is 4 cm, then what is the length of chord AB?

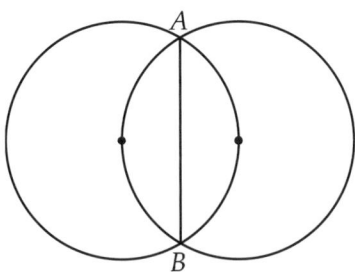

4. Equidistant Chord Theorem

※ Equidistant Chord Theorem

Equidistant Chord Theorem (Equidistant from center $\rightleftarrows$ $\cong$ chords)

Within a circle or in congruent circles, two chords are equidistant from the center if and only if they are congruent.

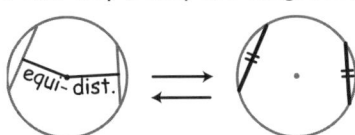

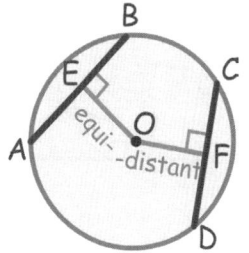

ex) If $\overline{OE} \cong \overline{OF}$ then $\overline{AB} \cong \overline{CD}$.

If $\overline{AB} \cong \overline{CD}$ then $\overline{OE} \cong \overline{OF}$.

☺ Proof :

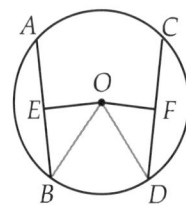

Given:

$\overline{OE} \cong \overline{OF}$, $\overline{OE} \perp \overline{AB}$, $\overline{OF} \perp \overline{CD}$

Prove: $\overline{AB} \cong \overline{CD}$

Statements	Reasons
1. $\overline{OE} \cong \overline{OF}$, $\overline{OE} \perp \overline{AB}$, $\overline{OF} \perp \overline{CD}$	1. Given
2. ∠OEB, ∠OFD are right ∠s	2. Definition of ⊥ lines
3. △OEB, △OFD are right △s	3. Definition of right △s
4. $\overline{OB} \cong \overline{OD}$	4. All radii are ≅ in ⊙
5. △OEB ≅ △OFD	5. HL Theorem
6. $\overline{EB} \cong \overline{FD}$, EB = FD	6. CPCTC
7. 2EB = 2FD	7. Multiplication property
8. 2EB = AB, 2FD = CD	8. ⊥ to chord → bisect the chord
9. AB = CD, $\overline{AB} \cong \overline{CD}$	9. Substitution property

EXAMPLE 9. Find the value of the variable(s) in each figure.

①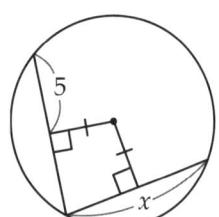

②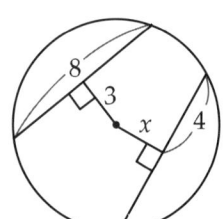

③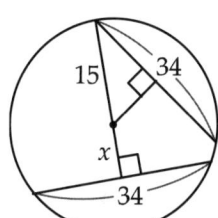

④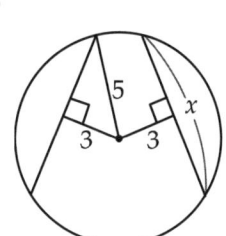

EXAMPLE 10. * Write a two column proof.

☺ Tip: Use the reason;
⊥ to chord ⇄ bisect the chord
Equidistant from center ⇄ ≅ chords

① Given: $\overline{AD} \perp \overline{BC}$
   Prove: $\overline{AD}$ bisect ∠BAC

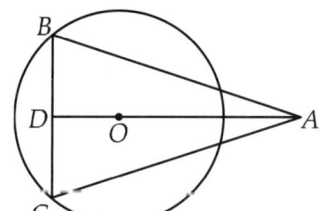

Statements	Reasons

② Given: $\overline{AO} \perp \overline{BC}$
   Prove: ∠B ≅ ∠C

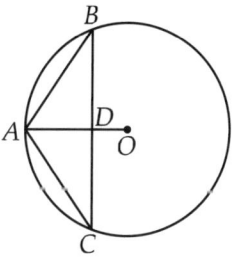

Statements	Reasons

Part 9_Circles 353

③ Given: $\overline{OD} \cong \overline{OE}$
$\overline{OD} \perp \overline{AB}, \overline{OE} \perp \overline{AC}$

Prove: $\angle B \cong \angle C$

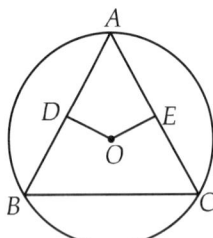

Statements	Reasons

④ Given: $\angle A \cong \angle B$
$\overline{OD} \perp \overline{AC}, \overline{OE} \perp \overline{BC}$

Prove: $\overline{OD} \cong \overline{OE}$

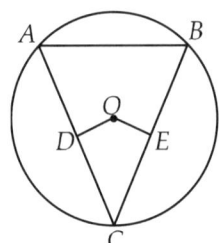

Statements	Reasons

Mia's Geometry
9.5 Inscribed Angles

1. Inscribed Angles

Inscribed Angle is an angle where the vertex is on the circle and the sides are chords of the circle.

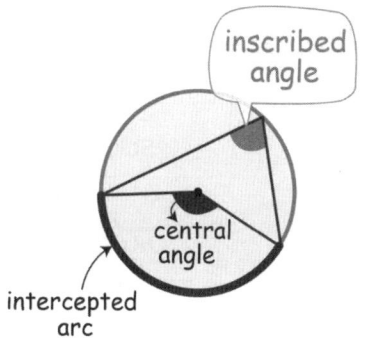

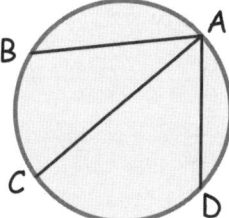

We say;

Inscribed $\angle BAC$ intercepts $\overset{\frown}{BC}$.

Inscribed $\angle BAD$ intercepts $\overset{\frown}{BCD}$.

※ Inscribed angle Theorem

Inscribed angle Theorem

An inscribed angle is half of the measure of intercepted arc (central angle).

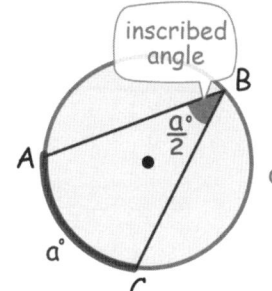 or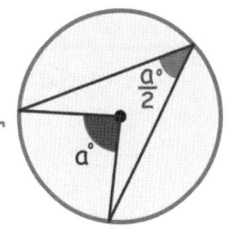

ex) $m\angle ABC = $ ①_____ or

$2m\angle ABC = $ ②_____

Blank : ① $\frac{1}{2} = m\overset{\frown}{AC}$ ② $m\overset{\frown}{AC}$

☺ Proof :

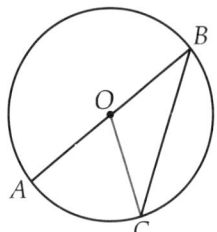

Given: ∠ABC is an inscribed angle

Prove: $m\angle B = \frac{1}{2}m\widehat{AC}$

Statements	Reasons
1. ∠ABC is an inscribed angle	1. Given
2. $\overline{OB} \cong \overline{OC}$	2. All radii are ≅ in ⊙
3. ∠B ≅ ∠C, m∠B = m∠C	3. ① _____
4. m∠B + m∠C = m∠AOC	4. ② _____
5. 2m∠B = m∠AOC	5. Substitution Property
6. $m\angle B = \frac{1}{2}m\angle AOC$	6. Division Property
7. $m\angle B = \frac{1}{2}m\widehat{AC}$	7. Definition of $m\widehat{AC}$

Blank : ① Isosceles △ thm.   ② Exterior ∠ thm.

EXAMPLE 1. Find the value of the variable(s) in each figure. The figures are not drawn to scale.

①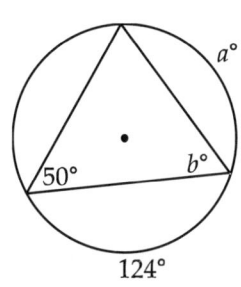

②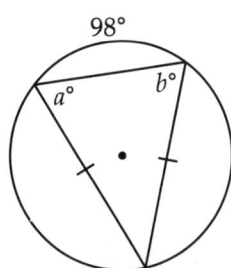

③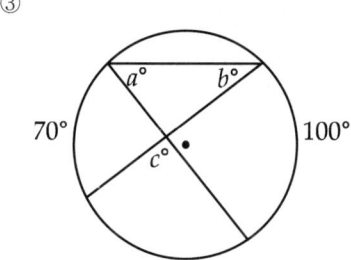

④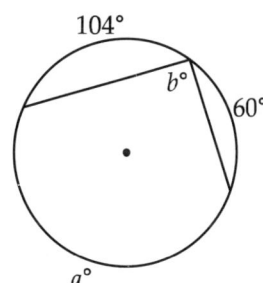

⑤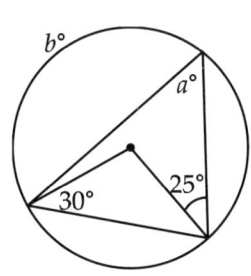

⑥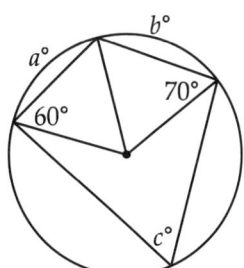

※ Facts about Inscribed Angle (1)

An angle inscribed in a semicircle is always

① _____

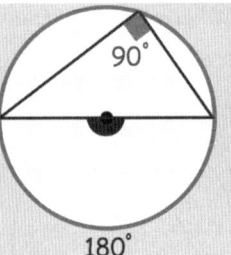

EXAMPLE 2. Find the value of the variable(s) in each figure. The figures are not drawn to scale.

①
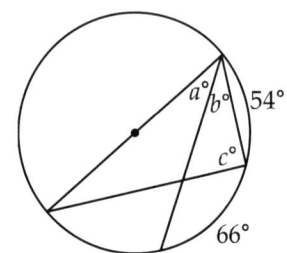

②
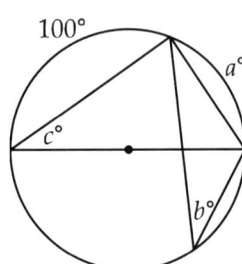

③
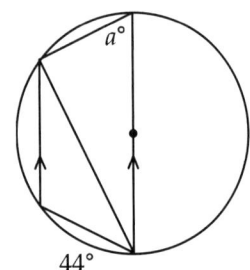

④
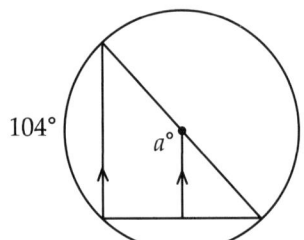

Blank : ① 90°

※ Facts about Inscribed Angle (2)

Two inscribed angles that intercept the same arc are ① _____.

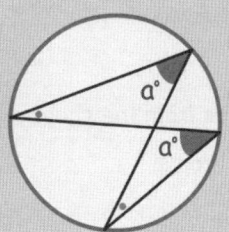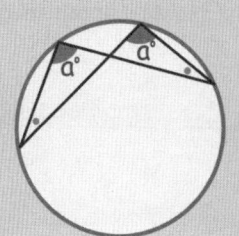

EXAMPLE 3. Find the value of the variable(s) in each figure. The figures are not drawn to scale.

①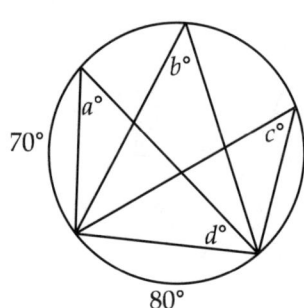

②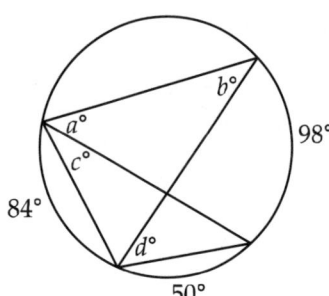

③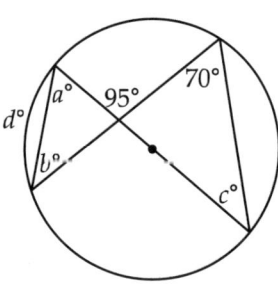

④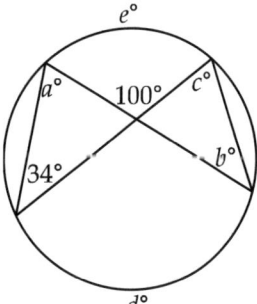

⑤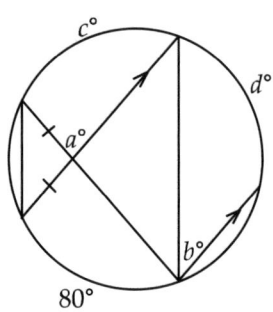

⑥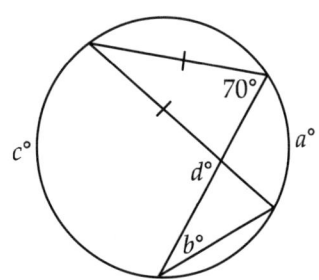

Blank : ① congruent

※ Facts about Inscribed Angle (3)

Inscribed angles from the congruent arc or chord are always ① _____.

EXAMPLE 4. Find the value of the variable(s) in each figure. The figures are not drawn to scale.

①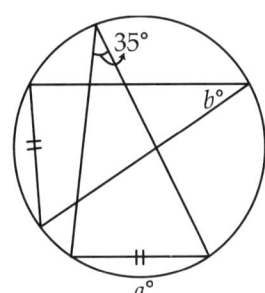

②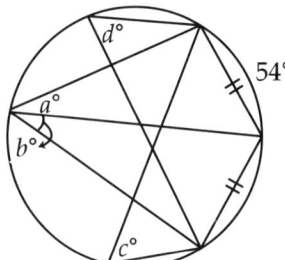

③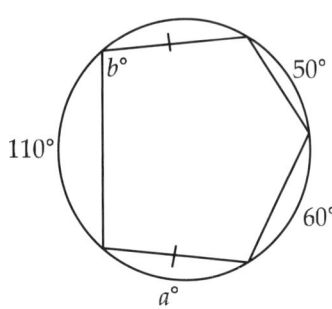

④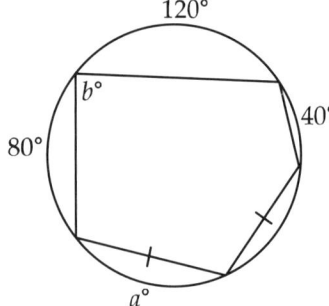

⑤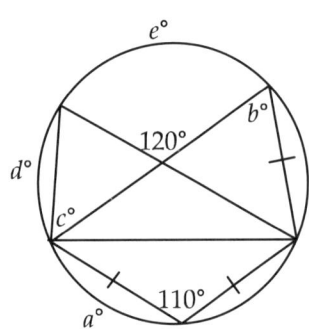

⑥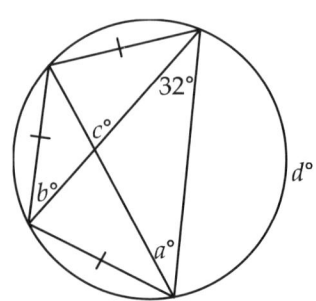

Blank : ① congruent

※ Facts about Inscribed Angle (4)

If a quadrilateral is inscribed in a circle,
then its opposite angles are ① _____.

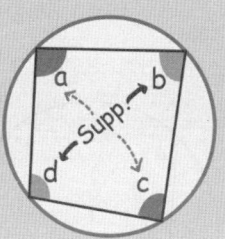

☺ Proof:

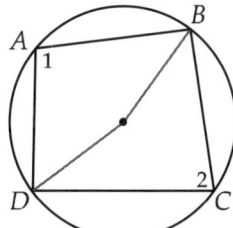

$m\widehat{DAB} + m\widehat{BCD} =$ ② _____

$m\widehat{DAB} = 2m\angle 2$, $m\widehat{BCD} =$ ③ _____ (inscribed ∠ thm)

$2m\angle 2 + 2m\angle 1 =$ ④ _____ (substitution prop)

$m\angle 2 + m\angle 1 =$ ⑤ _____ (division prop.)

∠1 and ∠2 are supplementary

※ Facts about Inscribed Angle (5)

The exterior angle of a quadrilateral inscribed in a circle
is equal to the interior opposite angle.

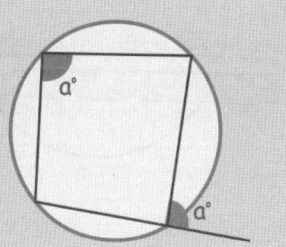

☺ Proof:

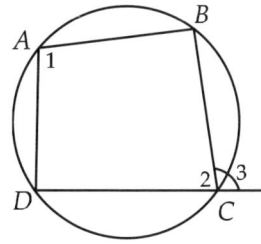

∠1 and ∠2 are supplementary

∠2 and ∠3 are supplementary (linear pair post.)

∠1 ≅ ∠3   (≅ suppl. thm)

Blank : ① supplementary   ② 360°   ③ 2m∠1   ④ 360°   ⑤ 180°

EXAMPLE 5. Find the value of the variable(s) in each figure. The figures are not drawn to scale.

①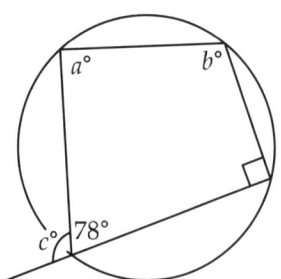

②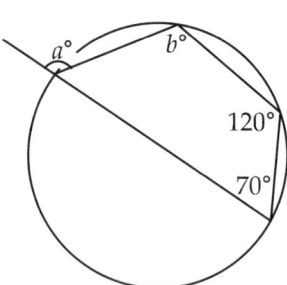

③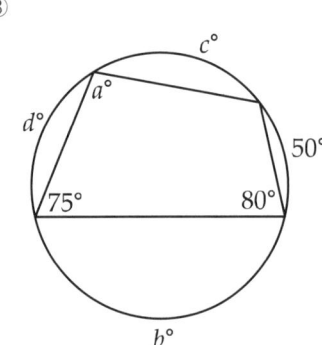

④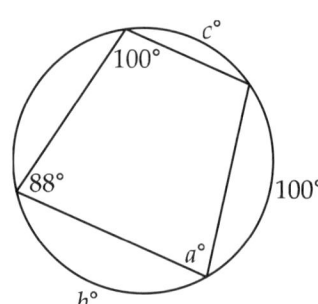

⑤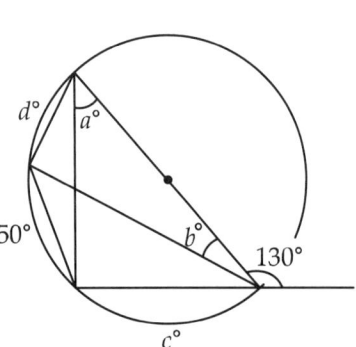

⑥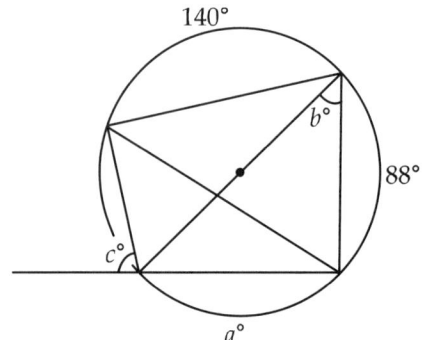

⑦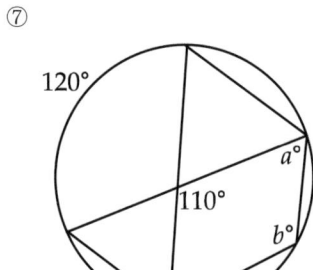

⑧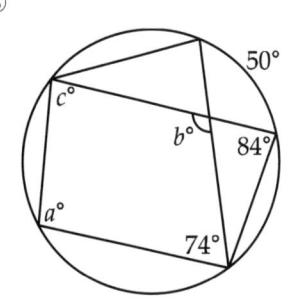

⑨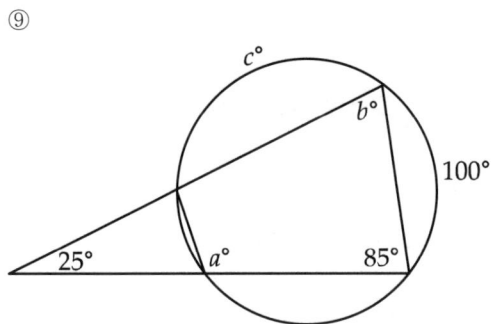

⑩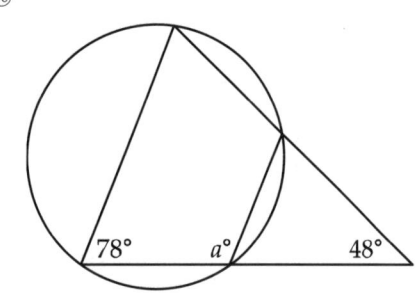

※ Facts about Inscribed Angle (6)

If $m\angle ABC = a°$, then

$m\widehat{ADC}$ = ①_____

$m\widehat{ABC}$ = ②_____

$m\angle AOC$ = ③_____

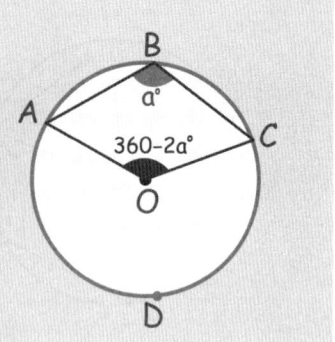

EXAMPLE 6. Find the value of the variable(s) in each figure. The figures are not drawn to scale.

①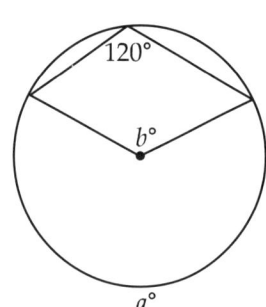

②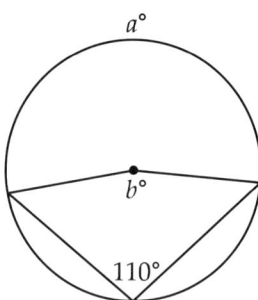

③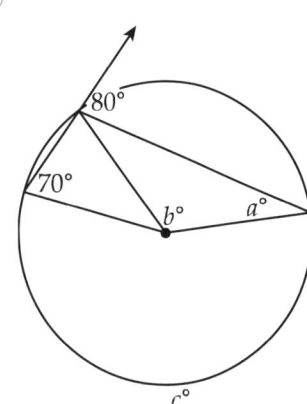

④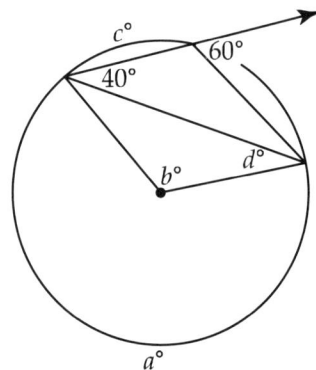

Blank : ① $2a°$ ② $(360 - 2a)°$ ③ $(360 - 2a)°$

364 Mia's Geometry

EXAMPLE 7. If $m\widehat{AB}:m\widehat{BC}:m\widehat{CD}:m\widehat{DE}:m\widehat{EA}=1:2:3:4:5$, what is $m\angle AED$?

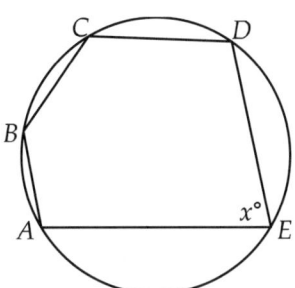

EXAMPLE 8. * For the given figure, $\overline{AE}$ is the diameter of the circle. What is $x+y+z$?

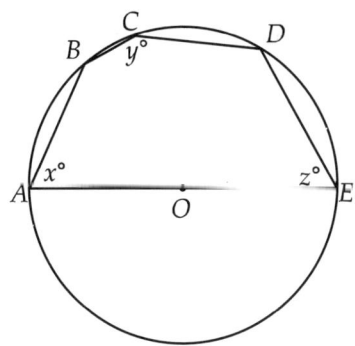

2. Tangent Chord Theorem

An inscribed angle $\angle ABC$ is shown.

If we move $\overline{BC}$ as shown;

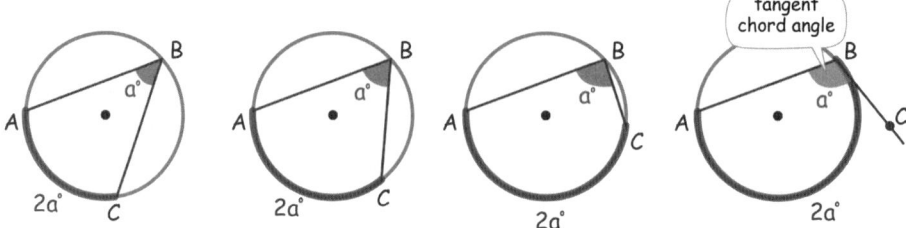

then $\overline{BC}$ will finally become a tangent and we have an angle formed by tangent and chord.

※ Tangent Chord Theorem

Tangent Chord Theorem

The measure of an angle formed by a chord and a tangent is equal to half the measure of the intercepted arc.

ex) $m\angle BAD = \dfrac{1}{2}m\widehat{AB}$ or $2m\angle BAD = $ ① _____

The angle formed by a chord and a tangent is congruent to the angle opposite the chord.

ex) $m\angle BAD = m\angle BCA$

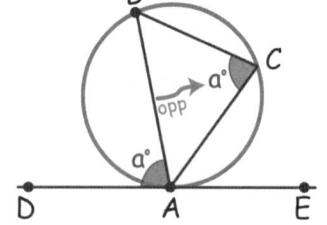

Blank : ① $m\widehat{AB}$

☺ Memorizing Tip:

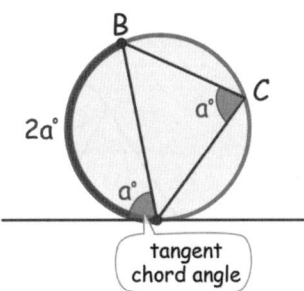

tangent chord angle

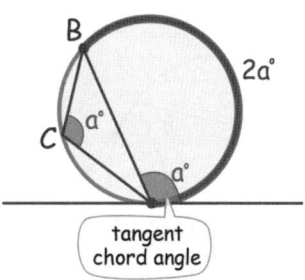

tangent chord angle

EXAMPLE 9. Find the value of the variable(s) in each figure. The figures are not drawn to scale.

①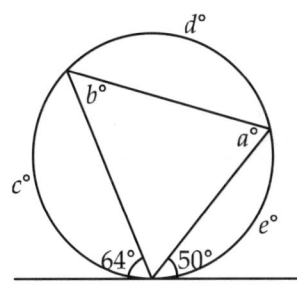

②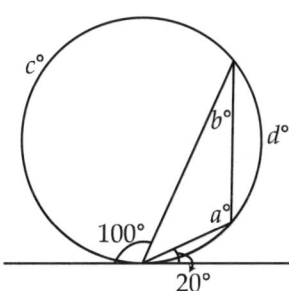

③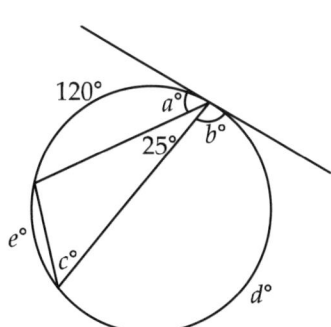

④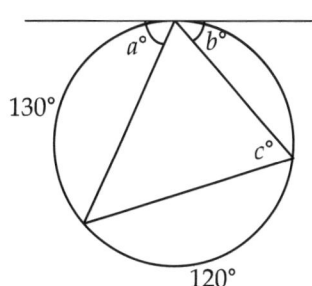

Part 9_Circles 367

⑤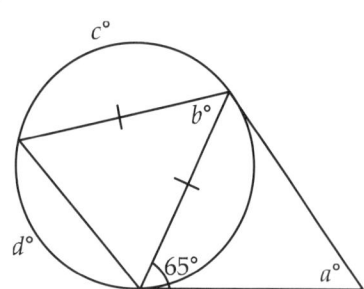

⑥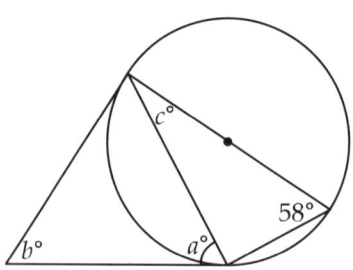

⑦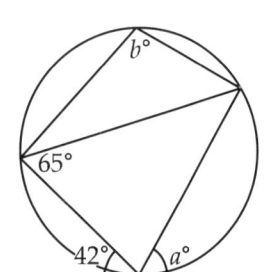

⑧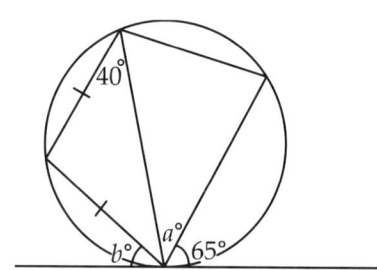

⑨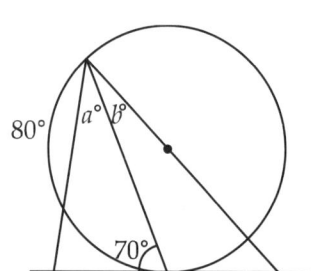

⑩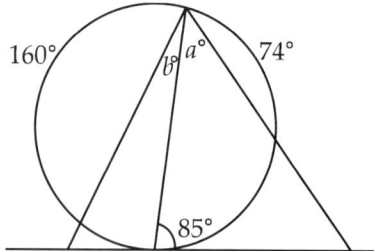

⑪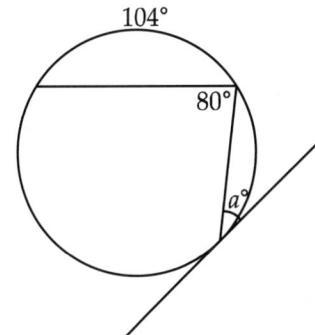

⑫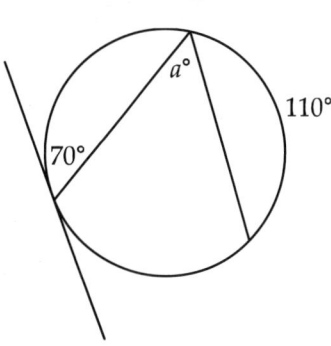

⑬ *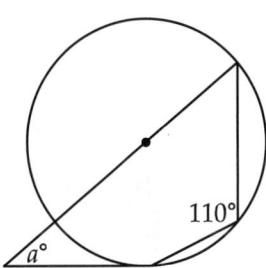

⑭ *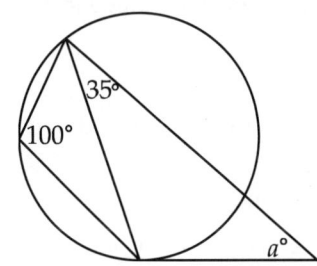

⑮ *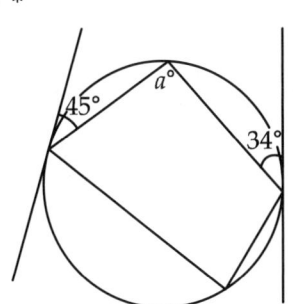

3. When there are Two Circles

※ Facts about Quadrilateral inscribed in Two intersecting Circles

Fact 1) $m\angle 1 = m\angle 2 = m\angle 3$

Fact 2) $\overline{AB} \parallel \overline{EF}$

    since $\angle 1 \cong \angle 3$ (Alt. int. $\angle$s)

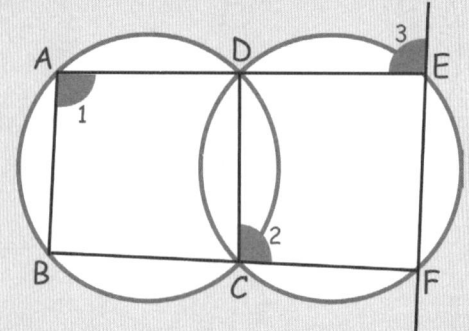

※ Facts about Triangle inscribed in Two Tangent Circles

Fact 1) $m\angle 1 = m\angle 2 = m\angle 3 = m\angle 4$

Fact 2) $\overline{AB} \parallel \overline{CD}$

    since $\angle 1 \cong \angle 4$ (Alt. int. $\angle$s)

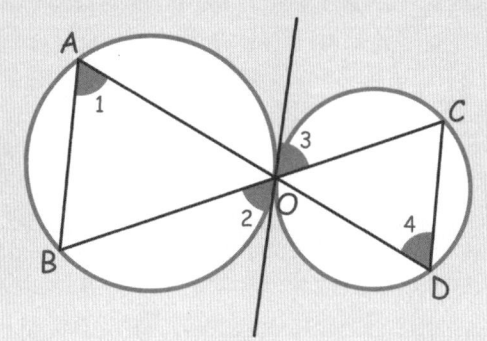

※ Facts about Triangle inscribed in Two Tangent Circles

Fact 1) $m\angle 1 = m\angle 2 = m\angle 3$

Fact 2) $\overline{AB} \parallel \overline{CD}$

    since $\angle 1 \cong \angle 2$ (Corresp. $\angle$s)

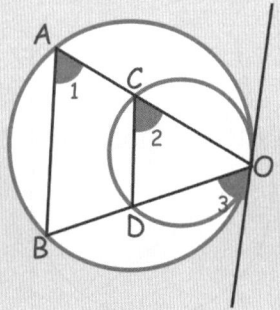

EXAMPLE 10. Find the value of the variable(s) in each figure. The figures are not drawn to scale.

①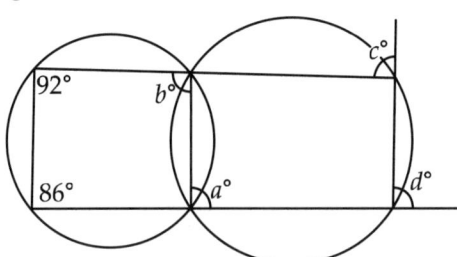

②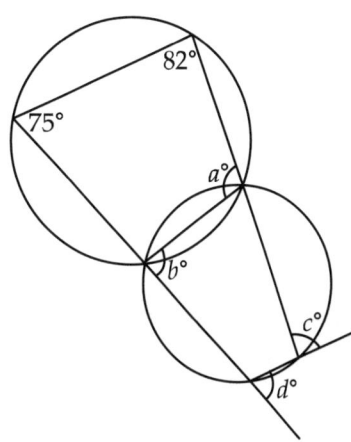

③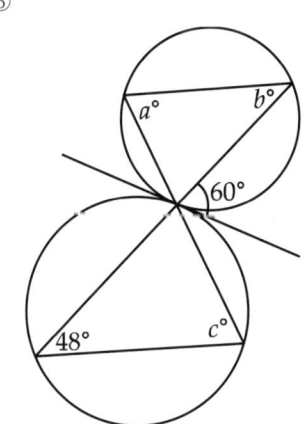

④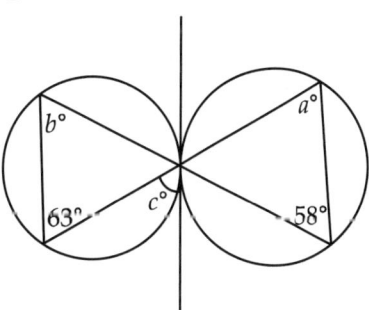

Part 9_Circles 371

⑤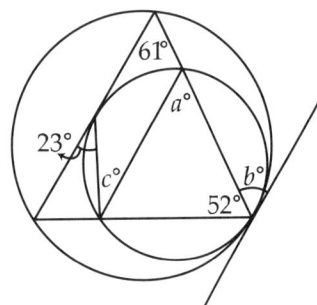

⑥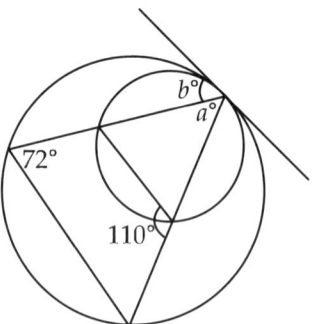

EXAMPLE 11. What is x?

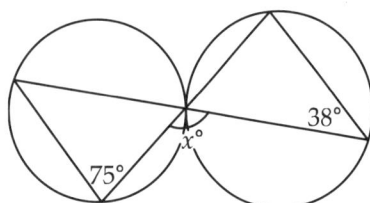

Mia's Geometry
9.6 Secants, Tangents, and Angle Measure

1. Intersection Inside a Circle

In this chapter, we will explore how to determine the measure of angle formed when drawing secants or tangents to a circle.

※ Intersecting chords Angle Measure Theorem

Intersecting chords Angle Measure Theorem

If two secants intersect inside a circle, the measure of the angle formed is half the sum of the measures of the arcs intercepted by the angle and its vertical angle.

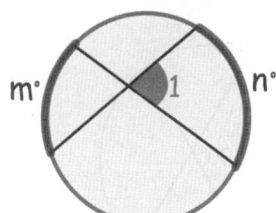

$m\angle 1 = \dfrac{1}{2}(m° + n°)$

☺ Proof :

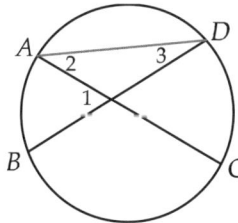

Given: Chord $\overline{AC}$ and $\overline{BD}$ intersect inside the circle

Prove: $m\angle 1 = \dfrac{1}{2}(m\widehat{AB} + m\widehat{CD})$

Statements	Reasons
1. Chord $\overline{AC}$ and $\overline{CD}$ intersect inside the circle	1. Given
2. $m\angle 1 = m\angle 2 + m\angle 3$	2. ① _____
3. $m\angle 2 = \dfrac{1}{2}m\widehat{CD}$, $m\angle 3 = \dfrac{1}{2}m\widehat{AB}$	3. ② _____
4. $m\angle 1 = \dfrac{1}{2}m\widehat{AB} + \dfrac{1}{2}m\widehat{CD}$	4. Substitution Property
5. $m\angle 1 = \dfrac{1}{2}(m\widehat{AB} + m\widehat{CD})$	5. Distribution Property

Blank : ① Exterior ∠ thm.   ② Inscribed ∠ thm

EXAMPLE 1. Find the value of the variable(s) in each figure. The figures are not drawn to scale.

①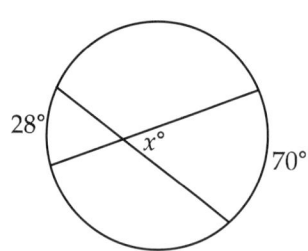

②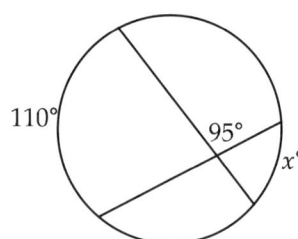

③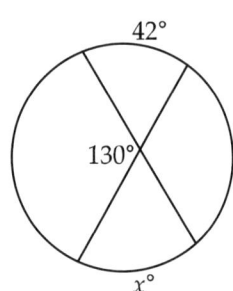

④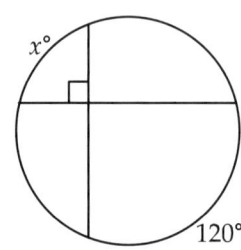

⑤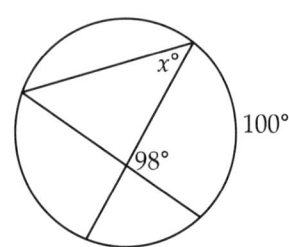

⑥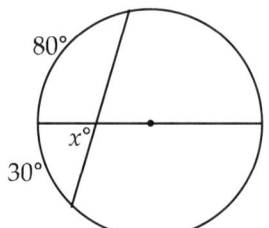

2. Intersection Outside a Circle

※ Angle Formed by Secants and Tangents Theorem

Angle Formed by Secants and Tangents Theorem

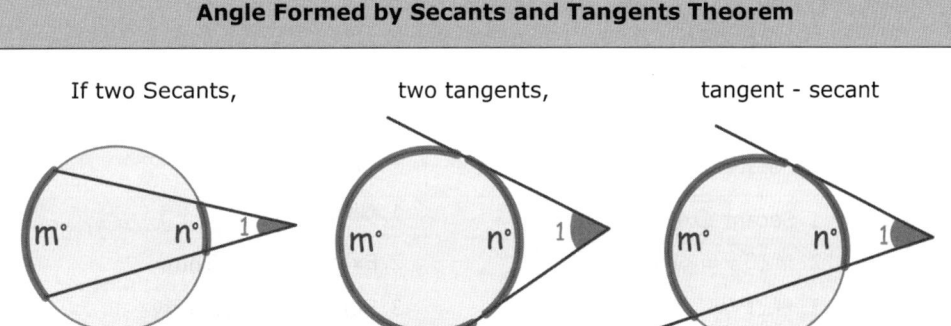

If two Secants, two tangents, tangent - secant intersect outside a circle, then the measure of the angle formed is one-half the positive difference of the measures of the intercepted arcs.

$$m\angle 1 = \frac{1}{2}(m° - n°)$$

☺ Memorizing Tip:

Measure of the angle = $\frac{1}{2}$ (Measure of larger arc − measure of smaller arc)

☺ Proof :

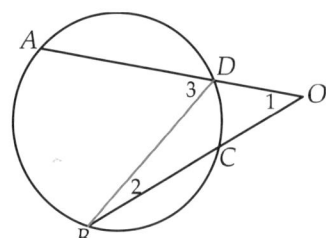

Given: Secant $\overline{OA}$ and $\overline{OB}$

Prove: $m\angle 1 = \frac{1}{2}(m\widehat{AB} - m\widehat{CD})$

Statements	Reasons
1. Secant $\overline{OA}$ and $\overline{OB}$	1. Given
2. $m\angle 3 = m\angle 1 + m\angle 2$	2. Exterior Angle Thm.
3. $m\angle 1 = m\angle 3 - m\angle 2$	3. Subtraction Property
4. $m\angle 2 = \frac{1}{2}m\widehat{CD}, m\angle 3 = \frac{1}{2}m\widehat{AB}$	4. ①_____
5. $m\angle 1 = \frac{1}{2}m\widehat{AB} - \frac{1}{2}m\widehat{CD}$	5. Substitution Property
6. $m\angle 1 = \frac{1}{2}(m\widehat{AB} - m\widehat{CD})$	6. Distribution Property

EXAMPLE 2. Find the value of the variable(s) in each figure. The figures are not drawn to scale.

①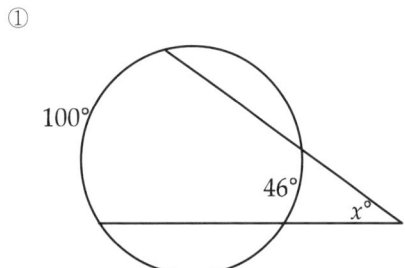

②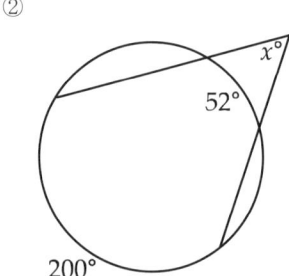

Blank : ① Inscribed ∠ thm

③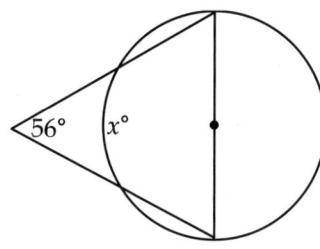

④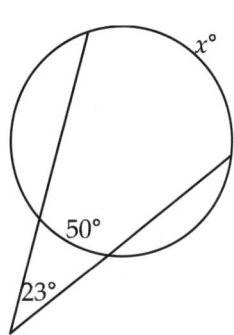

⑤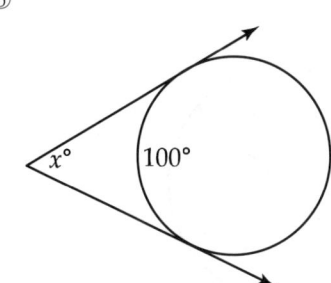

⑥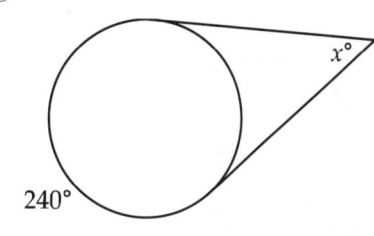

⑦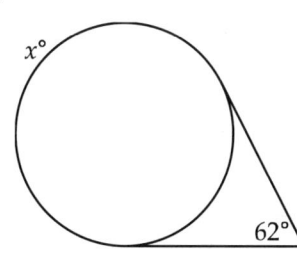

⑧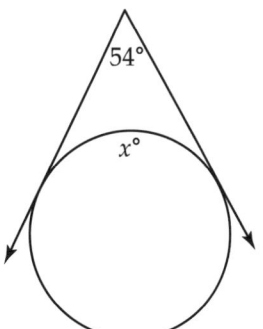

Part 9_Circles 377

⑨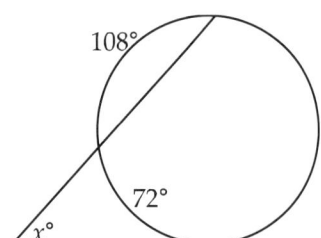

⑩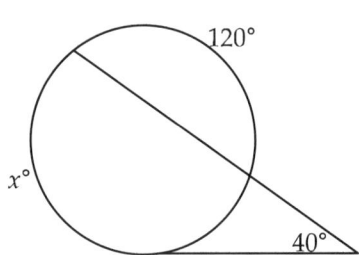

⑪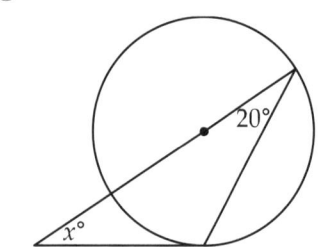

⑫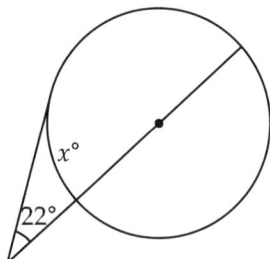

⑬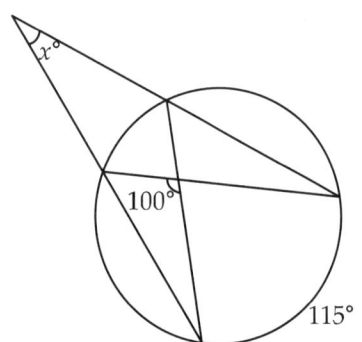

⑭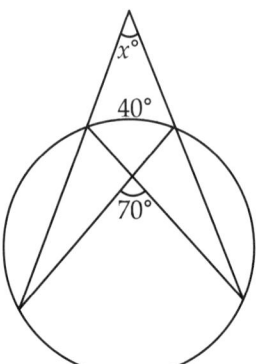

EXAMPLE 3. Two concentric circles are given as shown. Find x.

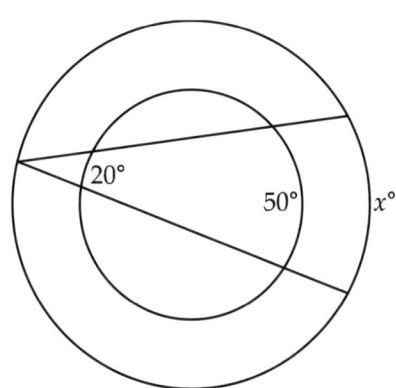

EXAMPLE 4. For the given figure, find $m\widehat{BC}$ and $m\widehat{ED}$.

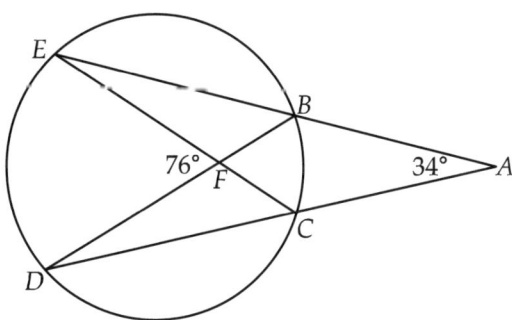

Part 9_Circles 379

EXAMPLE 5. * For the given figure, $m\widehat{ABC} = 250°$. Find $m\widehat{ADC}$.

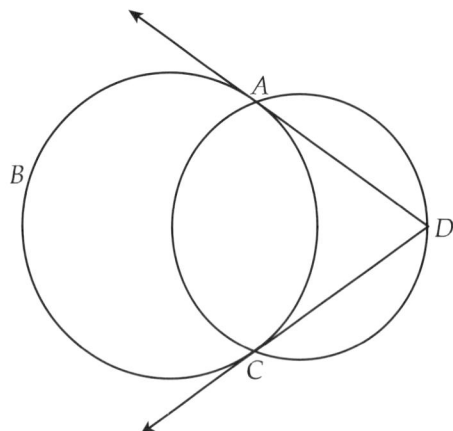

EXAMPLE 6. * For the given figure, $m\widehat{ADC} = 130°$. Find $m\angle BAC$.

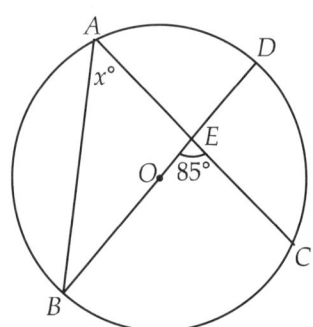

EXAMPLE 7. * For the given figure, $m\widehat{DE} = 20°$, $m\widehat{DF} = 100°$ and $m\angle ABC = 60°$. Find x and y.

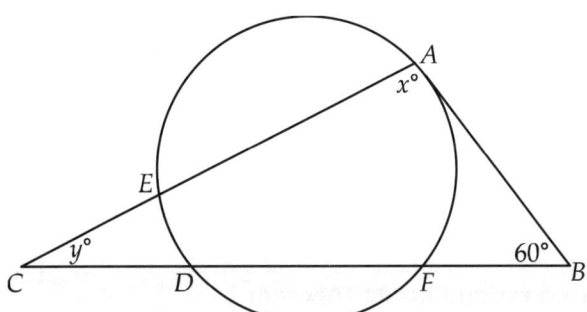

Mia's Geometry

9.7 Secants, Tangents, and Segments

1. Intersection Inside a Circle

In this chapter, we will explore how to determine the length of segment formed when drawing secants or tangents to a circle.

※ Intersecting Chords Theorem

Intersecting Chords Theorem
If two chords intersect inside a circle, then the products of the measures of the segments of the chords are equal. 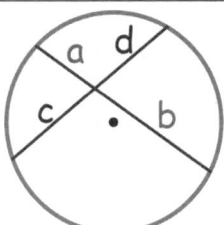 $ab = cd$

☺ Careful! It is NOT $a : b = c : d$.

☺ Proof :

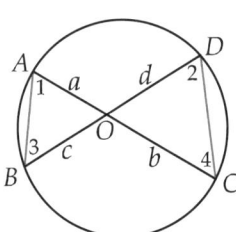

Given: $\overline{AC}$ and $\overline{BD}$ intersect at O

Prove: $ab = cd$

Statements	Reasons
1. $\overline{AC}$ and $\overline{BD}$ intersect at O	1. Given
2. $\angle 1 \cong \angle 2$, $\angle 3 \cong \angle 4$	2. Two inscribed $\angle$s that intercept the same arc are $\cong$.
3. $\triangle ABO \sim \triangle DCO$	3. ① _____
4. $\dfrac{a}{c} = \dfrac{d}{b}$	4. ② _____
5. ③ _____	5. Cross Product Property

Blank : ① AA ~ post.   ② Corresp. sides are proportional in ~ △   ③ $ab = cd$

EXAMPLE 1. Find the value of the variable(s) in each figure. The figures are not drawn to scale.

①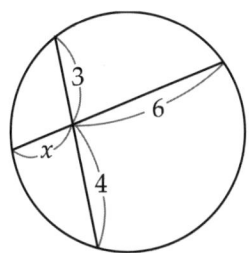

②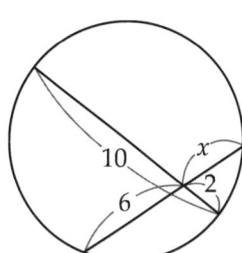

③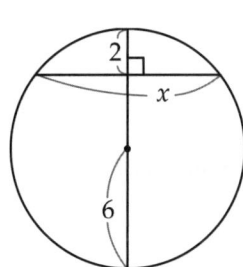

④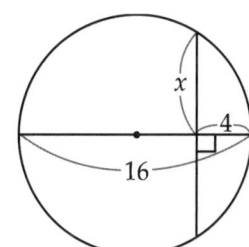

⑤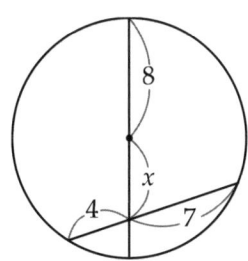

⑥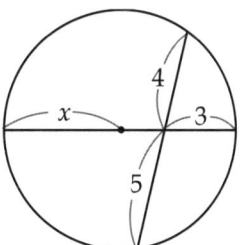

⑦ 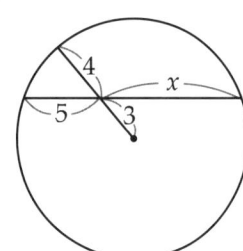   ⑧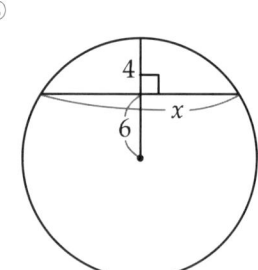

EXAMPLE 2. Two circles intersect at two points A and B as shown. What is x?

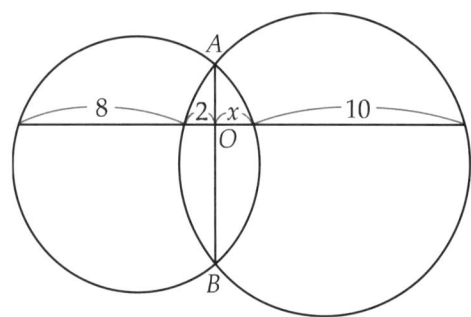

2. Intersection Outside a Circle

※ Two Secants Theorem, Tangent - Secant Theorem

Two Secants Theorem	Two tangents Theorem	Tangent - Secant Theorem
$ab = cd$	$a = c$	$a^2 = bc$

☺ Careful! It is NOT $a : b = c : d$.

☺ Proof :

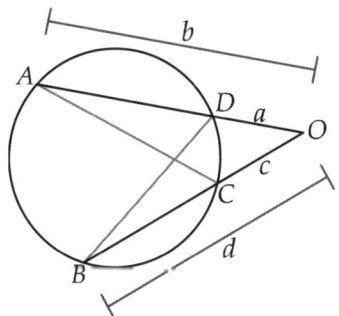

Given: $\overline{OA}$ and $\overline{OB}$ are drawn
Prove: $ab = cd$

Statements	Reasons
1. $\overline{OA}$ and $\overline{OB}$ are drawn	1. Given
2. $\angle A \cong \angle B$	2. Two inscribed $\angle$s that intercept the same arc are $\cong$.
3. $\angle O \cong \angle O$	3. Reflexive Property
4. $\triangle ACO \sim \triangle BDO$	4. ① _____
5. ② _____	5. Corres. sides are prop. in $\sim \triangle$
6. $ab = cd$	6. Cross Product Property

Blank : ① AA $\sim$ post.   ② $\dfrac{a}{d} = \dfrac{c}{b}$

☺ Proof :

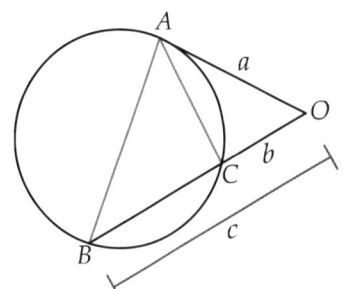

Given: $\overline{OA}$ and $\overline{OB}$ are drawn

Prove: $a^2 = bc$

Statements	Reasons
1. $\overline{OA}$ and $\overline{OB}$ are drawn	1. Given
2. $\angle O \cong \angle O$	2. Reflexive Property
3. ① _____	3. ② _____
4. $\triangle OAC \sim \triangle OBA$	4. ③ _____
5. ④ _____	5. Corres. sides are prop. in $\sim \triangle$
6. $a^2 = bc$	6. Cross Product Property

EXAMPLE 3. Find the value of the variable(s) in each figure. The figures are not drawn to scale.

①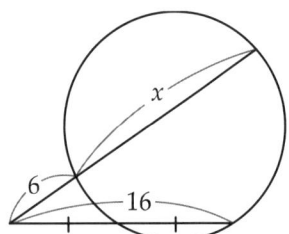

②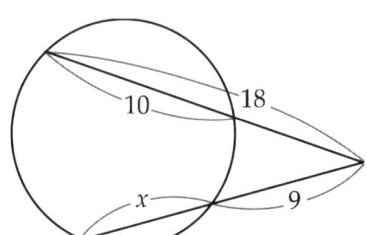

Blank : ① $\angle OAC \cong \angle OBA$ ② tangent chord thm. ③ AA $\sim$ post, ④ $\dfrac{a}{b} = \dfrac{c}{a}$

386 Mia's Geometry

③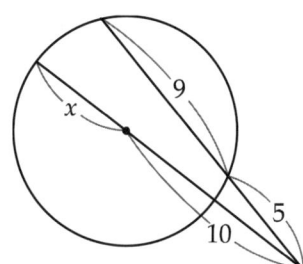

④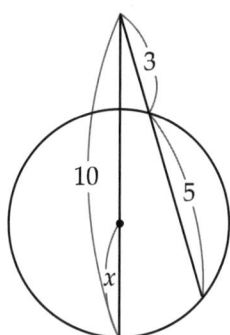

⑤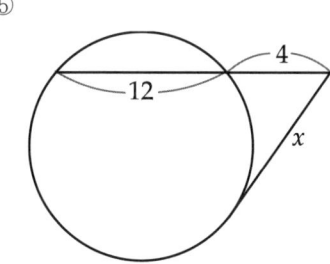

⑥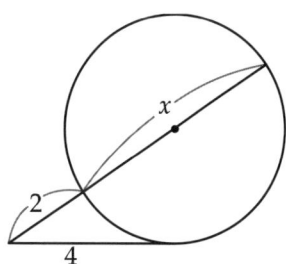

⑦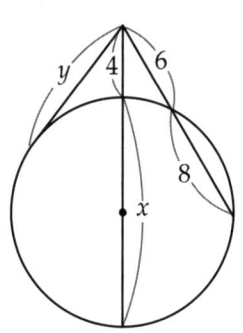

⑧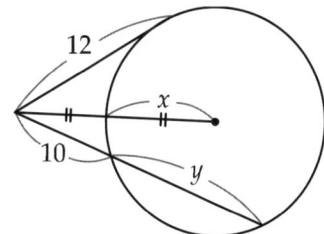

⑨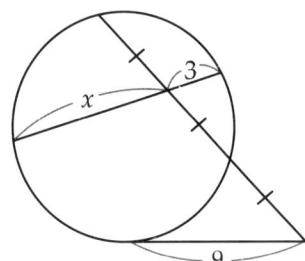

⑩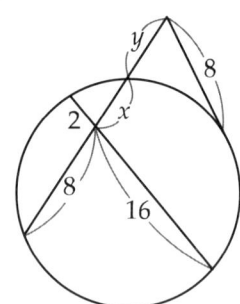

⑪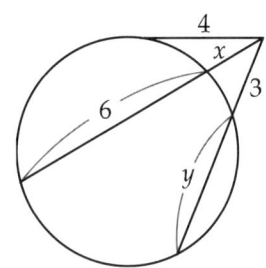

⑫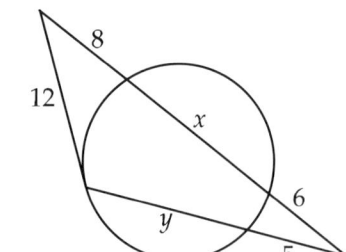

EXAMPLE 4. Two circles intersect at two points A and B as shown. What is x?

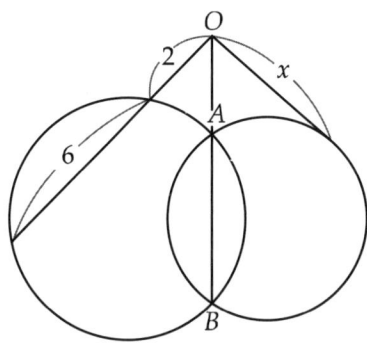

EXAMPLE 5. * Two circles are tangent at point P and $\overline{OP}$ is tangent to both circles. If $OB = 5$, $AB = 7$, $OC = 4$, $CE = 2$, and $DF = 4$, what is EF?

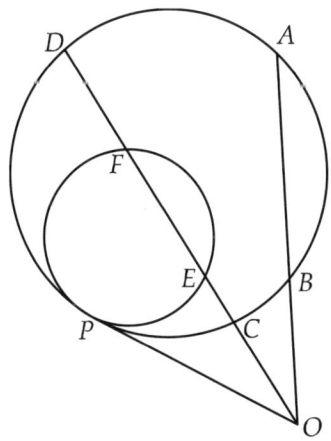

Mia's Geometry

Postulates, Theorems from CH9

All in One (sorted by Miamath)

When there is a tangent..	
Tangent radius Theorem If a line is tangent to a circle, then the line is perpendicular to the radius.	
Converse of Tangent radius Theorem If a line is perpendicular to a radius of a circle at its endpoint on the circle, then the line is a tangent to the circle.	
Two tangents Theorem The two tangents to a circle from a point outside the circle are congruent.	

When there is a circle..	
All radii are ≅ in ⊙. All radii of a circle are congruent.	
Arc Addition Postulate The measure of an arc formed by two adjacent arcs is the sum of the measures of the two arcs.	$m\widehat{AB} + m\widehat{BC} = m\widehat{ABC}$

Congruent Arcs Theorem

(≅ arcs ⇄ ≅ central ∠s)

Within a circle or in congruent circles, two arcs are congruent if and only if their central angles are congruent.

Perpendicular Diameter Theorem

(⊥ to chord → bisect the chord)

If a diameter of a circle is perpendicular to a chord, then the diameter bisects the chord.

Converse of Perpendicular Diameter Theorem

(bisect the chord → ⊥ to chord)

If a diameter bisects a chord, then the diameter is perpendicular to the chord.

Equidistant Chord Theorem

(Equidistant from center ⇄ ≅ chords)

Within a circle or in congruent circles, two chords are equidistant from the center if and only if they are congruent.

Inscribed angle Theorem

An inscribed angle is half of the measure of intercepted arc (central angle).

Tangent Chord Theorem

The measure of an angle formed by a chord and a tangent is equal to half the measure of the intercepted arc.

Theorems about circles

Fill in the blanks.

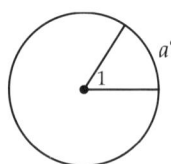   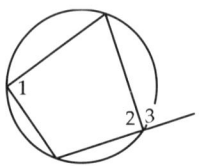

$m\angle 1 =$ ①_____ $m\angle 1 =$ ②_____ $m\angle 1 =$ ③_____ $m\angle 1 =$ ⑤_____
$m\angle 1 + m\angle 2 =$ ④_____

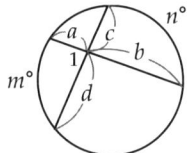   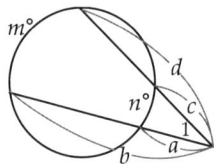   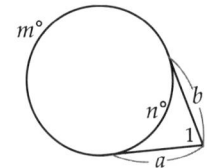   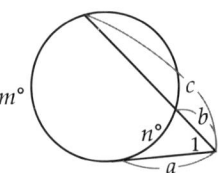

$m\angle 1 =$ ⑥_____ $m\angle 1 =$ ⑦_____ $m\angle 1 = \dfrac{1}{2}(m° - n°)$ $m\angle 1 = \dfrac{1}{2}(m° - n°)$

⑧_____   ⑨_____   ⑩_____   ⑪_____

Blank: ① a°   ② a/2°   ③ m∠3   ④ 180°   ⑤ a°   ⑥ $\dfrac{1}{2}(m° + n°)$ ⑦ $\dfrac{1}{2}(m° - n°)$

⑧ ab = cd   ⑨ ab = cd   ⑩ a = b   ⑪ a² = bc

Part 10
Areas of Plane Figures

10.1 Area of polygons

10.2 Area of regular polygons

10.3 Area of Circles and Sectors

10.4 Areas and Ratios

Mia's Geometry
10.1 Area of polygons

1. Area of Polygons

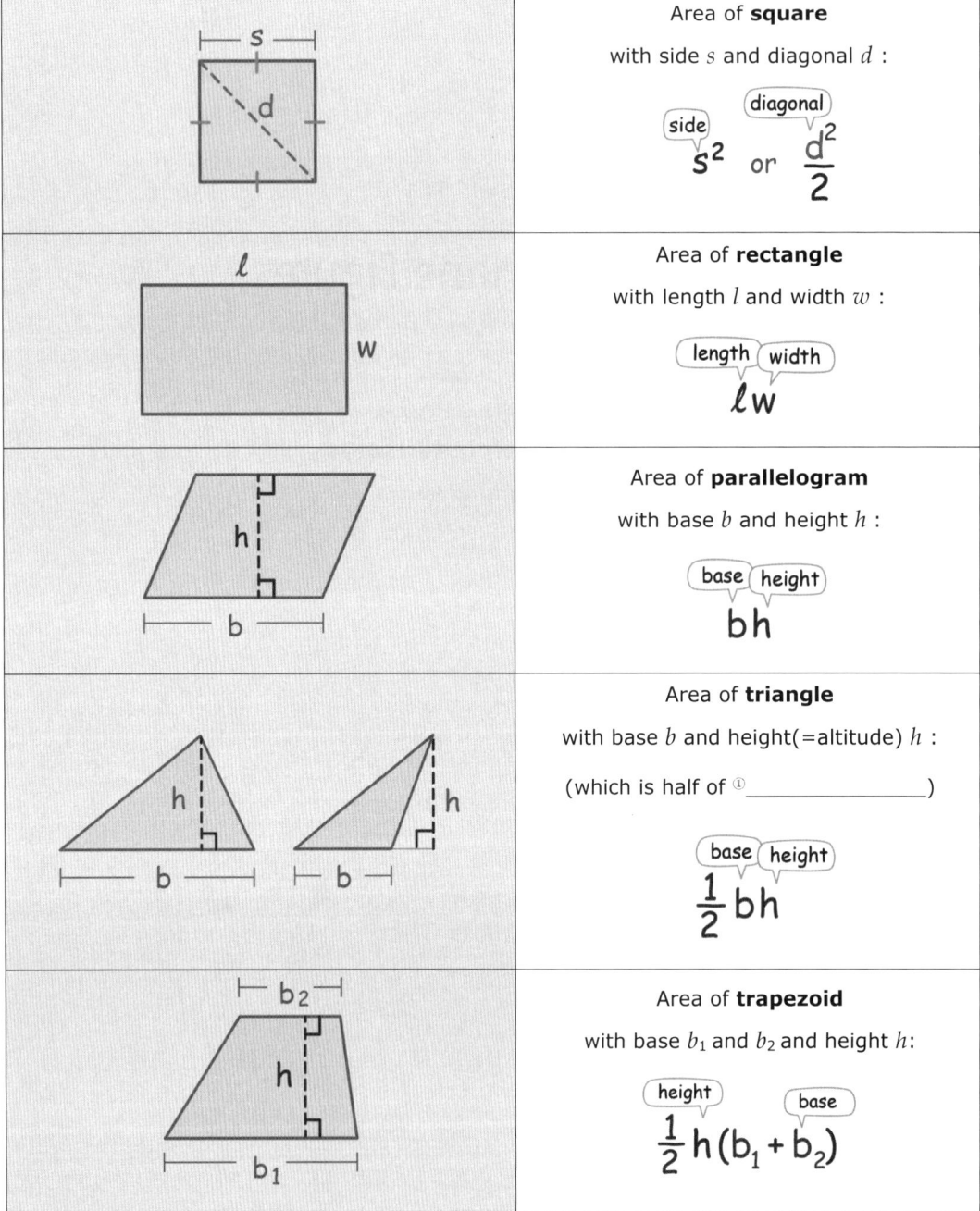

(square with side s and diagonal d)	**Area of square** with side s and diagonal d: s^2 or $\dfrac{d^2}{2}$
(rectangle with length l and width w)	**Area of rectangle** with length l and width w: lw
(parallelogram with base b and height h)	**Area of parallelogram** with base b and height h: bh
(triangles with base b and height h)	**Area of triangle** with base b and height(=altitude) h: (which is half of ① _____) $\dfrac{1}{2}bh$
(trapezoid with bases b_1, b_2 and height h)	**Area of trapezoid** with base b_1 and b_2 and height h: $\dfrac{1}{2}h(b_1+b_2)$

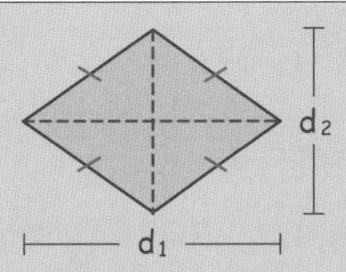

Area of rhombus

with diagonal d_1 and d_2 :

$$\frac{1}{2}d_1 d_2 \quad \text{(diagonals)}$$

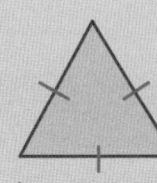

Area of equilateral triangle

with side s :

$$\frac{\sqrt{3}}{4}s^2 \quad \text{(side)}$$

☺ Proof: Area of parallelogram

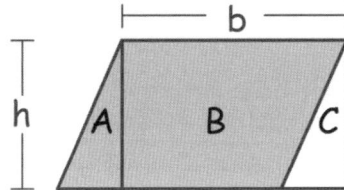

triangle $A \cong$ triangle C (HL theorem)

Area of Parallelogram

$= A + B$

$=$ ② _____ $+ B$

$= bh$

☺ Proof: Area of Trapezoid

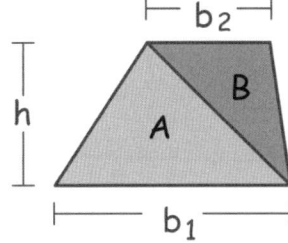

Area of Trapezoid

$=$ triangle $A +$ triangle B

$= \dfrac{1}{2}b_1 h +$ ③ _____

$= \dfrac{1}{2}h(b_1 + b_2)$

Blank : ① parallelogram　② C　③ $\dfrac{1}{2}b_2 h$

Part 10_Areas of Plane Figures 395

☺ Proof: Area of Rhombus

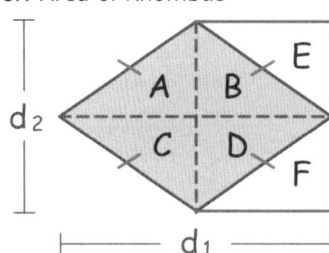

triangle $A \cong$ triangle E

triangle $C \cong$ triangle F (HL theorem)

Area of parallelogram

$= A + B + C + D$

$= $ ①____ $+ B + $ ②____ $+ D = \frac{1}{2}d_1 d_2$

☺ Proof: Area of Equilateral Triangle

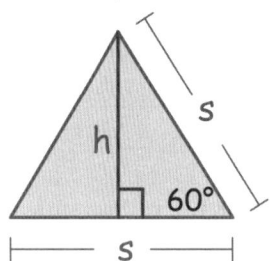

From 30-60-90 triangle

$h = $ ③____

Area of equilateral triangle

$= \frac{1}{2}(base)(height)$

$= \frac{1}{2}($ ④____$)($ ⑤____$) = \frac{\sqrt{3}}{4}s^2$

EXAMPLE 1. Find the area of the shaded region. The figures are not drawn to scale.

①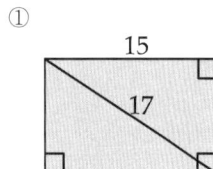

②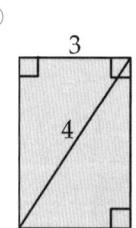

Blank : ① E   ② F   ③ $\frac{\sqrt{3}}{2}s$ ④ s   ⑤ $\frac{\sqrt{3}}{2}s$

③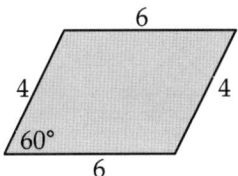

④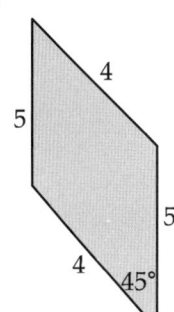

⑤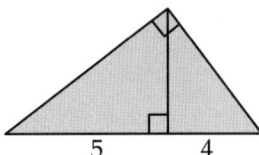

⑥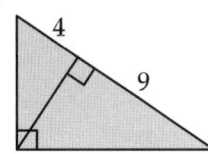

⑦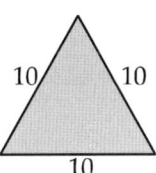

⑧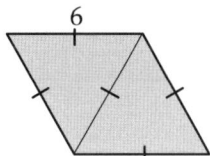

⑨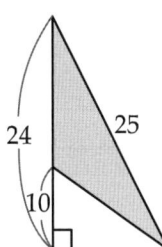

⑩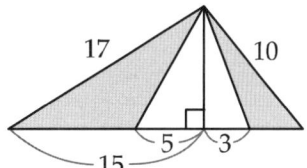

⑪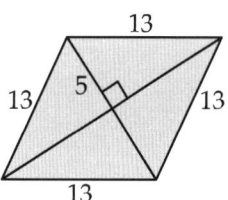

⑫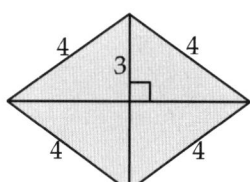

⑬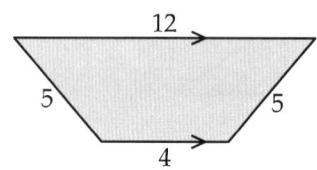

⑭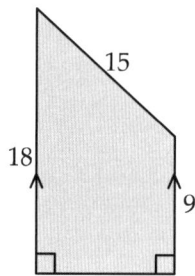

⑮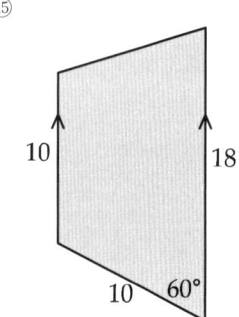

⑯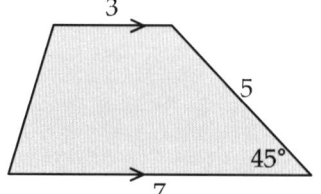

398 Mia's Geometry

EXAMPLE 2. Find the area of trapezoid $ABCD$.

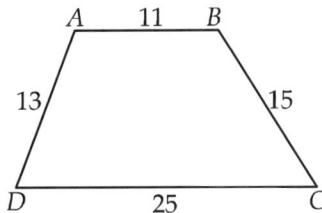

EXAMPLE 3. $\overline{AB} \parallel \overline{DE}$ and F is the midpoint of $\overline{AE}$. What is the area of quadrilateral $ABCD$?

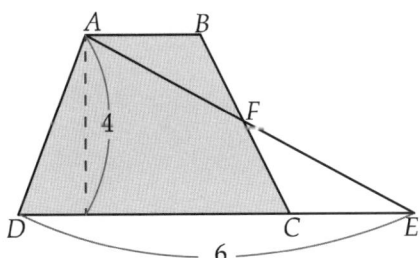

EXAMPLE 4. The square $ABCD$ has a side of 4 cm and the larger square $EFGH$ has a side of 6 cm. If the vertex E is at the center of the square $ABCD$, then what is the area of the overlapping region?

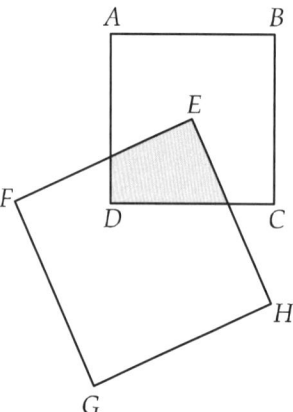

EXAMPLE 5. An isosceles trapezoid $ABCD$ with base $AB=6$ and $DC=8$ is inscribed in a circle with radius 5. The center of the circle lies in the interior of the trapezoid. Find the area of the trapezoid $ABCD$.

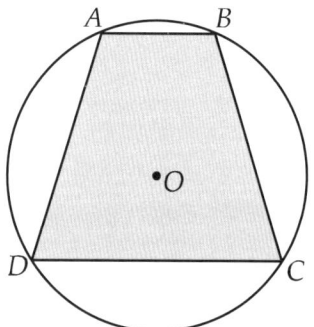

EXAMPLE 6. * A circle with radius 5 is inscribed in a trapezoid $ABCD$. If $AD = 13$ and $BC = 11$, then what is the area of the trapezoid $ABCD$?

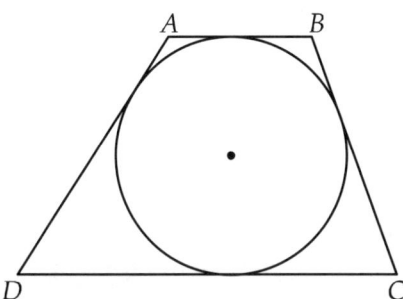

EXAMPLE 7. * A square is inscribed in a right triangle ABC, where $\dfrac{AB}{BC} = \dfrac{4}{3}$. What fraction of the area of the right triangle is the area of the square?

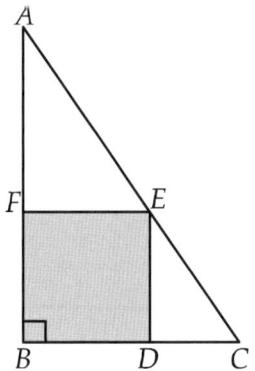

Mia's Geometry
10.2 Area of regular polygons

1. Circumcircle, Incircle, Radius and Apothem

When we have a polygon, we can draw a circumcircle and an incircle.

A ① _____ is a circle that passes through all vertices (corner points) of a polygon.
('*circum-*' means 'around')

The radius of the circumcircle is also the
② _____ of the polygon.

An ③ _____ is a circle that fits the inside of a polygon. ('*in-*' means 'inside')

The radius of the incircle is the ④ _____ of the polygon.

Blank : ① circumcircle   ② radius   ③ incircle   ④ apothem

2. Area of a Regular Polygon

We can break a n-sided regular polygon into n congruent ① _____ ;

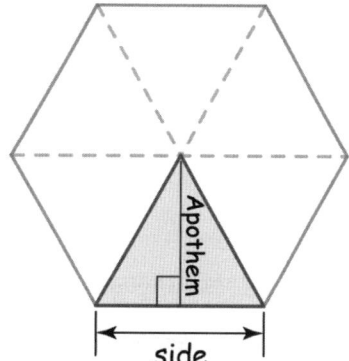

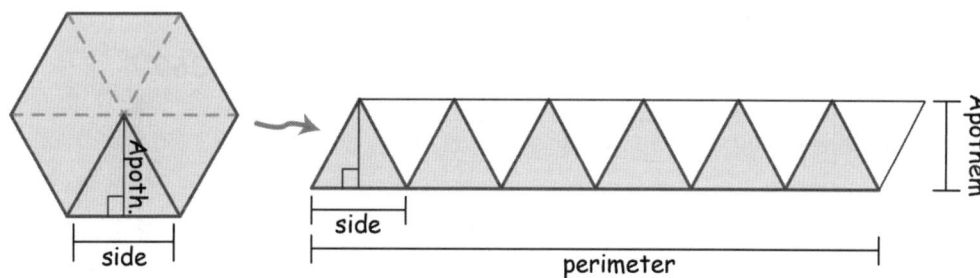

If we gather up $2n$ congruent isosceles triangles, then we can make a parallelogram with base = ② _____, height = ③ _____.

Therefore the area of regular polygon = ④ _____

※ **Area of Regular Polygon**

The area of a **n-sided regular polygon** with apothem a and side length of s;

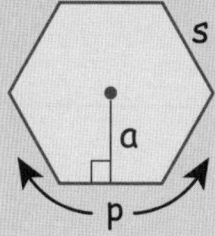

$$A = \frac{1}{2}ap = \frac{1}{2}ans$$

(apothem, perimeter, side)

Blank : ① isosceles △   ② perimeter   ③ apothem   ④ $\frac{1}{2}$ (perimeter)(apothem)

3. When Apothem is Given

Find the area of the regular hexagon with the apothem 8.

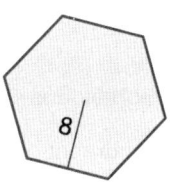

Break into 12 right triangles.

The angle on the center will be $\dfrac{360°}{\boxed{①}} = \boxed{②}$.

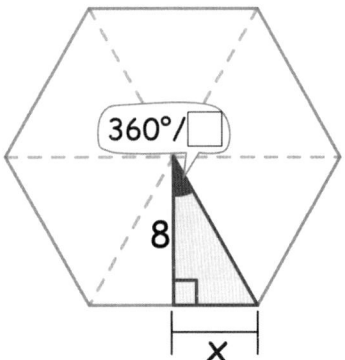

Since $\tan 30° = \dfrac{\boxed{③}}{}$ and $x = \boxed{④} \cdot \tan 30° = \boxed{⑤}$

the side length of the hexagon will be ⑥ _____.

Therefore the area of the hexagon is;

$\dfrac{1}{2}ap = \dfrac{1}{2}ans = \dfrac{1}{2}\boxed{⑦}\boxed{⑧}\boxed{⑨} = \boxed{⑩}$

Blank: ① 12   ② 30°   ③ $\dfrac{x}{8}$ ④ 8   ⑤ 4.1688   ⑥ 9.2376   ⑦ 8   ⑧ 6   ⑨ 9.2376   ⑩ 221.7025

EXAMPLE 1. Find the area of the shaded region. Round to the nearest tenth.

①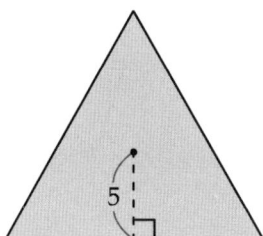

②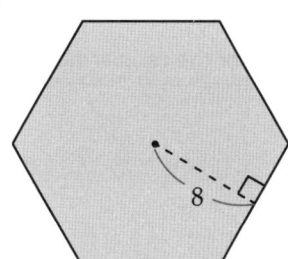

③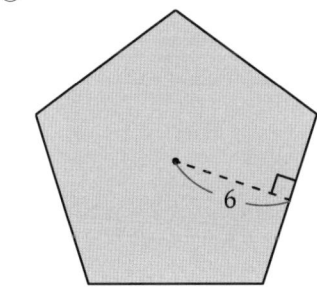

④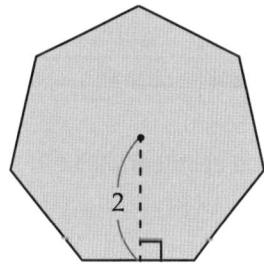

4. When Radius is Given

📱 Find the area of the regular hexagon with the radius 8.

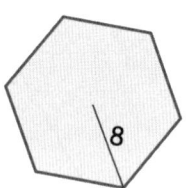

Break into 12 right triangles.

The angle on the center will be $\dfrac{360°}{\boxed{①}} = \boxed{②}$.

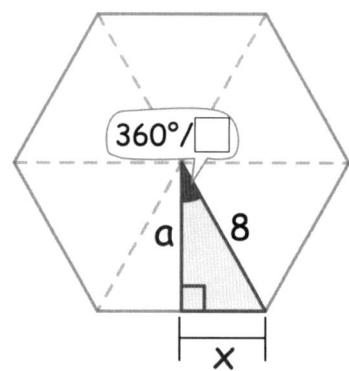

Since $\sin 30° = \dfrac{\boxed{③}}{\boxed{}}$ and $x = \boxed{④} \cdot \sin 30° = \boxed{⑤}$

the side length of the hexagon will be ⑥_____.

Since $\cos 30° = \dfrac{\boxed{⑦}}{\boxed{}}$ and $a = \boxed{⑧} \cdot \cos 30° = \boxed{⑨}$

the length of the apothem will be ⑩_____.

Therefore the area of the hexagon is;

$\dfrac{1}{2}ap = \dfrac{1}{2}ans = \dfrac{1}{2}\boxed{⑪}\boxed{⑫}\boxed{⑬} = \boxed{⑭}$

Blank : ① 12   ② 30°   ③ $\dfrac{x}{8}$ ④ 8   ⑤ 4   ⑥ 8   ⑦ $\dfrac{a}{8}$ ⑧ 8   ⑨ 6.9282   ⑩ 6.9282
⑪ 6.9282   ⑫ 6   ⑬ 8   ⑭ 166.2768

EXAMPLE 2. Find the area of the shaded region. Round to the nearest tenth.

①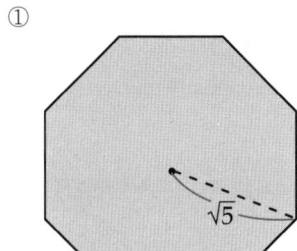

②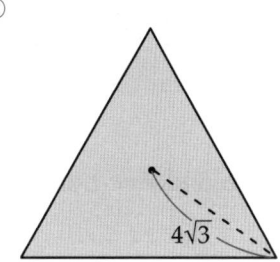

③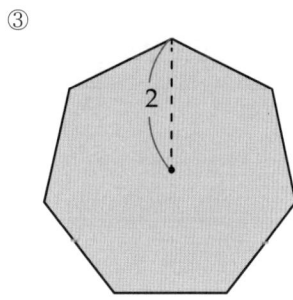

Mia's Geometry

10.3 Area of Circles and Sectors

1. Circumference and Arc Length

The number ① _____ (pi)

is the ratio of the circumference C of a circle to its diameter d.

$$\pi = \frac{C}{d} \Rightarrow C = d\pi \Rightarrow C = ②\underline{}$$

Arc length is the length of the arc. (≠ Measure of arc)

In a circle, the ratio of the arc length to the circumference is equal to the ratio of the measure of the arc to 360°.

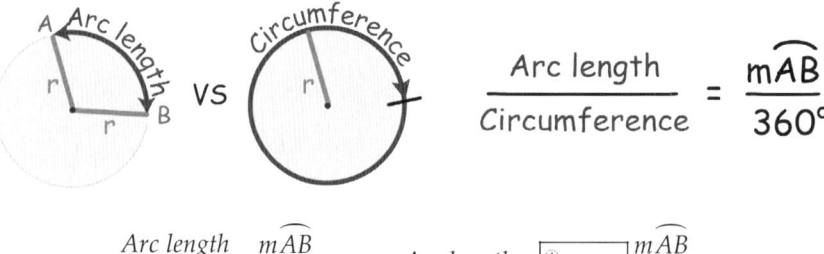

$$\frac{Arc\ length}{③} = \frac{m\widehat{AB}}{360°} \Rightarrow Arc\ length = ④\boxed{} \frac{m\widehat{AB}}{360°}$$

※ Formula for the Circumference and the Arc Length

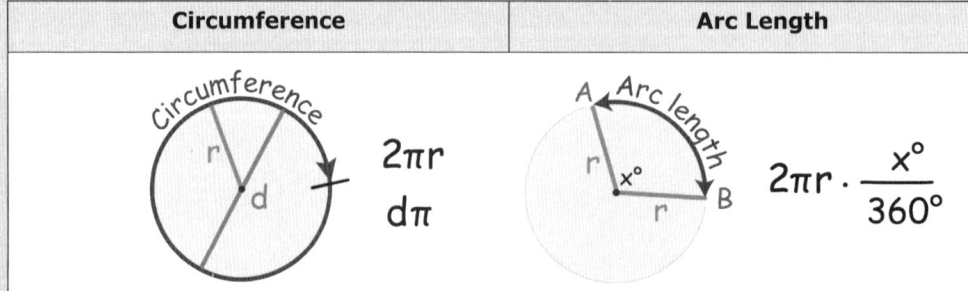

Blank : ① π ② 2πr ③ 2πr ④ 2πr

EXAMPLE 1. Find the arc length of the shaded sector.

①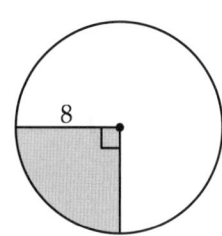

②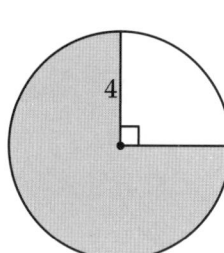

③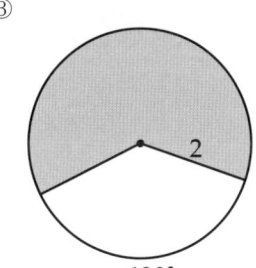

④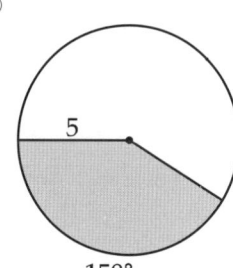

EXAMPLE 2. Find the perimeter of the shaded region.

①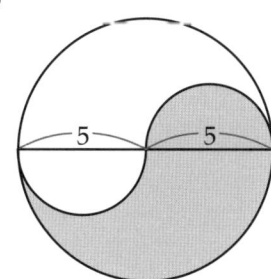

②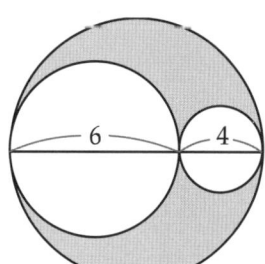

③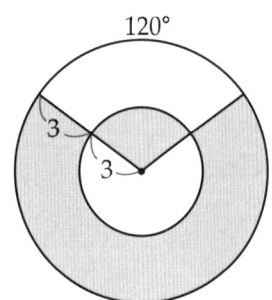

④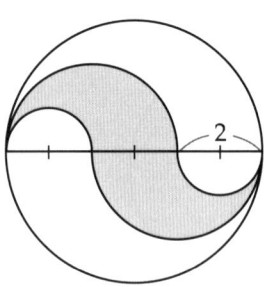

⑤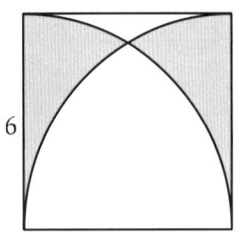

⑥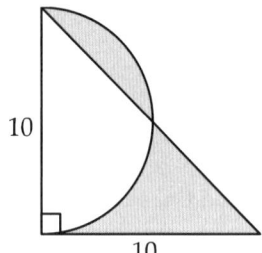

EXAMPLE 3. *The belt fits tightly around two pulleys which have radii 8 cm and 2 cm, respectively. The distance of the centers of each pulley is 12cm. (The figure is not drawn in scale)

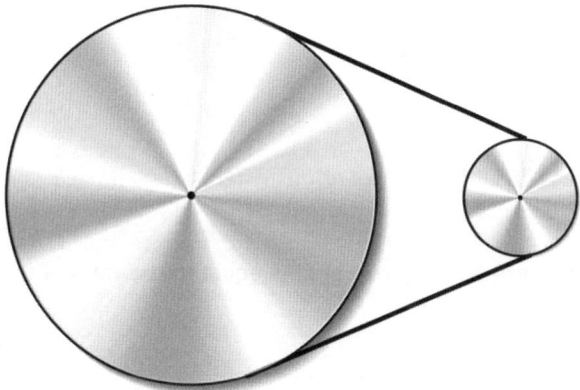

What is the length of the belt? (Ignore the thickness of the belt.)

2. Area of the Circle and Sector

Take a circle, and break it down to several wedges.
Gather up all those sectors and make a parallelogram with base length of ①_____ and height of ②_____.

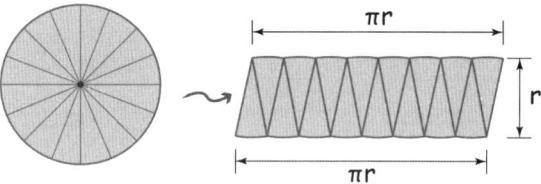

$$\text{Circle Area} = \text{Area of the wedges} = (\text{base})(\text{height}) = \text{③}\underline{\qquad}$$

The ratio of the sector area to the circle area is equal to the ratio of the measure of the arc to 360°.

$$\frac{\text{Sector Area}}{\text{Circle Area}} = \frac{m\widehat{AB}}{360°}$$

$$\frac{\text{Sector Area}}{\text{④}} = \frac{m\widehat{AB}}{360°} \Rightarrow \text{Sector Area} = \text{⑤}\boxed{} \cdot \frac{m\widehat{AB}}{360°}$$

※ Formula for the Circle area and the Sector Area

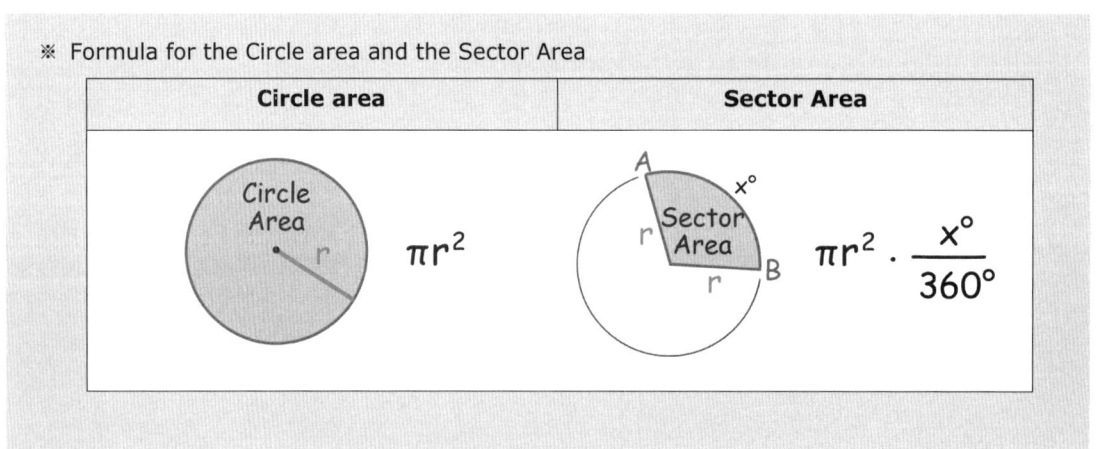

Blank : ① πr   ② r   ③ πr²   ④ πr²   ⑤ πr²

412 Mia's Geometry

EXAMPLE 4. Find the area of the shaded region.

①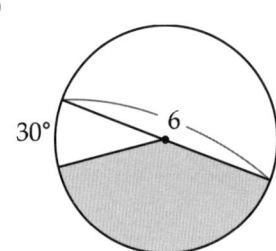

②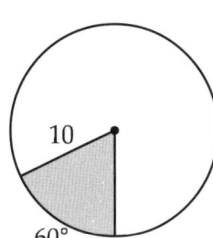

③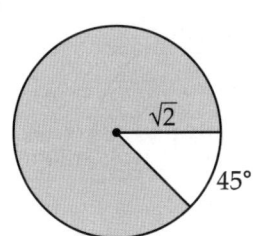

④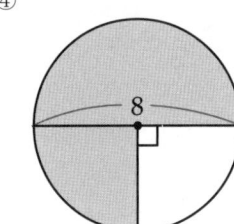

⑤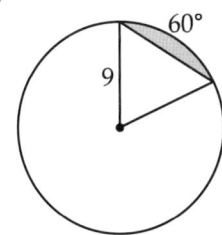

⑥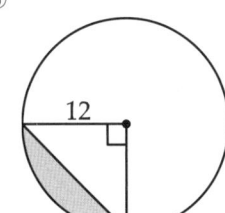

⑦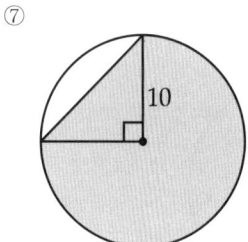

⑧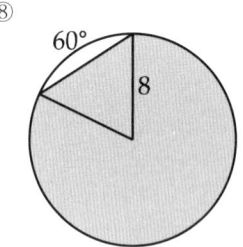

⑨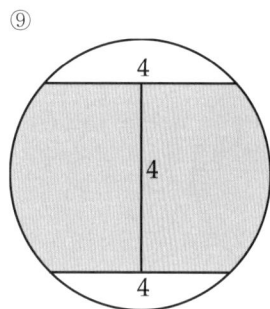

⑩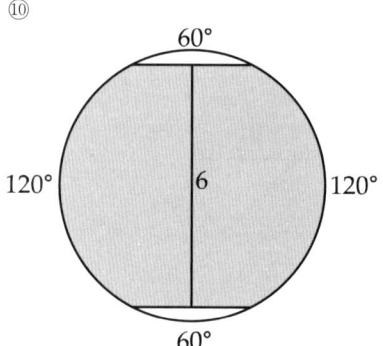

⑪ Square *ABCD*

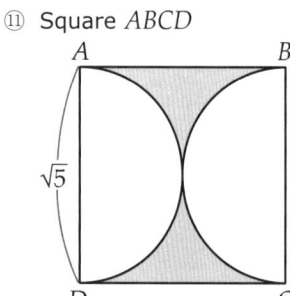

⑫ Square *ABCD*

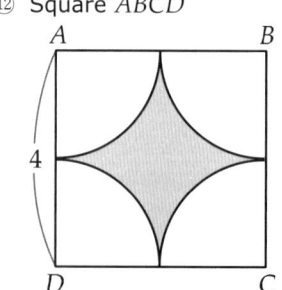

⑬ Square *ABCD*

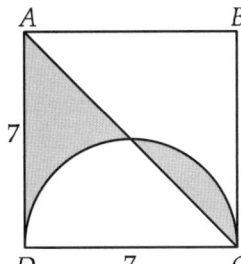

⑭ m∠*ABC* = 90°

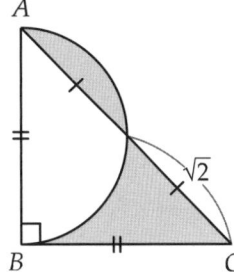

⑮ m∠*ABC* = 90°

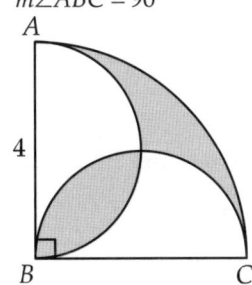

⑯ Square *ABCD*

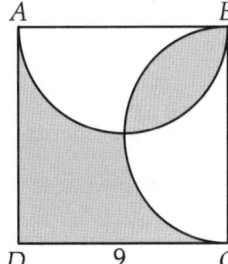

⑰

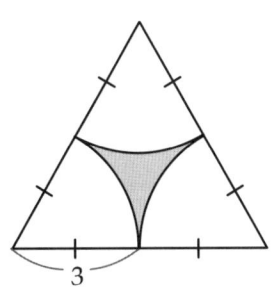

⑱ Square *ABCD*

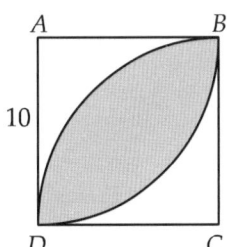

EXAMPLE 5. Square ABCD has a side length of 6. Find the area of the shaded region.

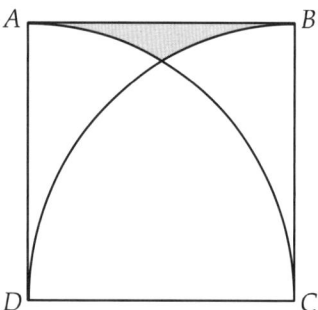

EXAMPLE 6. ABC is a right triangle. Semicircles are drawn on $\overline{AB}$, $\overline{BC}$, and $\overline{CA}$. If $AB = 6$, $BC = 10$, then what is the area of the shaded region?

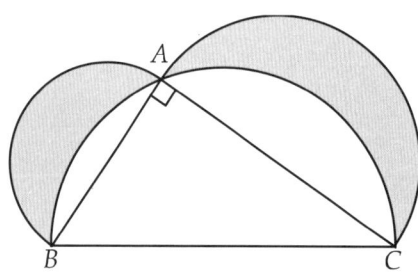

EXAMPLE 7. A sheep is tied to the corner of a barn by 15 m rope. The barn measures 20 m by 10 m as shown in the figure. Find the area which the sheep can feed on.

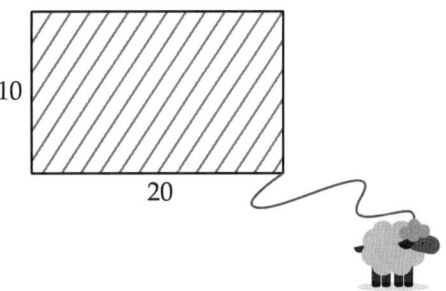

EXAMPLE 8. *Two circles pass through each other's centers as shown. If the radius of one circle is 4 cm, then what is the area of the shaded region?

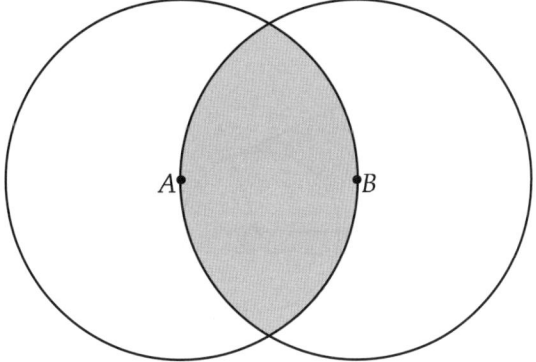

EXAMPLE 9. *Find the area of the shaded region.

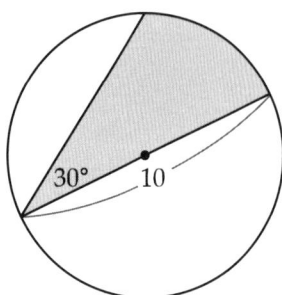

EXAMPLE 10. * Circles A and B with radii 12 cm and 4 cm are tangent to each other. Find the area of the shaded region.

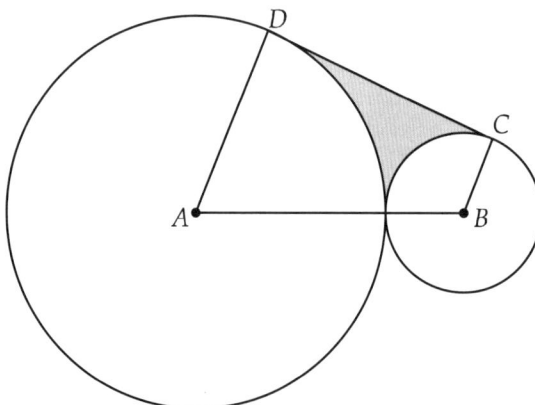

Mia's Geometry

10.4 Areas and Ratios

1. Ratios and Areas

When two triangles have equal height;

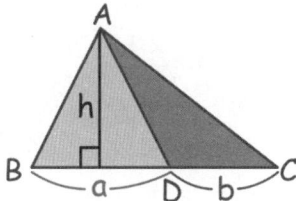

$$\frac{\text{Area of } \triangle ABD}{\text{Area of } \triangle ADC} = \frac{\frac{1}{2}ah}{①} = \boxed{②}$$

When two triangles have equal base;

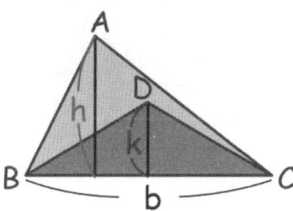

$$\frac{\text{Area of } \triangle ABC}{\text{Area of } \triangle DBC} = \frac{\frac{1}{2}bh}{③} = \boxed{④}$$

When two triangles are similar;

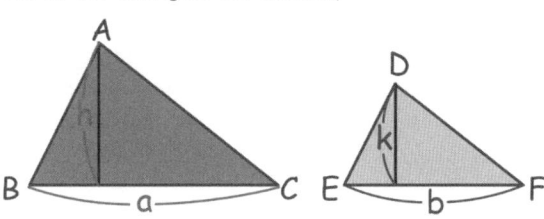

Since corresponding sides are proportional in ~ △s, $\dfrac{a}{b} = \boxed{⑤}$

$$\frac{\text{Area of } \triangle ABC}{\text{Area of } \triangle DEF} = \frac{\frac{1}{2}ah}{⑥}$$

$$= \frac{ah}{⑦} = \boxed{⑧}$$

Blank : ① $\dfrac{1}{2}bh$ ② $\dfrac{a}{b}$ ③ $\dfrac{1}{2}bk$ ④ $\dfrac{h}{k}$ ⑤ $\dfrac{h}{k}$ ⑥ $\dfrac{1}{2}bk$ ⑦ bk ⑧ $\dfrac{a^2}{b^2}$

※ Ratios and Areas

When two triangles have *equal height*,
the ratio of the areas are equals the ratio of the bases.

$$\frac{\text{Area of triangle A}}{\text{Area of triangle B}} = \frac{a}{b}$$

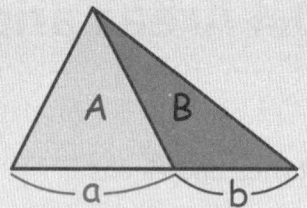

When two triangles have *equal base*,
the ratio of the areas are equals the ratio of the heights.

$$\frac{\text{Area of big triangle}}{\text{Area of small triangle}} = \frac{h}{k}$$

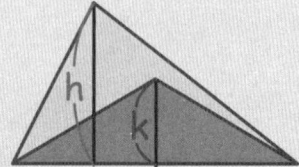

When two triangles are similar,
then the ratio of their areas equals the square of their scale factors.

$$\frac{\text{Area of big triangle}}{\text{Area of small triangle}} = \frac{a^2}{b^2}$$

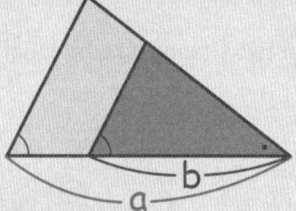

EXAMPLE 1. Find the ratio of the areas of triangles and fill in the blanks.

①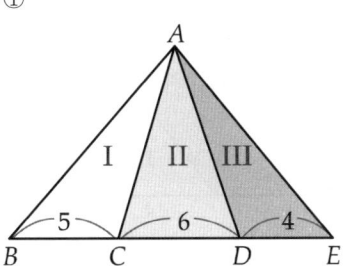

a) I : II = _____

b) I : III = _____

c) △ABD : △ACE = _____

②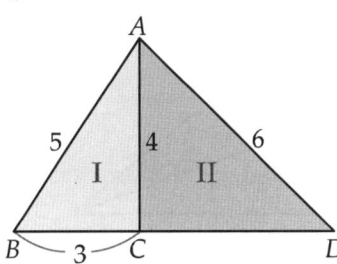

a) I : II = _____

b) △ABD : II = _____

③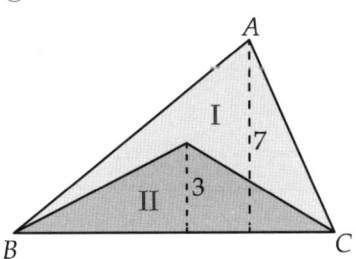

a) △ABC : II = _____

b) I : II = _____

④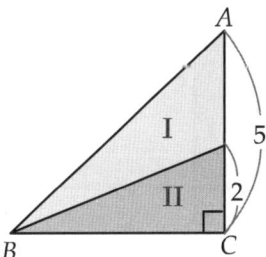

a) I : △ABC = _____

b) I : II = _____

⑤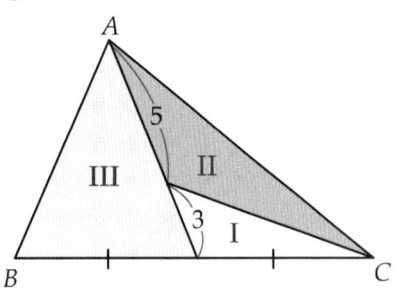

a) I : II = _____

b) I : III = _____

c) I : △ABC = _____

d) II : III = _____

⑥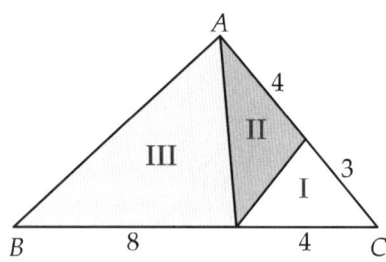

a) I : II = _____

b) I : III = _____

c) II : △ABC = _____

d) II : III = _____

⑦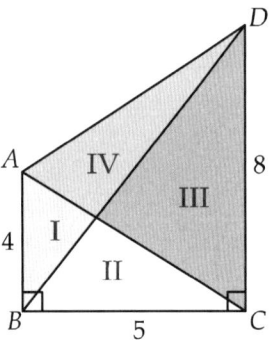

a) I : II = _____

b) I : III = _____

c) I : IV = _____

d) I : □ABCD = _____

⑧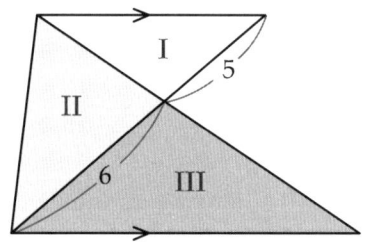

a) I : II = _____

b) I : III = _____

c) II : III = _____

422 Mia's Geometry

⑨ Parallelogram ABCD

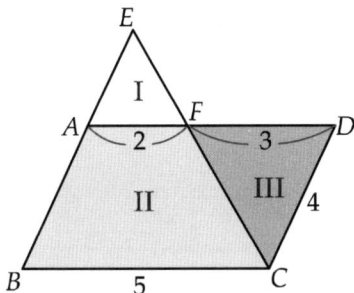

a) I : II = _____

b) I : III = _____

c) I : ▱ABCD = _____

⑩ Parallelogram ABCD

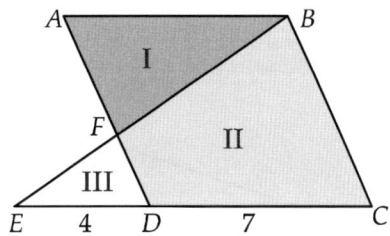

a) I : III = _____

b) III : △BEC = _____

c) III : II = _____

d) I : II = _____

EXAMPLE 2. In the figure, $ABCD$ is a parallelogram with area 80 cm^2. If $3AP = 5PD$, then what is the area of triangle APE?

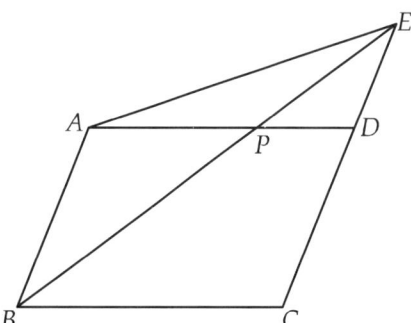

EXAMPLE 3. * In the figure, $ABCD$ is a trapezoid and diagonal $\overline{AC}$ and $\overline{BD}$ meets at point P. If the area of triangle APB is 4 and area of triangle DPC is 25, then what is the area of the trapezoid $ABCD$?

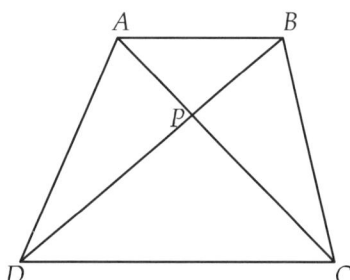

2. Area and Median

☺ Remind:

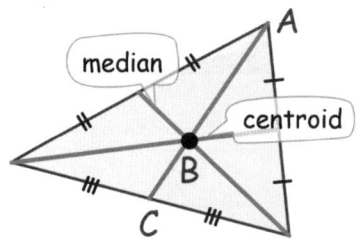

※ Definition of Median:

Median is a segment from a *vertex* to the

① _____ of the opposite side.

※ Centroid Theorem:

The centroid of a triangle is located **two-third** of the distance from a vertex to the midpoint of the side opposite the vertex on a median.

※ Area of a triangle from the medians

A triangle is divided into 6 ② _____ areas by its medians.

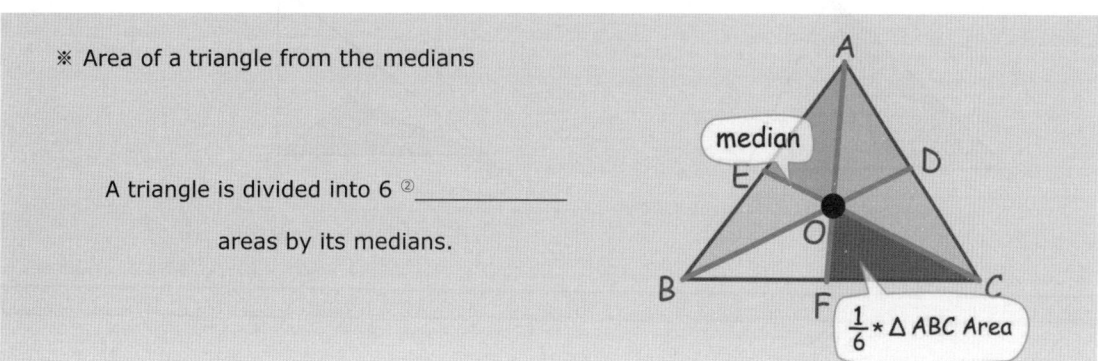

$\frac{1}{6}$ * △ ABC Area

EXAMPLE 4. Point O is the centroid of △ ABC. If the area of △ ABC is 12cm², find the area of the shaded region.

①
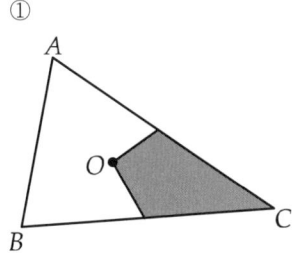

②
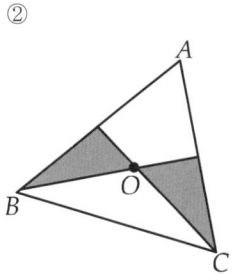

Blank : ① midpoint   ② congruent

③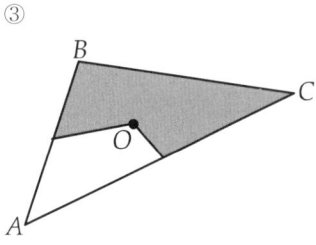

④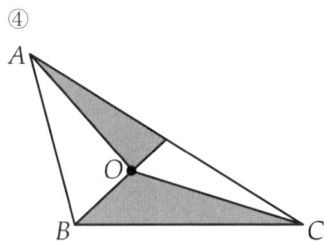

⑤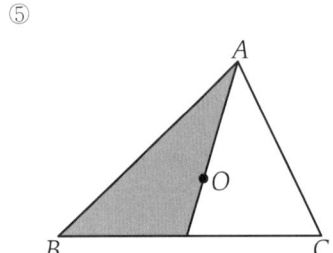

⑥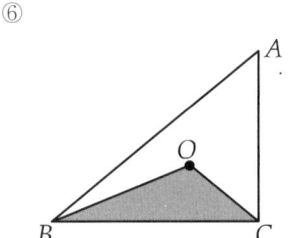

EXAMPLE 5. Point O is the centroid of $\triangle ABC$ and Point M is the centroid of $\triangle OBC$. If the area of $\triangle ABC$ is 24 cm², find the area of the shaded region.

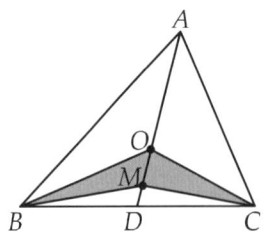

EXAMPLE 6. *In the figure, $ABCD$ is a parallelogram with area 60 cm². If P is the midpoint of $\overline{AD}$ and Q is the midpoint of $\overline{DC}$ as shown. What is the area of the shaded region?

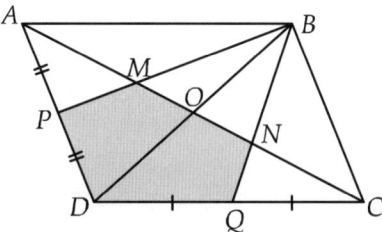

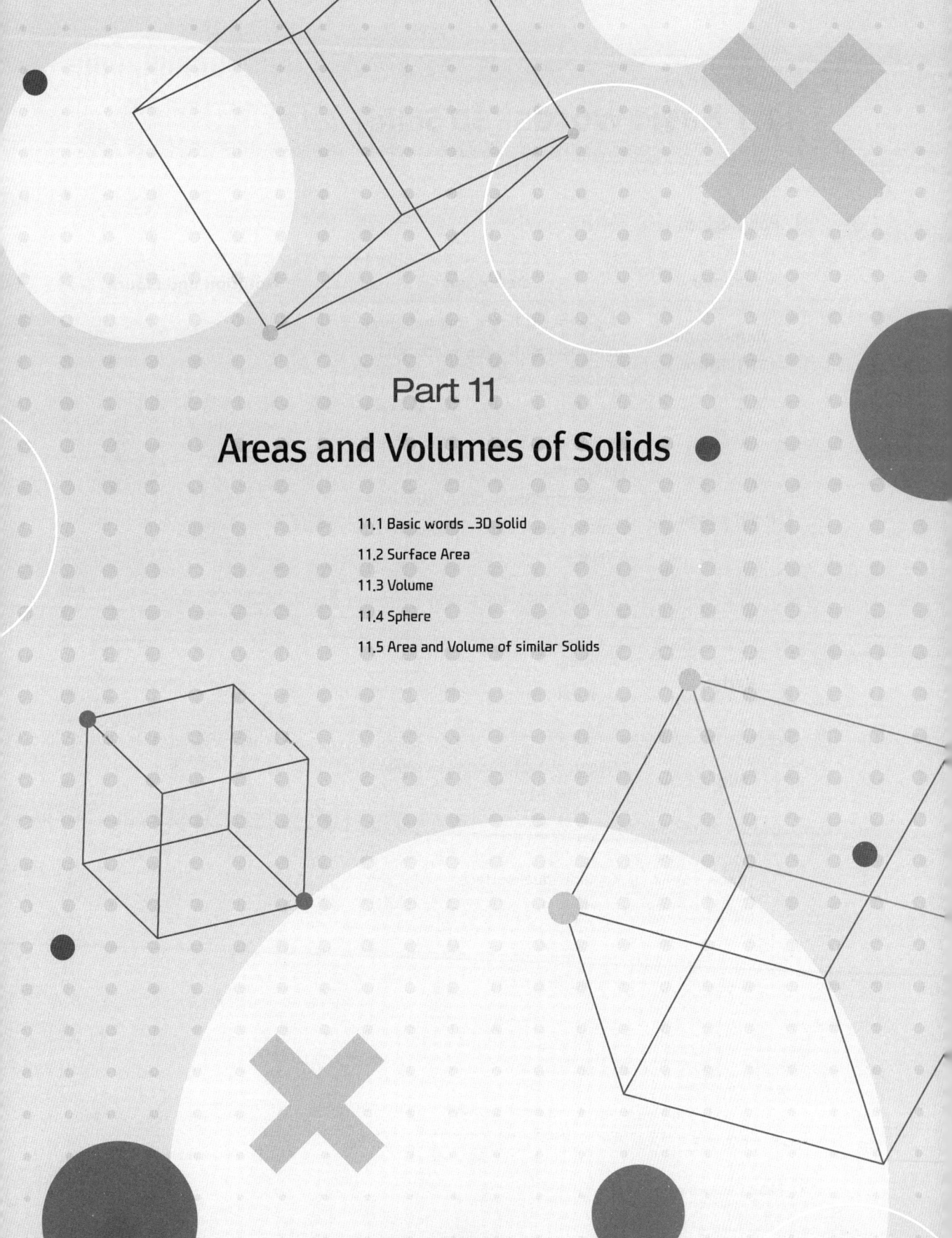

Mia's Geometry

11.1 Basic words _3D Solid

1. Polyhedron

Vocabulary	Definition	Notation and Figure
3 dimensional (3D) figure	A geometric figure that has three dimensions: length, width, and height (or depth).	
Polyhedron	A 3D figure whose surfaces are polygons. (From the Greek poly- meaning "many" and -edron meaning "face"). ex) pyramids and prisms	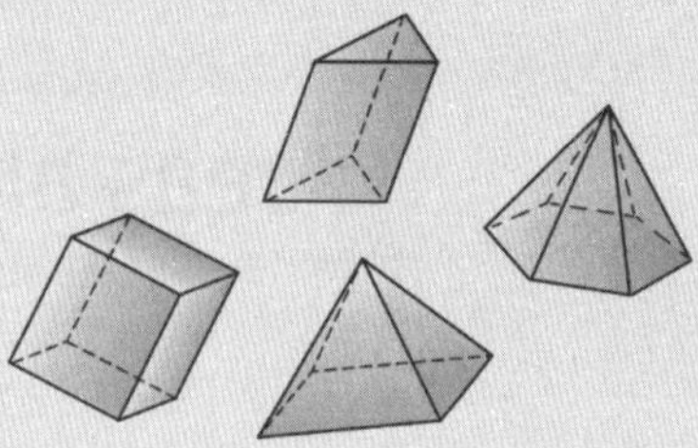
Vertex	A corner. • plural : ①_____	
Edge	Segment that joins one vertex with another.	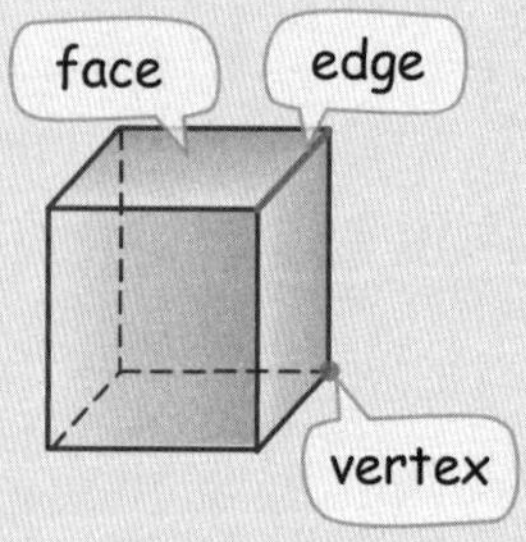
Face	An individual surface.	

Blank : ① vertices

2. Prism

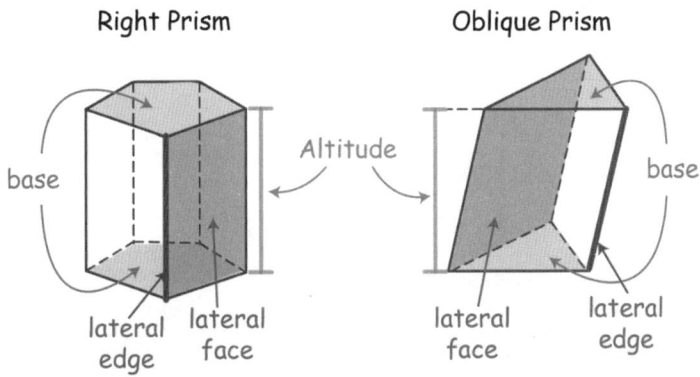

Right Prism   Oblique Prism

Vocabulary	Definition
Prism	Polyhedron with two congruent and parallel faces. • A prism may either be ①_____ or ②_____. • The shape of the bases give the prism its name; ex) cube triangular prism pentagonal prism
Base	Two congruent and parallel faces
Lateral faces	The faces that are not bases. • Lateral faces are ③_____.
Altitude	Perpendicular distance between the two parallel bases.
Height	The length of the ④_____.

Blank : ① right   ② oblique   ③ parallelogram   ④ altitude

3. Pyramids

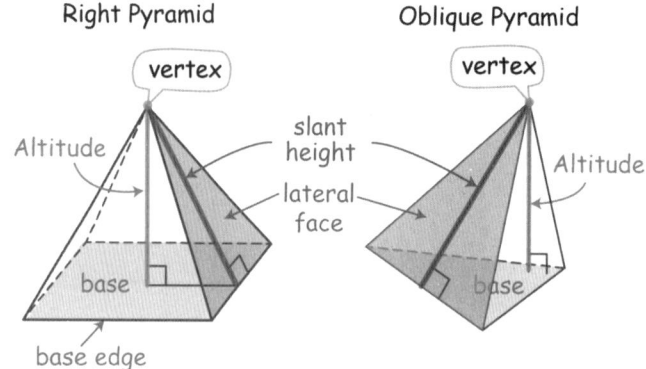

Vocabulary	Definition
Pyramid	Polyhedron with a polygon base and triangular lateral faces that meet at one point. • A pyramid may either be ①_____ or ②_____. • The shape of the base gives the pyramid its name; ex) triangular pyramid, Square pyramid, hexagonal pyramid
Base	A face at the bottom of the pyramid.
Vertex	The single point at the top where all the triangular faces meet.
Lateral faces	The triangular faces that is not base.
Altitude	Perpendicular distance from the vertex to the bases.
Height	The length of the altitude.
Slant Height	The height of the triangular lateral faces.
Regular pyramid	A regular pyramid has a regular polygon as its base • Lateral faces are ③_____ in a right regular pyramid. • The altitude meets the base at the ④_____ of the base.

Blank : ① right   ② oblique   ③ isosceles △   ④ center

432 Mia's Geometry

4. Cylinder and Cone

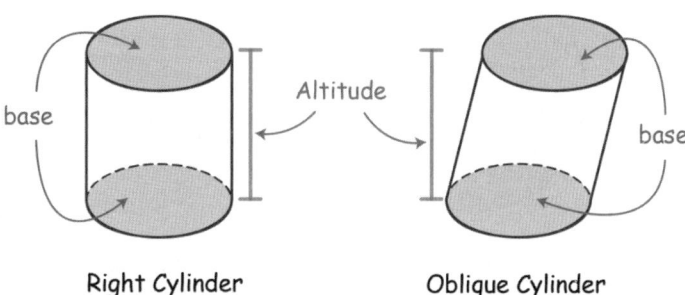

Right Cylinder   Oblique Cylinder

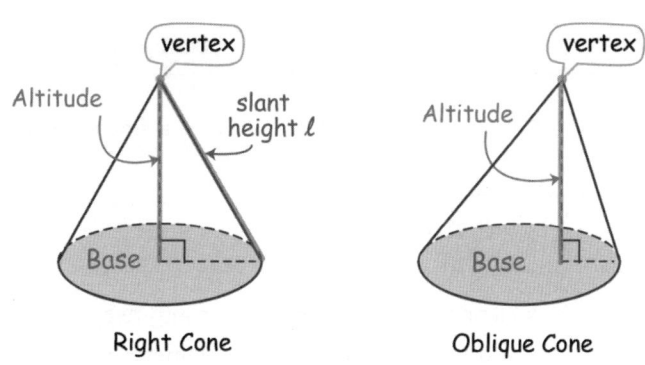

Right Cone   Oblique Cone

Vocabulary	Definition
Cylinder	3D figure with two congruent, parallel, and ① _____ bases. • A cylinder is **not** a polyhedron.
Cone	3D figure with a circular base and a single vertex. • A lateral face of a cone is a ② _____.

Blank : ① circular   ② sector

5. Sphere

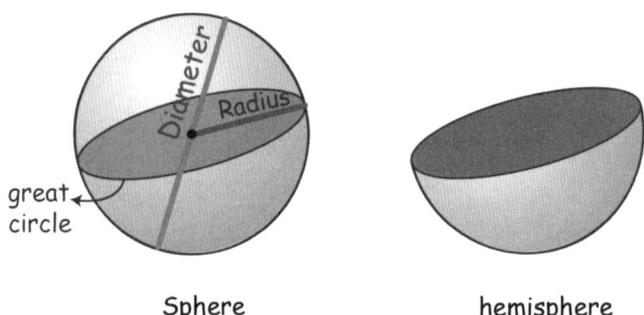

Sphere   hemisphere

Vocabulary	Definition
Sphere	Set of all points equidistant from a single point in space.
Hemisphere	A half of a sphere.
Great Circle	A circle that divides the sphere into two equal halves. • A great circle contains the diameter of the sphere.

Mia's Geometry

11.2 Surface Area

1. Surface Area of Prism

The Surface area is the total area of the surface of a 3D figure.

All you need to do is ① _____ all the area of the ② _____.

You can find the surface area by looking at a ③ _____.

A **net** is a 3D shape unfolded and laid out flat to show all its faces.

Let's find the surface area of a prism.

If we see the net of the prism, you can see the lateral face should be a ④ _____.

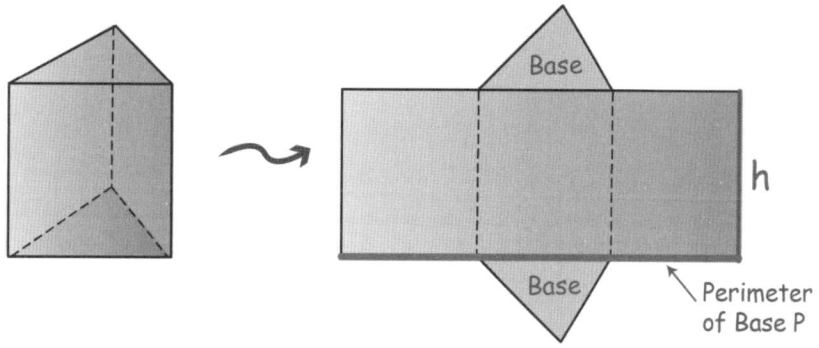

Surface area   = bases area + lateral area

             = ⑤ _____ + ⑥ _____ × ⑦ _____

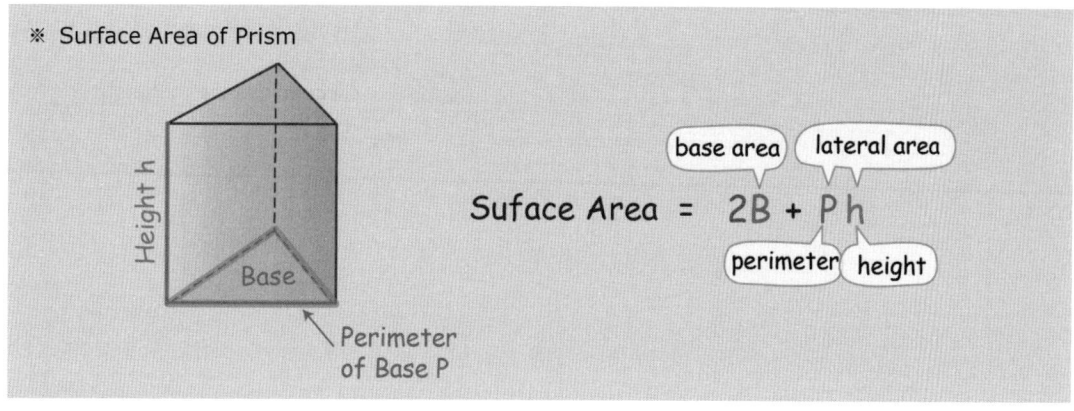

Blank : ① add   ② faces   ③ net   ④ rectangle   ⑤ 2(base)   ⑥ perimeter of base   ⑦ height

2. Surface Area of Cylinder

If we 'unroll' a right cylinder, you can see the lateral face should be a ①_____.

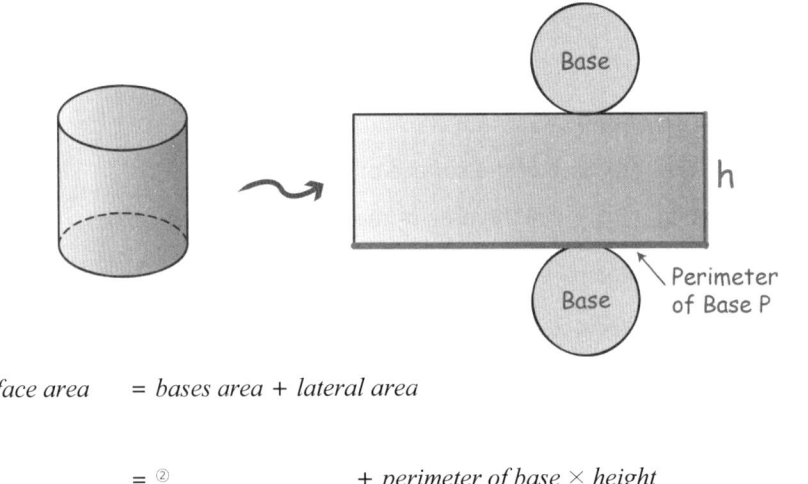

$$\begin{aligned}
\textit{Surface area} \quad &= \textit{bases area} + \textit{lateral area} \\
&= \text{②}\underline{\qquad\qquad} + \textit{perimeter of base} \times \textit{height} \\
&= \text{③}\underline{\qquad\qquad} + \text{④}\underline{\qquad\qquad} \times \textit{height}
\end{aligned}$$

※ Surface Area of Cylinder

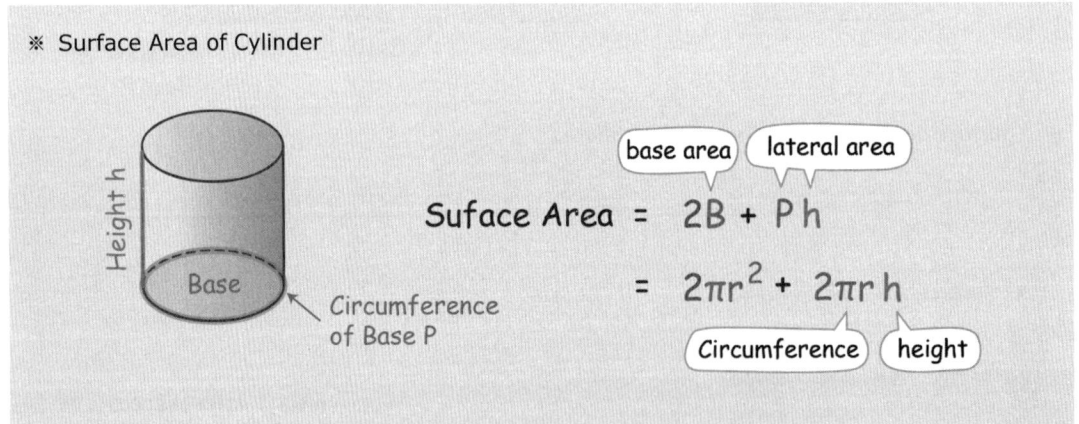

Blank : ① rectangle ② $2(\pi r^2)$ ③ $2(\pi r^2)$ ④ $2\pi r$

EXAMPLE 1. Find the surface area.

① Cube

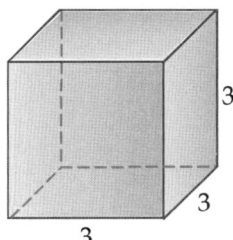

② Triangular prism

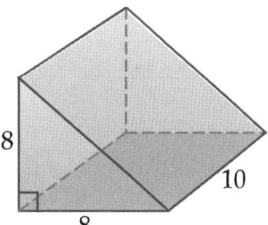

③ Regular hexagonal prism

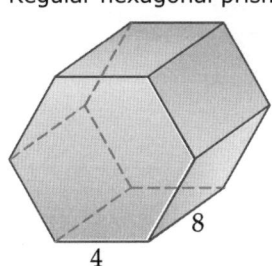

④ Isosceles Trapezoidal prism

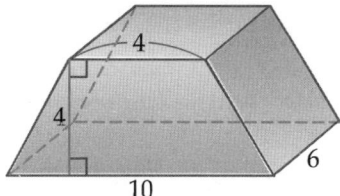

⑤ Cylinder

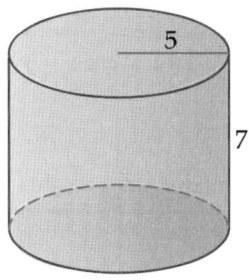

⑥ Cylinder

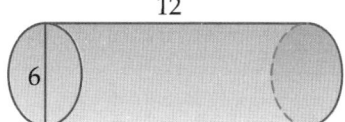

3. Surface Area of Pyramids

If we see the net of the pyramid, you can see the lateral face can be half of a

① _____.

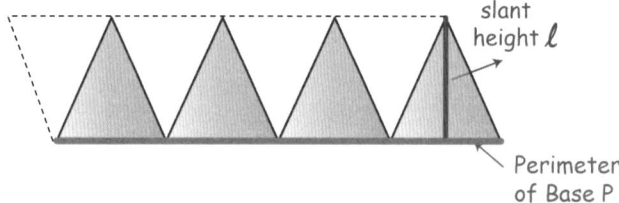

Surface area = *base area* + *lateral area*

    = *base area* + ② _____

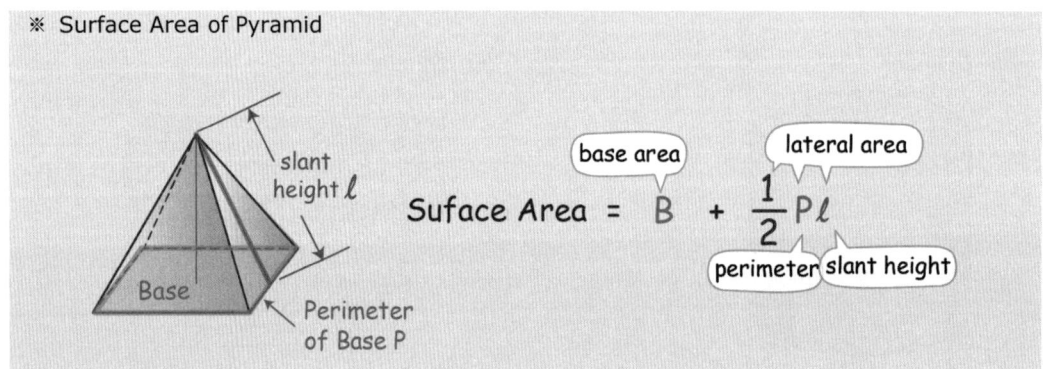

※ **Surface Area of Pyramid**

Surface Area = B + $\frac{1}{2}$ Pℓ

(base area) (lateral area)
(perimeter)(slant height)

Blank : ① parallelogram   ② $\frac{1}{2}$ (perimeter of base) (slant height)

4. Surface Area of Cone

If we see the net of the cone, you can notice that ;
the perimeter of the base
= circumference of the base
= ①_____ of the lateral face.

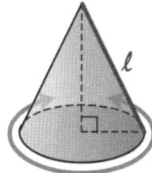
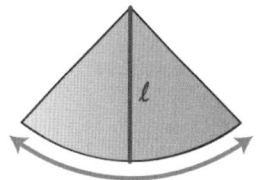

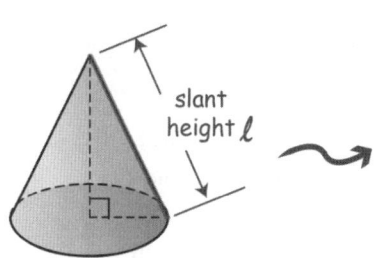
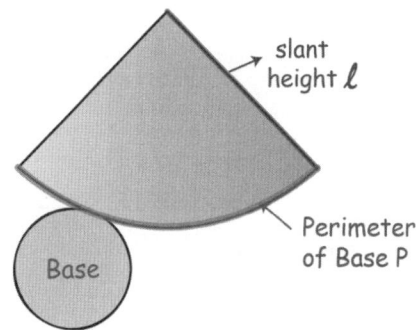

$$\text{Surface area} = \text{base area} + \text{lateral area}$$
$$= \text{base area} + \frac{1}{2}pl$$
$$= \text{②}\underline{\hspace{3cm}} + \text{③}\underline{\hspace{3cm}}$$

※ Surface Area of Cone

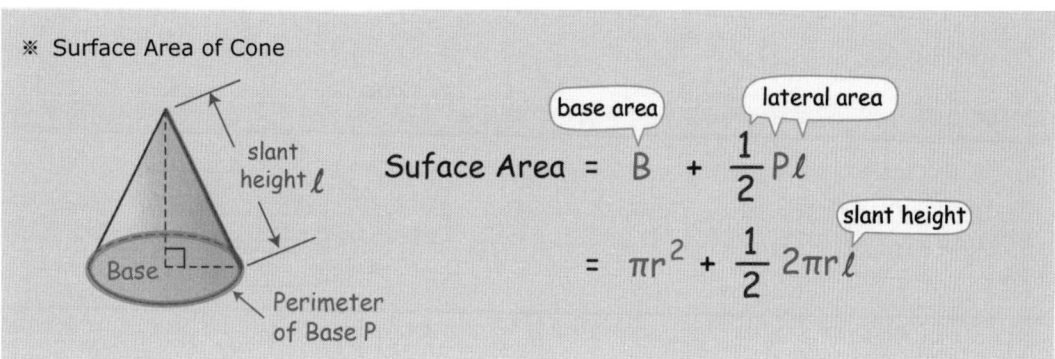

$$\text{Surface Area} = \underbrace{B}_{\text{base area}} + \underbrace{\frac{1}{2}Pl}_{\text{lateral area}}$$
$$= \pi r^2 + \frac{1}{2}\, 2\pi r\, \underbrace{l}_{\text{slant height}}$$

Blank : ① arc length   ② πr^2 ③ $\frac{1}{2}(2\pi r)(\text{slant height})$

EXAMPLE 2. Find the surface area.

① Square Pyramid

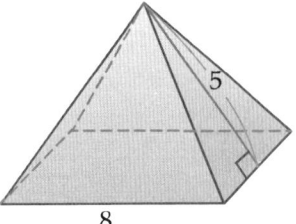

② Regular hexagonal Pyramid

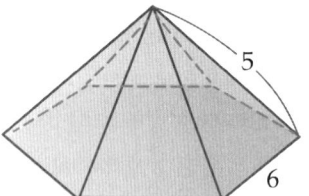

③ Cone

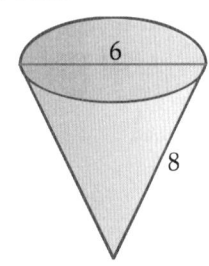

④ Square Pyramid

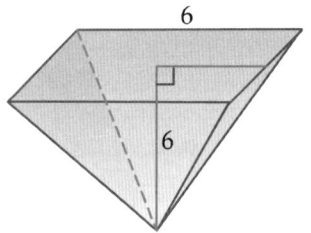

⑤ Cone

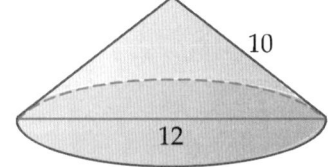

EXAMPLE 3. A cylindrical vessel, without a lid, needs to be tin-coated on both its inner and outer surfaces. If the diameter of the base is 14 cm and the height is 10 cm, what is the cost of tin coating the vessel if it costs $0.10 per cm²? Ignore the thickness of the vessel.

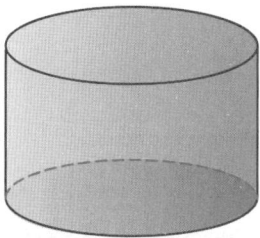

EXAMPLE 4. A silo is being painted from the outside, excluding the bottom. Calculate the area to be painted. One can of paint covers 6π m². If the cost of one can is $25, what is the total cost of the paint can?

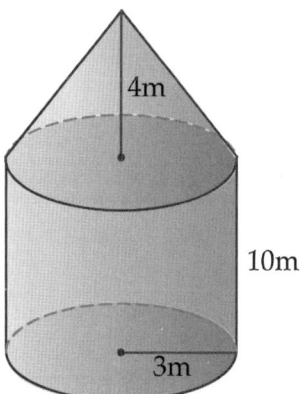

EXAMPLE 5. A cone is made by rolling a piece of paper as shown in the figure.

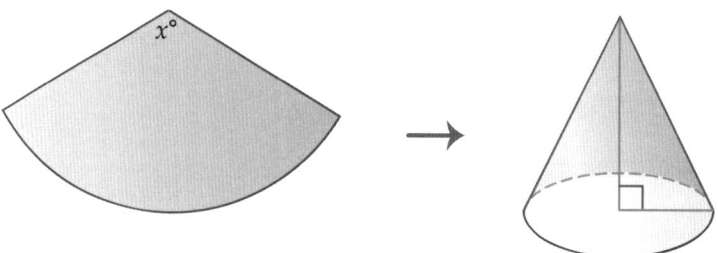

If the cone has a height 4 cm and base diameter 6 cm, find the size of the angle marked x.

EXAMPLE 6. *A *frustum* of a cone is formed when a right circular cone is sliced parallel to its base. Find the total surface area of the given *frustum*. The figure is not drawn to scale.

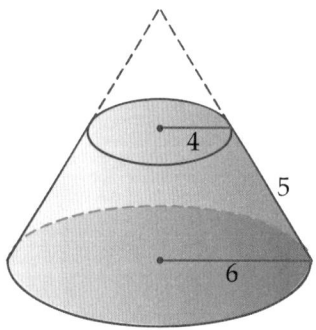

Mia's Geometry
11.3 Volume

1. Volume of Prism and Cylinder

Volume is the amount of space a 3D shape takes up. It represents how much material or substance an object can hold inside it.

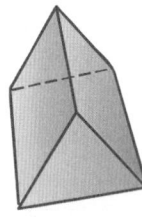
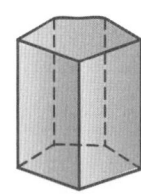

For the volume of prism and cylinder, you can just do (base area) x (height).

※ Volume of Prism and Cylinder

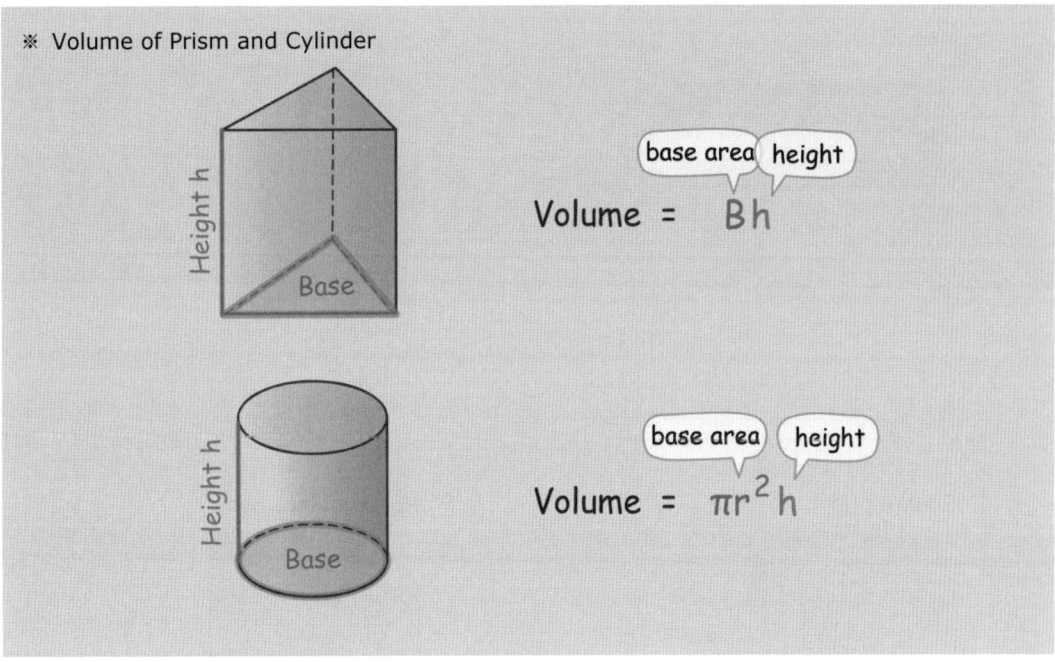

Volume = Bh (base area × height)

Volume = $\pi r^2 h$ (base area × height)

EXAMPLE 1. Find the volume of the 3D figure.

① Trapezoidal prism

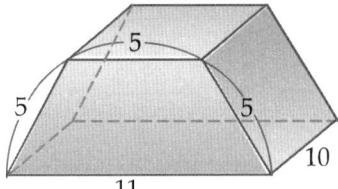

② Hexagonal prism

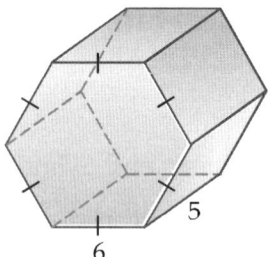

③ Cylinder

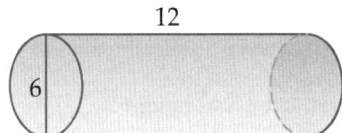

④ Cylinder

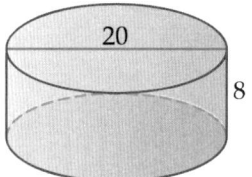

⑤ Square prism

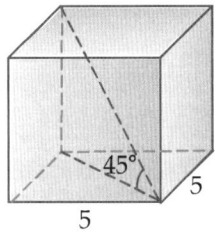

⑥ Rectangular prism

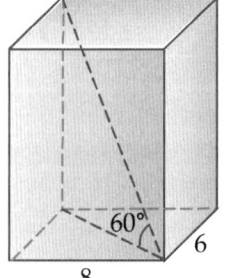

⑦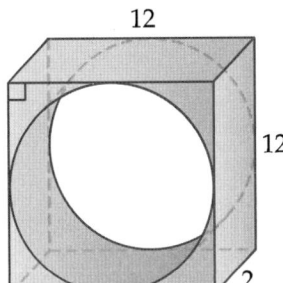

⑧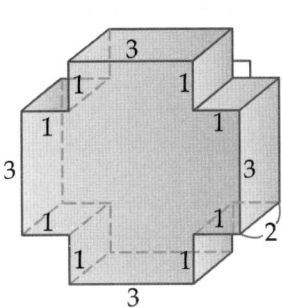

⑨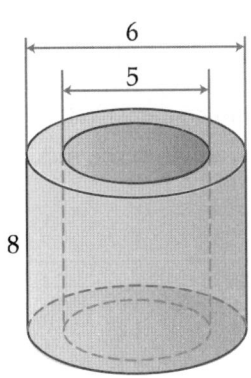

⑩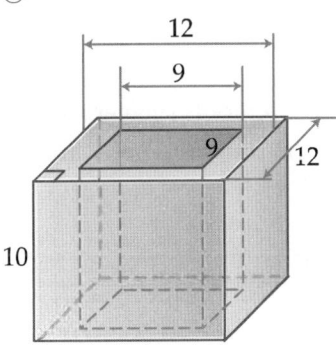

⑪ Oblique rectangular prism

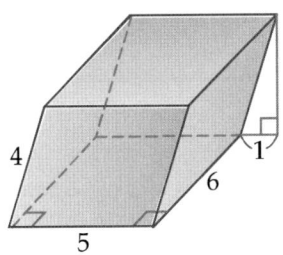

⑫ Oblique cylinder

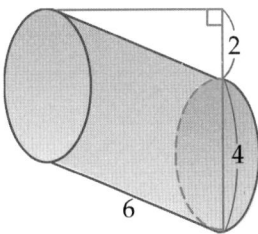

EXAMPLE 2. A cylinder has a volume of 250π in^3. What is the radius of this cylinder if its altitude equals the diameter of its base?

EXAMPLE 3. A rock is submerged in water in a rectangular prism container with a base of 20 cm by 30 cm. If the water level rises by 2 cm, what is the volume of the rock?

EXAMPLE 4. A square prism is inscribed in a cylinder with radius 8 and height of 10cm. Find the volume of the prism.

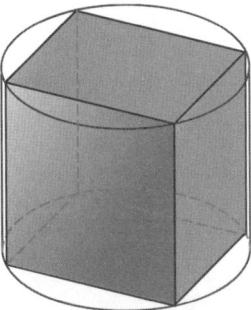

EXAMPLE 5. A 5 in. by 6 in. by 10. in rectangular prism is given in the figure. The vase has a solid base of height of 2 inches and the sides are each 0.5 inches thick. What is the volume of the vase?

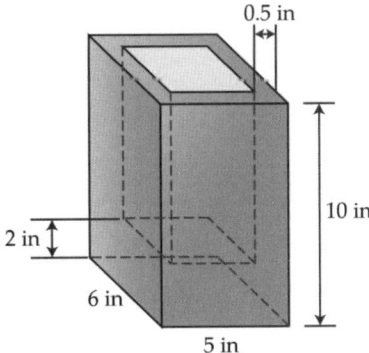

Part 11_Areas and Volumes of Solids 447

EXAMPLE 6. * Cube with length of 5 inches is given. A hole in the shape of square prism with a dimension 2 in. by 2 in. by 5 in. is drilled through the middle of the cube in three sides as shown in the figure. What is the volume?

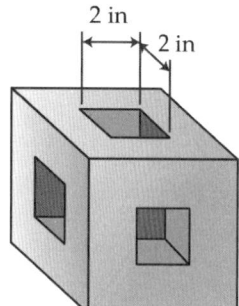

2. Diagonals of Prisms

※ Face Diagonal : Diagonal of a face (2D)

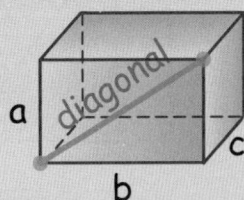 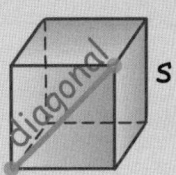

diag. = ① _____   diag. = ② _____

※ Body Diagonal : Diagonal of the whole solid (3D)

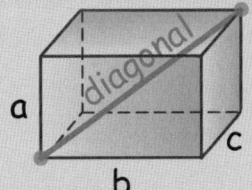 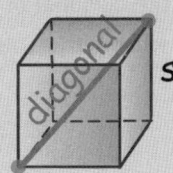

diag. = ③ _____   diag. = ④ _____

EXAMPLE 7. Find the length of the following segments AB and AC.

①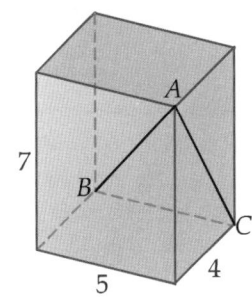

②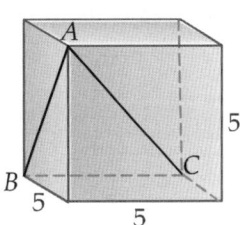

Blank : ① $\sqrt{a^2+b^2}$ ② $\sqrt{2}s$ ③ $\sqrt{a^2+b^2+c^2}$ ④ $\sqrt{3}s$

③ 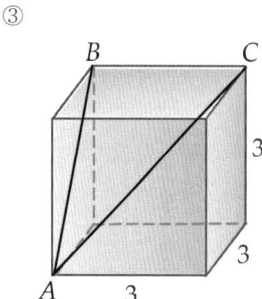   ④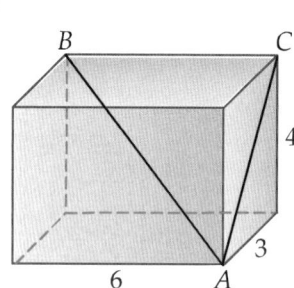

EXAMPLE 8. If the diagonal of a cube (diagonal that joins two vertices not in the same face) is 6 cm, what is the volume of the cube?

EXAMPLE 9. If the area of the triangle AHF in the figure is $16\sqrt{3}$ cm^2, what is the volume of the cube?

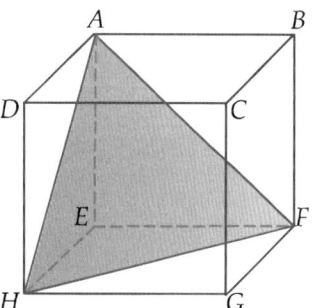

3. Volume of Pyramid and Cone

The ratio of the volume of a prism to the volume of a pyramid is ①_____, when the prism and pyramid have the same base and height. This means that the volume of a pyramid is one-third of the volume of a prism.

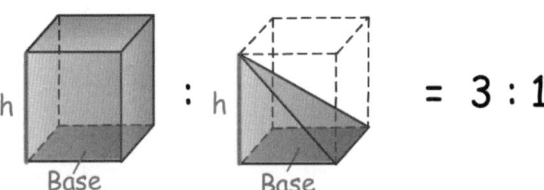

※ Volume of Pyramid and Cone

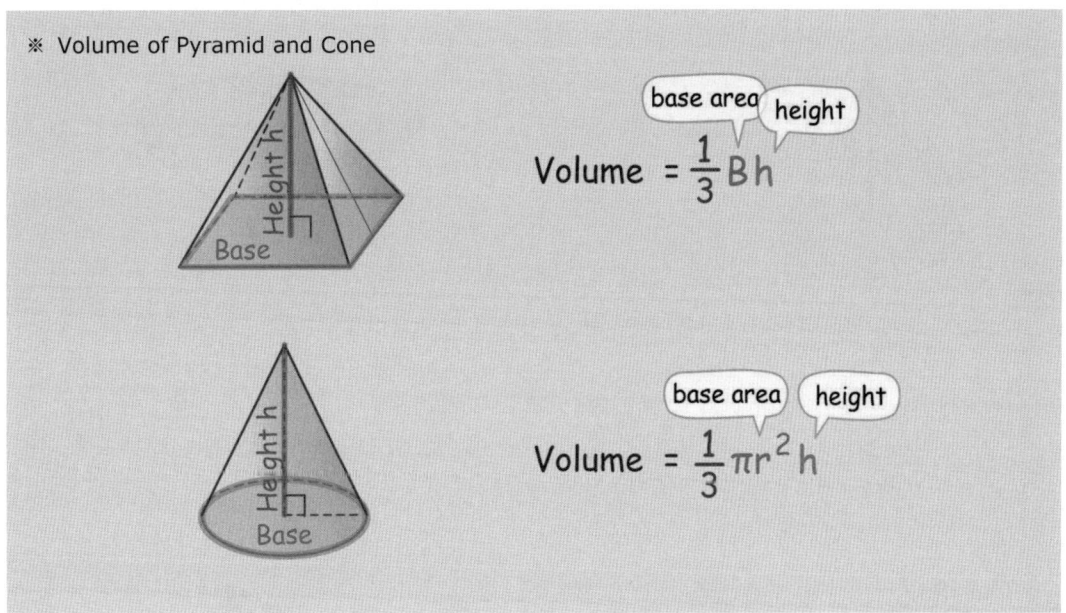

Volume = $\frac{1}{3}Bh$ (base area, height)

Volume = $\frac{1}{3}\pi r^2 h$ (base area, height)

Blank : ① 3 : 1

EXAMPLE 10.   Find the volume of the 3D figure.

① Square pyramid

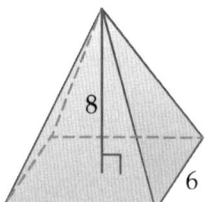

② Rectangular pyramid

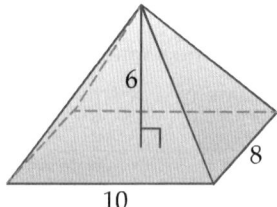

③

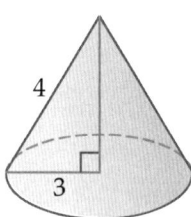

④

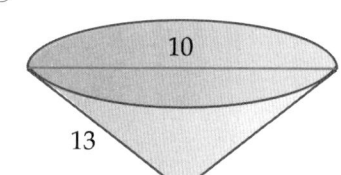

⑤

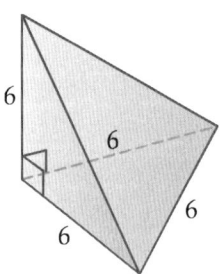

⑥

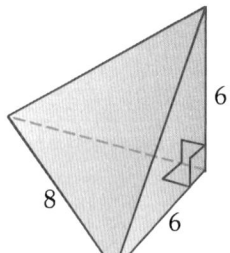

⑦ Oblique regular hexagonal pyramid   ⑧ Oblique cone

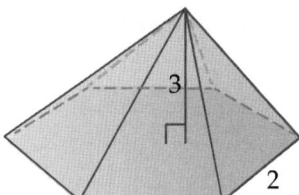 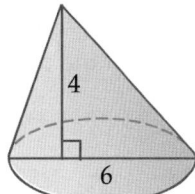

⑨ 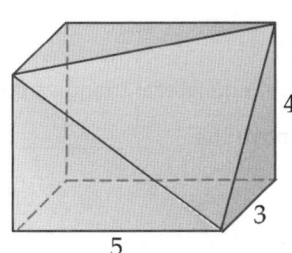   ⑩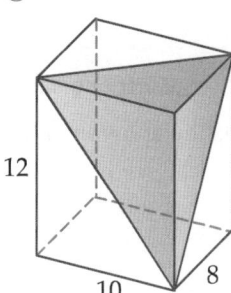

⑪ 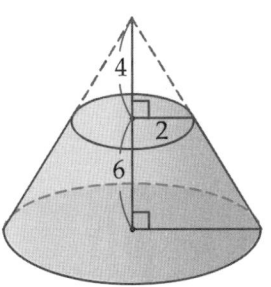   ⑫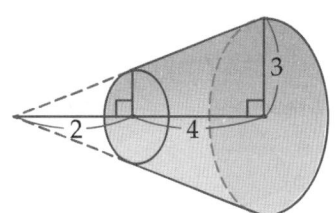

EXAMPLE 11.   *A right regular triangular pyramid is a three-dimensional shape with four equilateral triangles faces. If a lateral edge of a right regular triangular pyramid is 6 cm, what is the volume of the pyramid?

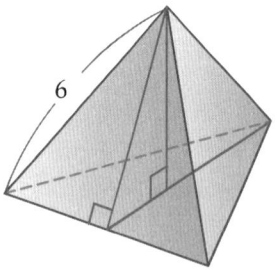

※ Fact about Right regular triangular pyramid (Pyramid with 4 equilateral triangles faces) :
A right regular triangular pyramid has its vertex directly above the ①_____
of its base.

EXAMPLE 12.   *A sector containing an angle of 120° is cut off from a circle of radius 9cm and folded into a cone. Find the volume of the cone.

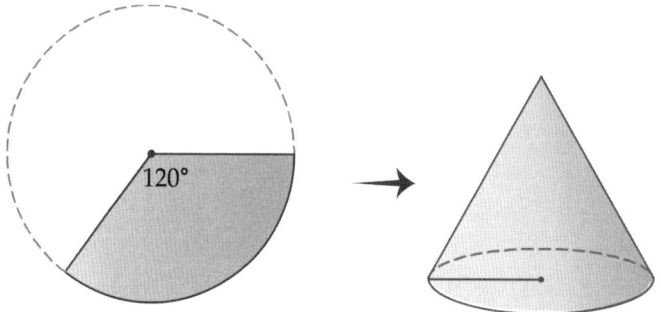

Blank : ① centroid

EXAMPLE 13.   *If the radius of a right circular cone is reduced by 10% and the height is reduced by 20%, by what percent must the volume of the cone be reduced?

> ☺ Tip:
>   x is increased by r% : ① _____
>   x is decreased by r% : ② _____

EXAMPLE 14.   *A right cylinder is inscribed in a right cone of height 8 cm and radius 6 cm. Express the volume of the cylinder in terms of its base radius r.

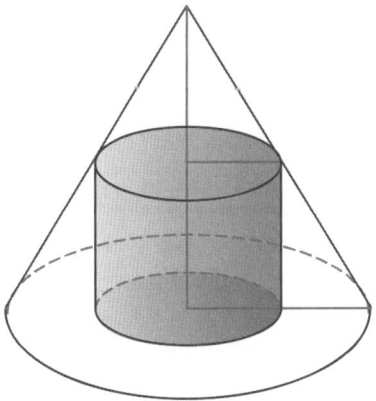

Blank : ① $x(1 + r/100)$ ② $x(1 - r/100)$

Mia's Geometry

11.4 Sphere

1. Surface Area of Sphere

Two pieces of leather fabric are wrapped around each other to make a baseball.

The total area of the leather fabric is roughly equal to the total area of ①_____ circles, which is equivalent to the surface area of a baseball.

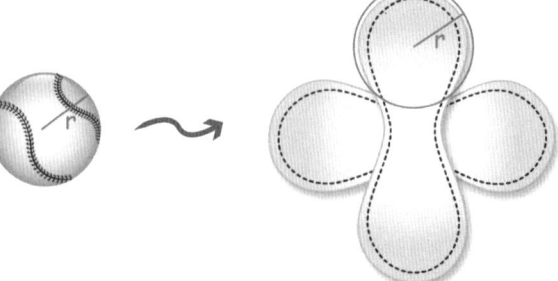

※ Surface Area of Sphere

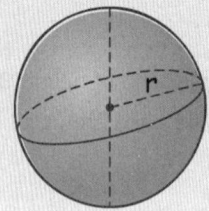

Suface Area = $4\pi r^2$

EXAMPLE 1. Find the surface area of the 3D figure.

①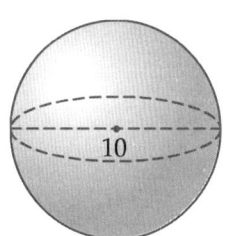

②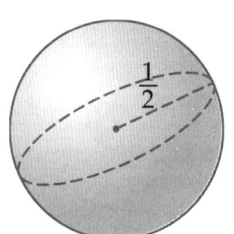

Blank : ① four

③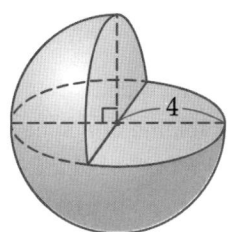

④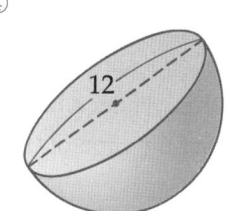

EXAMPLE 2. A silo consists of a cylinder capped by a hemispherical dome. About two cans of paint are needed to cover the hemispherical dome. How many cans are needed to paint the rest of the silo, excluding the bottom?

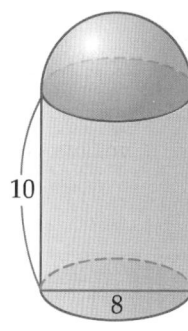

2. Volume of Sphere

Let's fit a cylinder around a sphere.

We must now make the cylinder's height 2r so the sphere fits perfectly inside.

Then we can notice that the ratio of the volume of a cylinder to the volume of a sphere is
①_____.

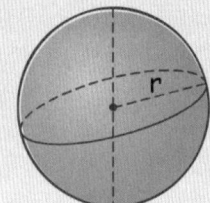 = 3 : 2

②_____ : *Volume of Sphere* = 3 : 2

Volume of Sphere = ③_____

※ Volume of Sphere

Volume = $\frac{4}{3}\pi r^3$

Blank : ① 3 : 2   ② $2\pi r^2$ ③ $\frac{4}{3}\pi r^3$

EXAMPLE 3. Find the volume of the sphere.

①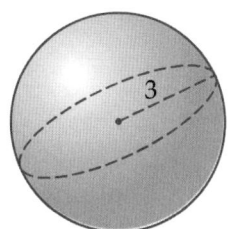

②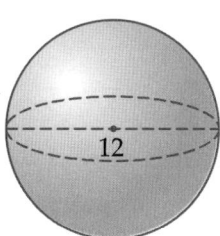

③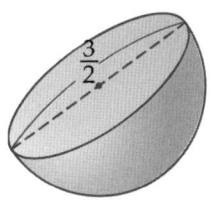

④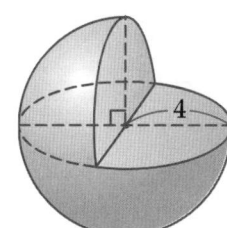

⑤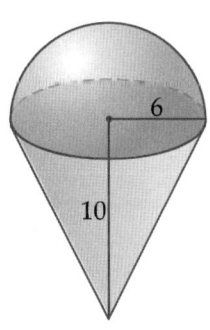

⑥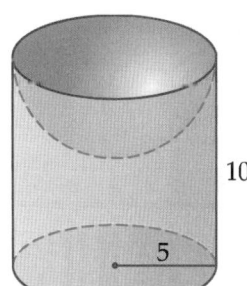

EXAMPLE 4. Two identical balls are packed tightly into a cylindrical tube with a volume 32π cm³. Find the volume of one ball.

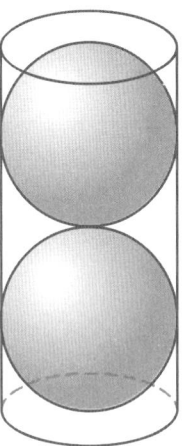

EXAMPLE 5. A sphere with radius r is inscribed in a cylinder. Show that the surface area of the sphere equals the lateral area of the cylinder.

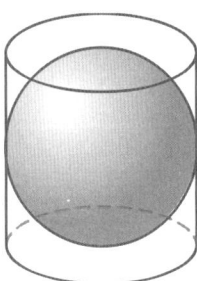

※ Volume of Sphere

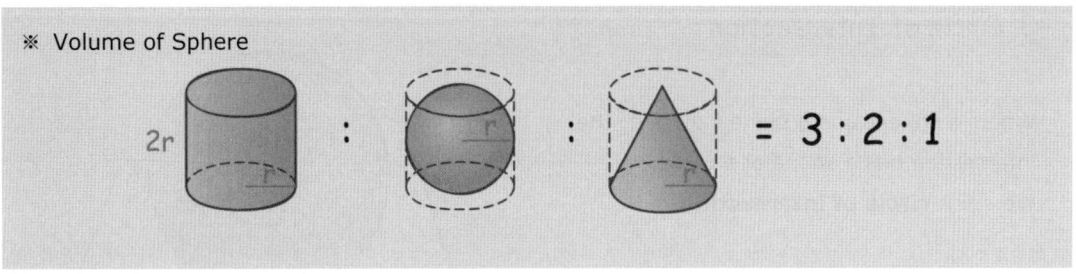

EXAMPLE 6. A cone and a sphere are inscribed in a cylinder as shown. If the volume of the sphere is 30m³, then what is the volume of the cone and cylinder?

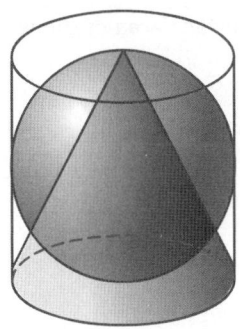

EXAMPLE 7. * A sphere and square pyramid are inscribed in a cube. What is the ratio of the volume of cube, sphere, and square pyramid?

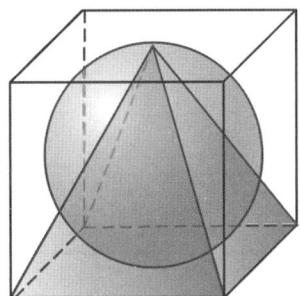

3. Circle of Intersection

Where a sphere and a plane intersect, the intersection has a shape of a circle.
We call it **circle of intersection**.

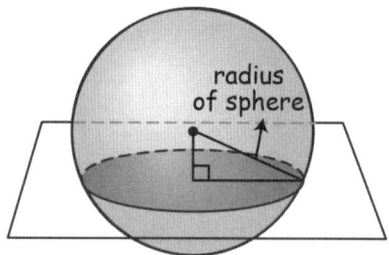

EXAMPLE 8. *A bowl of water, being a hemisphere has a radius of 10 cm. Water is filled in the bowl and has depth of 6 cm. Find the exposed surface area of the water?

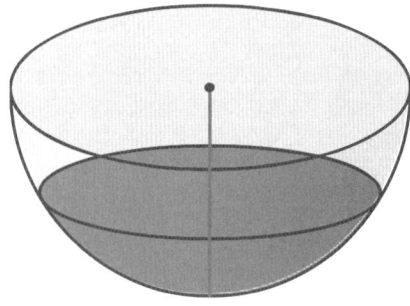

EXAMPLE 9. *A cylinder with height 12 and base radius 8 is inscribed in a sphere. Find the volume of the sphere.

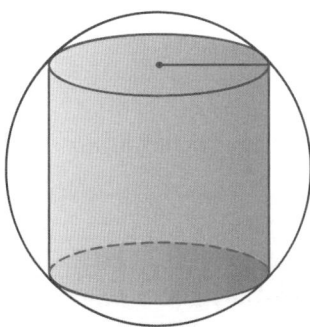

EXAMPLE 10. *A cone is inscribed in a sphere with radius 6 cm. If the center of the sphere is located 3cm above the base of the cone, what is the volume of cone?

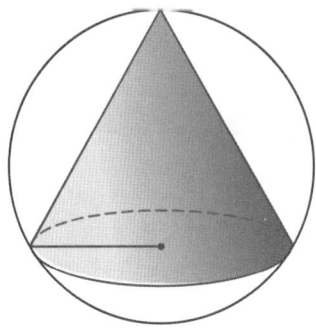

Mia's Geometry
11.5 Area and Volume of similar Solids

1. Similar 3D Figures

Two solids(3D figures) are ①_____ if the corresponding dimensions (such as length, width, height, radius, or diameter) are proportional.

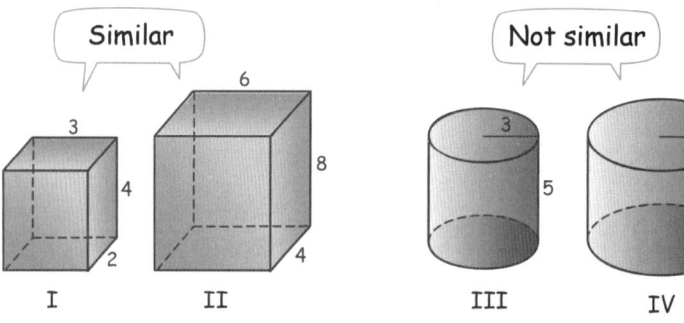

ex)   I and II are ②_____ since the scale ratio is ③_____.

   III and IV are ④_____.

EXAMPLE 1. Determine whether each pair of solids are similar or not. If similar, find the scale ratio. The figures are not drawn to scale.

①

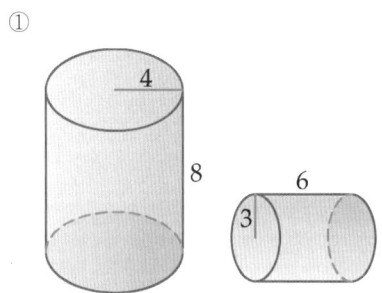

②

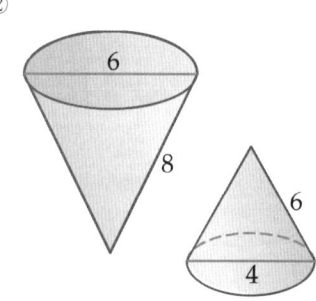

Blank : ① similar   ② similar   ③ 1 : 2   ④ not similar

③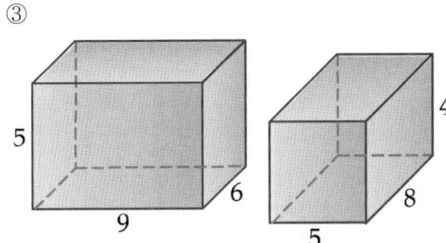

④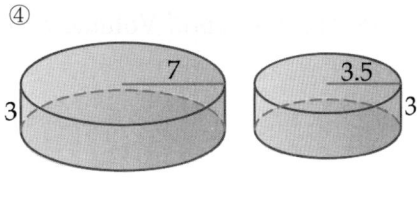

⑤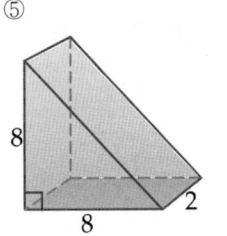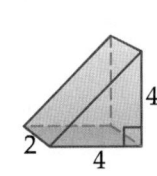

⑥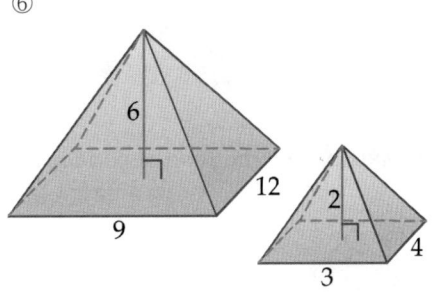

⑦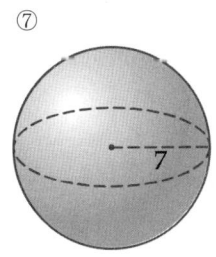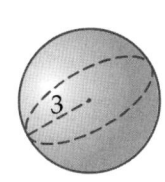

⑧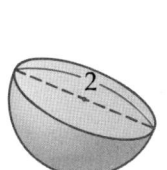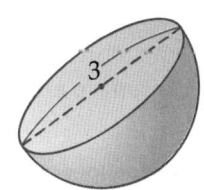

2. Perimeter, Area, and Volume of a Similar Solids

※ Perimeter, Area, and Volume of a Similar Solids

If the similarity ratio of two similar figures is $a : b$, then

the ratio of their **perimeters** is $a : b$,

the ratio of their **areas** is $a^2 : b^2$,

the ratio of their **volumes** is $a^3 : b^3$.

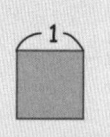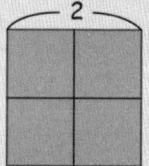
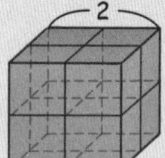

EXAMPLE 2. Find the ratio of surface areas and volumes of each pair of similar figures.

①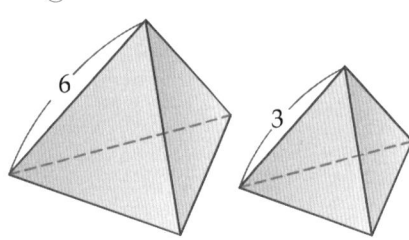

Ratio of the surface areas = _____

Ratio of the volumes = _____

②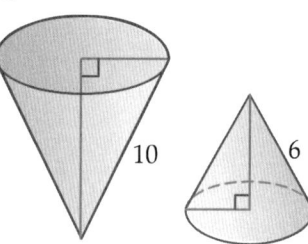

Ratio of the surface areas = _____

Ratio of the volumes = _____

③ 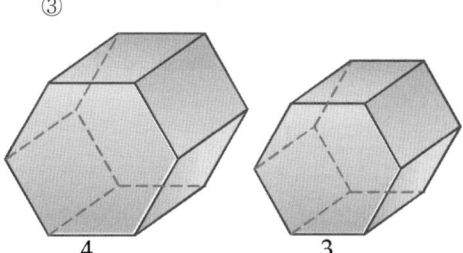   ④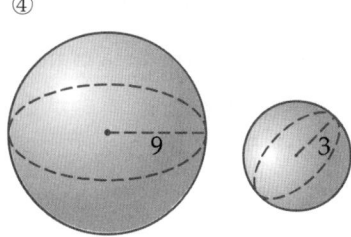

Ratio of the surface areas = _____   Ratio of the surface areas = _____

Ratio of the volumes = _____   Ratio of the volumes = _____

EXAMPLE 3. Fill in the table.

	Ratio of perimeters	Ratio of surface areas	Ratio of volumes
①	1 : 3		
②	6 : 10		
③		8 : 18	
④		9 : 16	
⑤			128 : 54
⑥			27 : 125
⑦		3 : 5	
⑧		2 : 3	

Part 11_Areas and Volumes of Solids 467

EXAMPLE 4. The shorter side of one rectangle is 6 ft. The shorter side of another similar rectangle is 9 ft. The area of the smaller rectangle is 48 ft^2. What is the area of another similar rectangle?

EXAMPLE 5. A diagonal of a cube is 3 cm and a diagonal of another cube is 4 cm. If the larger cube has a volume 192 cm^3, what is the volume of the smaller cube?

EXAMPLE 6. Two similar pyramids have base areas 8 m^2 and 50 m^2. If the volume of the smaller pyramid is 24 m^3, what is the volume of the larger pyramid?

EXAMPLE 7. There are two spherical candies with diameters of 2 cm and 6 cm, respectively. If the larger candy is melted down, how many candies of the same size as the smaller one can be made?

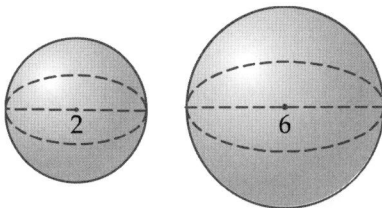

EXAMPLE 8. Water was filled up to two-thirds of the height in a conical shaped container with a volume of 81 cm³. What is the volume of the water?

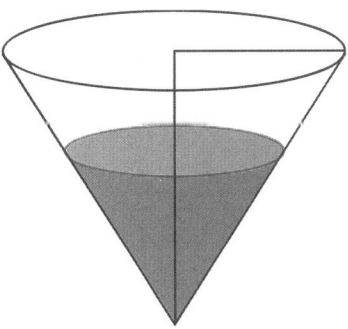

EXAMPLE 9. Half of the height of a large cone was sliced off from the top. What fraction of the cone's original volume remains?

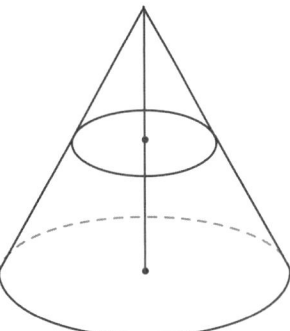

EXAMPLE 10. *If the lengths of the edges of a cube are increased by 20%, the volume of the cube will increased by how many percent?

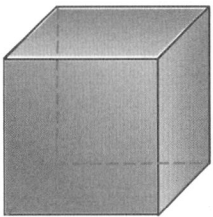

EXAMPLE 11. * Water is being filled at a constant rate into a conical shaped container as shown. If it takes 5 minutes to fill up 1/3 of the total height, how much *more* time will it take to completely fill the conical shaped container?

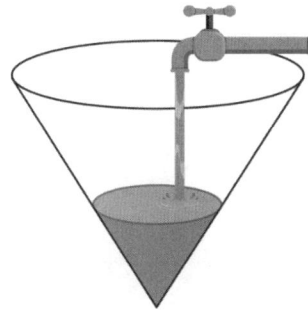

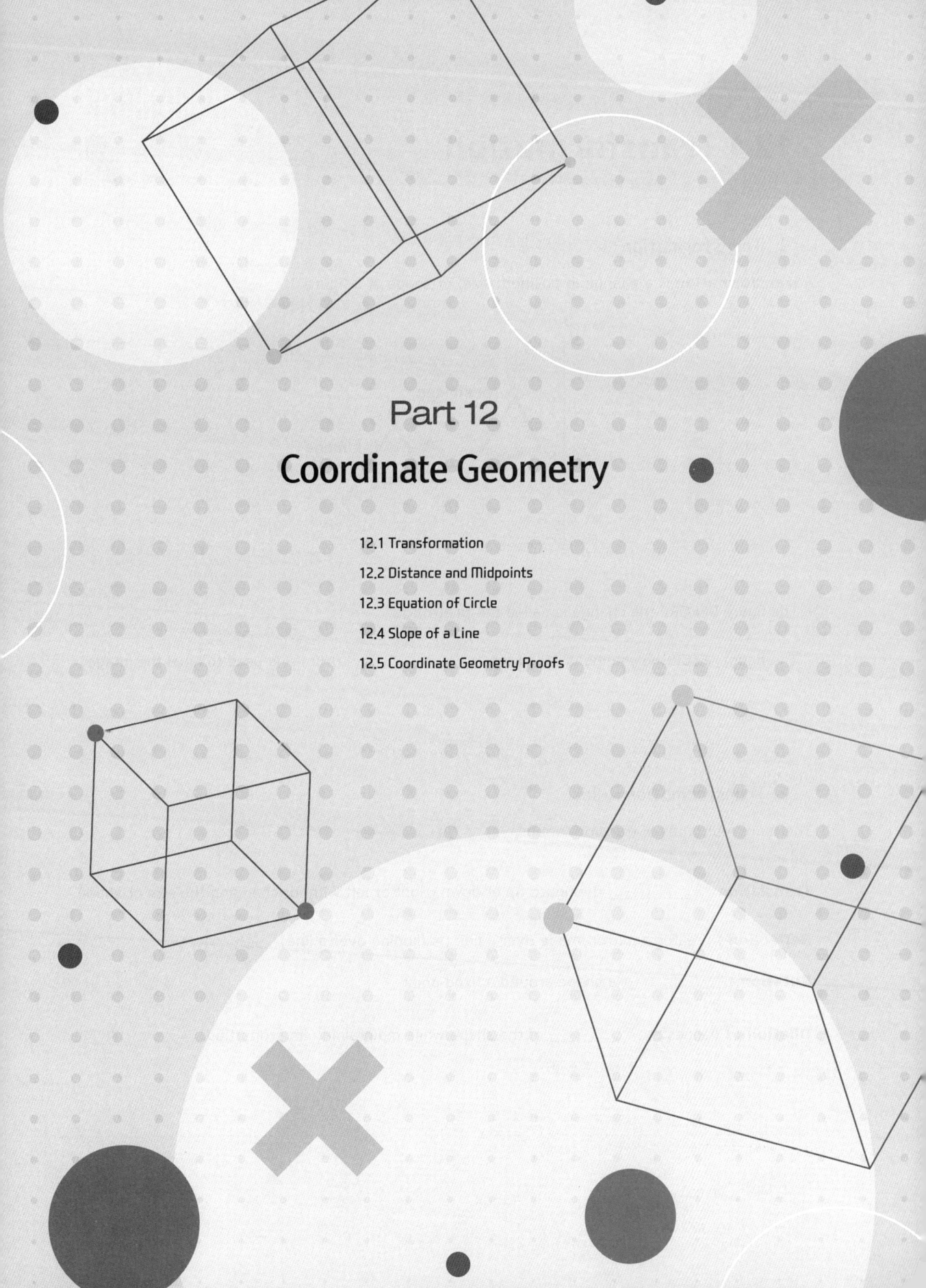

Mia's Geometry
12.1 Transformation

1. Transformation

A **transformation** is a change in position, size, or shape of a figure.

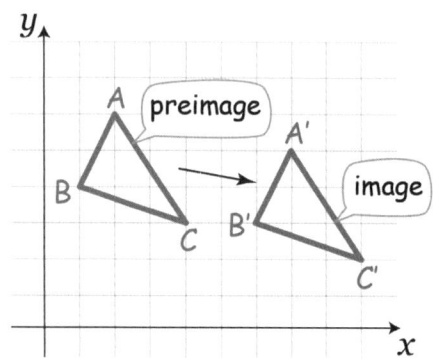

The figure BEFORE the change is called the **preimage**.

The figure AFTER the change is called the ①_____. ' (prime) is used to label the image

2. Transformation Rules

There are four types of transformations.

Translation : ②_____ the figure up or down, right or left without changing the size or shape

Reflection : Creates a mirror image over a line (= flipping over a line)

Rotation : ③_____ a shape around a fixed point

Dilation : Changes the ④_____ of the shape while maintaining its proportion.

Blank : ① image ② Move ③ Rotate ④ size

Type	In details	Rules of Transformation	
Translation	Move right a units up b units (If left or down, then subtract)	$(x, y) \to (x+a, y+b)$	
Reflection	Reflection over x axis	$(x, y) \to (x, -y)$	
	Reflection over y axis	$(x, y) \to (-x, y)$	
	Reflection over origin	$(x, y) \to (-x, -y)$	
	Reflection over y = x	$(x, y) \to (y, x)$	
	Reflection over y = -x	$(x, y) \to (-y, -x)$	

Rotation	Rotation 90° CCW about the origin	$(x, y) \rightarrow (-y, x)$	
	Rotation 180° CCW about the origin (=Reflection over origin)	$(x, y) \rightarrow (-x, -y)$	
	Rotation 270° CCW about the origin	$(x, y) \rightarrow (y, -x)$	
Dilation	Dilation with scale factor of k with respect to the origin	$(x, y) \rightarrow (kx, ky)$	

- CCW means Counterclockwise.
- Rotation 180° CCW about the origin = Reflection about origin

EXAMPLE 1. Find the coordinate of the image of the point using the transformation without using a coordinate plane.

① A(-2, 3), reflection over x-axis

② B(5, -1), 180° CCW rotation

③ C(4, -8), translation 2 units left and 3 units up.

④ D(-4, -10), reflection over y-axis

⑤ E(-7, -1), 270° CCW rotation

⑥ F(4, -7), move 4 units right and 1 unit down.

⑦ G(0, -4), reflection over origin

⑧ H(-2, 4), dilation with scale factor of $\frac{1}{2}$ with respect to origin

⑨ I(-1, 7), dilation with scale factor of 3 with respect to origin

⑩ J(4, 0), reflection over y = -x

⑪ K(-5, 3), reflection over y = -x

⑫ L(-4, -2), 90° CCW rotation

EXAMPLE 2. Graph the image △A'B'C' using the transformation.

① Reflection over y = x

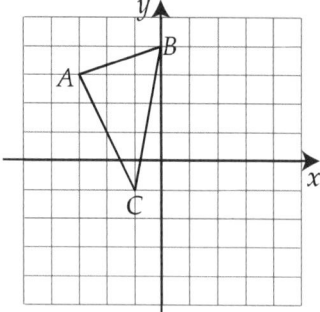

② Reflection over origin

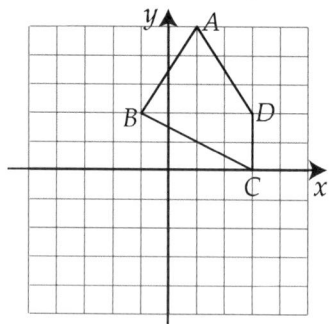

③ 90° CCW rotation.

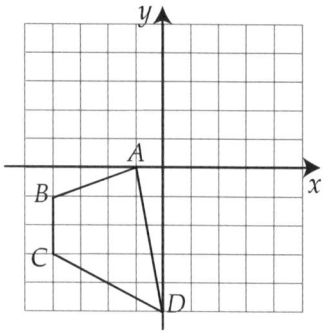

④ 270° CCW rotation

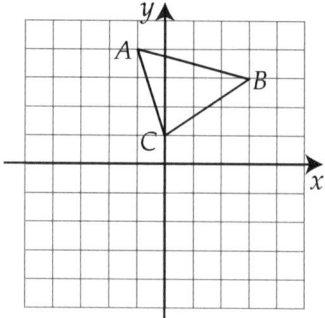

EXAMPLE 3. Write a transformation rule for the following graphs.

①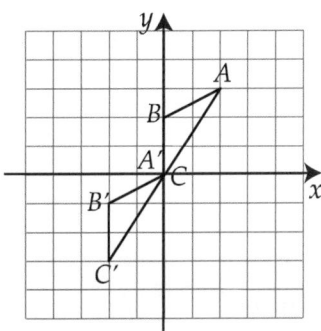

②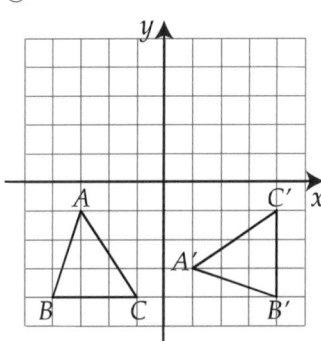

③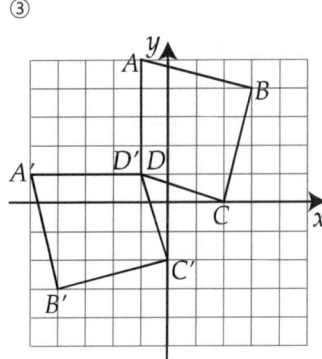

④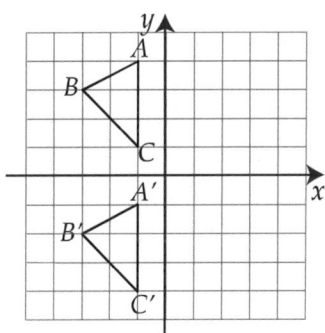

⑤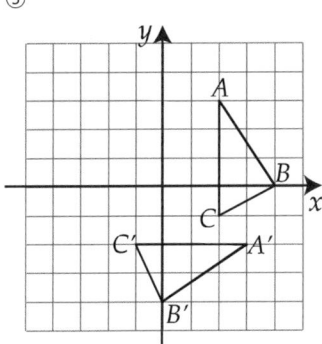

⑥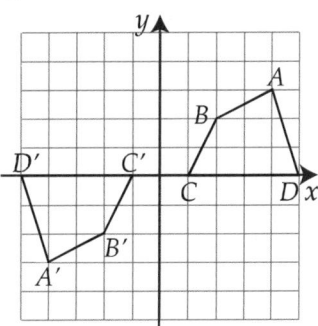

3. Composition of Transformation

Sometimes we want to perform two or more transformations on a given preimage. We call this a
①_____ of transformation.

EXAMPLE 4. Graph the image $\triangle A''B''C''$ using the transformations.

① a. $(x,y) \to (x-1, y+2)$
   b. 180° CCW rotation

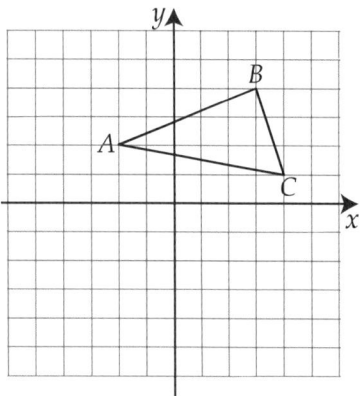

② a. 90° CCW rotation
   b. Reflection over x axis

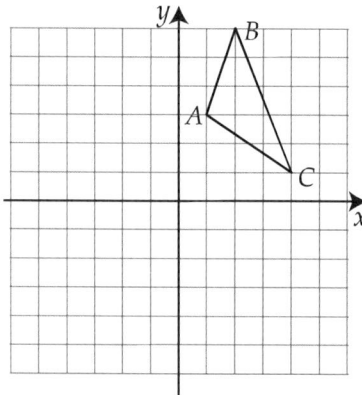

Blank : ① composition

③ a. 270° CCW rotation.

b. $(x,y) \rightarrow (2x, 2y)$

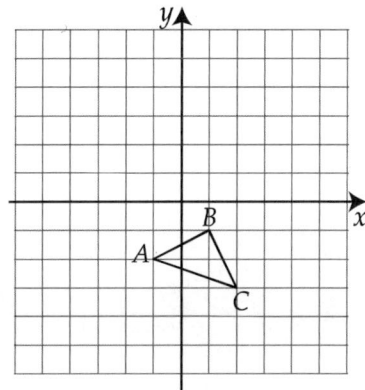

④ a. Reflection over y = -x

b. $(x,y) \rightarrow (x+3, y-1)$

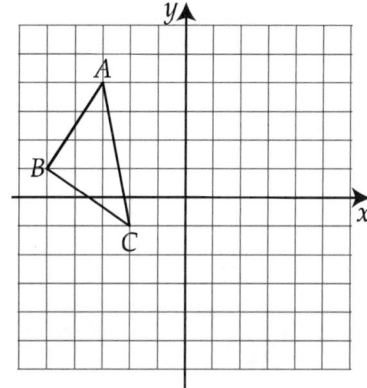

⑤ a. Reflection over y = -x

b. 90° CCW rotation.

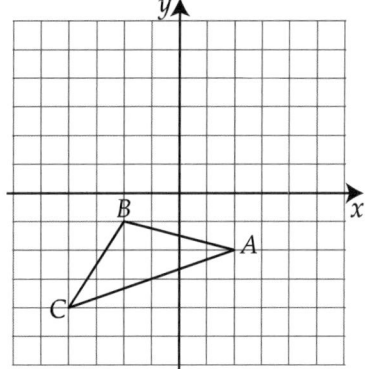

⑥ a. $(x,y) \rightarrow (0.5x, 0.5y)$

b. 180° CCW rotation.

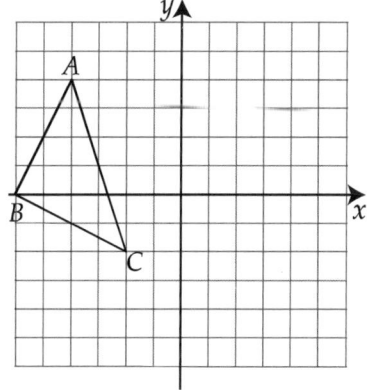

Mia's Geometry
12.2 Distance and Midpoints

1. Midpoint Formula

※ Midpoint Formula

The **midpoint** between any two points (x_1, y_1) and (x_2, y_2) is;

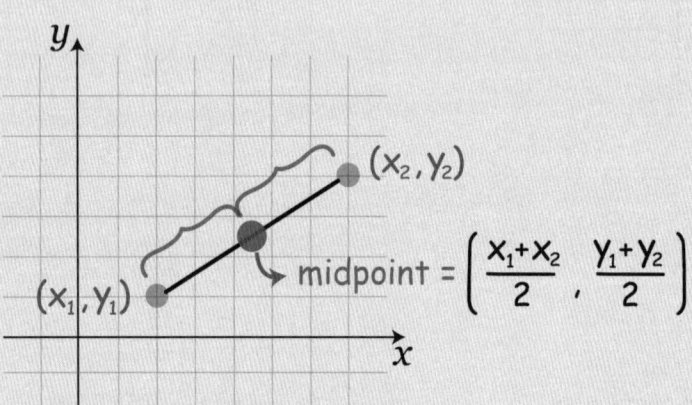

EXAMPLE 1. Find the midpoint.

① $(5,2),(2,4)$ ② $(-2,-4),(4,4)$

③ $(\sqrt{3},3),(-\sqrt{3},-3)$ ④ $(0,\sqrt{5})(1,2\sqrt{5})$

⑤ $(2+\sqrt{3}, 1+\sqrt{7}), (-2+\sqrt{3}, 1-\sqrt{7})$ ⑥ $(1-4\sqrt{2}, -\sqrt{3}), (1-6\sqrt{2}, 5\sqrt{3})$

⑦ $(a, ab), (b, -ab)$ ⑧ $(a+b, a-b), (a-b, a+b)$

EXAMPLE 2. The diameter of a circle connects two points (2 , -3) and (6 , 4) on the circle. Find the coordinates of the center of the circle.

2. Distance Formula

Let's say we have two points (x_1, y_1) and (x_2, y_2).

Vertical distance between two points; ①_____

Horizontal distance between two points; ②_____

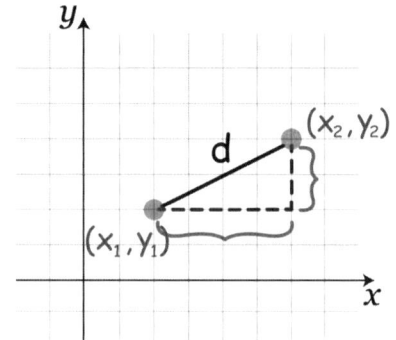

Then according to Pythagorean Theorem the distance between two points is;

③_____

※ **Distance Formula**

The **distance d** between any two points (x_1, y_1) and (x_2, y_2) is;

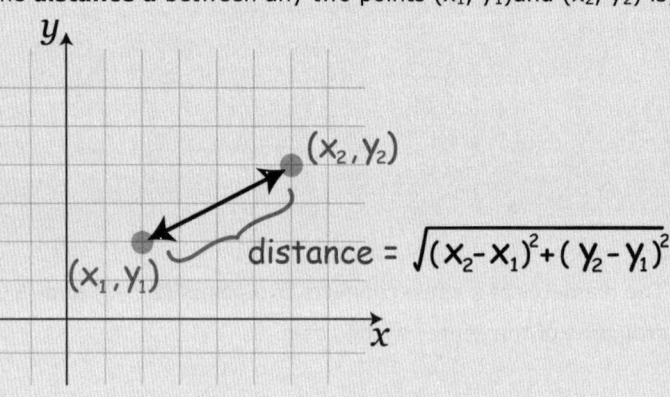

$$\text{distance} = \sqrt{(x_2-x_1)^2 + (y_2-y_1)^2}$$

EXAMPLE 3. Find the distance.

① $(5,2), (2,4)$ ② $(-2,-4), (4,4)$

Blank: ① $y_2 - y_1$ ② $x_2 - x_1$ ③ $\sqrt{(x_2 - x_1)^2 + (y_2 - y_1)^2}$

③ $(\sqrt{3}, 3), (-\sqrt{3}, -3)$ ④ $(0, \sqrt{5})(1, 2\sqrt{5})$

⑤ $(2, \sqrt{7}), (-2, \sqrt{7})$ ⑥ $(1-4\sqrt{2}, -\sqrt{3}), (1-6\sqrt{2}, 5\sqrt{3})$

EXAMPLE 4. The diameter of a circle connects two points (2, -3) and (6, 4) on the circle. Find the radius of the circle.

Mia's Geometry
12.3 Equation of Circle

1. Equation of a circle

A **circle** is a set of all points on a plane that are ① _____ from a center.

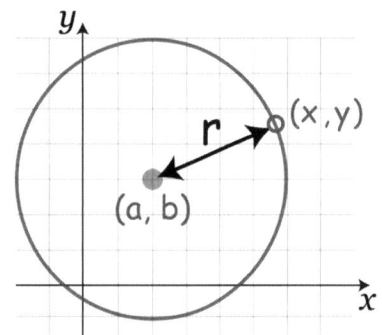

The circle is **all the points** ② _____ that are "③ ____" away from the center ④ _____.

It means
the distance between (x, y) and (a, b) is r;

⑤ _____

※ **Equation of a Circle**

$$(x-a)^2 + (y-b)^2 = r^2$$

center (a, b)   radius r

A circle with center (a,b) and radius r.

Blank: ① equidistant   ② (x, y)   ③ r   ④ (a, b)   ⑤ $r = \sqrt{(x-a)^2 + (y-b)^2}$

EXAMPLE 1. Find the center and radius of the circle with the given equation. Then graph the circle.

① $(x-1)^2 + (x+3)^2 = 9$

② $(x+2)^2 + (y-4)^2 = 4$

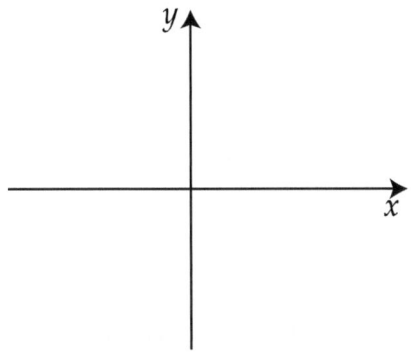
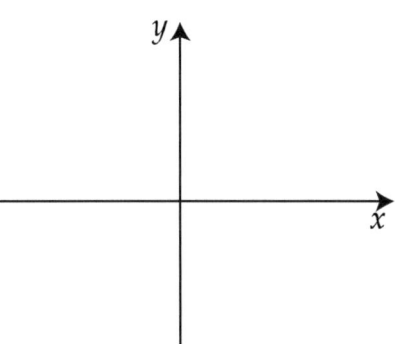

③ $(x+2)^2 + y^2 = 16$

④ $x^2 + (y-4)^2 = 16$

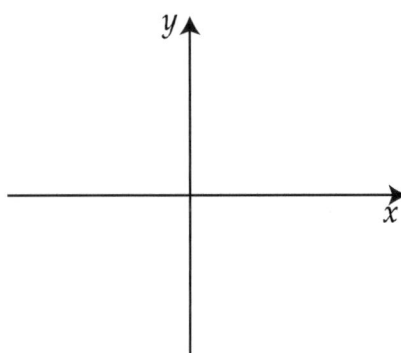
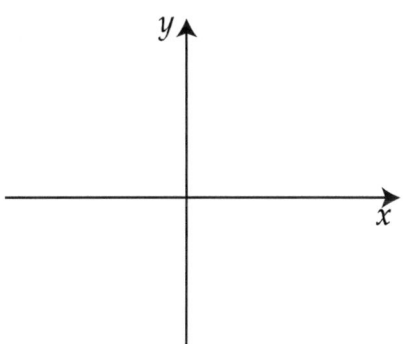

⑤ $x^2 + y^2 = 27$

⑥ $x^2 + (y+1)^2 = 12$

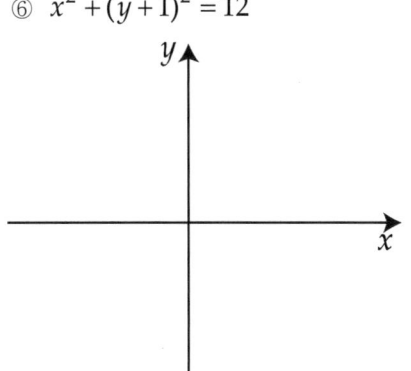

EXAMPLE 2. Write an equation for the circle that satisfies each set of conditions.

① center (3, -7) and radius 5

② center (0, 2) and radius 3

③ center (0, 0) and radius $\sqrt{5}$

④ center (-1, 7) and radius $\sqrt{2}$

⑤ center (0, -3) and diameter $\sqrt{8}$

⑥ center (-2, 0) and diameter 8

⑦ center (-2, 3) and passes through origin

⑧ center (-5, 2) and passes through (-9, 4)

⑨ endpoints of a diameter at (0, 6) and (-8, -2)

⑩ endpoints of a diameter at (-4, -2) and (8, 6)

⑪ * center (-8, -5) and tangent to x-axis

⑫ * center (5, -4) and tangent to y-axis

2. Completing the square

※ How to 'complete the square'? (= making perfect square trinomial)

Take ① _____ and ② _____ the number in front of x!

Perfect square trinomial: $x^2 - 6x + \boxed{③}$ = Perfect square: $(x-3)^2$

take the half → square it!

EXAMPLE 3. Find the value of c that makes each a perfect square trinomial. Then write the trinomial as a perfect square.

① $x^2 + 10x + c$ ② $x^2 - 12x + c$

③ $x^2 - 22x + c$ ④ $x^2 + 18x + c$

⑤ $x^2 + 3x + c$ ⑥ $x^2 - x + c$

⑦ $x^2 - 0.8x + c$ ⑧ $x^2 + 2.2x + c$

⑨ $x^2 + \dfrac{3}{5}x + c$ ⑩ $x^2 - \dfrac{x}{2} + c$

Blank : ① half ② square ③ 9

3. General Form of the Equation of a Circle

More *neat* way to show it?

※ General Form of the Equation of a Circle

$$x^2 + y^2 + Ax + By + C = 0$$

EXAMPLE 4. Find the center and radius of the circle with the given equation.

☺ Tip: Try to complete the square!

① $x^2 + y^2 - 10x + 8y + 16 = 0$

② $x^2 + y^2 + 2x + 6y + 2 = 0$

③ $x^2 - 6x + y^2 = 12$

④ $x^2 + y^2 + 10y + 14 = 0$

⑤ $x^2 + y^2 + 5x + 3y - 25 = 0$ ⑥ $x^2 + y^2 + 3x - 7y = 0$

Mia's Geometry
12.4 Slope of a Line

1. Slope of a Line

※ **Slope** shows the ①_____ of a line and is represented by the letter **m**

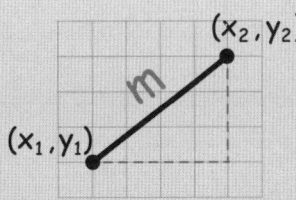

$$\text{slope} = m = \boxed{②} = \frac{y_2 - y_1}{x_2 - x_1}$$

※ Types of Slopes

Positive Slope ($m>0$) : The line rises from left to right.

Negative Slope ($m<0$) : The line falls from left to right.

Zero Slope ($m=0$) : The line is horizontal

Undefined Slope : The line is vertical

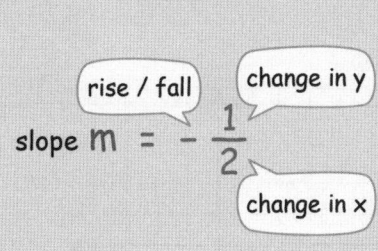

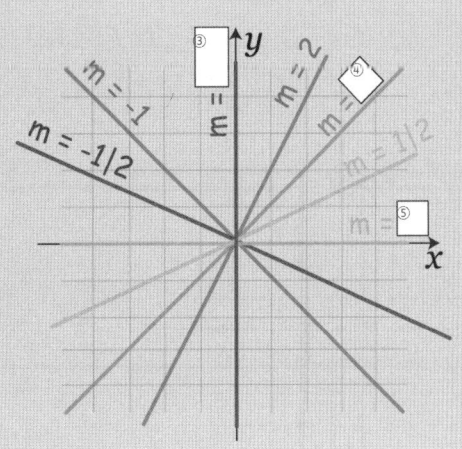

Blank : ① steepness   ② $\frac{\text{rise}}{\text{run}}$ ③ undefined   ④ 1   ⑤ 0

EXAMPLE 1. Find the slope of the line.

①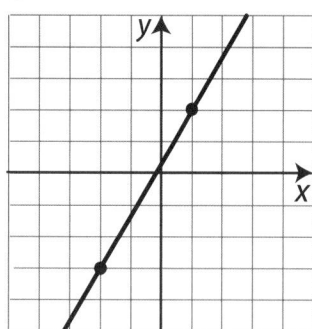

②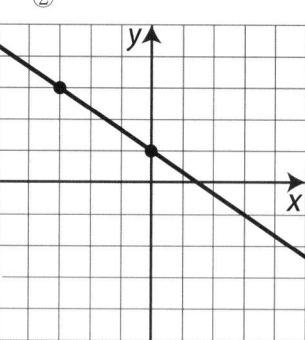

③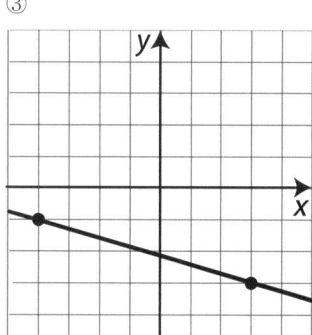

④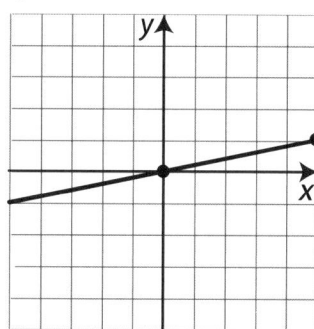

⑤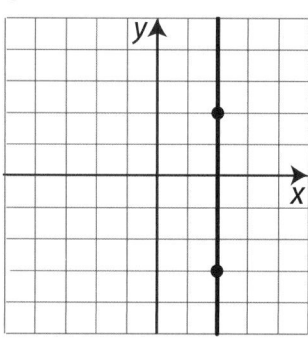

⑥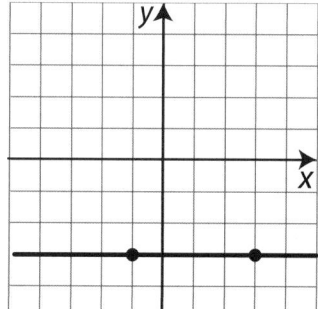

⑦
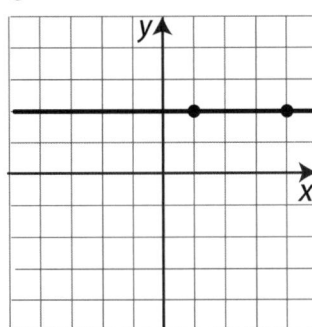

EXAMPLE 2. Find the slope of the line that passes through each pair of points.

☺ Tip: Make sure to subtract in the same order
in both the numerator and the denominator.

① $(1,5), (-1,-3)$

② $(1,9), (0,6)$

③ $(0,2), (3,0)$

④ $(8,-5), (4,-2)$

⑤ $\left(-\dfrac{5}{2},-4\right), (1,2)$

⑥ $(2,-3), \left(\dfrac{3}{2},-4\right)$

⑦ (5,2),(−3,2)   ⑧ (8,2),(8,−1)

2. Two Linear Graphs

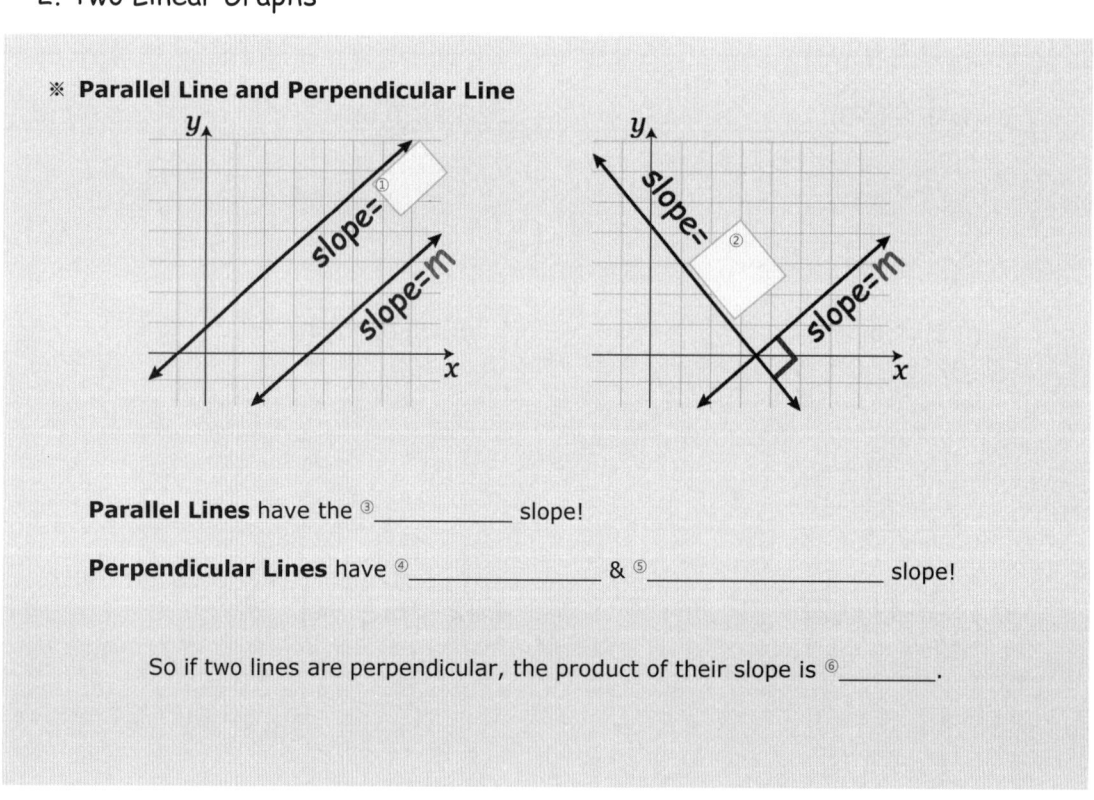

Parallel Line and Perpendicular Line

Parallel Lines have the ③_____ slope!

Perpendicular Lines have ④_____ & ⑤_____ slope!

So if two lines are perpendicular, the product of their slope is ⑥_____.

Blank : ① m ② $-\dfrac{1}{m}$ ③ same ④ opposite ⑤ reciprocal ⑥ -1

EXAMPLE 3. Two lines are given. Are the lines parallel, perpendicular, or neither?

① Line passes (2, –5) and (6, 2)
   Line passes (4, –3) and (8, 4).

② Line passes (7, 3) and (2, 4).
   Line passes (1, 1) and (0, 6).

③ Line passes (4, –3) and (6, 2).
   Line passes (3, –2) and (13, 2).

④ Line passes (2, 7) and (3, –1).
   Line passes (6, –4) and (–2, –5).

⑤ Line passes (–1, –4) and (2, 2).
   Line passes (4, 3) and (2, 4).

⑥ Line passes (5, –2) and (–3, –4).
   Line passes (3, –4) and (7, –3).

Mia's Geometry

12.5 Coordinate Geometry Proofs

1. Formulas for Coordinate Geometry proof

Midpoint Formula	$\left(\dfrac{x_1+x_2}{2}, \dfrac{y_1+y_2}{2}\right)$
Distance Formula	$\sqrt{(x_2-x_1)^2+(y_2-y_1)^2}$
Slope Formula	$\dfrac{y_2-y_1}{x_2-x_1}$
Parallel Lines have the ①_____ slope	
Perpendicular Lines have ②_____ and ③_____ slope	

2. Proving a triangle is a right triangle

※ Proving a triangle is a right triangle

    Method 1: Using the Distance Formula
        (Pythagorean Theorem)

    Method 2: Using the Slope Formula
        (Perpendicular Slopes)

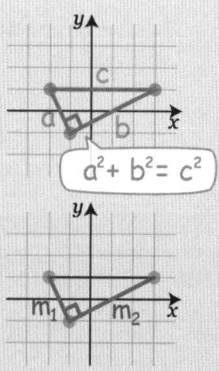

Blank : ① same   ② opposite   ③ reciprocal

EXAMPLE 1. Prove that the polygon with coordinates $A(1, 3)$, $B(5, 6)$, and $C(4, -1)$ is an isosceles right triangle.

EXAMPLE 2. Prove that the polygon with coordinates $A(5, 6)$, $B(2, -3)$, and $C(8, 5)$ is an isosceles right triangle.

3. Proving a Quadrilateral is a Parallelogram

※ Proving a Quadrilateral is a Parallelogram

Method 1: Show both pairs of opposite sides are parallel
(Using slopes)

Method 2: Show both pairs of opposite sides are equal
(Using distance formula)

Method 3: Show the diagonals bisect each other
(Using midpoint formula, <u>Recommend</u>!)

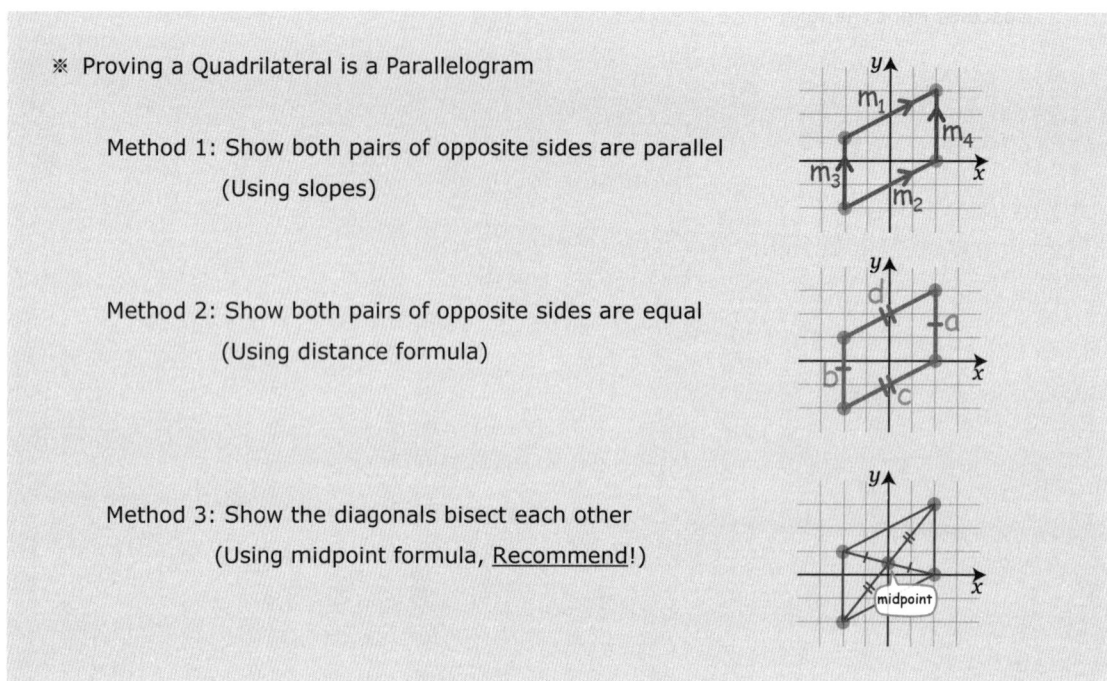

EXAMPLE 3. Prove that the polygon with coordinates $A(-1, 1)$, $B(-3, 4)$, $C(1, 5)$ and $D(3, 2)$ is a parallelogram.

EXAMPLE 4. Prove that the polygon with coordinates $R(3, 2)$, $S(6, 2)$, $T(0, -2)$ and $U(-3, -2)$ is a parallelogram.

4. Proving a Quadrilateral is a Rectangle

※ Proving a Quadrilateral is a Rectangle

First, prove that it is a *parallelogram*, then

Method 1: Show that the diagonals are congruent.
 (Using Distance Formula, <u>Recommend</u>!)

Method 2: Show that it has one right angle.
 (Using Slopes)

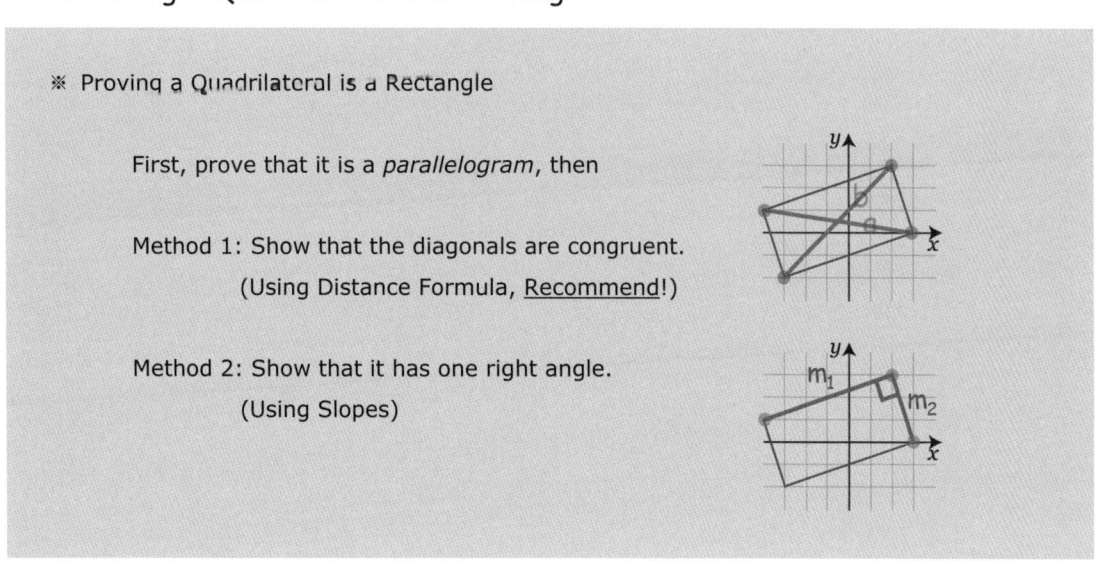

EXAMPLE 5. Prove that the polygon with coordinates $A(0, 4)$, $B(4, 2)$, $C(1, -4)$, and $D(-3, -2)$ is a parallelogram.

EXAMPLE 6. Prove that the polygon with coordinates $G(1, 1)$, $H(5, 3)$, $I(4, 5)$ and $J(0, 3)$ is a rectangle.

5. Proving a Quadrilateral is a Rhombus

※ Proving a Quadrilateral is a Rhombus

First, prove that it is a *parallelogram*, then

Method 1: Prove that the diagonals are perpendicular.
(Using perpendicular slopes, <u>Recommend</u>!)

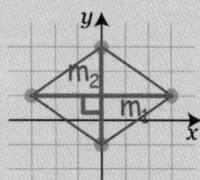

Method 2: Prove that all four sides are equal or prove that a pair of adjacent sides is equal.
(Using distance formula)

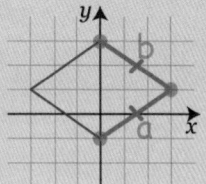

EXAMPLE 7. Prove that the polygon with coordinates $Q\ (6, 7)$, $R\ (11, 7)$, $S\ (8, 3)$, $T\ (3, 3)$ is a rhombus.

EXAMPLE 8. Prove that the polygon with coordinates $A(-1, 4)$, $B(2, 6)$, $C(5, 4)$ and $D(2, 2)$ is a rhombus.

6. Proving that a Quadrilateral is a Square

There are many ways to do this. I recommend proving the diagonals bisect each other (parallelogram), are equal (rectangle) and perpendicular (rhombus).

EXAMPLE 9. Prove that the polygon with coordinates $A(0, 0)$, $B(4, 3)$, $C(7, -1)$ and $D(3, -4)$ is a square.

EXAMPLE 10. Prove that the polygon with coordinates $A(1, 3)$, $B(2, 0)$, $C(5, 1)$ and $D(4, 4)$ is a square.

7. Proving a Quadrilateral is a Trapezoid

Show one pair of sides are parallel (same slope) and one pair of sides are not parallel (different slopes).

EXAMPLE 11. Prove that the polygon with coordinates $A(1, 5)$, $B(4, 7)$, $C(7, 3)$ and $D(1, -1)$ is a trapezoid.

EXAMPLE 12. Prove that the polygon with coordinates $J(4, 7)$, $K(11, 0)$, $L(7, 0)$, and $M(4, 3)$ is an isosceles trapezoid.

Mia's Geometry
Abbreviation

Abbreviation	Meaning
add.	addition
alt. ext. ∠	alternate interior angle
alt. int. ∠	alternate exterior angle
bisct.	bisect, bisector
compl.	complementary
consec. int ∠	consecutive interior angle
conv.	converse
corresp.∠	corresponding angle
CPCTC	Corresponding parts of congruent triangles are congruent.
def.	definition
diag.	diagonal
div.	division
ext. ∠	exterior angle
iff	if and only if
ineq. inequal.	inequality
int. ∠	interior angle
isos.	isosceles
m∠A	measure of angle A
midpt.	midpoint
midseg.	midsegment
mult.	multiplication
n-gon	polygon with n sides
post.	postulate

prop.	property
pt.	point
quad.	quadrilateral
rect.	rectangle
rhm.	rhombus
rt. ∠	right angle
seg.	segment
substi.	substitution
subtra.	subtraction
suppl.	supplementary
thm.	theorem
trans.	transversal
trap.	trapezoid
vert. ∠	vertical angle
∠	angle
∥	parallel, is parallel to
⊥	perpendicular, is perpendicular to
△	triangle
▱	parallelogram
▫	Quadrilateral
≅	congruent
~	similar, is similar to
⊙	circle
r	radius
∴	Therefore

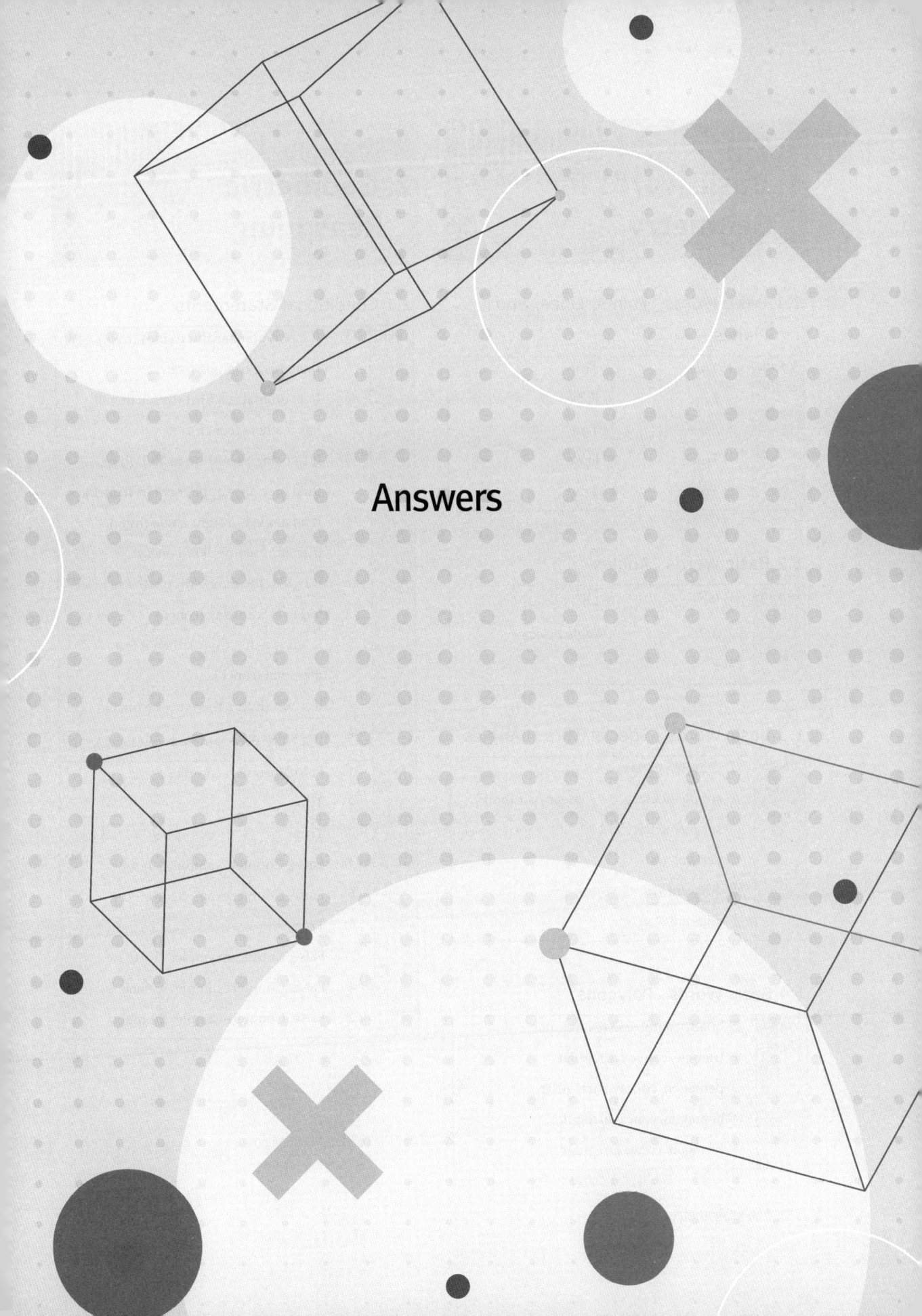

Answers

Answers

1. Basic words for Geometry

1.1 Basic Words_ Points, Lines, and Planes

Vocab check	① True	② True
	③ False	④ False
	⑤ False	⑥ True
	⑦ True	⑧ False
	⑨ True	⑩ True

1.2 Basic Words_ Angles

Vocab check	① 90°	② $\overrightarrow{OC}, \overrightarrow{OD}$
	③ AOE	④ angle bisector
	⑤ 4	

1.3 Basic Words_ Special Pairs of Angles

Vocab check	① complementary ∠s
	② supplementary ∠s , linear pair (both)
	③ supplementary ∠s
	④ vertical ∠s
	⑤ adjacent ∠s
	⑥ adjacent ∠s

1.4 Basic Words_ Polygons

Vocab check	① quadrilateral, convex, regular
	② triangle, convex, irregular
	③ pentagon, concave, irregular
	④ heptagon, concave, regular
	⑤ hexagon, convex, regular

Answers

2. Geometric Reasoning

2.1 Conditional Statements

Ex1.	①	If a polygon has three sides (hyp.), then it is a triangle (concl.).
	②	If an animal is a bird (hyp.), then it has feathers (concl.).
	③	If two angles add up to 180° (hyp.), then they are supplementary (concl.).
	④	If an angle is a right angle (hyp.), then it measures 90° (concl.).
	⑤	If I go to the movie (hyp.), then today is Saturday (concl.).
	⑥	If Jeff is a dog (hyp.), then it is a mammal (concl.).
	⑦	If $x > 5$ (hyp.), then $x > 1$ (concl.).
	⑧	If $x^2 = 4$ (hyp.), then $x = 2$ (concl.).
Ex2.	①	False, Counterexample: $x = 2$
	②	True
	③	True
	④	False, Counterexample: $x = 3$
	⑤	False, Counterexample: $x = -6$
	⑥	True
	⑦	False, Counterexample: $B = 0$
	⑧	False, Counterexample: scalene △
	⑨	False, Counterexample: rhombus

2.2 Inverses and Contrapositives

Ex1.

① If $x \neq 2$, then $x^2 \neq 4$ (False)
Converse: If $x^2 \neq 4$, then $x \neq 2$. (True)
Inverse: If $x = 2$, then $x^2 = 4$. (True)
Contrapositive: If $x^2 = 4$, then $x = 2$. (False)

② If $x^2 = 9$, then $x = -3$ (False)
Converse: If $x = -3$, then $x^2 = 9$. (True)
Inverse: If $x^2 \neq 9$, then $x \neq -3$. (True)
Contrapositive: If $x \neq -3$, then $x^2 \neq 9$. (False)

③ If x is positive, then x is at least 2. ($x > 0 \rightarrow x \geq 2$, False)
Converse : If x is at least 2, then x is positive. (or $x \geq 2 \rightarrow x > 0$, True)
Inverse : If x is not positive, then x is not at least 2. (or $x \leq 0 \rightarrow x < 2$, True)
Contrapositive : If x is not at least 2, then x is not positive. (or $x < 2 \rightarrow x \leq 0$, False)

④ If $x > 2$, then $x > 5$ (False)
Converse : If $x > 5$, then $x > 2$. (True)
Inverse : If $x \leq 2$, then $x \leq 5$. (True)
Contrapositive: If $x \leq 5$, then $x \leq 2$. (False)

⑤ If a polygon is not a rectangle, then it is not a square (True)
Converse : If a polygon is not a square, then it is not a rectangle. (False)
Inverse : If a polygon is a rectangle, then it is a square. (False)
Contrapositive : If a polygon is a square, then it is a rectangle. (True)

⑥ If two angles are supplemntary, then the sum of their measures is 180° (True)
Converse : If the sum of two angles is 180°, then they are supplementary. (True)
Inverse : If two angles are not supplementary, then the sum of their measures is not 180°. (True)
Contrapositive : If the sum of two angles is not 180°, then they are not supplementary. (True)

Ex2.

① *Converse*: If an angle is an acute angle, then it measures less than 90°. (True)
Biconditional: An angle is acute if and only if it measures less than 90°.

② *Converse*: If two angles are complementary, then the sum of their measures is 90°. (True)
Biconditional: Two angles are complementary if and only if the sum of their measures is 90°.

③ *Converse*: If an animal lives in the forest, then it is an owl. (False, many animals live in the forest.)
Not able to write biconditional statement.

④ *Converse*: If an animal is black and white, then it is a penguin. (False, zebras are black and white)
Not able to write biconditional statement.

⑤ *Converse*: If $\overline{AB} \cong \overline{CD}$, then $AB = CD$ (True)
Biconditional : $\overline{AB} \cong \overline{CD}$ if and only if $AB = CD$.

⑥ *Converse*: If a circle has an area of πr², then its radius is r. (True)
Biconditional: A circle has an area of πr² if and only if its radius is r.

⑦ *Converse*: If two lines intersect to form right angles, then they are perpendicular. (True)
Biconditional: Two lines are perpendicular if and only if they intersect to form right angles.

2.3 Postulates and Theorems

Ex1.
① G ② July
③ 24 ④ $-\frac{1}{16}$
⑤ (triangle) ⑥ (dot pattern)

Ex2.
① deductive ② inductive
③ inductive ④ deductive
⑤ deductive ⑥ inductive

Ex3.
① never ② always
③ sometimes ④ sometimes
⑤ always ⑥ sometimes
⑦ sometimes ⑧ never
⑨ sometimes ⑩ never
⑪ always ⑫ sometimes

2.4 Writing Proofs

Ex1.
① Symmetric prop.
② Reflexive prop.
③ Substitution prop.
④ Division prop.
⑤ Transitive prop.
⑥ Transitive prop.
⑦ Reflexive prop.
⑧ Symmetric prop.
⑨ Multiplication prop.
⑩ Substitution prop.
⑪ Substitution prop.
⑫ Addition prop.
⑬ Transitive prop.
⑭ Subtraction prop.
⑮ Subtraction prop.

Ex2.

①

Statements	Reasons
1. $2x+6=7x-14$	1. Given
2. $6=5x-14$	2. Subtraction prop.
3. $20=5x$	3. Addition prop.
4. $4=x$	4. Division prop.
5. $x=4$	5. Symmetric prop.

②

Statements	Reasons
1. $\frac{9x-6}{3}=4$	1. Given
2. $9x-6=12$	2. Multipl. prop.
3. $9x=18$	3. Addition prop.
4. $x=2$	5. Division prop.

③

Statements	Reasons
1. $3(x+4)=15$; $x+y=10$	1. Given
2. $x+4=5$	2. Division prop.
3. $x=1$	3. Subtraction prop.
4. $1+y=10$	4. Substitution prop.
5. $y=9$	5. Subtraction prop.

④

Statements	Reasons
1. $2(-y-1)=14$; $y=2x+1$	1. Given
2. $-2y-2=14$	2. Distribution prop.
3. $-2y=16$	3. Addition prop.
4. $y=-8$	4. Division prop.
5. $-8=2x+1$	5. Substitution prop.
6. $-9=2x$	6. Subtraction prop.
7. $x=-9/2$	7. Division prop.

⑤

Statements	Reasons
1. $\overline{AB} \cong \overline{AC}$	1. Given
2. $AB=AC$	2. Def. of $\cong$ seg
3. $2x+1=3x-10$	3. Substitution prop.
4. $2x+11=3x$	4. Addition prop.
5. $11=x$	5. Subtraction prop.
6. $x=11$	5. Symmetric prop.

⑥ Statements	Reasons
1. $\angle A \cong \angle B$	1. Given
2. $m\angle A = m\angle B$	2. Def. of $\cong \angle$
3. $2x = 10$	3. Substitution prop.
4. $x = 5$	5. Division prop.

2.5 Segments and Angle Relationships

Ex1.
① Definition of Midpoint
② Midpoint Theorem
③ Midpoint Theorem
④ Segment Addition Postulate
⑤ Segment Addition Postulate
⑥ Definition of Midpoint
⑦ Definition of Segment Bisector
⑧ Definition of Segment Bisector
⑨ Segment Addition Postulate
⑩ Segment Addition Postulate

Ex2.

①
Statements	Reasons
$BC = DE$	Given
$AB + BC = AC$	Seg. add. post.
$AB + DE = AC$	Substitution prop.

②
Statements	Reasons
$AB = CD$	Given
$BC = BC$	Reflexive prop.
$AB + BC = CD + BC$	Addition prop.
$AC = BD$	Seg. add. post.

③
Statements	Reasons
B is midpoint of $\overline{AC}$	Given
C is midpoint of $\overline{BD}$	Given
$AB = BC$	Def. of midpt.
$BC = CD$	Def. of midpt.
$AB + BC = BC + CD$	Addition prop.
$AC = BD$	Seg. add. post.

④
Statements	Reasons
$AB = CD$	Given
$AO + BO = CO + DO$	Seg. add. post
$AO = CO$	Given
$BO = DO$	Subtraction prop.
$DO = BO$	Symmetric prop.

⑤
Statements	Reasons
$AB = CD$	Given
M is midpoint of $\overline{AB}$	Given
M is midpoint of $\overline{CD}$	Given
$AM = \frac{1}{2}AB$	Midpoint thm.
$CM = \frac{1}{2}CD$	Midpoint thm.
$2AM = AB$	Multipl. prop.
$2CM = CD$	Multipl. prop.
$2AM = 2CM$	Substitution prop.
$AM = CM$	Division prop.

⑥
Statements	Reasons
$AC = DF$	Given
B is midpoint of $\overline{AC}$	Given
E is midpoint of $\overline{DF}$	Given
$BC = \frac{1}{2}AC$	Midpoint thm.
$EF = \frac{1}{2}DF$	Midpoint thm.
$2BC = AC$	Multipl. prop.
$2EF = DF$	Multipl. prop.
$2BC = 2EF$	Substitution prop.
$BC = EF$	Division prop.

⑦
Statements	Reasons
$\overline{AD}$ bisects $\overline{CE}$	Given
$CD = DE$	Def. of seg. bisct.
$BC = EF$	Given
$BC + CD = DE + EF$	Addition prop.
$BD = DF$	Seg. add. post

⑧

Statements	Reasons
$\overline{BE}$ bisects $\overline{AC}$ and $\overline{DF}$	Given
$AB = BC$	Def. of seg. bisct.
$DE = EF$	Def. of seg. bisct.
$BC = EF$	Given
$AB = DE$	Substitution prop.

⑨

Statements	Reasons
$\overline{AC} \cong \overline{BD}$	Given
$AC = BD$	Def. of $\cong$ seg.
$AB + BC = BC + CD$	Seg. add. post
$BC = BC$	Reflexive prop.
$AB = CD$	Subtraction prop.

⑩

Statements	Reasons
$AC = DF$	Given
$AB + BC = DE + EF$	Seg. add. post.
$AB = EF$	Given
$BC = DE$	Subtraction prop.

Ex3.
① Midpoint thm.   ② $\angle$ add. post.
③ Def. of $\angle$ bisector   ④ Def. of midpt.
⑤ $\angle$ add. post.   ⑥ Def. of $\angle$ bisector
⑦ $\angle$ bisector thm.   ⑧ Seg. add. post.

Ex4.
①

Statements	Reasons
$\angle 1 \cong \angle 3$	Given
$m\angle 1 = m\angle 3$	Def. of $\cong$ $\angle$
$m\angle 2 = m\angle 2$	Reflexive prop.
$m\angle 1 + m\angle 2$ $= m\angle 3 + m\angle 2$	Addition prop.
$m\angle DAB = m\angle CAE$	$\angle$ add. post.

②

Statements	Reasons
$\angle ABC \cong \angle ABD$	Given
$m\angle ABC = m\angle ABD$	Def. of $\cong$ $\angle$
$m\angle 1 + m\angle 2$ $= m\angle 3 + m\angle 4$	$\angle$ add. post.
$m\angle 2 = m\angle 4$	Given
$m\angle 1 = m\angle 3$	Subtraction prop.

③

Statements	Reasons
$m\angle DAB = m\angle CAE$	Given
$m\angle 1 + m\angle 2$ $= m\angle 2 + m\angle 3$	$\angle$ add. post.
$m\angle 2 = m\angle 2$	Reflexive prop.
$m\angle 1 = m\angle 3$	Subtraction prop.

④

Statements	Reasons
$m\angle 1 = m\angle 3$	Given
$m\angle 2 = m\angle 4$	Given
$m\angle 1 + m\angle 2$ $= m\angle 3 + m\angle 4$	Addition prop.
$m\angle ABC = m\angle ABD$	$\angle$ add. post.
$\angle ABC \cong \angle ABD$	Def. of $\cong$ $\angle$

⑤

Statements	Reasons
$m\angle 1 + m\angle 2 = 180°$	$\angle$ add. post.
$m\angle 3 + m\angle 4 = 180°$	$\angle$ add. post.
$m\angle 1 + m\angle 2$ $= m\angle 3 + m\angle 4$	Substitution prop.
$m\angle 2 = m\angle 3$	Given
$m\angle 1 = m\angle 4$	Subtraction prop.

⑥

Statements	Reasons
$\overrightarrow{BD}$ bisects $\angle ABC$	Given
$\overrightarrow{FH}$ bisects $\angle EFG$	Given
$m\angle 1 = \frac{1}{2} m\angle ABC$	$\angle$ bisector thm.
$m\angle 3 = \frac{1}{2} m\angle EFG$	$\angle$ bisector thm.
$2m\angle 1 = m\angle ABC$	Multipl. prop.
$2m\angle 3 = m\angle EFG$	Multipl. prop.
$m\angle ABC = m\angle EFG$	Given
$2m\angle 1 = 2m\angle 3$	Substitution prop.
$m\angle 1 = m\angle 3$	Division prop.

⑦

Statements	Reasons
$\overrightarrow{BE}$ bisects $\angle ABC$	Given
$\overrightarrow{CD}$ bisects $\angle ACB$	Given
$m\angle 1 = \frac{1}{2} m\angle ABC$	$\angle$ bisector thm.
$m\angle 2 = \frac{1}{2} m\angle ACB$	$\angle$ bisector thm.
$2m\angle 1 = m\angle ABC$	Multipl. prop.

$2m\angle 2 = m\angle ACB$	Multipl. prop.
$m\angle ABC = m\angle ACB$	Given
$2m\angle 1 = 2m\angle 2$	Substitution prop.
$m\angle 1 = m\angle 2$	Division prop.

2.6 Special Pairs of Angles

Ex1.		
	①	Def. of compl. ∠s
	②	Linear pair post. (Suppl. thm)
	③	∠ add. post.
	④	Def. of suppl. ∠s
	⑤	Linear pair post. (Suppl. thm)
	⑥	Def. of compl. ∠s
	⑦	Def. of suppl. ∠s
	⑧	Compl. thm
	⑨	Compl. thm
	⑩	Vertical ∠s thm.
	⑪	Vertical ∠s thm.

Ex2.		
	① $x = 20$	② $x = 55, y = 40$
	③ $x = 16$	④ $x = 50$
	⑤ $x = 80, y = 91$	⑥ $x = 75, y = 70$

Ex3.	50
Ex4.	120

Ex5.

①
Statements	Reasons
$\angle 1 \cong \angle 4$	Given
$\angle 1 \cong \angle 2$	Vert. ∠s thm.
$\angle 3 \cong \angle 4$	Vert. ∠s thm.
$\angle 2 \cong \angle 3$	Substitution prop.

②
Statements	Reasons
$m\angle AOC = m\angle FOD$	Vert. ∠s thm.
$m\angle 1 + m\angle 2$ $= m\angle 3 + m\angle 4$	∠ add. post.
$m\angle 1 = m\angle 3$	Given
$m\angle 2 = m\angle 4$	Subtraction prop.

③
Statements	Reasons
$\overrightarrow{OB}$ bisects $\angle AOC$	Given
$\angle 1 \cong \angle 2$	Def. of ∠ bisct.
$\angle 1 \cong \angle 3$	Vert. ∠s thm.
$\angle 2 \cong \angle 3$	Substitution prop.

④
Statements	Reasons
$m\angle 1 + m\angle 2 = 90°$	Given
$\angle 1, \angle 2$ are compl.	Def. of compl. ∠s
$\angle 1 \cong \angle 3$	Vert. ∠s thm.
$\angle 2, \angle 3$ are compl.	Substitution prop.

⑤
Statements	Reasons
$\overrightarrow{OA} \perp \overrightarrow{OC}$	Given
$\angle 1, \angle 2$ are compl.	Compl. thm.
$\angle 2 \cong \angle 3$	Vert. ∠s thm.
$\angle 1, \angle 3$ are compl.	Substitution prop.

⑥
Statements	Reasons
$\angle 1, \angle 2$ form linear pair	Given
$\angle 1, \angle 2$ are suppl.	Linear pair post.
$\angle 1 \cong \angle 3$	Vert. ∠s thm.
$\angle 3 \cong \angle 4$	Given
$\angle 1 \cong \angle 4$	Transitive prop.
$\angle 2, \angle 4$ are suppl.	Substitution prop.

⑦
Statements	Reasons
$\angle 1, \angle 2$ form linear pair	Given
$\angle 1, \angle 2$ are suppl.	Linear pair post.
$\angle 1 \cong \angle 3$	Vert. ∠s thm.
$\angle 3 \cong \angle 5$	Given
$\angle 1 \cong \angle 5$	Transitive prop.
$\angle 2 \cong \angle 4$	Given
$\angle 4, \angle 5$ are suppl.	Substitution prop.

Ex6.	① never	② sometimes
	③ sometimes	④ sometimes
	⑤ sometimes	⑥ sometimes
	⑦ sometimes	⑧ always
	⑨ always	⑩ never
	⑪ sometimes	

2.7 Perpendicular Lines

Ex1.	①	Def. of ⊥ lines
	②	⊥ lines thm.
	③	⊥ lines thm.
	④	Def. of ⊥ lines
	⑤	Def. of ⊥ lines
	⑥	Def. of compl. ∠s
	⑦	Conv. of ⊥ lines thm.
	⑧	Conv. of ⊥ lines thm.
	⑨	Def. of compl. ∠s

Ex2.

①
Statements	Reasons
$\overline{AB} \perp \overline{BC}$	Given
$m\angle B = 90°$	Def. of ⊥ lines
$\overline{BC} \perp \overline{CD}$	Given
$m\angle C = 90°$	Def. of ⊥ lines
$\angle B \cong \angle C$	All right ∠s are ≅

②
Statements	Reasons
$\overline{AC} \perp \overline{AB}$	Given
$\overline{BD} \perp \overline{CD}$	Given
$m\angle A = 90°$	Def. of ⊥ lines
$m\angle D = 90°$	Def. of ⊥ lines
$\angle A \cong \angle D$	All right ∠s are ≅
$\angle A \cong \angle C$	Given
$\angle D \cong \angle B$	Given
$\angle B \cong \angle C$	Substitution prop.

③
Statements	Reasons
$m\angle 1 = m\angle 2$	Given
$m\angle 3 = m\angle 4$	Given
$m\angle 1 + m\angle 3 = m\angle 2 + m\angle 4$	Addition prop.
$m\angle AOB = m\angle AOC$	∠ add. post.
$\overrightarrow{BC} \perp \overrightarrow{OA}$	Conv. of ⊥ lines thm.

④
Statements	Reasons
$\overline{AB} \perp \overline{CD}$	Given
$\angle 1 \cong \angle 2$	⊥ lines thm.
$\angle 1 \cong \angle 3$	Given
$\angle 2 \cong \angle 4$	Given
$\angle 3 \cong \angle 4$	Substitution prop.

⑤
Statements	Reasons
$\overline{AB} \perp \overline{CD}$	Given
$\angle 1 \cong \angle 2$	⊥ lines thm.
$\angle 1 \cong \angle 3$	Given
$\angle 2 \cong \angle 3$	Substitution prop.

2.8 Theorems about Special Pairs of Angles

Ex1.	①	$\angle 1 \cong \angle 5$, ≅ suppl. thm
	②	$\angle 8 \cong \angle 9$, ≅ compl. thm.
	③	$\angle 7 \cong \angle 9$, ≅ compl. thm.
	④	$\angle 11 \cong \angle 12$, ⊥ lines thm.
	⑤	$\angle 13 \cong \angle 12$, ⊥ lines thm.
	⑥	$\angle 3 \cong \angle 5$, ≅ suppl. thm
	⑦	$\angle 9 \cong \angle 10$, Def. of ∠ bisector

Ex2.

①

Statements	Reasons
$\overrightarrow{OA} \perp \overrightarrow{OC}$	Given
∠1 is compl. to ∠2	Compl. thm.
∠2 is compl. to ∠3	Given
∠1 ≅ ∠3	≅ compl. thm.

②

Statements	Reasons
$\overline{AB} \perp \overline{BC}$	Given
$\overline{ED} \perp \overline{EF}$	Given
∠1 is compl. to ∠2	Compl. thm.
∠3 is compl. to ∠4	Compl. thm.
∠2 ≅ ∠4	Given
∠1 ≅ ∠3	≅ compl. thm.

③

Statements	Reasons
$m\angle 1 + m\angle 3 = 180°$	Given
∠1 is suppl. to ∠3	Def. of suppl. ∠s
∠2 is suppl. to ∠4	Given
∠1 ≅ ∠2	Vert. ∠s thm.
∠3 ≅ ∠4	≅ suppl. thm.

④

Statements	Reasons
∠1 is compl. to ∠2	Given
∠3 is compl. to ∠4	Given
∠2 ≅ ∠3	Vert. ∠s thm.
∠1 ≅ ∠4	≅ compl. thm.

⑤

Statements	Reasons
∠2 is suppl. to ∠3	Given
∠1 is suppl. to ∠2	Linear pair post.
∠1 ≅ ∠3	≅ suppl. thm.

⑥

Statements	Reasons
$m\angle 1 + m\angle 3 = 180°$	Given
∠1 is suppl. to ∠3	Def. of suppl. ∠s
∠1 is suppl. to ∠2	Linear pair post.
∠2 ≅ ∠3	≅ suppl. thm.

⑦

Statements	Reasons
∠1 ≅ ∠4	Given
∠1 is suppl. to ∠2	Linear pair post.
∠3 is suppl. to ∠4	Linear pair post.
∠2 ≅ ∠3	≅ suppl. thm.

⑧

Statements	Reasons
∠2 ≅ ∠3	Given
∠1 is suppl. to ∠2	Linear pair post.
∠3 is suppl. to ∠4	Linear pair post.
∠1 ≅ ∠4	≅ suppl. thm.

⑨

Statements	Reasons
$\overrightarrow{OC}$ bisects ∠AOB	Given
∠1 ≅ ∠2	Def. of ∠ bisector
∠1 is suppl. to ∠3	Linear pair post
∠2 is suppl. to ∠4	Linear pair post
∠3 ≅ ∠4	≅ suppl. thm.

⑩

Statements	Reasons
$\overline{AD} \perp \overline{BC}$	Given
∠1 is compl. to ∠3	Compl. thm.
∠2 is compl. to ∠4	Compl. thm.
∠3 ≅ ∠4	Given
∠1 ≅ ∠2	≅ compl. thm.

⑪

Statements	Reasons
$\overline{AD} \perp \overline{DC}$	Given
$\overline{BC} \perp \overline{DC}$	Given
∠1 is compl. to ∠2	Compl. thm.
∠3 is compl. to ∠4	Compl. thm.
∠1 ≅ ∠3	Given
∠2 ≅ ∠4	≅ compl. thm.

⑫

Statements	Reasons
Two lines intersect at one point	Given
∠1 is suppl. to ∠2	Linear pair post.
∠3 is suppl. to ∠2	Linear pair post.
∠1 ≅ ∠3	≅ suppl. thm.

Answers

3. Parallel Lines

3.1 Parallel Lines and Transversals

Ex1.	① plane $FGHIJ$
	② plane $ABCDE$
	(or $DIHC$, $EAFJ$, $JIHGF$)
	③ $\overline{BC}$ (or $\overline{BG}, \overline{AE}, \overline{AF}$)
	④ $\overline{DI}$ (or $\overline{CH}, \overline{BG}, \overline{AF}$)
	⑤ $\overline{CD}$ (or $\overline{DE}, \overline{AE}, \overline{HI}, \overline{IJ}, \overline{FJ}$)
	⑥ $\overline{AB}$ (or $\overline{BC}, \overline{CD}, \overline{FG}, \overline{GH}, \overline{HI}$)
	⑦ $\overline{BC}$ or $\overline{BA}$
Ex2.	① sometimes ② always
	③ never ④ never
	⑤ never ⑥ sometimes
	⑦ never ⑧ sometimes
	⑨ always ⑩ sometimes
	⑪ sometimes ⑫ always
Ex3.	① i) lines: a, b transversal: c
	ii) lines: c, d transversal: a
	② i) lines: b, c transversal: a
	ii) lines: b, d transversal: a
	③ i) lines: a, b transversal: c
	ii) lines: c, a transversal: b
	④ i) lines: $\overrightarrow{AC}, \overrightarrow{CB}$ transversal: $\overline{AB}$
	ii) lines: $\overrightarrow{AC}, \overrightarrow{AB}$ transversal: $\overline{CB}$
	⑤ i) lines: $\overline{AB}, \overline{CD}$ transversal: $\overline{BC}$
	ii) lines: $\overline{DE}, \overline{CE}$ transversal: $\overline{DC}$
	⑥ i) lines: c, d transversal: b
	ii) lines: a, d transversal: c

Ex4.	① Corresp. ∠s	② Corresp. ∠s
	③ Consec. int ∠s	④ Consec. int ∠s
	⑤ Alt. int. ∠s	⑥ Alt. int. ∠s
	⑦ Alt. ext. ∠s	⑧ Alt. ext. ∠s
Ex5.	242°	

3.2 Angles and Parallel Lines

Ex1.	① ∥ → consec. int ∠s are suppl.
	② ∥ → alt. int. ∠s are ≅
	③ ∥ → corresp. ∠s are ≅
	④ ∥ → consec. int ∠s are suppl.
	⑤ ∥ → alt. ext. ∠s are ≅
	⑥ ∥ → corresp. ∠s are ≅
	⑦ ∥ → alt. int. ∠s are ≅
	⑧ ⊥ to one ∥, ⊥ to other (⊥trans.thm)
	⑨ ⊥ to one ∥, ⊥ to other (⊥trans.thm)
	⑩ Vert. ∠s thm.
Ex2.	① $x = 85, y = 95, z = 85$
	② $x = 130, y = 50, z = 50$
	③ $x = 128, y = 68, z = 112$
	④ $x = 30, y = 105, z = 45$
	⑤ $x = 50, y = 60, z = 50$
	⑥ $x = 80, y = 130, z = 95$
	⑦ $x = 58, y = 42, z = 80$
	⑧ $x = 72, y = 60, z = 48$
	⑨ $x = 20, y = 45, z = 40$
Ex3.	① $x = 26$ ② $x = 87$
	③ $x = 100$ ④ $x = 85$
	⑤ $x = 75$ ⑥ $x = 70$
	⑦ $x = 120$ ⑧ $x = 130$
	⑨ $x = 68$ ⑩ $x = 64$
Ex4.	180

3.3 Proving Lines Parallel

Ex1.
① $c \parallel d$ (Consec. int ∠s are suppl. → ∥)
② $a \parallel b$ (Alt. int ∠s are ≅ → ∥)
③ $a \parallel c$ (Corresp. ∠s are ≅ → ∥)
④ $a \parallel b$ (Alt. int ∠s are ≅ → ∥)
   $c \parallel e$ (Corresp. ∠s are ≅ → ∥)
⑤ $c \parallel b$ (Alt. int ∠s are ≅ → ∥)
   $d \parallel e$ (Alt. int ∠s are ≅ → ∥)

Ex2.
① $b \parallel a$, Two ⊥s make ∥ (Two ⊥s thm.)
② $b \parallel c$, Two ⊥s make ∥ (Two ⊥s thm.)
③ none
④ none
⑤ $c \parallel e$, Two ⊥s make ∥ (Two ⊥s thm.)
   $a \parallel b$, Two ⊥s make ∥ (Two ⊥s thm.)
⑥ $c \parallel b$, Two ⊥s make ∥ (Two ⊥s thm.)

Ex3.

①
Statements	Reasons
∠1 ≅ ∠2	Given
∠2 ≅ ∠3	Vert. ∠s thm.
∠3 ≅ ∠4	Given
∠1 ≅ ∠4	Transitive prop.
$\overline{AB} \parallel \overline{DE}$	Alt. int. ∠s ≅ → ∥

②
Statements	Reasons
$m\angle 3 + m\angle 8 = 180°$	Given
∠3, ∠8 suppl.	Def. of suppl. ∠s
∠8 ≅ ∠5	Vert. ∠s thm.
∠3, ∠5 suppl.	Substitution prop.
$a \parallel b$	Consec. int ∠s are suppl. → ∥

③
Statements	Reasons
∠1 ≅ ∠5	Given
∠4 ≅ ∠5	Given
∠1 ≅ ∠4	Substitution prop.
$b \parallel a$	Alt. int. ∠s ≅ → ∥
∠3 ≅ ∠5	∥ → alt. int. ∠s ≅

④
Statements	Reasons
$m\angle 4 + m\angle 7 = 180°$	Given
∠4, ∠7 suppl.	Def. of suppl. ∠s
$b \parallel c$	Consec. int ∠s are suppl. → ∥
∠4 ≅ ∠5	∥ → alt. int. ∠s ≅

⑤
Statements	Reasons
∠1 ≅ ∠5	Given
∠9 ≅ ∠18	Given
$d \parallel f$	Corresp. ∠s ≅ → ∥
$f \parallel e$	Alt. ext. ∠s ≅ → ∥
$d \parallel e$	Transitive prop. of ∥ lines
∠20 is suppl. to ∠21	∥ → consec. int ∠s are suppl.
∠21 ≅ ∠26	Vert. ∠s thm.
∠20 is suppl. to ∠26	Substitution prop.

⑥
Statements	Reasons
∠2 ≅ ∠4	Given
∠4 ≅ ∠7	Vert. ∠s thm.
∠7 ≅ ∠10	Given
∠2 ≅ ∠10	Transitive prop.
$a \parallel b$	Corresp. ∠s ≅ → ∥

⑦
Statements	Reasons
$a \parallel b$	Given
∠3 is suppl. to ∠11	∥ → consec. int ∠s are suppl.
∠8 is suppl. to ∠9	Linear pair post.
∠3 ≅ ∠8	Given
∠9 ≅ ∠11	≅ suppl. thm.
$\overline{AE} \parallel \overline{BD}$	Corresp. ∠s ≅ → ∥
∠2 is suppl. to ∠5	∥ → consec. int ∠s are suppl.
$m\angle 2 + m\angle 5 = 180°$	Def. of suppl. ∠s

⑧ Statements	Reasons
$\overline{BC}$ bisects $\angle ABE$	Given
$\angle 1 \cong \angle 2$	Def. of ∠ bisector
$\angle 1 \cong \angle 3$	Given
$\angle 3 \cong \angle 2$	Substitution prop.
$\overline{BC} \parallel \overline{DE}$	Alt. int. ∠s ≅ → ∥

⑨ Statements	Reasons
$a \perp d$	Given
$b \perp d$	Given
$a \parallel b$	Two ⊥s make ∥ (Two ⊥s thm.)
$\angle 1 \cong \angle 2$	∥ → alt. int. ∠s ≅

⑩ Statements	Reasons
$a \perp c$	Given
$b \perp c$	Given
$a \parallel b$	Two ⊥s make ∥ (Two ⊥s thm.)
$\angle 1$ is suppl. to $\angle 2$	∥ → consec. int ∠s are suppl.
$m\angle 1 + m\angle 2 = 180°$	Def. of suppl. ∠s

Ex3.		
	① $x = 70$	② $x = 65$
	③ $x = 83$	④ $x = 85$
	⑤ $x = 20$	⑥ $x = \dfrac{85}{3}$
	⑦ $x = 50, y = 20$	⑧ $x = 120, y = 20$

Ex4.	
	① $x = 100, y = 80, z = 100$
	② $x = 140, y = 40$
	③ $x = 135, y = 45$
	④ $x = 132$
	⑤ $x = 50, y = 55$
	⑥ $x = 111$
	⑦ $x = 145, y = 70, z = 60$
	⑧ $x = 122, y = 85$
	⑨ $x = 127$
	⑩ $x = 105$
	⑪ $x = 85, y = 40$
	⑫ $x = 120, y = 98$

Ex5.	180

3.4 Angles of Triangles

Ex1.	① V	② VI
	③ IV	④ II
	⑤ I	⑥ VII
	⑦ III	
Ex2.	① sometimes	② sometimes
	③ always	④ never
	⑤ never	⑥ sometimes
	⑦ sometimes	⑧ sometimes

Answers

4. Congruent triangles

'*' indicates the 'S' part or 'A' part of SSS, SAS, ASA, etc

4.1 Congruent Polygons

Ex1.	① ∠F	② $\overline{ED}$
	③ $\overline{AB}$	④ ∠C
	⑤ ∠BAD	⑥ ∠ADE
	⑦ □EDAF	
Ex2.	① △ABC ≅ △DEC	
	② △MNO ≅ △QPO	
	③ △EFG ≅ △HGF	
	④ △MNO ≅ △MPO	
	⑤ △ABC ≅ △EDC	
	⑥ △HIJ ≅ △KJI	
	⑦ □UVXW ≅ □YZXW	
	⑧ □SPQR ≅ □SUTR	

4.2 Proving Congruence_ SSS, SAS, ASA

Ex1.	① SSS post.	② SAS post.
	③ Not possible	④ Not possible
	⑤ SAS post.	⑥ ASA post.
	⑦ ASA post.	⑧ ASA post.
	⑨ Not possible	⑩ Not possible
	⑪ SAS post.	⑫ SSS post.

Ex2.

①
Statements	Reasons
$\overline{AB} \perp \overline{AC}$	Given
$\overline{CE} \perp \overline{DE}$	Given
C is midpoint of $\overline{AE}$	Given
$m\angle A = m\angle E = 90°$	Def. of ⊥ lines
∠A ≅ ∠E *	All right ∠s are ≅
∠ACB ≅ ∠ECD *	Vert. ∠s thm.
$\overline{AC} \cong \overline{EC}$ *	Def. of midpt.
△ABC ≅ △EDC	ASA post. (*)

②
Statements	Reasons
$\overline{BC} \cong \overline{CD}$ *	Given
$\overline{AC} \perp \overline{BD}$	Given
$m\angle ACB = m\angle ACD$ = 90°	Def. of ⊥ lines
∠ACB ≅ ∠ACD *	All right ∠s are ≅
$\overline{AC} \cong \overline{AC}$ *	Reflexive prop.
△ABC ≅ △ADC	SAS post. (*)

③
Statements	Reasons
$\overline{AB}$ and $\overline{DF}$ bisect each other	Given
$\overline{AE} \cong \overline{BE}$ *	Def. of seg. bisct.
$\overline{DE} \cong \overline{FE}$ *	Def. of seg. bisct.
∠AEF ≅ ∠BED *	Vert. ∠s thm.
△AEF ≅ △BED	SAS post. (*)

④
Statements	Reasons
$\overline{AB} \cong \overline{AD}$ *	Given
$\overline{AC}$ bisects $\overline{BD}$	Given
$\overline{BC} \cong \overline{DC}$ *	Def. of seg. bisct.
$\overline{AC} \cong \overline{AC}$ *	Reflexive prop.
△ABC ≅ △ADC	SSS post. (*)

⑤
Statements	Reasons
$\overline{AB} \parallel \overline{DC}$	Given
∠BAM ≅ ∠DCN *	∥ → alt. int. ∠s ≅
$\overline{AB} \cong \overline{DC}$ *	Given
$\overline{AN} \cong \overline{MC}$	Given
AN = MC	Def. of ≅ seg.
AM + MN = MN + NC	Seg. add. post.
MN = MN	Reflexive prop.
AM = NC *	Subtraction prop.
△ABM ≅ △CDN	SAS post. (*)

⑥

Statements	Reasons
$\overline{BD}$ bisects $\angle ABC$	Given
$\angle ABD \cong \angle CBD$ *	Def. of $\angle$ bisector
$\overline{AB} \cong \overline{CB}$ *	Given
$\overline{BD} \cong \overline{BD}$ *	Reflexive prop.
$\triangle ABD \cong \triangle CBD$	SAS post. (*)

⑦

Statements	Reasons
$\overline{BC} \cong \overline{DE}$ or $BC = DE$	Given
$CD = CD$	Reflexive prop.
$BC + CD = DE + CD$	Addition prop.
$BD = CE$ *	Seg. add. post.
$\overline{AB} \cong \overline{AE}$ *	Given
$\overline{AD} \cong \overline{AC}$ *	Given
$\triangle ABD \cong \triangle AEC$	SSS post. (*)

⑧

Statements	Reasons
$\overline{AF} \parallel \overline{BE}$	Given
$\angle FAC \cong \angle EBD$ *	$\parallel \rightarrow$ corresp. $\angle$s $\cong$
$\overline{CF} \parallel \overline{DE}$	Given
$\angle ACF \cong \angle BDE$ *	$\parallel \rightarrow$ corresp. $\angle$s $\cong$
$AB = CD$	Given
$BC = BC$	Reflexive prop.
$AB + BC = CD + BC$	Addition prop.
$AC = BD$ *	Seg. add. post.
$\triangle AFC \cong \triangle BED$	ASA post. (*)

⑨

Statements	Reasons
H is midpoint of $\overline{AB}$	Given
$\overline{AH} \cong \overline{BH}$ *	Def. of midpt.
$\angle A \cong \angle B$ *	Given
$\angle 1 \cong \angle 2$, $m\angle 1 = m\angle 2$	Given
$m\angle 3 = m\angle 3$	Reflexive prop.
$m\angle 1 + m\angle 3 = m\angle 2 + m\angle 3$	Addition prop.
$m\angle AHE = m\angle BHD$ *	$\angle$ add. post.
$\triangle AHE \cong \triangle BHD$	ASA post. (*)

⑩

Statements	Reasons
$AB = AE$ *	Given
$BC = ED$	Given
$AB + BC = AE + ED$	Addition prop.
$AC = AD$ *	Seg. add. post.
$\angle A \cong \angle A$ *	Reflexive prop.
$\triangle ACE \cong \triangle ADB$	SAS post. (*)

⑪

Statements	Reasons
$\angle 1 \cong \angle 2$	Given
$\angle 1$ is suppl. to $\angle BAD$	Linear pair post.
$\angle 2$ is suppl. to $\angle CDA$	Linear pair post.
$\angle BAD \cong \angle CDA$ *	$\cong$ suppl. thm.
$\overline{AB} \cong \overline{CD}$ *	Given
$\overline{AD} \cong \overline{AD}$ *	Reflexive prop.
$\triangle ABD \cong \triangle DCA$	SAS post. (*)

⑫

Statements	Reasons
$\overline{AB} \cong \overline{AE}$ *	Given
$\angle 1 \cong \angle 4$	Given
$\angle 1$ is suppl. to $\angle 2$	Linear pair post.
$\angle 3$ is suppl. to $\angle 4$	Linear pair post.
$\angle 2 \cong \angle 3$ *	$\cong$ suppl. thm.
$\angle 5 \cong \angle 7$, $m\angle 5 = m\angle 7$	Given
$m\angle 6 = m\angle 6$	Reflexive prop.
$m\angle 5 + m\angle 6 = m\angle 7 + m\angle 6$	Addition prop.
$m\angle BAD = m\angle EAC$ *	$\angle$ add. post.
$\triangle BAD \cong \triangle EAC$	ASA post. (*)

4.3 Proving Congruence_ AAS, HL

Ex1.
① AAS thm. ② HL thm.
③ HL thm. ④ Not possible
⑤ Not possible ⑥ AAS thm.
⑦ HL thm. ⑧ AAS thm.

Ex2.

①

Statements	Reasons
$\overline{AD} \cong \overline{BE}$ *	Given
$\angle A \cong \angle E$ *	Given
$\angle C \cong \angle C$ *	Reflexive prop.
$\triangle ACD \cong \triangle ECB$	AAS thm. (*)

②

Statements	Reasons
$\angle A \cong \angle C$ *	Given
$\overline{BD}$ bisects $\angle ABC$	Given
$\angle ABD \cong \angle CBD$ *	Def. of $\angle$ bisector
$\overline{BD} \cong \overline{BD}$ *	Reflexive prop.
$\triangle ABD \cong \triangle CBD$	AAS thm. (*)

③

Statements	Reasons
$\overline{AB} \perp \overline{CD}$	Given
$\overline{AC} \perp \overline{BE}$	Given
$m\angle CDB = m\angle BEC = 90°$	Def. of $\perp$ lines
$\angle BEC \cong \angle CDB$ *	All right $\angle$s are $\cong$
$\angle EBC \cong \angle DCB$ *	Given
$\overline{BC} \cong \overline{BC}$ *	Reflexive prop.
$\triangle DCB \cong \triangle EBC$	AAS thm. (*)

④

Statements	Reasons
$\overline{AB} \cong \overline{AE}$ *	Given
$\angle C \cong \angle D$ *	Given
$\angle A \cong \angle A$ *	Reflexive prop.
$\triangle ACE \cong \triangle ADB$	AAS thm. (*)

⑤

Statements	Reasons
$\overline{BD}$ bisects $\overline{AE}$	Given
$\overline{AC} \cong \overline{EC}$ *	Def. of seg. bisct.
$\overline{AB} \parallel \overline{DE}$	Given
$\angle A \cong \angle E$ *	$\parallel \to$ alt. int. $\angle$s $\cong$
$\angle B \cong \angle D$ *	$\parallel \to$ alt. int. $\angle$s $\cong$
$\triangle ABC \cong \triangle EDC$	AAS thm. (*)

⑥

Statements	Reasons
$\angle A, \angle D$ are right $\angle$s	Given
$\triangle ABC, \triangle DCB$ are right $\triangle$s *	Def of right $\triangle$ s
$\overline{AC} \cong \overline{DB}$ *	Given
$\overline{BC} \cong \overline{BC}$ *	Reflexive prop.
$\triangle ABC \cong \triangle DCB$	HL thm. (*)

⑦

Statements	Reasons
$\overline{AB} \perp \overline{AC}$	Given
$\overline{DE} \perp \overline{DF}$	Given
$m\angle A = m\angle D = 90°$	Def. of $\perp$ lines
$\triangle ABC, \triangle DFE$ are right $\triangle$ *	Def of right $\triangle$
$\overline{AB} \cong \overline{DF}$ *	Given
$\overline{BE} \cong \overline{FC}, BE = FC$	Given
$EC = EC$	Reflexive prop.
$BE + EC = FC + EC$	Addition prop.
$BC = EF$ *	Seg. add. post.
$\triangle ABC \cong \triangle DFE$	HL thm. (*)

⑧

Statements	Reasons
$\angle 1, \angle 2$ are right $\angle$s	Given
$\triangle BCE, \triangle DAF$ are right $\triangle$s *	Def of right $\triangle$
$\overline{BC} \cong \overline{DA}$ *	Given
$\overline{FC} \cong \overline{EA}, FC = EA$	Given
$EF = EF$	Reflexive prop.
$FC + EF = EA + EF$	Addition prop.
$CE = AF$ *	Seg. add. post.
$\triangle BCE \cong \triangle DAF$	HL thm. (*)

⑨ Statements	Reasons
$\overline{AE} \perp \overline{BD}$	Given
$m\angle ACB = m\angle ECD$ $= 90°$	Def. of $\perp$ lines
$\triangle ABC, \triangle EDC$ are right $\triangle$ *	Def of right $\triangle$
C is midpoint of $\overline{BD}$	Given
$\overline{BC} \cong \overline{DC}$ *	Def. of midpt.
$\overline{AB} \cong \overline{ED}$ *	Given
$\triangle ABC \cong \triangle EDC$	HL thm. (*)

4.4 CPCTC

Ex1.

① Statements	Reasons
$\overline{AB} \cong \overline{BC}$ *	Given
$\overline{AD} \cong \overline{CD}$ *	Given
$\overline{DB} \cong \overline{DB}$ *	Reflexive prop.
$\triangle ADB \cong \triangle CDB$	SSS post. (*)
$\angle A \cong \angle C$	CPCTC

② Statements	Reasons
$\overline{AC}$ and $\overline{DE}$ bisect each other	Given
$\overline{AB} \cong \overline{BC}$ *	Def. of seg. bisct.
$\overline{DB} \cong \overline{EB}$ *	Def. of seg. bisct.
$\angle DBA \cong \angle EBC$ *	Vert. $\angle$s thm.
$\triangle DBA \cong \triangle EBC$	SAS post. (*)
$\angle D \cong \angle E$	CPCTC

③ Statements	Reasons
$\overline{AC} \perp \overline{BD}$	Given
$m\angle ACB = m\angle ACD$ $= 90°$	Def. of $\perp$ lines
$\triangle ABC, \triangle ADC$ are right $\triangle$ *	Def of right $\triangle$
$\overline{AB} \cong \overline{AD}$ *	Given
$\overline{AC} \cong \overline{AC}$ *	Reflexive prop.
$\triangle ABC \cong \triangle ADC$	HL thm. (*)
$\overline{BC} \cong \overline{DC}$	CPCTC

④ Statements	Reasons
$\overline{AB} \parallel \overline{DE}$	Given
$\angle A \cong \angle E$ *	$\parallel \rightarrow$ alt. int. $\angle$s $\cong$
$\angle B \cong \angle D$ *	$\parallel \rightarrow$ alt. int. $\angle$s $\cong$
$\overline{AC} \cong \overline{EC}$ *	Given
$\triangle ABC \cong \triangle EDC$	AAS thm. (*)
$\overline{AB} \cong \overline{ED}$	CPCTC

⑤ Statements	Reasons
$\overline{AC}$ bisects $\overline{BD}$	Given
$\overline{BC} \cong \overline{DC}$ *	Def. of seg. bisct.
$\overline{AB} \cong \overline{AD}$ *	Given
$\overline{AC} \cong \overline{AC}$ *	Reflexive prop.
$\triangle ABC \cong \triangle ADC$	SSS post. (*)
$\angle ACB \cong \angle ACD$	CPCTC
$\overline{AC} \perp \overline{BD}$	Conv. of $\perp$ lines thm.

⑥ Statements	Reasons
$\overline{AB} \cong \overline{DC}$ *	Given
$\overline{AD} \cong \overline{BC}$ *	Given
$\overline{BD} \cong \overline{BD}$ *	Reflexive prop.
$\triangle ADB \cong \triangle CBD$	SSS post. (*)
$\angle ABD \cong \angle CDB$	CPCTC
$\overline{AB} \parallel \overline{DC}$	Alt. int. $\angle$s $\cong \rightarrow \parallel$

⑦ Statements	Reasons
B is midpoint of $\overline{AC}$	Given
B is midpoint of $\overline{DE}$	Given
$\overline{AB} \cong \overline{CB}$ *	Def. of midpt.
$\overline{DB} \cong \overline{EB}$ *	Def. of midpt.
$\angle DBA \cong \angle EBC$ *	Vert. $\angle$s thm.
$\triangle DBA \cong \triangle EBC$	SAS post. (*)
$\angle D \cong \angle E$	CPCTC
$\overline{AD} \parallel \overline{EC}$	Alt. int. $\angle$s $\cong \rightarrow \parallel$

⑧
Statements	Reasons
$\overline{AC} \perp \overline{BD}$	Given
$m\angle ACB = m\angle ACD = 90°$	Def. of $\perp$ lines
$\triangle ACB \cong \triangle ACD$ are right $\triangle s$*	Def of right $\triangle$
$\overline{AB} \cong \overline{AD}$*	Given
$\overline{AC} \cong \overline{AC}$*	Reflexive prop.
$\triangle ACB \cong \triangle ACD$	HL thm. (*)
$\overline{BC} \cong \overline{DC}$	CPCTC
$\overline{AC}$ bisects $\overline{BD}$	Def. of seg. bisct.

⑨
Statements	Reasons
$\overline{BE} \cong \overline{DF}$, $BE = DF$	Given
$EF = EF$	Reflexive prop.
$BE + EF = DF + EF$	Addition prop.
$BF = DE$*	Seg. add. post.
$\overline{AE} \cong \overline{CF}$*	Given
$\angle 1 \cong \angle 4$	Given
$\angle 1$ is suppl. to $\angle 2$	Linear pair post.
$\angle 3$ is suppl. to $\angle 4$	Linear pair post.
$\angle 2 \cong \angle 3$*	$\cong$ suppl. thm.
$\triangle ADE \cong \triangle CBF$	SAS post. (*)
$\angle FBC \cong \angle EDA$	CPCTC

⑩
Statements	Reasons
$\overline{AC} \cong \overline{EC}$*	Given
$\angle 1 \cong \angle 4$	Given
$\angle 1$ is suppl. to $\angle 2$	Linear pair post.
$\angle 4$ is suppl. to $\angle 3$	Linear pair post.
$\angle 2 \cong \angle 3$*	$\cong$ suppl. thm.
$\angle C \cong \angle C$*	Reflexive prop.
$\triangle ADC \cong \triangle EBC$	AAS thm. (*)
$\overline{AD} \cong \overline{EB}$	CPCTC

⑪
Statements	Reasons
Draw $\overline{AM}$	Auxiliary line
M is midpoint of $\overline{BC}$	Given
$\overline{BM} \cong \overline{CM}$*	Def. of midpt.
$\overline{AM} \cong \overline{AM}$*	Reflexive prop.
$\overline{AB} \cong \overline{AC}$*	Given
$\triangle ABM \cong \triangle ACM$	SSS post. (*)
$\angle 2 \cong \angle 3$	CPCTC
$\angle 1$ is suppl. to $\angle 2$	Linear pair post.
$\angle 3$ is suppl. to $\angle 4$	Linear pair post.
$\angle 1 \cong \angle 4$	$\cong$ suppl. thm.

⑫
Statements	Reasons
Draw $\overline{AC}$	Auxiliary line
$\overline{AB} \cong \overline{AD}$*	Given
$\overline{BC} \cong \overline{DC}$*	Given
$\overline{AC} \cong \overline{AC}$*	Reflexive prop.
$\triangle ACB \cong \triangle ACD$	SSS post. (*)
$\angle 2 \cong \angle 3$	CPCTC
$\angle 1$ is suppl. to $\angle 2$	Linear pair post.
$\angle 3$ is suppl. to $\angle 4$	Linear pair post.
$\angle 1 \cong \angle 4$	$\cong$ suppl. thm.

⑬
Statements	Reasons
$\overline{AB} \perp \overline{BC}$	Given
$\overline{DC} \perp \overline{BC}$	Given
$\angle 1$ is compl. to $\angle 2$	Compl. thm.
$\angle 3$ is compl. to $\angle 4$	Compl. thm.
$\angle 1 \cong \angle 3$	Given
$\angle 2 \cong \angle 4$*	$\cong$ compl. thm.
$\angle AEB \cong \angle DEC$*	Vert. $\angle$s thm.
$\overline{AB} \cong \overline{DC}$	Given
$\triangle AEB \cong \triangle DEC$	AAS thm. (*)
$\overline{BE} \cong \overline{CE}$	CPCTC

⑭
Statements	Reasons
$\overline{AD} \perp \overline{DC}$	Given
$\overline{BC} \perp \overline{DC}$	Given
$\overline{AD} \parallel \overline{BC}$	Two $\perp$s make $\parallel$ (Two $\perp$s thm.)
$\angle ADB \cong \angle CBD$*	$\parallel \rightarrow$ alt. int. $\angle$s $\cong$
$\overline{AD} \cong \overline{BC}$*	Given
$\overline{DB} \cong \overline{DB}$*	Reflexive prop.
$\triangle ADB \cong \triangle CBD$	SAS post. (*)
$\overline{AB} \cong \overline{CD}$	CPCTC

⑮ Statements	Reasons
$\overline{AB} \perp \overline{BC}$	Given
$\overline{DC} \perp \overline{BC}$	Given
$\overline{AB} \parallel \overline{DC}$	Two ⊥s make ∥ (Two ⊥s thm.)
$\angle A \cong \angle DCE$ *	∥ → alt. int. ∠s ≅
$\overline{DE} \perp \overline{EC}$	Given
$m\angle B = m\angle DEC = 90°$	Def. of ⊥ lines
$\angle B \cong \angle DEC$ *	All right ∠s are ≅
$\overline{EC} \cong \overline{AB}$ *	Given
$\triangle ABC \cong \triangle CED$	ASA post. (*)
$\overline{BC} \cong \overline{ED}$	CPCTC

4.5 Isosceles Triangles

Ex1.
① $\angle B \cong \angle C$ (Isosceles △ thm.)
② $\angle DFE \cong \angle DEF$ (Isosceles △ thm.)
③ $\angle HEC \cong \angle HCE$ (Isosceles △ thm.)
④ $\angle A \cong \angle EDA$ (Isosceles △ thm.)
⑤ $\overline{DE} \cong \overline{DF}$ (Conv. of isos.△ thm.)
⑥ $\overline{FG} \cong \overline{FH}$ (Conv. of isos.△ thm.)
⑦ $\overline{AD} \cong \overline{AE}$ (Conv. of isos.△ thm.)
⑧ $\overline{CA} \cong \overline{CB}$ (Conv. of isos.△ thm.)

Ex2.
① $x = 8$ ② $y = 5$
③ $x = 20$ ④ $x = 53$
⑤ $x = 115$ ⑥ $x = 80$
⑦ $x = 150$ ⑧ $x = 60$
⑨ $x = 41$ ⑩ $x = 35$
⑪ $x = 21$ ⑫ $x = 45/2 = 22.5$

Ex3.

①
Statements	Reasons
$\overline{AB} \cong \overline{BC}$	Given
$\angle 2 \cong \angle 3$	Isosceles △ thm.
$\angle 1 \cong \angle 2$	Vert. ∠s thm.
$\angle 3 \cong \angle 4$	Vert. ∠s thm.
$\angle 1 \cong \angle 4$	Substitution prop.

②
Statements	Reasons
$\angle C \cong \angle D$	Given
$AC = AD$	Conv. isos.△ thm.
$AB + BC = AE + ED$	Seg. add. post.
$BC = ED$	Given
$AB = AE$	Subtraction prop.
$\angle 1 \cong \angle 2$	Isosceles △ thm.

③
Statements	Reasons
$\overline{AB} \cong \overline{AC}$	Given
$\overline{BD}$ bisects $\angle ABC$	Given
$\overline{CD}$ bisects $\angle ACB$	Given
$m\angle B = m\angle C$	Isosceles △ thm.
$m\angle DBC = \frac{1}{2} m\angle B$	∠ bisector thm.
$m\angle DCB = \frac{1}{2} m\angle C$	∠ bisector thm.
$2m\angle DBC = m\angle B$	Multipl. prop.
$2m\angle DCB = m\angle C$	Multipl. prop.
$2m\angle DBC = 2m\angle DCB$	Substitution prop.
$m\angle DBC = m\angle DCB$	Division prop.
$\overline{BD} \cong \overline{CD}$	Conv. isos.△ thm.

④
Statements	Reasons
$\overline{AB} \cong \overline{AC}$	Given
$\angle 3 \cong \angle 2$	Isosceles △ thm.
$\angle 2 \cong \angle 1$	Vert. ∠s thm.
$\angle 3 \cong \angle 1$	Transitive prop.

⑤
Statements	Reasons
$\overline{AO} \cong \overline{DO}$ *	Given
$\angle A \cong \angle D$ *	Given
$\angle AOB \cong \angle DOC$ *	Vert. ∠s thm.
$\triangle AOB \cong \triangle DOC$	ASA post. (*)
$\overline{OB} \cong \overline{OC}$	CPCTC
$\angle 1 \cong \angle 2$	Isosceles △ thm.

⑥
Statements	Reasons
$\overline{CE} \cong \overline{BD}$ *	Given
$\overline{AC} \cong \overline{AD}$ *	Given
$\angle 2 \cong \angle 3$ *	Isosceles △ thm.
$\triangle ACE \cong \triangle ADB$	SAS post. (*)
$\overline{AE} \cong \overline{AB}$	CPCTC

⑦
Statements	Reasons
$\angle 3 \cong \angle 6$ *	Given
$\angle 3$ is suppl. to $\angle 4$	Linear pair post.
$\angle 5$ is suppl. to $\angle 6$	Linear pair post.
$\angle 4 \cong \angle 5$	≅ suppl. thm
$\overline{AC} \cong \overline{AD}$ *	Conv. isos. △ thm.
$\angle 1 \cong \angle 2$ *	Given
$\triangle ABC \cong \triangle AED$	ASA post. (*)
$\overline{AB} \cong \overline{AE}$	CPCTC

⑧
Statements	Reasons
$\overline{FB} \cong \overline{DC}$ *	Given
$\overline{FG} \cong \overline{DE}$ *	Given
$\angle 2 \cong \angle 3$	Given
$\angle 1$ is suppl. to $\angle 2$	Linear pair post
$\angle 3$ is suppl. to $\angle 4$	Linear pair post
$\angle 1 \cong \angle 4$ *	≅ suppl. thm.
$\triangle FGB \cong \triangle DEC$	SAS post. (*)
$\angle B \cong \angle C$	CPCTC
$\overline{AB} \cong \overline{AC}$	Conv. isos. △ thm.

⑨
Statements	Reasons
$\overline{AB} \cong \overline{AC}$, $AB = AC$	Given
E is midpoint of $\overline{AB}$	Given
D is midpoint of $\overline{AC}$	Given
$EB = \frac{1}{2}AB, DC = \frac{1}{2}AC$	Midpoint thm.
$2EB = AB, 2DC = AC$	Multipl. prop.
$2EB = 2DC$	Substitution prop.
$EB = DC$ *	Division prop.
$\angle ABC \cong \angle ACB$ *	Isosceles △ thm.
$\overline{BC} \cong \overline{BC}$ *	Reflexive prop.
$\triangle EBC \cong \triangle DCB$	SAS post. (*)
$\angle ECB \cong \angle DBC$	CPCTC
$\overline{OB} \cong \overline{OC}$	Conv. isos. △ thm.

4.6 Using Congruent Triangles

Ex1.
①
Statements	Reasons
$\overline{AO} \cong \overline{DO}$ *	Given
$\overline{CO} \cong \overline{FO}$ *♥	Given
$\angle AOC \cong \angle DOF$ *	Vert. ∠s thm.
$\triangle AOC \cong \triangle DOF$	SAS post. (*)
$\angle C \cong \angle F$ ♥	CPCTC
$\angle BOC \cong \angle EOF$ ♥	Vert. ∠s thm.
$\triangle BOC \cong \triangle EOF$	ASA post. (♥)
$\overline{BC} \cong \overline{EF}$	CPCTC

② Statements	Reasons
$\overline{AD} \cong \overline{BC}$ *	Given
$\angle A \cong \angle B$ *	Given
F is midpoint of $\overline{AB}$	Given
$\overline{AF} \cong \overline{BF}$ *	Def. of midpt.
$\triangle FAD \cong \triangle FBC$	SAS post. (*)
$\overline{DF} \cong \overline{CF}$ ♥	CPCTC
$\overline{FE} \perp \overline{DC}$	Given
$m\angle FED = m\angle FEC = 90°$	Def. of $\perp$ lines
$\triangle FED, \triangle FEC$ are right $\triangle$ ♥	Def of right $\triangle$
$\overline{FE} \cong \overline{FE}$ ♥	Reflexive prop.
$\triangle FED \cong \triangle FEC$	HL thm. (♥)
$\angle DFE \cong \angle CFE$	CPCTC

③ Statements	Reasons
Draw $\overline{BD}, \overline{FD}$	Auxiliary line
$\overline{AD}$ bisects $\angle BAF$	Given
$\angle BAD \cong \angle FAD$ *	Def. of $\angle$ bisector
$\overline{AB} \cong \overline{AF}$ *	Given
$\overline{AD} \cong \overline{AD}$ *	Reflexive prop.
$\triangle BAD \cong \triangle FAD$	SAS post. (*)
$\overline{BD} \cong \overline{FD}$ ♥	CPCTC
$\overline{BC} \cong \overline{FE}$ ♥	Given
$m\angle C = m\angle E = 90°$	Given
$\triangle CBD, \triangle EFD$ are right $\triangle$s ♥	Def of right $\triangle$
$\triangle CBD \cong \triangle EFD$	HL thm. (♥)
$\overline{CD} \cong \overline{ED}$	CPCTC

④ Statements	Reasons
$\overline{AB} \cong \overline{AD}$ *	Given
$\overline{CB} \cong \overline{CD}$ *♥	Given
$\overline{AC} \cong \overline{AC}$ *	Reflexive prop.
$\triangle ABC \cong \triangle ADC$	SSS post. (*)
$\angle BCE \cong \angle DCE$ ♥	CPCTC
$\overline{EC} \cong \overline{EC}$ ♥	Reflexive prop.
$\triangle BCE \cong \triangle DCE$	SAS post. (♥)
$\overline{EB} \cong \overline{ED}$	CPCTC

⑤ Statements	Reasons
Draw $\overline{OB}$	Auxiliary line
$\overline{AB} \cong \overline{CB}$ *♥	Given
$\overline{AO} \cong \overline{CO}$ *	Given
$\overline{OB} \cong \overline{OB}$ *	Reflexive prop.
$\triangle AOB \cong \triangle COB$	SSS post. (*)
$\angle A \cong \angle C$ ♥	CPCTC
$\overline{AE} \cong \overline{CD}$ ♥	Given
$\triangle AEB \cong \triangle CDB$	SAS post. (♥)
$\overline{EB} \cong \overline{DB}$	CPCTC

⑥ Statements	Reasons
$\overline{AC} \cong \overline{AD}$ *	Given
$\overline{AB} \cong \overline{AE}$ *	Given
$\angle A \cong \angle A$ *	Reflexive prop.
$\triangle ACE \cong \triangle ADB$	SAS post. (*)
$\angle ACO \cong \angle ADO$ ♥	CPCTC
$\angle BOC \cong \angle EOD$ ♥	Vert. $\angle$s thm.
$AC = AD$	Def. of $\cong$ seg.
$AB + BC = AE + ED$	Seg. add. post.
$AB = AE$	Def. of $\cong$ seg.
$BC = ED$ ♥	Subtraction prop.
$\triangle BOC \cong \triangle EOD$	AAS thm. (♥)
$\overline{OC} \cong \overline{OD}$	CPCTC

Answers

5. Relationships in Triangles

5.1 Median, Altitude, and Bisectors

Ex1.
① Median: $\overline{IK}$ Altitude: $\overline{GJ}$
  Perp. bisct.: $\overline{JK}$ ∠bisct.: $\overline{HL}$
② Median: $\overline{HJ}$ Altitude: $\overline{IL}$
  Perp. bisct.: $\overline{MK}$ ∠bisct.: $\overline{GN}$
③ Median: $\overline{BD}$ Altitude: $\overline{AE}$
  Perp. bisct.: $\overline{FD}$ ∠bisct.: $\overline{AG}$
④ Median: $\overline{CD}$ Altitude: $\overline{AB}$
  Perp. bisct.: $\overline{DF}$ ∠bisct.: $\overline{AE}$

Ex2.
① $x = 8$, ⊥ bisct. thm.
② $x = 6$, Conv. of ⊥ bisct. thm.
③ $x = \dfrac{7}{2}$, Conv. of ⊥ bisct. thm.
④ $x = 3$, ⊥ bisct. thm.
⑤ $x = 23$, ∠ bisct. thm.
⑥ $x = 10$, Conv. of ∠ bisct. thm.
⑦ $x = 57$, Conv. of ∠ bisct. thm.
⑧ $x = 6$, ∠ bisct. thm.

Ex3.

①
Statements	Reasons
$\overline{DA} \cong \overline{DB}$	Given
$\overline{OC} \perp \overline{AB}$	Given
$\overline{OC}$ is ⊥ bisct.	Conv. ⊥ bisct. thm.
$\overline{AC} \cong \overline{BC}$	⊥ bisct. thm.

②
Statements	Reasons
$\overline{AE}$ is ⊥ bisct. of $\overline{DB}$	Given
$\overline{BE}$ is ⊥ bisct. of $\overline{AC}$	Given
$\overline{AD} \cong \overline{AB}$	⊥ bisct. thm.
$\overline{BC} \cong \overline{AB}$	⊥ bisct. thm.
$\overline{AD} \cong \overline{BC}$ *	Substitution prop.
$\overline{AB} \cong \overline{AB}$ *	Reflexive prop.
$\angle BAD \cong \angle ABC$ *	Given
$\triangle BAD \cong \triangle ABC$	SAS post.(*)

③
Statements	Reasons
$\triangle OAB$ is isos. △	Given
$\overline{AO}$ bisects $\angle CAB$	Given
$\overline{BO}$ bisects $\angle DBA$	Given
$\overline{CO} \cong \overline{BO}$	∠ bisct. thm.
$\overline{BO} \cong \overline{AO}$	Def. of isos △
$\overline{AO} \cong \overline{DO}$	∠ bisct. thm.
$\overline{CO} \cong \overline{DO}$	Transitive prop.

5.2 Centers of Triangles

Ex1.
① $x = 20, y = 25, z = 15$
② $x = 15, y = 11, z = 15$
③ $x = 5, y = 7, z = 7$
④ $x = 3.5, y = 16$
⑤ $x = 20, y = 12$
⑥ $x = 6, y = 10$
⑦ $x = 10, y = 15$
⑧ $x = 9, y = 8$
⑨ $x = 7, y = 32, z = 38$
⑩ $x = 4, y = 10$

Ex2.
① $x = 22, y = 3$
② $x = 18, y = 7$
③ $x = 2, y = 30$
④ $x = 5, y = 57$
⑤ $x = 40$
⑥ $x = 30$

Ex3.	① $x=3, y=6, z=5$
	② $x=6, y=6$
	③ $x=14, y=8, z=15$
	④ $x=18, y=5, z=11$
Ex4.	6
Ex5.	① centroid　　② incenter
	③ incenter　　④ circumcenter
	⑤ circumcenter　⑥ circumcenter
	⑦ orthocenter　⑧ incenter
	⑨ circumcenter　⑩ centroid
	⑪ orthocenter

5.3 Midsegment Theorem

Ex1.	① $x=80, y=62, z=14$
	② $x=75, y=12$
	③ $x=75, y=55, z=10$
	④ $x=58, y=8, z=10$
	⑤ $x=9, y=8$
	⑥ $x=14, y=12$
	⑦ $x=5, y=6, z=4$
	⑧ $x=20, y=24, z=16$
	⑨ $x=10, y=15$
	⑩ $x=3, y=9$
	⑪ $x=\dfrac{32}{3}, y=20$
	⑫ $x=8, y=6$
Ex2.	8
Ex3.	12 cm
Ex4.	9 cm

5.4 Properties of Inequalities

Ex1.	① True　　② True
	③ False　　④ False
	⑤ True　　⑥ True
	⑦ False　　⑧ False
	⑨ True　　⑩ False
	⑪ False　　⑫ True
	⑬ True　　⑭ False
	⑮ True　　⑯ True
Ex2.	① Yes　　② Yes
	③ No　　④ Yes
	⑤ Yes　　⑥ Yes
	⑦ No

Ex3.

①
Statements	Reasons
$OA < OC$	Given
$OB < OD$	Given
$OA + OB < OC + OD$	Prop. of inequal. (or add. prop of ineq)
$AB < CD$	Seg. add. post.

②
Statements	Reasons
$AC < BD$	Given
$AB + BC < BC + CD$	Seg. add. post.
$BC = BC$	Reflexive prop.
$AB < CD$	Prop. of inequal. (or subtr. prop of ineq)

③
Statements	Reasons
$\angle 1, \angle 2$ are vert. $\angle$s	Given
$m\angle 1 = m\angle 2$	Vert. $\angle$s thm.
$m\angle 1 + m\angle AOE > m\angle 2$	Prop. of inequal.
$m\angle AOB > m\angle 2$	$\angle$ add. post.

④
Statements	Reasons
$m\angle AOB = m\angle DOC$	Given
$m\angle AOB + m\angle BOC > m\angle DOC$	Prop. of inequal.
$m\angle AOC > m\angle DOC$	$\angle$ add. post.

Ex4.	① ∠2	② ∠7
	③ ∠6	④ ∠14
	⑤ ∠12	⑥ ∠8

Ex5.	① ∠6,7,9,10,12,13	② ∠12,13
	③ ∠6,5,3,2	④ ∠8,9,5,6,2,3
	⑤ ∠11,14	⑥ ∠11,14,7,4,1
	⑦ ∠8,11,14,4,1	⑧ ∠7,4,1

Ex6.

①
Statements	Reasons
∠3, ∠4 are vert. ∠s	Given
$m\angle 3 = m\angle 4$	Vert. ∠s thm.
$m\angle 2 < m\angle 3$	Ext. ∠ ineq. thm.
$m\angle 1 = m\angle 2$	Vert. ∠s thm.
$m\angle 1 < m\angle 4$	Substitution prop.

②
Statements	Reasons
$\overline{AB} \perp \overline{BC}$	Given
$m\angle B = 90°$	Def. of ⊥ lines
$m\angle ACD > m\angle B$	Ext. ∠ ineq. thm.
$m\angle ACD > 90°$	Substitution prop.

5.5 Inequalities in One Triangle

Ex1.	① ∠C, ∠B, ∠A	② ∠C, ∠A, ∠B
	③ ∠A, ∠B, ∠C	④ ∠A, ∠B, ∠C

Ex2.	① $a<c<b$	② $a<c<b$
	③ $c<b<a$	④ $c<b<a$
	⑤ $b<a<c<e<d$	
	⑥ $d<c<b<a$	⑦ $a<b<c$

Ex3.	① yes	② no
	③ no	④ no
	⑤ no	⑥ yes

Ex4.

①
Statements	Reasons
$\angle 1 \cong \angle 2$	Given
$BC = CD$	Conv. isos. △ thm.
$AB + AC > BC$	△ ineq. thm.
$AB + AC > CD$	Substitution prop.

②
Statements	Reasons
$AD + AC > CD$	△ ineq. thm.
$AB = AC$	Given
$AD + AB > CD$	Substitution prop.

③
Statements	Reasons
$BE = ED$	Given
$AB + AC > CB*$	△ ineq. thm.
$CE + ED > CD$	△ ineq. thm.
$CE + BE > CD$	Substitution prop.
$CB > CD*$	Seg. add. post.
$AB + AC > CD$	Prop. of inequal. (Transitive) (*)

④
Statements	Reasons
M is midpoint of $\overline{AD}$	Given
$AM = MD$	Def. of midpt.
$AM + BM > AB$	△ ineq. thm.
$MD + BM > AB$	Substitution prop.

⑤
Statements	Reasons
$\overline{PS} \parallel \overline{QR}$	Given
$\angle PSQ \cong \angle RQS*$	∥ → alt. int. ∠s ≅
$\angle P \cong \angle R*$	Given
$\overline{SQ} \cong \overline{SQ}*$	Reflexive prop.
$\triangle PSQ \cong \triangle RQS$	AAS thm. (*)
$PQ = SR$	CPCTC
$PS + PQ > QS$	△ ineq. thm.
$PS + SR > QS$	Substitution prop.

⑥ Statements	Reasons
$\overline{JM}$ bisects $\angle KJL$	Given
$\angle KJM \cong \angle LJM$ *	Def. of $\angle$ bisector
$\angle JMK \cong \angle JML$ *	Given
$\overline{JM} \cong \overline{JM}$ *	Reflexive prop.
$\triangle KJM \cong \triangle LJM$	ASA post. (*)
$\overline{JK} \cong \overline{JL}$	CPCTC
$JK = JL$	Def. of $\cong$ seg.
$JK < JM + MK$	$\triangle$ ineq. thm.
$JL < JM + MK$	Substitution prop.

5.6 Inequalities in Two Triangles

Ex1.
① $AB < BC$ (SAS ineq. thm.)
② $BC > EF$ (SAS ineq. thm.)
③ $AB > AC$ (SAS ineq. thm.)
④ $AD < BC$ (SAS ineq. thm.)
⑤ $BD < DC$ (SAS ineq. thm.)
⑥ $m\angle ACB < m\angle CBD$ (SSS ineq. thm.)
⑦ $m\angle COB < m\angle AOB$ (SSS ineq. thm.)
⑧ $m\angle ABC < m\angle EDC$ (SSS ineq. thm.)
⑨ $m\angle ABD < m\angle CBD$ (SSS ineq. thm.)

Ex2.
① $OA > OC$ (SAS ineq. thm.)
　$OA > 10$ ($\angle$-Side rel. thm.)
　$OA + OB > 10$ ($\triangle$ ineq. thm.)
② $AB < DE$ (SAS ineq. thm.)
　$m\angle BOC > m\angle DOC$ (SSS ineq. thm.)
　$AB < 24$ ($\triangle$ ineq. thm.)
③ $m\angle AOB < m\angle COD$ (SSS ineq. thm.)
　$m\angle BOC < m\angle BCE$
　(Ext. $\angle$ ineq. thm.)
　$m\angle ABO < m\angle OAB$
　($\angle$-Side rel. thm.)

④ $m\angle AOB < m\angle BOC$ (SSS ineq. thm.)
　$m\angle A < m\angle AOB$ ($\angle$-Side rel. thm.)
　$m\angle A < m\angle AOP$ (Ext. $\angle$ ineq. thm.)

Ex3.

① Statements	Reasons
$AB = DC$ *	Given
$DB = DB$ *	Reflexive prop.
$m\angle 1 < m\angle 2$ *	Given
$AD < BC$	SAS ineq. thm. (*)

② Statements	Reasons
$AB = AD$ *	Given
$AC = AC$ *	Reflexive prop.
$BC > CD$ *	Given
$m\angle 1 > m\angle 2$	SSS ineq. thm. (*)

③ Statements	Reasons
D is midpoint of $\overline{EC}$	Given
$ED = CD$ *	Def. of midpt.
$m\angle 1 = m\angle 2$	Given
$AD = BD$ *	Conv. isos. $\triangle$ thm.
$AE < BC$ *	Given
$m\angle 3 < m\angle 4$	SSS ineq. thm. (*)

④ Statements	Reasons
$m\angle 3 = m\angle 4$	Given
$AB = AC$ *	Conv. isos. $\triangle$ thm.
$AD = AD$ *	Reflexive prop.
$m\angle 1 > m\angle 2$ *	Given
$BD > DC$	SAS ineq. thm. (*)

⑤ Statements	Reasons
$AD = BE$ *	Given
$DC = EC$ *	Given
$m\angle 1 < m\angle 2$	Given
$AC > BC$ *	$\angle$-Side rel. thm.
$m\angle 3 > m\angle 4$	SSS ineq. thm. (*)

⑥ Statements	Reasons
$AB = CD*$	Given
$BD = BD*$	Reflexive prop.
$\angle DBA < \angle BDC*$	Ext. $\angle$ ineq. thm.
$AD < BC$	SAS ineq. thm. (*)

⑦ Statements	Reasons
$m\angle B = m\angle ACB$	Given
$AC = AB*$	Conv. isos. △ thm.
$AC = DC*$	Given
$m\angle BAC < m\angle ACD*$	Ext. $\angle$ ineq. thm.
$CB < AD$	SAS ineq. thm. (*)

Answers

6. Quadrilaterals

6.1 Angles of Polygons

Ex1.	①	720, 360, 120, 60
	②	1440, 360, 144, 36
	③	7, 360, 128.6, 51.4
	④	8, 360, 135, 45
	⑤	12, 1800, 360, 30
	⑥	24, 3960, 360, 15
	⑦	36, 6120, 360, 170
	⑧	18, 2880, 360, 160
Ex2.	① 180	② 15
	③ 80	④ 410
	⑤ 45	⑥ 120
	⑦ 150	⑧ 133
Ex3.	36	
Ex4.	720°	
Ex5.	180°	
Ex6.	720°	

6.2 Parallelograms

Ex1.	①	▱ → diag. bisct.
	②	▱ → diag. bisct.
	③	Def. of ▱
	④	Def. of ▱
	⑤	▱ → opp. sides ≅
	⑥	▱ → opp. ∠s ≅
	⑦	▱ → opp. ∠s ≅
	⑧	Def. of ▱
		∥ → consec. int ∠s suppl.

Answers 533

	⑨	Def. of ▱	
		∥ → alt. int. ∠s ≅	
	⑩	▱ → opp. sides ≅	
Ex2.	① $a=60, b=120, c=6, d=4$		
	② $a=70, b=75, c=9, d=11$		
	③ $a=77, b=23, c=7$		
	④ $a=82, b=58, c=9$		
	⑤ $a=55$	⑥ $a=70$	
	⑦ $a=120$	⑧ $a=20$	

Ex3.

①
Statements	Reasons
▱ABCD	Given
▱DEFG	Given
∠B ≅ ∠ADC	▱ → opp. ∠s ≅
∠ADC ≅ ∠EDG	Vert. ∠s thm.
∠EDG ≅ ∠F	▱ → opp. ∠s ≅
∠B ≅ ∠F	Transitive prop.

②
Statements	Reasons
▱ABCD	Given
▱CDEF	Given
$\overline{AB} \cong \overline{DC}$	▱ → opp. sides ≅
$\overline{DC} \cong \overline{EF}$	▱ → opp. sides ≅
$\overline{AB} \cong \overline{EF}$	Transitive prop.

③
Statements	Reasons
▱ABCD	Given
$\overline{BE}$ bisects ∠ABC	Given
∠1 ≅ ∠2 *	Def. of ∠ bisector
$\overline{AD} \parallel \overline{BC}$	Def. of ▱
$\overline{AB} \parallel \overline{EC}$	Def. of ▱
∠2 ≅ ∠AFB	∥ → alt. int. ∠s ≅
∠AFB ≅ ∠EFD	Vert. ∠s thm.
∠2 ≅ ∠EFD *	Transitive prop.
∠1 ≅ ∠DEF *	∥ → alt. int. ∠s ≅
∠EFD ≅ ∠DEF	Substitution prop.(*)
$\overline{FD} \cong \overline{ED}$	Conv. isos. △ thm.

④
Statements	Reasons
▱ABCD	Given
$\overline{AD} \parallel \overline{BC}$	Def. of ▱
∠B ≅ ∠DAE	∥ → corresp. ∠s ≅
$\overline{AD} \cong \overline{DE}$	Given
∠DAE ≅ ∠E	Isosceles △ thm.
∠B ≅ ∠E	Transitive prop.

⑤
Statements	Reasons
▱ABCD	Given
$\overline{MN}$ passes point O	Given
$\overline{BO} \cong \overline{DO}$ *	▱ → diag. bisct.
∠MOD ≅ ∠NOB *	Vert. ∠s thm.
$\overline{AD} \parallel \overline{BC}$	Def. of ▱
∠MDO ≅ ∠NBO *	∥ → alt. int. ∠s ≅
△MDO ≅ △NBO	ASA post. (*)
$\overline{MO} \cong \overline{NO}$	CPCTC

⑥
Statements	Reasons
▱ABCD	Given
$\overline{AO} \cong \overline{CO}$ *	▱ → diag. bisct.
∠AOM ≅ ∠CON *	Vert. ∠s thm.
$\overline{AB} \parallel \overline{CD}$	Def. of ▱
∠AMO ≅ ∠CNO *	∥ → alt. int. ∠s ≅
△AMO ≅ △CNO	AAS thm. (*)
$\overline{MO} \cong \overline{NO}$	CPCTC

⑦
Statements	Reasons
▱ABCD	Given
$\overline{EB} \perp \overline{ED}, \overline{FD} \perp \overline{FB}$	Given
$m\angle E = m\angle F = 90°$	Def. of ⊥ lines
∠E ≅ ∠F *	All right ∠s are ≅
$\overline{AD} \cong \overline{BC}$ *	▱ → opp. sides ≅
∠2 ≅ ∠3	▱ → opp. ∠s ≅
∠1 is suppl. to ∠2	Linear pair post.
∠3 is suppl. to ∠4	Linear pair post.
∠1 ≅ ∠4 *	≅ suppl. thm.
△EDA ≅ △FBC	AAS thm. (*)
∠EDA ≅ ∠FBC	CPCTC

⑧

Statements	Reasons
A, B, D are midpoint	Given
$\overline{FA} \cong \overline{AE}$ *	Def. of midpt.
$\overline{FB} \cong \overline{BC}$	Def. of midpt.
$\overline{ED} \cong \overline{DC}$	Def. of midpt
$\overline{AB} \cong \overline{DC}$	$\square \to$ opp. sides $\cong$
$\overline{AD} \cong \overline{BC}$	$\square \to$ opp. sides $\cong$
$\overline{AB} \cong \overline{ED}$ *	Substitution prop.
$\overline{AD} \cong \overline{FB}$ *	Substitution prop.
$\triangle FAB \cong \triangle AED$	SSS post. (*)

⑨

Statements	Reasons
$\square ABCD$	Given
M is midpoint of $\overline{AD}$	Given
$\overline{AO} \cong \overline{OC}$	$\square \to$ diag. bisct.
$\overline{AM} \cong \overline{MD}$	Def. of midpt.
$\overline{MO} \parallel \overline{DC}$	$\triangle$ midseg. thm.

6.3 Tests for Parallelograms

Ex1.
① Yes, Def. of $\square$
② No
③ Yes, One pair sides is $\cong$ and $\parallel \to \square$
④ Yes, Opp. sides $\cong \to \square$
⑤ No
⑥ Yes, Opp. $\angle$s $\cong \to \square$
⑦ Yes, Opp. sides $\cong \to \square$
⑧ No
⑨ No
⑩ Yes, Diag. bisct. $\to \square$
⑪ No
⑫ Yes, One pair sides is $\cong$ and $\parallel \to \square$

Ex2.
①

Statements	Reasons
$\square ABCD$	Given
$\overline{FB} \parallel \overline{ED}$	Def. of $\square$
$\angle FDB \cong \angle EBD$	Given
$\overline{DF} \parallel \overline{BE}$	Alt. int. $\angle$s $\cong \to \parallel$
$FBED$ is $\square$	Def. of $\square$

②

Statements	Reasons
$\square ABCD$	Given
$\square BEFC$	Given
$\overline{AD} \parallel \overline{BC}$	Def. of $\square$
$\overline{BC} \parallel \overline{EF}$	Def. of $\square$
$\overline{AD} \parallel \overline{EF}$	Transitive prop. of $\parallel$ lines
$AEFD$ is $\square$	Def. of $\square$

③

Statements	Reasons
$\square ABCD$	Given
$\overline{FB} \parallel \overline{DE}$	Def. of $\square$
$AB = DC$	$\square \to$ opp. sides $\cong$
$\overline{AF} \cong \overline{CE}$, $AF = CE$	Given
$AB + AF = DC + CE$	Addition prop.
$FB = DE$	Seg. add. post.
$FBED$ is $\square$	One pair sides is $\cong$ and $\parallel \to \square$

④

Statements	Reasons
$\square ABCD$	Given
$\overline{AE} \parallel \overline{FC}$	Def. of $\square$
$\overline{AE} \cong \overline{FC}$	Given
$AEFC$ is $\square$	One pair sides is $\cong$ and $\parallel \to \square$

⑤

Statements	Reasons
$\overline{AE}$ is seg.bisct. of $\overline{BC}$	Given
F is midpoint of $\overline{AE}$	Given
$\overline{BF} \cong \overline{CF}$	Def. of seg. bisct.
$\overline{AF} \cong \overline{EF}$	Def. of midpt.
$ACEB$ is $\square$	Diag. bisct. $\to \square$

⑥ Statements	Reasons
▱ABCD	Given
AO = CO	▱ → diag. bisct.
BO = DO	▱ → diag. bisct.
E, F, G, H is midpoint	Given
$EO = \frac{1}{2}AO, GO = \frac{1}{2}CO$	Midpoint thm.
$FO = \frac{1}{2}BO, HO = \frac{1}{2}DO$	Midpoint thm.
2EO = AO, 2GO = CO	Multipl. prop.
2FO = BO, 2HO = DO	Multipl. prop.
2EO = 2GO	Substitution prop.
2FO = 2HO	Substitution prop.
EO = GO	Division prop.
FO = HO	Division prop.
EFGH is ▱	Diag. bisct. → ▱

⑦ Statements	Reasons
▱ABCD	Given
$\overline{AB} \cong \overline{DC}$ *	▱ → opp. sides ≅
$\overline{AB} \parallel \overline{DC}$	Def. of ▱
∠ABM ≅ ∠CDN *	∥ → alt. int. ∠s ≅
$\overline{AM} \parallel \overline{CN}$	Given
∠AMB ≅ ∠CND *	∥ → alt. ext. ∠s ≅
△AMB ≅ △CND	AAS thm. (*)
$\overline{AM} \cong \overline{CN}$	CPCTC
AMCN is ▱	One pair sides is ≅ and ∥ → ▱

⑧ Statements	Reasons
$\overline{AC} \perp \overline{DE}$	Given
$\overline{AC} \perp \overline{BF}$	Given
m∠AED = m∠CFB = 90°	Def. of ⊥ lines
∠AED ≅ ∠CFB *	All right ∠s are ≅
▱ABCD	Given
$\overline{AD} \cong \overline{BC}$ *	▱ → opp. sides ≅
$\overline{AD} \parallel \overline{BC}$	Def. of ▱
∠DAE ≅ ∠BCF *	∥ → alt. int. ∠s ≅
△DAE ≅ △BCF	AAS thm. (*)
$\overline{DE} \cong \overline{BF}$	CPCTC
$\overline{DE} \parallel \overline{BF}$	Two ⊥s make ∥ (Two ⊥s thm.)
BEDF is ▱	One pair sides is ≅ and ∥ → ▱

⑨ Statements	Reasons
▱ABCD	Given
$\overline{BO} \cong \overline{DO}$	▱ → diag. bisct.
AO = CO	▱ → diag. bisct.
AE + EO = CF + FO	Seg. add. post.
AE = FC	Given
EO = FO	Subtraction prop.
DEBF is ▱	Diag. bisct. → ▱

6.4 Rectangles, Rhombi and Squares

Ex1.
① Yes, Rect → opp. sides ∥
② Yes, Rect → diag. bisct.
③ Yes, Rect → diag. bisct.
④ No
⑤ Yes, Def. of rectangle
⑥ Yes, Def. of rectangle
⑦ Yes, Rect → diag. ≅
⑧ Yes, Rect → diag. ≅
⑨ No
⑩ No

Ex2.
① x = 27, y = 63, z = 54
② x = 25, y = 65
③ x = 6, y = 55
④ x = 4, y = 72

Ex3.

①
Statements	Reasons
ABCD is rect.	Given
$\overline{AD} \cong \overline{BC}$ *	Rect → opp. sides ≅
$\overline{AC} \cong \overline{BD}$ *	Rect → diag. ≅
$\overline{DC} \cong \overline{DC}$ *	Reflexive prop.
△ADC ≅ △BCD	SSS post. (*)
∠1 ≅ ∠2	CPCTC

②
Statements	Reasons
ABCD is rect.	Given
$\overline{AD} \cong \overline{BC}$ *	Rect → opp. sides ≅
E is midpoint of $\overline{DC}$	Given
$\overline{DE} \cong \overline{CE}$ *	Def. of midpt.
m∠D = m∠C = 90°	Def. of rectangle
∠D ≅ ∠C *	All right ∠s are ≅
△ADE ≅ △BCE	SAS post. (*)
$\overline{AE} \cong \overline{BE}$	CPCTC

③
Statements	Reasons
ABCD is rect.	Given
BCED is a ▱	Given
$\overline{AC} \cong \overline{BD}$	Rect → diag. ≅
$\overline{BD} \cong \overline{CE}$	▱ → opp. sides ≅
$\overline{AC} \cong \overline{CE}$	Transitive prop.
∠CAD ≅ ∠CED	Isosceles △ thm.

④
Statements	Reasons
ABCD is rect.	Given
$\overline{AD} \cong \overline{BC}$ *	Rect → opp. sides ≅
∠A, ∠B are right ∠s	Def. of rectangle
∠A ≅ ∠B *	All right ∠s are ≅
AE = BF	Given
EF = EF	Reflexive prop.
AE + EF = BF + EF	Addition prop.
AF = BE *	Seg. add. post.
△AFD ≅ △BEC	SAS post. (*)
∠AFD ≅ ∠BEC	CPCTC
$\overline{EG} \cong \overline{FG}$	Conv. isos. △ thm.

⑤
Statements	Reasons
▱ABCD	Given
$\overline{AD} \cong \overline{BC}$ *	Rect → opp. sides ≅
$\overline{DG} \cong \overline{CG}$ *	Given
∠ADF, ∠BCE are right ∠s	Def. of rectangle
m∠ADF = m∠BCE	All right ∠s are ≅
m∠FDG = m∠ECG	Isosceles △ thm.
m∠ADF + m∠FDG = m∠ECG + m∠BCE	Addition prop.
m∠ADG = m∠BCG *	∠ add. post.
△ADG ≅ △BCG	SAS post. (*)
$\overline{AG} \cong \overline{BG}$	CPCTC

Ex4.
① Yes, Rhombus → diag. ⊥
② Yes, Rhombus → diag. bisct.
③ Yes, Def. of rhombus
④ No
⑤ Yes, Rhombus → diag. bisects opp. ∠s
⑥ Yes, Rhombus → diag. bisects opp. ∠s
⑦ No
⑧ Yes, Rhombus → diag. ⊥
⑨ No
⑩ Yes, Def. of rhombus

Ex5.
① a = 40, b = 100, c = 40, d = 10
② a = 65, b = 65, c = 50, d = 5
③ a = 90, b = 47, c = 47, d = 43, e = 7
④ a = 55, b = 35, c = 90, d = 55, e = 11

Ex6.

①
Statements	Reasons
ABCD is a rhombus	Given
$\overline{AB} \cong \overline{AD}$ *	Def. of rhombus
$\overline{BO} \cong \overline{DO}$ *	Rhm → diag. bisct.
$\overline{AO} \cong \overline{AO}$ *	Reflexive prop.
△BAO ≅ △DAO	SSS post. (*)

②

Statements	Reasons
ABCD is a rhombus	Given
$\overline{BD} \perp \overline{AC}$	Rhm → diag. ⊥
$m\angle DPC = 90°$	Def. of ⊥ lines
$m\angle DPC + m\angle 1 + m\angle 2 = 180°$	△ sum thm.
$90° + m\angle 1 + m\angle 2 = 180°$	Substitution prop.
$m\angle 1 + m\angle 2 = 90°$	Subtraction prop.
∠1, ∠2 are compl.	Def. of compl.

③

Statements	Reasons
ABCD is a rhombus	Given
$m\angle ADP = m\angle ABQ$	Given
$m\angle 1 + m\angle 2 = m\angle 6 + m\angle 5$	∠ add. post.
$m\angle 1 = m\angle 6$	Rhm → opp. ∠s ≅
$m\angle 2 = m\angle 5$ *	Subtraction prop.
$m\angle 3 = m\angle 4$ *	Vert. ∠s thm.
$\overline{DC} \cong \overline{BC}$ *	Def. of rhombus
$\triangle DCP \cong \triangle BCQ$	ASA post. (*)
$\overline{CP} \cong \overline{CQ}$	CPCTC

④

Statements	Reasons
ABCD is rhombus	Given
$\overline{DC} \cong \overline{BC}$ *	Def. of rhombus
$\overline{CP} \cong \overline{CP}$ *	Reflexive prop.
$\overline{DP} \cong \overline{BP}$ *	Given
$\triangle DCP \cong \triangle BCP$	SSS post. (*)
$\angle DCP \cong \angle BCP$	CPCTC

⑤

Statements	Reasons
ABCD is rhombus	Given
F is midpoint of $\overline{AE}$	Given
$\overline{AB} \parallel \overline{DE}$	Rhm → opp. sides ∥
$\angle ABF \cong \angle ECF$ *	∥ → alt. int. ∠s ≅
$\angle AFB \cong \angle EFC$ *	Vert. ∠s thm.
$\overline{AF} \cong \overline{EF}$ *	Def. of midpt.
$\triangle ABF \cong \triangle ECF$	AAS thm. (*)
$\overline{AB} \cong \overline{CE}$	CPCTC
$\overline{AB} \cong \overline{AD}$	Def. of rhombus
$\overline{AD} \cong \overline{CE}$	Substitution prop.

⑥

Statements	Reasons
ABCD is rhombus	Given
$\overline{AO} \cong \overline{CO}$ *	Rhm → diag. bisct.
$\overline{OP} \cong \overline{OP}$ *	Reflexive prop.
$\overline{PO} \perp \overline{AC}$	Rhm → diag. ⊥
$m\angle POA = m\angle POC = 90°$	Def. of ⊥ lines
$\angle POA \cong \angle POC$ *	All right ∠s are ≅
$\triangle POA \cong \triangle POC$	SAS post. (*)
$\overline{PA} \cong \overline{PC}$	CPCTC
△APC is isos.	Def. of isos △

Ex7.

	▱	rect	rhm	squ
Two opp sides ∥	○	○	○	○
opp. sides ≅	○	○	○	○
opp. ∠s ≅	○	○	○	○
equilateral			○	○
equiangular		○		○
diag. bisct.	○	○	○	○
diag. ≅		○		○
diag. ⊥			○	○
diag. bisct. opp. ∠s			○	○

6.5 Trapezoids

Ex1.
① Yes, Def. of isos. trap.
② No
③ Yes, Isos.trap.→ diag. ≅
④ Yes, Def. of isos. trap.
⑤ Yes, Isos.trap.→ base ∠s ≅
⑥ No
⑦ No
⑧ Yes, Isos.trap.→ diag. ≅
⑨ Yes, Def. of isos. trap.
⑩ Yes, Isos.trap.→ base ∠s ≅

Ex2.

①
Statements	Reasons
Isos. trap. $ABCD$	Given
$\angle D \cong \angle C$	Isos.trap.→ base ∠s ≅
$\overline{AB} \parallel \overline{DC}$	Def. of isos. trap.
$\angle C$ is suppl. to $\angle B$	∥ →consec. int ∠s are suppl.
$\angle D$ is suppl. to $\angle B$	Substitution prop.

②
Statements	Reasons
Isos. trap. $ABCD$	Given
$\angle B \cong \angle C$	Isos.trap.→base ∠s ≅
$\overline{DC} \cong \overline{DE}$	Given
$\angle C \cong \angle DEC$	Isosceles △ thm.
$\angle B \cong \angle DEC$	Transitive prop.
$\overline{AB} \parallel \overline{DE}$	Corresp. ∠s ≅ → ∥
$\overline{AD} \parallel \overline{BE}$	Def. of isos. trap.
$ABED$ is ▱	Def. of ▱

③
Statements	Reasons
Isos. trap. $ABCD$	Given
$\overline{AD} \cong \overline{BC}$ *	Def. of isos. trap.
$\overline{DC} \cong \overline{DC}$ *	Reflexive prop.
$\angle D \cong \angle C$ *	Isos.trap.→base ∠s ≅
$\triangle ADC \cong \triangle BCD$	SAS post. (*)
$\angle DAC \cong \angle CBD$	CPCTC

④
Statements	Reasons
Isos. trap. $ABCD$	Given
$\overline{AD} \cong \overline{BC}$ *	Def. of isos. trap.
$\angle BAD \cong \angle ABC$ *	Isos.trap.→base ∠s ≅
$\overline{AB} \cong \overline{AB}$ *	Reflexive prop.
$\triangle BAD \cong \triangle ABC$	SAS post. (*)
$\angle DBA \cong \angle CAB$	CPCTC
$\overline{AO} \cong \overline{BO}$	Conv. isos. △ thm.
$\triangle ABO$ is isos.	Def. of isos △

⑤
Statements	Reasons
Isos. trap. $ABCD$	Given
$\angle ADP \cong \angle BCP$ *	Given
$\angle APD \cong \angle BPC$ *	Vert. ∠s thm.
$\overline{AD} \cong \overline{BC}$ *	Def. of isos. trap.
$\triangle ADP \cong \triangle BCP$	AAS thm. (*)
$\overline{DP} \cong \overline{CP}$	CPCTC
$\triangle DPC$ is isos.	Def. of isos △

Ex3.
① $x = 13$ ② $x = 14$
③ $x = 5$ ④ $x = 12$
⑤ $x = 8, y = 5$ ⑥ $x = 7, y = 4$
⑦ $x = 5$ ⑧ $x = 6$

Ex4.
A : Parallelogram
B : Square
C : Rhombus
D : Trapezoid

Ex5.
① always   ② never
③ always   ④ always
⑤ sometimes   ⑥ sometimes
⑦ sometimes   ⑧ sometimes
⑨ never   ⑩ always
⑪ always   ⑫ sometimes
⑬ sometimes   ⑭ never

Answers

7. Similarity

7.1 Proportions

Ex1.	① 24 ft, 32 ft, 48 ft
	② 21 in, 27 in, 36 in

Ex2.	① 54°, 36° ② 40°, 140°
	③ 48°, 60°, 72°

Ex3.	① $\dfrac{5}{2}$	② $\dfrac{7}{n}$
	③ $\dfrac{4}{9}$	④ $\dfrac{2}{1}$
	⑤ $\dfrac{3}{11}$	⑥ $\dfrac{11}{13}$
	⑦ $\dfrac{b}{5}$	⑧ $\dfrac{r}{3}$

Ex4.	① $x = 5$	② $x = 10$
	③ $x = 13$	④ $x = 21$
	⑤ $x = 4$ or 6	⑥ $x = -1$ or 9
	⑦ $x = \dfrac{16}{3}$	⑧ $x = -9$

7.2 Identify Similar Figures

Ex1.	① $\angle G$	② $\angle N$
	③ $\dfrac{EF}{FG}$	④ $\dfrac{LM}{MN}$
	⑤ $\angle S$	⑥ $\angle Z$
	⑦ $\dfrac{ST}{TR}$	⑧ $\dfrac{XY}{XZ}$

Ex2.	① $a = 40$, $b = 70$, $c = \dfrac{35}{4}$
	$\triangle ABC \sim \triangle OZW$
	② $a = 23$, $b = 67$, $c = 10$
	$\triangle ABC \sim \triangle WOR$
	③ $a = 140$, $b = 85$, $c = \dfrac{10}{3}$
	$\square ABCD \sim \square XSMQ$
	④ $a = 92$, $b = 88$, $c = 11$
	$\square ABCD \sim \square HSOL$
	⑤ $a = 50$, $b = \dfrac{10}{3}$
	$\triangle ABC \sim \triangle EDC$
	⑥ $a = 125$, $b = \dfrac{21}{4}$
	$\square ABCD \sim \square AOQS$

Ex3.	① sometimes	② sometimes
	③ always	④ always
	⑤ sometimes	⑥ sometimes
	⑦ always	⑧ sometimes (If number of sides is different, then not similar)
	⑨ never	⑩ sometimes
	⑪ sometimes	⑫ sometimes
	⑬ always	⑭ always
	⑮ sometimes	

7.3 Proving Similar Triangles

Ex1.	① AA ~ post.	② SAS ~ thm.
	③ SSS ~ thm.	④ AA ~ post.
	⑤ Not similar	⑥ Not similar
	⑦ SAS ~ thm.	⑧ AA ~ post.
	⑨ AA ~ post.	⑩ SSS ~ thm.
	⑪ AA ~ post.	⑫ Not similar

Ex2.

①
Statements	Reasons
▱ABCD	Given
$\overline{AB} \parallel \overline{CE}$	Def. of ▱
∠BAF ≅ ∠FEC*	∥ → alt. int. ∠s ≅
∠BFA ≅ ∠CFE*	Vert. ∠s thm.
△ABF ~ △ECF	AA ~ post. (*)

②
Statements	Reasons
∠ADE ≅ ∠ABC*	Given
∠A ≅ ∠A*	Reflexive prop.
△ADE ~ △ABC	AA ~ post. (*)

③
Statements	Reasons
$\overline{AB} \perp \overline{BF}, \overline{DF} \perp \overline{BF}$	Given
m∠B = m∠F = 90°	Def. of ⊥ lines
∠B ≅ ∠F*	All right ∠s are ≅
∠1 ≅ ∠4	Given
∠1 is suppl. to ∠2	Linear pair post.
∠3 is suppl. to ∠4	Linear pair post.
∠2 ≅ ∠3*	≅ suppl. thm.
△ABC ~ △DFE	AA ~ post. (*)

④
Statements	Reasons
▱ABCD	Given
∠A ≅ ∠C*	▱ → opp. ∠s ≅
$\overline{AB} \perp \overline{ED}, \overline{FG} \perp \overline{BC}$	Given
m∠AED = m∠CGF = 90°	Def. of ⊥ lines
∠AED ≅ ∠CGF*	All right ∠s are ≅
△AED ~ △CGF	AA ~ post. (*)

⑤
Statements	Reasons
D is midpoint of $\overline{AB}$	Given
E is midpoint of $\overline{AC}$	Given
$AD = \frac{1}{2} AB$	Midpoint thm.
$AE = \frac{1}{2} AC$	Midpoint thm.
$\frac{AD}{AB} = \frac{1}{2}$	Division prop.
$\frac{AE}{AC} = \frac{1}{2}$	Division prop.
$\frac{AD}{AB} = \frac{AE}{AC}$ *	Substitution prop.
∠A ≅ ∠A*	Reflexive prop.
△ABC ~ △ADE	SAS ~ thm. (*)

⑥
Statements	Reasons
$\overline{AB} \cong \overline{AC}$	Given
∠B ≅ ∠C*	Isosceles △ thm.
▱AEDF	Given
∠1 ≅ ∠3	▱ → opp. ∠s ≅
∠1 is suppl. to ∠2	Linear pair post.
∠3 is suppl. to ∠4	Linear pair post.
∠2 ≅ ∠4*	≅ suppl. thm.
△DEB ~ △DFC	AA ~ post. (*)

⑦
Statements	Reasons
$\overline{DE} \perp \overline{BC}$	Given
$\overline{DE} \parallel \overline{FG}$	Given
$\overline{FG} \perp \overline{BC}$	⊥ to one ∥, ⊥ to other (from ch3.2)
m∠DEB = m∠FGC = 90°	Def. of ⊥ lines
∠DEB ≅ ∠FGC*	All right ∠s are ≅
$\overline{AB} \cong \overline{AC}$	Given
∠B ≅ ∠C*	Isosceles △ thm.
△DEB ~ △FGC	AA ~ post. (*)

⑧
Statements	Reasons
$\overline{BC}$ bisects ∠ACD	Given
∠ACB ≅ ∠DCE*	Def. of ∠ bisector
AC · CE = DC · BC	Given
$\frac{AC}{BC} = \frac{DC}{CE}$ *	Division prop.
△ABC ~ △DEC	SAS ~ thm. (*)

⑨

Statements	Reasons
E is midpoint of $\overline{AB}$	Given
D is midpoint of $\overline{AC}$	Given
F is midpoint of $\overline{BC}$	Given
$ED = \frac{1}{2}BC$	△ midseg. thm.
$DF = \frac{1}{2}AB$	△ midseg. thm.
$EF = \frac{1}{2}AC$	△ midseg. thm.
$\frac{ED}{BC} = \frac{1}{2}$	Division prop.
$\frac{DF}{AB} = \frac{1}{2}$	Division prop.
$\frac{EF}{AC} = \frac{1}{2}$	Division prop.
$\frac{ED}{BC} = \frac{DF}{AB} = \frac{EF}{AC}$ *	Substitution prop.
$\triangle ABC \sim \triangle EDF$	SSS ~ thm. (*)

Ex3.

①

Statements	Reasons
$\frac{AB}{AD} = \frac{AC}{AE}$ *	Given
$\angle A \cong \angle A$ *	Reflexive prop.
$\triangle ABC \sim \triangle ADE$	SAS ~ thm. (*)
$\angle ADE \cong \angle B$	Corresp. ∠s are ≅ in ~△s
$\overline{DE} \parallel \overline{BC}$	Corresp. ∠s ≅ → ∥

②

Statements	Reasons
$\frac{AC}{EC} = \frac{BC}{DC}$ *	Given
$\angle ACB \cong \angle ECD$ *	Vert. ∠s thm.
$\triangle ACB \sim \triangle ECD$	SAS ~ thm. (*)
$\angle A \cong \angle E$	Corresp. ∠s are ≅ in ~△s
$\overline{AB} \parallel \overline{DE}$	Alt. int. ∠s ≅ → ∥

③

Statements	Reasons
$\frac{AC}{AB} = \frac{AB}{AD} = \frac{BC}{DB}$ *	Given
$\triangle ABC \sim \triangle ADB$	SSS ~ thm. (*)
$\angle C \cong DBA$	Corresp. ∠s are ≅ in ~△s

④

Statements	Reasons
$\frac{AB}{CD} = \frac{BC}{DE} = \frac{CA}{EC}$ *	Given
$\triangle ABC \sim \triangle CDE$	SSS ~ thm. (*)
$\angle BCA \cong \angle DEC$	Corresp. ∠s are ≅ in ~△s
$\overline{BC} \parallel \overline{DE}$	Alt. int. ∠s ≅ → ∥

⑤

Statements	Reasons
$\overline{AB} \perp \overline{BC}$	Given
$\overline{AD} \perp \overline{DB}$	Given
$m\angle ABC = m\angle ADB = 90°$	Def. of ⊥ lines
$\angle ABC \cong \angle ADB$ *	All right ∠s are ≅
$\angle A \cong \angle A$ *	Reflexive prop.
$\triangle ABC \sim \triangle ADB$	AA ~ post. (*)
$\frac{AB}{AD} = \frac{AC}{AB}$	Corresp. sides are prop. in ~△s
$AB^2 = AC \cdot AD$	Mean-ext. prop.

⑥

Statements	Reasons
$\overline{ED} \parallel \overline{BC}$	Given
$\angle 1 \cong \angle B$ *	∥ → corresp. ∠s ≅
$\angle 2 \cong \angle 2$ *	Reflexive prop.
$\triangle AEF \sim \triangle ABG$	AA ~ post. (*)
$\frac{EF}{BG} = \frac{AF}{AG}$	Corresp. sides are prop. in ~△s
$\angle 4 \cong \angle C$ *	∥ → corresp. ∠s ≅
$\angle 3 \cong \angle 3$ *	Reflexive prop.
$\triangle ADF \sim \triangle ACG$	AA ~ post. (*)
$\frac{AF}{AG} = \frac{FD}{GC}$	Corresp. sides are prop. in ~△s
$\frac{EF}{BG} = \frac{FD}{GC}$	Transitive prop.

⑦ Statements	Reasons
$\overline{AB} \perp \overline{BC}$	Given
$\overline{DC} \perp \overline{BC}$	Given
$\overline{AB} \parallel \overline{DC}$	Two $\perp$s make $\parallel$ (Two $\perp$s thm.)
$\angle A \cong \angle DCE$ *	$\parallel \to$ alt. int. $\angle$s $\cong$
$m\angle B = m\angle DEC = 90°$	Def. of $\perp$ lines
$\angle B \cong \angle DEC$ *	All right $\angle$s are $\cong$
$\triangle ABC \sim \triangle CED$	AA $\sim$ post. (*)
$\dfrac{AB}{CE} = \dfrac{BC}{ED}$	Corresp. sides are prop. in $\sim \triangle$ s

⑧ Statements	Reasons
$ABCD$ is trap.	Given
$\overline{AB} \parallel \overline{DC}$	Def. of trapezoids
$\angle BAE \cong \angle DCE$ *	$\parallel \to$ alt. int. $\angle$s $\cong$
$\angle ABE \cong \angle CDE$ *	$\parallel \to$ alt. int. $\angle$s $\cong$
$\triangle ABE \sim \triangle CDE$	AA $\sim$ post. (*)
$\dfrac{AE}{CE} = \dfrac{BE}{DE}$	Corresp. sides are prop. in $\sim \triangle$s

Ex4.
① $x = 8$ ② $x = 12$
③ $x = 3$ ④ $x = 16$
⑤ $x = 10$ ⑥ $x = 12$
⑦ $x = 3$ ⑧ $x = 6$
⑨ $x = 9$ ⑩ $x = \dfrac{72}{13}$
⑪ $x = 4$ ⑫ $x = 12$

Ex5. $x = \dfrac{99}{20}$

Ex6. $x = 4, y = 8$

7.4 More Theorems about Similar Triangles

Ex1.
① $x = 3$ ② $x = \dfrac{10}{3}$
③ $x = \dfrac{15}{2}, y = \dfrac{14}{3}$ ④ $x = \dfrac{21}{2}, y = 8$
⑤ $x = \dfrac{7}{3}, y = \dfrac{5}{3}$ ⑥ $x = 15, y = \dfrac{3}{2}$
⑦ $x = 6, y = \dfrac{10}{3}$ ⑧ $x = 20, y = 8$
⑨ $x = 15$ ⑩ $x = 9$
⑪ $x = \dfrac{18}{5}, y = \dfrac{24}{5}$ ⑫ $x = \dfrac{8}{3}, y = \dfrac{10}{3}$
⑬ $x = \dfrac{12}{5}, y = 10$ ⑭ $x = 14, y = \dfrac{32}{3}$
⑮ $x = \dfrac{35}{8}$ ⑯ $x = \dfrac{36}{5}$
⑰ $x = 4, y = 9$ ⑱ $x = 6$

Ex2.
① $x = 9, y = \dfrac{16}{5}$ ② $x = \dfrac{20}{3}, y = 6$
③ $x = \dfrac{20}{3}, y = \dfrac{8}{3}$ ④ $x = 20, y = \dfrac{72}{5}$

Ex3.
① $x = \dfrac{16}{3}$ ② $x = \dfrac{50}{7}$
③ $x = 22$ ④ $x = 18$
⑤ $x = 6$ ⑥ $x = \dfrac{60}{11}$
⑦ $x = \dfrac{120}{23}$

Answers

8. Right Triangles and Trigonometry

8.1 Right Triangle Similarity

Ex1.	① $x=6, y=2\sqrt{13}, z=3\sqrt{13}$
	② $x=\dfrac{\sqrt{2}}{4}, y=\dfrac{\sqrt{3}}{4}, z=\dfrac{\sqrt{6}}{4}$
	③ $x=5, y=4, z=2\sqrt{5}$
	④ $x=16, y=8\sqrt{3}, z=4\sqrt{3}$
	⑤ $x=5, y=\sqrt{14}, z=\sqrt{35}$
	⑥ $x=1, y=\sqrt{42}, z=\sqrt{6}$
Ex2.	20
Ex3.	① $x=\dfrac{24}{5}$　② $x=\dfrac{120}{17}$
	③ $x=\dfrac{60}{13}$　④ $x=\dfrac{\sqrt{2}}{2}$
Ex4.	$DH=\dfrac{12}{5}$

8.2 The Pythagorean Theorem

Ex1.	① $x=5$	② $x=\sqrt{61}$
	③ $x=\sqrt{7}$	④ $x=\sqrt{119}$
	⑤ $x=2\sqrt{7}$	⑥ $x=\sqrt{39}$
	⑦ $x=\sqrt{5}$	⑧ $x=2$
	⑨ $x=\sqrt{2}$	
Ex2.	① $x=25$	② $x=2$
	③ $x=6$	④ $x=26$
	⑤ $x=1$	⑥ $x=50$
	⑦ $x=16$	⑧ $x=5$

Ex3.	① $x=\sqrt{13}$	② $x=\sqrt{265}$
	③ $x=24$	④ $x=4$
	⑤ $x=\sqrt{71}$	⑥ $x=\sqrt{127}$
	⑦ $x=\dfrac{65}{17}$	⑧ $x=\dfrac{5}{2}$
	⑨ $x=\dfrac{9}{5}$	⑩ $x=\dfrac{144}{13}$
	⑪ $x=2\sqrt{5}$	⑫ $x=\dfrac{24}{5}=4.8$
	⑬ $x=\dfrac{3}{4}$	⑭ $x=\dfrac{20}{7}$
	⑮ $x=\sqrt{13}$	⑯ $x=\sqrt{10}$
	⑰ $x=1$	
Ex4.	$x=3$	
Ex5.	$x=10$	
Ex6.	① acute	② obtuse
	③ obtuse	④ acute
	⑤ obtuse	⑥ right

8.3 Special Right Triangles

Ex1.	① $x=4, y=4\sqrt{2}$	② $x=\sqrt{6}, y=\sqrt{3}$
	③ $x=2, y=\sqrt{2}$	④ $x=5\sqrt{2}, y=5\sqrt{2}$
	⑤ $x=3\sqrt{2}, y=3\sqrt{2}$	⑥ $x=2, y=2$
	⑦ $x=\dfrac{\sqrt{10}}{2}, y=\dfrac{\sqrt{10}}{2}$	
Ex2.	① $x=6, y=3\sqrt{3}$	② $x=3, y=2\sqrt{3}$
	③ $x=\dfrac{7}{2}, y=\dfrac{7\sqrt{3}}{2}$	④ $x=4, y=4\sqrt{3}$
	⑤ $x=\dfrac{8\sqrt{3}}{3}, y=\dfrac{4\sqrt{3}}{3}$	⑥ $x=2\sqrt{2}, y=\sqrt{2}$
	⑦ $x=\dfrac{\sqrt{10}}{2}, y=\dfrac{\sqrt{30}}{2}$	

Ex3.	① $a=3\sqrt{3}, b=3, c=9, d=6\sqrt{3}$
	② $a=2\sqrt{3}, b=4\sqrt{3}, c=2, d=4$
	③ $a=2\sqrt{2}, b=2\sqrt{2}, c=4\sqrt{2}, d=4$
	④ $a=\frac{7\sqrt{3}}{3}, b=\frac{14\sqrt{3}}{3}, c=7, d=7\sqrt{2}$
	⑤ $a=\frac{8\sqrt{3}}{3}, b=\frac{16\sqrt{3}}{3}, c=\frac{16}{3}, d=\frac{32}{3}$
	⑥ $a=8, b=3\sqrt{2}$
Ex4.	$a=5\sqrt{6},\ b=10\sqrt{2}$
Ex5.	$x=\frac{8\sqrt{3}}{3}$

Ex3.	① $x=10\sin\theta, y=10\cos\theta$	
	② $x=9\cos\theta, y=9\sin\theta$	
	③ $x=\frac{4.5}{\tan\theta}, y=\frac{4.5}{\sin\theta}$	
	④ $x=\frac{22}{\sin\theta}, y=\frac{22}{\tan\theta}$	
Ex4.	① $\frac{\sqrt{3}}{2}$	② $\frac{\sqrt{2}}{2}$
	③ $\frac{\sqrt{2}}{2}$	④ $\frac{\sqrt{3}}{2}$
	⑤ $\sqrt{3}$	⑥ 1
	⑦ $\frac{1}{2}$	⑧ $\frac{1}{2}$
	⑨ $\frac{\sqrt{2}}{2}$	⑩ $\frac{1}{2}$
	⑪ $\frac{\sqrt{2}+\sqrt{6}}{4}$	⑫ 0
	⑬ 1	⑭ 1

8.4 Trigonometry of Right Triangles

Ex1.	① $\frac{\pi}{2}$	② $\frac{5\pi}{9}$
	③ $\frac{2\pi}{3}$	④ $\frac{5\pi}{6}$
	⑤ 60°	⑥ 300°
	⑦ 240°	⑧ 15°
	⑨ $\frac{120°}{\pi}$	⑩ $\frac{1260°}{\pi}$
Ex2.	① $\sin\theta=\frac{5}{13}, \cos\theta=\frac{12}{13}, \tan\theta=\frac{5}{12}$	
	② $\sin\theta=\frac{2\sqrt{13}}{13}, \cos\theta=\frac{3\sqrt{13}}{13}, \tan\theta=\frac{2}{3}$	
	③ $\sin\theta=\frac{\sqrt{2}}{2}, \cos\theta=\frac{\sqrt{2}}{2}, \tan\theta=1$	
	④ $\sin\theta=\frac{\sqrt{6}}{6}, \cos\theta=\frac{\sqrt{30}}{6}, \tan\theta=\frac{\sqrt{5}}{5}$	
	⑤ $\sin\theta=\frac{2\sqrt{6}}{7}, \cos\theta=\frac{5}{7}, \tan\theta=\frac{2\sqrt{6}}{5}$	
	⑥ $\sin\theta=\frac{9}{11}, \cos\theta=\frac{2\sqrt{10}}{11}, \tan\theta=\frac{9\sqrt{10}}{20}$	

8.5 Angle of elevation or depression

Ex1.	315.150 ft	
Ex2.	7.464 mi	
Ex3.	14.339 ft	
Ex4.	81.355 ft	
Ex5.	8734.872 ft	
Ex6.	50.837 ft	
Ex7.	① 42°	② 77°
	③ 25°	④ 65°
Ex8.	17.458°	
Ex9.	40.365°	

Answers

9. Circles

9.1 Basic words _Circles and Arcs

Vocab check	① False	② True
	③ False	④ False
	⑤ True	⑥ False
	⑦ True	⑧ False
	⑨ False	⑩ True
	⑪ True	⑫ False

9.2 Tangent Lines

Ex1.	① $x = 134$	② $x = 80$
	③ $x = 28$	④ $x = 118$
	⑤ $x = \sqrt{39}$	⑥ $x = 9$
	⑦ $x = \dfrac{119}{10}$	⑧ $x = \dfrac{51}{14}$
	⑨ $x = \sqrt{55}$	
Ex2.	5	
Ex3.	$2\sqrt{33}$	
Ex4.	8	
Ex5.	$\dfrac{8\sqrt{3}}{3}$	
Ex6.	① 26	② 46
	③ 32	④ 38
	⑤ 56	⑥ 28
	⑦ 50	⑧ 38
	⑨ 44	⑩ 70
	⑪ 18	⑫ 12
	⑬ $6 + 2\sqrt{2}$	⑭ $16 + 2\sqrt{15}$

Ex7.	$x = \dfrac{3}{2}$
Ex8.	$r = 3$
Ex9.	$x = \dfrac{14}{3}$

9.3 Common Tangents and Tangent Circles

Ex1.	① (i) Internally tangent,
	(ii) common external tangent
	② (i) Externally tangent,
	(ii) common internal tangent
	③ (i) Externally tangent,
	(ii) common external tangent
	④ (i) Not tangent,
	(ii) common external tangent
	⑤ (i) Not tangent,
	(ii) neither
	⑥ (i) Not tangent,
	(ii) neither
	⑦ (i) Not tangent,
	(ii) common internal tangent
Ex2.	① $x = \sqrt{45} = 3\sqrt{5}$
	② $x = \sqrt{153} = 3\sqrt{17}$
	③ $x = 20, y = \sqrt{384} = 8\sqrt{6}$
	④ $x = \dfrac{15}{2}, y = \dfrac{\sqrt{189}}{2} = \dfrac{3\sqrt{21}}{2}$
	⑤ $x = \dfrac{25}{2}, y = 13, z = \dfrac{65}{2}$
	⑥ $x = \dfrac{45}{2}, y = 17, z = \dfrac{17}{2}$
	⑦ $x = \dfrac{15}{4}$
	⑧ $x = \dfrac{132}{10} = \dfrac{66}{5}$

Ex3.	3, 8, 5
Ex4.	$10 + 5\sqrt{3}$ cm
Ex5.	$10\sqrt{3} + 10$ cm
Ex6.	Smaller : $2\sqrt{17} - 4$, Larger : $2\sqrt{17} - 2$
Ex7.	$2\sqrt{2}$ cm

9.4 Chords and Arcs

Ex1.	① 5	② 10
	③ 40°	④ 110°
	⑤ 140°	⑥ 70°
	⑦ 210°	⑧ 150°
	⑨ 320°	⑩ 290°
Ex2.	① False	② False
	③ True	④ True
	⑤ False	⑥ True
	⑦ True	⑧ True
	⑨ True	⑩ True
Ex3.	① $m\overset{\frown}{CD} = 35°$ $m\overset{\frown}{AE} = 115°$	② $m\overset{\frown}{CD} = 40°$ $m\overset{\frown}{AE} = 75°$
	③ $m\overset{\frown}{CD} = 80°$ $CD = 10$	④ $m\overset{\frown}{BC} = 82°$
	⑤ $m\overset{\frown}{AB} = 50°$	⑥ $m\overset{\frown}{AB} = 60°$

Ex4.

①
Statements	Reasons
$\overline{AB} \parallel \overline{DC}$	Given
$\overline{OA} \cong \overline{OD}$ *	All radii $\cong$ in $\odot$
$\overline{OB} \cong \overline{OC}$ *	All radii $\cong$ in $\odot$
$\angle AOB \cong \angle DOC$ *	Vert. $\angle$ s thm.
$\triangle AOB \cong \triangle DOC$	SAS post. (*)
$\overline{AB} \cong \overline{DC}$	CPCTC
ABCD is $\square$	One pair sides is $\cong$ and $\parallel \rightarrow \square$

②
Statements	Reasons
Circle O	Given
$\overline{OA} \cong \overline{OC}$ *	All radii $\cong$ in $\odot$
$\overline{OD} \cong \overline{OB}$ *	All radii $\cong$ in $\odot$
$\angle AOD \cong \angle COB$ *	Vert. $\angle$ s thm.
$\triangle AOD \cong \triangle COB$	SAS post. (*)
$\angle 1 \cong \angle 4$	CPCTC

③
Statements	Reasons
$\angle B \cong \angle C$	Given
$\overline{AB} \cong \overline{AC}$	Conv. isos. $\triangle$ thm.
$\overset{\frown}{AB} \cong \overset{\frown}{AC}$	$\cong$ chords $\rightarrow \cong$ arcs

④
Statements	Reasons
$\overset{\frown}{AB} \cong \overset{\frown}{AC}$	Given
$\overline{AB} \cong \overline{AC}$	$\cong$ arcs $\rightarrow \cong$ chords
$\angle B \cong \angle C$	Isosceles $\triangle$ thm.

⑤
Statements	Reasons
$m\overset{\frown}{AC} = m\overset{\frown}{BD}$	Given
$m\overset{\frown}{AB} + m\overset{\frown}{BC} = m\overset{\frown}{BC} + m\overset{\frown}{CD}$	Arc add. post.
$m\overset{\frown}{AB} = m\overset{\frown}{CD}$	Subtraction prop.

⑥
Statements	Reasons
$m\overset{\frown}{AB} = m\overset{\frown}{CD}$	Given
$m\overset{\frown}{BC} = m\overset{\frown}{BC}$	Reflexive prop.
$m\overset{\frown}{AB} + m\overset{\frown}{BC} = m\overset{\frown}{CD} + m\overset{\frown}{BC}$	Addition prop.
$m\overset{\frown}{AC} = m\overset{\frown}{BD}$	Arc add. post.

Ex5.	① $5\sqrt{2}$	② $4\sqrt{10}$
	③ $4\sqrt{3}$	④ 4
	⑤ $\dfrac{15}{2}$	⑥ $\dfrac{29}{4}$
	⑦ $2\sqrt{61}$	⑧ 6
	⑨ 8	⑩ $2\sqrt{6}$
	⑪ $3\sqrt{3}$	⑫ $2\sqrt{3}$

Ex6.	7 cm
Ex7.	30 cm
Ex8.	$4\sqrt{3}$ cm
Ex9.	① 10 ② 3 ③ 8 ④ 8

Ex10.

①
Statements	Reasons
$\overline{AD} \perp \overline{BC}$	Given
$\overline{BD} \cong \overline{DC}$ *	⊥ to chords→bisct chords
$m\angle ADB = m\angle ADC = 90°$	Def. right ∠s
$\angle ADB \cong \angle ADC$ *	All right ∠s are ≅
$\overline{AD} \cong \overline{AD}$ *	Reflexive prop.
$\triangle ADB \cong \triangle ADC$	SAS post. (*)
$\angle BAD \cong \angle CAD$	CPCTC
$\overline{AD}$ bisect $\angle BAC$	Def. of ∠ bisct.

②
Statements	Reasons
$\overline{AO} \perp \overline{BC}$	Given
$m\angle ADB = m\angle ADC = 90°$	Def. of ⊥ lines
$\angle ADB \cong \angle ADC$ *	All right ∠s are ≅
$\overline{BD} \cong \overline{CD}$ *	⊥ to chords→bisct chords
$\overline{AD} \cong \overline{AD}$ *	Reflexive prop.
$\triangle ADB \cong \triangle ADC$	SAS post. (*)
$\angle B \cong \angle C$	CPCTC

③
Statements	Reasons
$\overline{OD} \cong \overline{OE}$	Given
$\overline{OD} \perp \overline{AB}$	Given
$\overline{OE} \perp \overline{AC}$	Given
$\overline{AB} \cong \overline{AC}$	Equidist.→ ≅ chords
$\angle B \cong \angle C$	Isosceles △ thm.

④
Statements	Reasons
$\angle A \cong \angle B$	Given
$\overline{OD} \perp \overline{AC}$	Given
$\overline{OE} \perp \overline{BC}$	Given
$\overline{AC} \cong \overline{BC}$	Conv. isos.△ thm.
$\overline{OD} \cong \overline{OE}$	≅ chords → equidist.

9.5 Inscribed Angles

Ex1.	① $a = 100, b = 68$
	② $a = b = \frac{131}{2} = 65.5$
	③ $a = 50, b = 35, c = 95$
	④ $a = 196, b = 98$
	⑤ $a = 60, b = 110$
	⑥ $a = 60, b = 40, c = 50$
Ex2.	① $a = 30, b = 33, c = 90$
	② $a = 80, b = 40, c = 40$
	③ $a = 68$
	④ $a = 142$
Ex3.	① $a = 40, b = 40, c = 40, d = 35$
	② $a = 49, b = 42, c = 25, d = 49$
	③ $a = 70, b = 25, c = 25, d = 40$
	④ $a = 66, b = 34, c = 66, d = 132, e = 68$
	⑤ $a = 80, b = 40, c = 80, d = 80$
	⑥ $a = 80, b = 40, c = 140, d = 110$
Ex4.	① $a = 70, b = 35$
	② $a = b = 27, c = d = 54$
	③ $a = 70, b = 90$
	④ $a = 60, b = 80$
	⑤ $a = 70, b = 70, c = 50, d = 50, e = 100$
	⑥ $a = 32, b = 32, c = 64, d = 168$

Ex5.	① $a=90, b=102, c=102$
	② $a=120, b=110$
	③ $a=100, b=150, c=100, d=60$
	④ $a=80, b=100, c=76$
	⑤ $a=40, b=25, c=80, d=50$
	⑥ $a=92, b=46, c=66$
	⑦ $a=70, b=130$
	⑧ $a=96, b=109, c=81$
	⑨ $a=110, b=70, c=120$
	⑩ $a=126$
Ex6.	① $a=240, b=120$
	② $a=220, b=140$
	③ $a=30, b=120, c=200$
	④ $a=240, b=120, c=40, d=30$
Ex7.	72°
Ex8.	270
Ex9.	① $a=64, b=50, c=128, d=132, e=100$
	② $a=100, b=20, c=200, d=120$
	③ $a=60, b=95, c=60, d=190, e=50$
	④ $a=65, b=55, c=65$
	⑤ $a=50, b=50, c=130, d=100$
	⑥ $a=58, b=64, c=32$
	⑦ $a=65, b=107$
	⑧ $a=35, b=40$
	⑨ $a=30, b=20$
	⑩ $a=48, b=15$
	⑪ $a=48$
	⑫ $a=55$
	⑬ $a=50$
	⑭ $a=45$
	⑮ $a=101$
Ex10.	① $a=92, b=94, c=92, d=86$
	② $a=105, b=82, c=82, d=75$
	③ $a=60, b=48, c=60$

	④ $a=63, b=58, c=58$
	⑤ $a=61, b=67, c=23$
	⑥ $a=38, b=70$
Ex11.	113

9.6 Secants, Tangents, and Angle Measures

Ex1.	① $x=49$	② $x=60$
	③ $x=58$	④ $x=60$
	⑤ $x=48$	⑥ $x=65$
Ex2.	① $x=27$	② $x=74$
	③ $x=68$	④ $x=96$
	⑤ $x=80$	⑥ $x=60$
	⑦ $x=242$	⑧ $x=126$
	⑨ $x=54$	⑩ $x=160$
	⑪ $x=50$	⑫ $x=68$
	⑬ $x=35$	⑭ $x=30$
Ex3.	30	
Ex4.	$m\widehat{BC}=42°, m\widehat{ED}=110°$	
Ex5.	220°	
Ex6.	55°	
Ex7.	$x=95, y=25$	

9.7 Secants, Tangents, and Segments

Ex1.	① $x = 2$	② $x = \dfrac{8}{3}$
	③ $a = 2\sqrt{5}$	④ $x = 4\sqrt{3}$
	⑤ $x = 6$	⑥ $x = \dfrac{29}{6}$
	⑦ $x = 8$	⑧ $x = 16$
Ex2.	$\dfrac{5}{2}$	
Ex3.	① $x = \dfrac{46}{3}$	② $x = 7$
	③ $x = \sqrt{30}$	④ $x = \dfrac{19}{5}$
	⑤ $x = 8$	⑥ $x = 6$
	⑦ $x = 17, y = 2\sqrt{2}$	⑧ $x = 4\sqrt{3}, y = \dfrac{22}{5}$
	⑨ $x = 9$	⑩ $x = 4, y = 4$
	⑪ $x = 2, y = \dfrac{7}{3}$	⑫ $x = 10, y = \dfrac{71}{5}$
Ex4.	$x = 4$	
Ex5.	4	

Answers

10. Areas of Plane Figures

10.1 Area of polygons

Ex1.	① 120	② $3\sqrt{7}$
	③ $12\sqrt{3}$	④ $10\sqrt{2}$
	⑤ $9\sqrt{5}$	⑥ 39
	⑦ $25\sqrt{3}$	⑧ $18\sqrt{3}$
	⑨ 49	⑩ 52
	⑪ 120	⑫ $6\sqrt{7}$
	⑬ 24	⑭ 162
	⑮ $70\sqrt{3}$	⑯ $\dfrac{25\sqrt{2}}{2}$
Ex2.	216	
Ex3.	12	
Ex4.	$4\ cm^2$	
Ex5.	49	
Ex6.	120	
Ex7.	$\dfrac{24}{49}$	

10.2 Area of regular polygons

Ex1.	① 129.9	② 221.7
	③ 130.8	④ 13.5
Ex2.	① 14.1	② 62.4
	③ 10.9	

10.3 Area of Circles and Sectors

Ex1.	① 4π	② 6π
	③ $\dfrac{8}{3}\pi$	④ $\dfrac{25}{6}\pi$
Ex2.	① 10π	② 20π
	③ $12+14\pi$	④ 6π
	⑤ $6\pi+12$	⑥ $10\sqrt{2}+10+5\pi$
Ex3.	$12\pi+12\sqrt{3}$ cm	
Ex4.	① $\dfrac{15}{4}\pi$	② $\dfrac{50}{3}\pi$
	③ $\dfrac{7}{4}\pi$	④ 12π
	⑤ $\dfrac{27}{2}\pi - \dfrac{81\sqrt{3}}{4}$	⑥ $36\pi-72$
	⑦ $50+75\pi$	⑧ $16\sqrt{3}+\dfrac{160}{3}\pi$
	⑨ $8+4\pi$	⑩ $6\sqrt{3}+8\pi$
	⑪ $5-\dfrac{5}{4}\pi$	⑫ $16-4\pi$
	⑬ $\dfrac{49}{4}$	⑭ 1
	⑮ $4\pi-8$	⑯ $\dfrac{81}{2}$
	⑰ $9\sqrt{3}-\dfrac{9}{2}\pi$	⑱ $50\pi-100$
Ex5.	$36-9\sqrt{3}-6\pi$	
Ex6.	24	
Ex7.	175π m^2	
Ex8.	$\dfrac{32}{3}\pi$ $8\sqrt{3}$ cm^2	
Ex9.	$\dfrac{25\sqrt{3}}{4}+\dfrac{25}{6}\pi$	
Ex10.	$64\sqrt{3}-\dfrac{88}{3}\pi$ cm^2	

10.4 Areas and Ratios

Ex1.	① a) $5:6$	b) $5:4$	c) $11:10$
	② a) $3:2\sqrt{5}$	b) $3+2\sqrt{5}:2\sqrt{5}$	
	③ a) $7:3$	b) $4:3$	
	④ a) $3:5$	b) $3:2$	
	⑤ a) $3:5$	b) $3:8$	
	c) $3:16$	d) $5:8$	
	⑥ a) $3:4$	b) $3:14$	
	c) $4:21$	d) $4:14=2:7$	
	⑦ a) $1:2$	b) $1:4$	
	c) $1:2$	d) $1:9$	
	⑧ a) $5:6$	b) $25:36$	c) $5:6$
	⑨ a) $4:21$	b) $4:9$	c) $4:30=2:15$
	⑩ a) $49:16$	b) $16:121$	
	c) $16:105$	d) $49:105=7:15$	
Ex2.	15 cm^2		
Ex3.	49		
Ex4.	① 4 cm^2	② 4 cm^2	
	③ 8 cm^2	④ 6 cm^2	
	⑤ 6 cm^2	⑥ 4 cm^2	
Ex5.	$\dfrac{16}{3} cm^2$		
Ex6.	$20 cm^2$		

Answers

11. Areas and Volumes of Solids

11.2 Surface Area

Ex1.	① 54	② $224 + 80\sqrt{2}$
	③ $48\sqrt{3} + 192$	④ 200
	⑤ 120π	⑥ 90π
Ex2.	① 144	② $54\sqrt{3} + 72$ (slant height = 4)
	③ 33π	④ $36 + 36\sqrt{5}$ (slant height = $3\sqrt{5}$)
	⑤ 96π	
Ex3.	$\$37.8\pi$	
Ex4.	$75\pi\, m^2$, $\$325$	
Ex5.	216	
Ex6.	102π	

Ex7.	① $AB = 3\sqrt{10}$, $AC = \sqrt{65}$	② $AB = 5\sqrt{2}$, $AC = 5\sqrt{3}$
	③ $AB = 3\sqrt{2}$, $AC = 3\sqrt{3}$	④ $AB = \sqrt{61}$, $AC = 5$
Ex8.	$24\sqrt{3}\, cm^3$	
Ex9.	$128\sqrt{2}\, cm^3$	
Ex10.	① 96	② 160
	③ $3\sqrt{7}\pi$	④ 100π
	⑤ $18\sqrt{3}$	⑥ $12\sqrt{7}$
	⑦ $6\sqrt{3}$	⑧ 12π
	⑨ 50	⑩ 160
	⑪ 78π	⑫ $\dfrac{52}{3}\pi$
Ex11.	$18\sqrt{2}\, cm^3$	
Ex12.	$18\sqrt{2}\pi\, cm^3$	
Ex13.	Reduced by 35.2%	
Ex14.	$\pi r^2 \left(8 - \dfrac{4}{3}r\right) cm^3$	

11.3 Volume

Ex1.	① 320	② $270\sqrt{3}$
	③ 108π	④ 800π
	⑤ $125\sqrt{2}$	⑥ $480\sqrt{3}$
	⑦ $288 - 72\pi$	⑧ 42
	⑨ 22π	⑩ 630
	⑪ $30\sqrt{15}$	⑫ $16\sqrt{2}\pi$
Ex2.	5 in	
Ex3.	$1200\, cm^3$	
Ex4.	$1280\, cm^3$	
Ex5.	$140\, in^3$	
Ex6.	$81\, in^3$	

11.4 Sphere

Ex1.	① 100π	② π
	③ 64π	④ 108π
Ex2.	5 cans	
Ex3.	① 36π	② 288π
	③ $\dfrac{9}{32}\pi$	④ 64π
	⑤ 264π	⑥ $\dfrac{500}{3}\pi$
Ex4.	$\dfrac{32}{3}\pi\, cm^3$	
Ex5.	Surface area of sphere = $4\pi r^2$	
	Lateral area of cylinder = $2\pi r(2r) = 4\pi r^2$	

Ex6.	Cone $15m^3$, Cylinder $45m^3$
Ex7.	$8:\dfrac{4\pi}{3}:\dfrac{8}{3}=24:4\pi:8$
Ex8.	$84\pi\,cm^2$
Ex9.	$\dfrac{4000}{3}\pi$
Ex10.	$81\pi\,cm^3$

Ex4.	$108\,ft^2$
Ex5.	$81\,cm^3$
Ex6.	$375\,m^3$
Ex7.	27 candies
Ex8.	$24\,cm^3$
Ex9.	$\dfrac{7}{8}$
Ex10.	Increased by 72.8%
Ex11.	2 hour 10 min (130 min)

11.5 Area and Volume of Similar Solids

Ex1.	① Similar, $4:3$ ② Not similar ③ Not similar ④ Not similar ⑤ Not similar ⑥ Similar, $3:1$ ⑦ Similar, $7:3$ ⑧ Similar, $2:3$
Ex2.	① Ratio of the surface areas = $4:1$ 　　Ratio of the volumes = $8:1$ ② Ratio of the surface areas = $25:9$ 　　Ratio of the volumes = $125:27$ ③ Ratio of the surface areas = $16:9$ 　　Ratio of the volumes = $64:27$ ④ Ratio of the surface areas = $9:1$ 　　Ratio of the volumes = $27:1$
Ex3.	① $1:9,\ 1:27$ ② $9:25,\ 27:125$ ③ $2:3,\ 8:27$ ④ $3:4,\ 27:64$ ⑤ $4:3,\ 16:9$ ⑥ $3:5,\ 9:25$ ⑦ $\sqrt{3}:\sqrt{5},\ 3\sqrt{3}:5\sqrt{5}$ ⑧ $\sqrt{2}:\sqrt{3},\ 2\sqrt{2}:3\sqrt{3}$

Answers

12. Coordinate Geometry

12.1 Transformation

Ex1.	① $A'(-2,-3)$	② $B'(-5,1)$
	③ $C'(2,-5)$	④ $D'(4,-10)$
	⑤ $E'(-1,7)$	⑥ $F'(8,-8)$
	⑦ $G'(0,4)$	⑧ $H'(-1,2)$
	⑨ $I'(-3,21)$	⑩ $J'(0,-4)$
	⑪ $K'(-3,5)$	⑫ $L'(2,-4)$

Ex2. ①
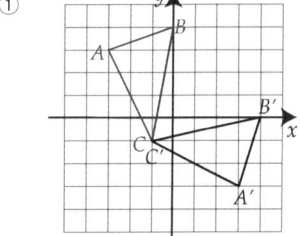

②
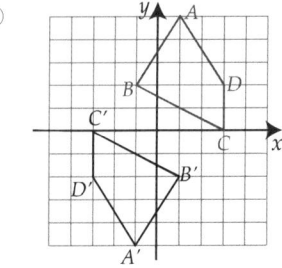

③
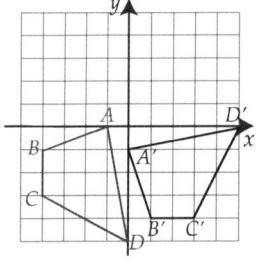

④
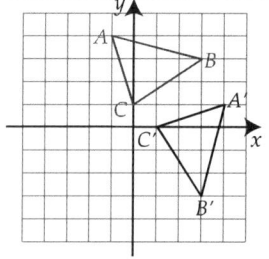

Ex3.
① Translation 2 units left, 3 units down
② Rotation 90° CCW
③ Reflection over $y = -x$
④ Translation 5 units down
⑤ Rotation 270° CCW
⑥ Reflection over origin
(or Rotation 180° CCW)

Ex4. ①
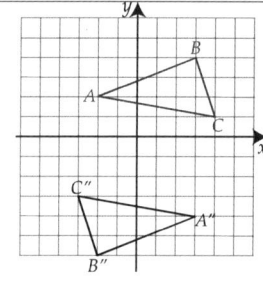

②
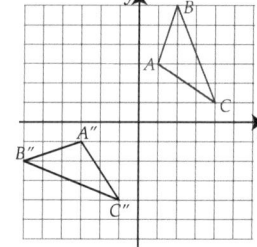

③
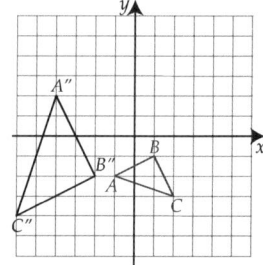

④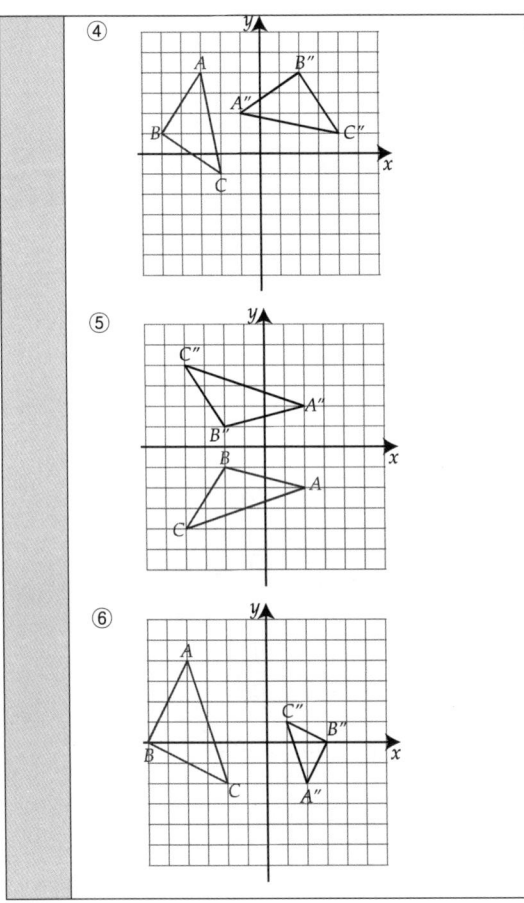

⑤

⑥

12.2 Distance and Midpoints

	① $\left(\dfrac{7}{2}, 3\right)$	② $(1, 0)$	
	③ $(0, 0)$	④ $\left(\dfrac{1}{2}, \dfrac{3\sqrt{5}}{2}\right)$	
	⑤ $(\sqrt{3}, 1)$	⑥ $(1-5\sqrt{2}, 2\sqrt{3})$	
	⑦ $\left(\dfrac{a+b}{2}, 0\right)$	⑧ (a, a)	
Ex2.	$\left(4, \dfrac{1}{2}\right)$		

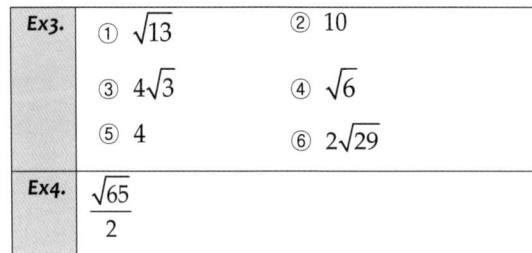

Ex3.	① $\sqrt{13}$	② 10
	③ $4\sqrt{3}$	④ $\sqrt{6}$
	⑤ 4	⑥ $2\sqrt{29}$
Ex4.	$\dfrac{\sqrt{65}}{2}$	

12.3 Equation of Circle

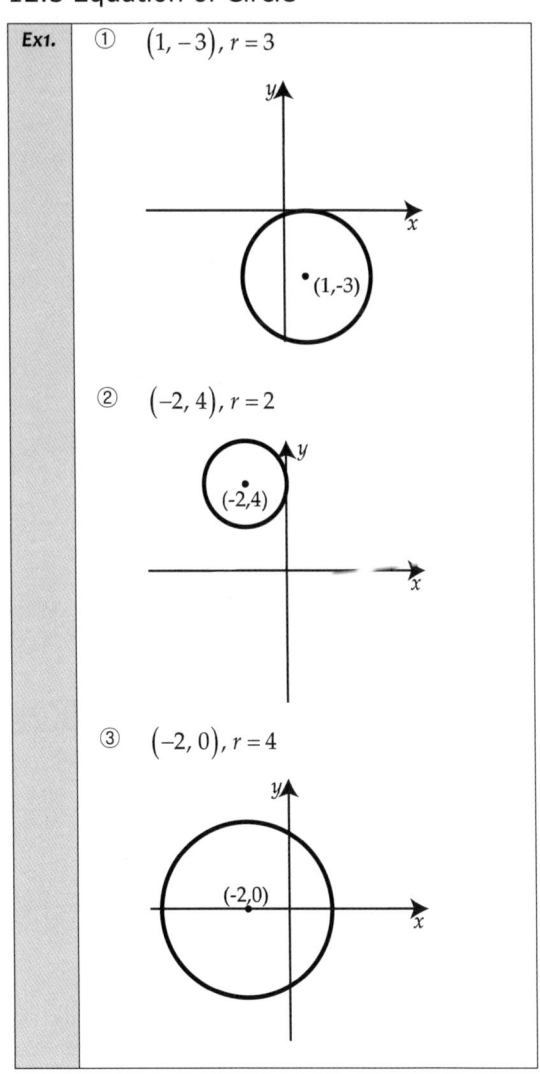

Answers 555

④ $(0, 4), r = 4$

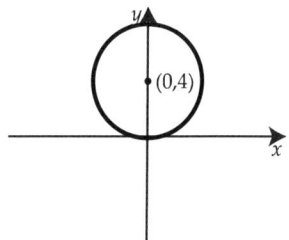

⑤ $(0, 0), r = 3\sqrt{3}$

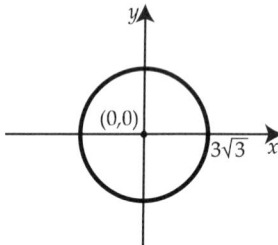

⑥ $(0, -1), r = 2\sqrt{3}$

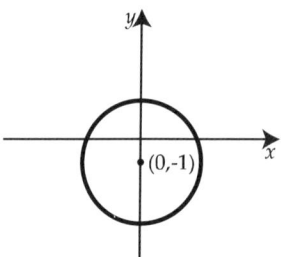

Ex2.
① $(x-3)^2 + (y+7)^2 = 25$
② $x^2 + (y-2)^2 = 9$
③ $x^2 + y^2 = 5$
④ $(x+1)^2 + (y-7)^2 = 2$
⑤ $x^2 + (y+3)^2 = 2$
⑥ $(x+2)^2 + y^2 = 16$
⑦ $(x+2)^2 + (y-3)^2 = 13$
⑧ $(x+5)^2 + (y-2)^2 = 20$

⑨ $(x+4)^2 + (y-2)^2 = 32$
⑩ $(x-2)^2 + (y-2)^2 = 52$
⑪ $(x+8)^2 + (y+5)^2 = 25$
⑫ $(x-5)^2 + (y+4)^2 = 25$

Ex3.
① $c = 25, (x+5)^2$
② $c = 36, (x-6)^2$
③ $c = 121, (x-11)^2$
④ $c = 81, (x+9)^2$
⑤ $c = \dfrac{9}{4}, \left(x+\dfrac{3}{2}\right)^2$
⑥ $c = \dfrac{1}{4}, \left(x-\dfrac{1}{2}\right)^2$
⑦ $c = 0.16, (x-0.4)^2$
⑧ $c = 1.21, (x+1.1)^2$
⑨ $c = \dfrac{9}{100}, \left(x+\dfrac{3}{10}\right)^2$
⑩ $c = \dfrac{1}{16}, \left(x-\dfrac{1}{4}\right)^2$

Ex4.
① $(5, -4), r = 5$
② $(-1, -3), r = 2\sqrt{2}$
③ $(3, 0), r = \sqrt{21}$
④ $(0, -5), r = \sqrt{11}$
⑤ $\left(-\dfrac{5}{2}, -\dfrac{3}{2}\right), r = \dfrac{\sqrt{134}}{2}$
⑥ $\left(-\dfrac{3}{2}, \dfrac{7}{2}\right), r = \dfrac{\sqrt{58}}{2}$

12.4 Slope of a Line

Ex1.	① $\dfrac{5}{3}$	② $-\dfrac{2}{3}$
	③ $-\dfrac{2}{7}$	④ $\dfrac{1}{5}$
	⑤ Undefined	⑥ 0
	⑦ 0	
Ex2.	① 4	② 3
	③ $-\dfrac{2}{3}$	④ $-\dfrac{3}{4}$
	⑤ $\dfrac{12}{7}$	⑥ 2
	⑦ 0	⑧ Undefined
Ex3.	① parallel	② neither
	③ neither	④ perpendicular
	⑤ perpendicular	⑥ parallel

12.5 Coordinate Geometry Proofs

Ex1.	$AB = 5, BC = 5\sqrt{2}, AC = 5$
	$AB = BC$, $BC^2 = AB^2 + AC^2$
	∴ ABC is isosceles right △.
Ex2.	$AB = 3\sqrt{10}, AC = \sqrt{10}, BC = 10$
	$BC^2 = AB^2 + AC^2$
	∴ ABC is a right △.
Ex3.	Midpt of A and C = (0,3)
	Midpt of B and D = (0,3)
	∴ Diag. bisct each other
	∴ ABCD is a parallelogram.

Ex4.	Midpt of R and T = $\left(\dfrac{3}{2}, 0\right)$
	Midpt of S and U = $\left(\dfrac{3}{2}, 0\right)$
	∴ Diag. bisct each other
	∴ RSTU is a parallelogram.
Ex5.	Midpt of A and C = (0.5, 0)
	Midpt of B and D = (0.5, 0)
	∴ Diag. bisct each other
	$AC = \sqrt{65}$, $BD = \sqrt{65}$
	∴ Diag. are ≅
	∴ ABCD is a rectangle.
Ex6.	Midpt of G and I = $\left(\dfrac{5}{2}, 3\right)$
	Midpt of H and J = $\left(\dfrac{5}{2}, 3\right)$
	∴ Diag. bisct each other
	GI = 5, HJ = 5
	∴ Diag. are ≅
	∴ GHIJ is a rectangle.
Ex7.	Midpt of Q and S = (7,5)
	Midpt of R and T = (7,5)
	∴ Diag. bisct each other
	Slope of $\overline{QS}$ = −2, Slope of $\overline{RT}$ = $\dfrac{1}{2}$
	∴ Diag. are ⊥
	∴ QRST is a rhombus.
Ex8.	Midpt of A and C = (2,4)
	Midpt of B and D = (2,4)
	∴ Diag. bisct each other
	Slope of $\overline{AC}$ = 0, Slope of $\overline{BD}$ = und
	∴ Diag. are ⊥
	∴ ABCD is a rhombus.

Answers 557

Ex9.	Midpt of A and C = $\left(\frac{7}{2}, -\frac{1}{2}\right)$ Midpt of B and D = $\left(\frac{7}{2}, -\frac{1}{2}\right)$ ∴ Diag. bisct each other AC = $5\sqrt{2}$, BD = $5\sqrt{2}$ ∴ Diag. are ≅ Slope of $\overline{AC}$ = $-\frac{1}{7}$, Slope of $\overline{BD}$ = 7 ∴ Diag. are ⊥ ∴ ABCD is a square.
Ex10.	Midpt of A and C = (3, 2) Midpt of B and D = (3, 2) ∴ Diag. bisct each other AC = $2\sqrt{5}$, BD = $2\sqrt{5}$ ∴ Diag. are ≅ Slope of $\overline{AC}$ = $-\frac{1}{2}$, Slope of $\overline{BD}$ = 2 ∴ Diag. are ⊥ ∴ ABCD is a square.
Ex11.	Slope of $\overline{AB}$ = $\frac{2}{3}$, Slope of $\overline{BC}$ = $-\frac{4}{3}$ Slope of $\overline{CD}$ = $\frac{2}{3}$, Slope of $\overline{DA}$ = und $\overline{AB}$ and $\overline{CD}$ are parallel. $\overline{BC}$ and $\overline{DA}$ are not parallel. ∴ ABCD is a trapezoid.
Ex12.	Slope of $\overline{JK}$ = -1, Slope of $\overline{KL}$ = 0 Slope of $\overline{LM}$ = -1, Slope of $\overline{MJ}$ = und $\overline{JK}$ and $\overline{LM}$ are parallel. $\overline{KL}$ and $\overline{MJ}$ are not parallel. KL = 4, MJ = 4 ∴ JKLM is a isosceles trapezoid.